Fate and Utopia in German Sociology, 1870–1923

Studies in Contemporary German Social Thought
Thomas McCarthy, General Editor

Fate and Utopia in German Sociology, 1870–1923

Harry Liebersohn

The MIT Press, Cambridge, Massachusetts, and London, England

This book was set in Baskerville by Graphic Composition, Inc., Athens, Georgia, and printed and bound by Halliday Lithograph in the United States of America.

Library of Congress Cataloging-in-Publication Data

Liebersohn, Harry.
  Fate and utopia in German sociology, 1870–1923.

  (Studies in contemporary German social thought)
  Bibliography: p.
  Includes index.
  1. Sociology—Germany—History—19th century.
  2. Sociology—Germany—History—20th century.
  I. Title. II. Series.
  HM22.G2L53 1988   301'.0943   87-26048
  ISBN 0-262-12133-6

For Dorothee

Contents

Contents

Acknowledgments

One of the pleasures of working on this book has been to confirm firsthand its thesis that the formation of ideas is inseparable from conversation about them. German friends generously listened to my questions about their culture and did their best to answer, while Americans tried to make sure that I rendered foreign concepts into a native idiom. My thanks to all the colleagues and friends who wished this to be, in Walter Benjamin's profound sense of the word, a work of translation.

Elizabeth Aldrich, Laura Boella, Norbert Bolz, Friedrich Wilhelm Graf, Michael Löwy, Martin Riesebrodt, and Michael Roth gave me valuable criticisms of individual chapters. Jürgen Zander and Cornelius Bickel generously shared their expertise on Tönnies with me.

Laszlo Deme's seminars on Hungarian history and refusal to separate it from the wider currents of German and European culture proved invaluable when my attention turned to Lukács. Jerrold Seigel steadily encouraged my interest in religion, and his biography of Marx shaped my approach to linking biography and social thought. Carl Schorske, my dissertation advisor at Princeton, challenged me again and again to bring the highest standards of rigor and imagination to my work; I thank him for years of teaching and friendship. Werner Conze's personal example as well as his criticisms refined my understanding of Germany's learned traditions. I am greatly saddened that he did not live to see the book.

As an Andrew W. Mellon Fellow in 1980–81, I enjoyed the rare intellectual conviviality of the Center for the Humanities at Wesleyan University. Grants from the German Academic Exchange Service (DAAD), American Council of Learned Societies, and American Philosophical Society provided financial support for much of the research and writing.

Cheerfully ignoring common sense, my parents believed that the book really would be finished one day. My father, Myer Liebersohn, taught me to think of sociology as a form of enlightenment, and this book is a continuation of my dialogue with him. He and my mother, Esther Liebersohn, kept me mindful of the need for readable prose.

My special thanks to William David Jones and Diane Trosino for their tireless, cheerful assistance in preparing the bibliography and correcting page proofs.

When we first met in Heidelberg twelve years ago, Dorothee Schneider took me for a walk on a mountain path—the *Philosophenweg,* as it happened—overlooking the town and university. Since then, she has always been happy to discuss the world of her grandfathers with me. She has also, with unfailing sensitivity, known when to lead me to landscapes lying beyond it.

September 1987

Fate and Utopia in German Sociology, 1870–1923

1
Introduction

Fate and Utopia in the Sociological Imagination

The Puritan *wanted* to work in a calling; we are *forced* to do so. . . . In Baxter's view the care for external goods should only lie on the shoulders of the saint 'like a light cloak, which can be thrown aside at any moment.' But fate declared that the cloak should become an iron cage.[1]

These lines from *The Protestant Ethic and the Spirit of Capitalism* state one of the central themes of German sociology before 1933: that capitalist society was a modern form of fate. In the ancient world fate came from the gods, in the modern world from humanity itself. Modernity's "iron cage" was the conditions of industrial production that confined individuals to a calling or specialized economic activity and cut them off from any larger cosmos of meaning. Max Weber contrasted modern fragmentation to the unity of ancient Athens and the age of Goethe. The special irony of humanity's departure from the "full and beautiful humanity" of earlier eras[2] was that a profoundly personal choice—not the will of the gods, not just impersonal accumulation of capital, but the Christian will to salvation—had created the iron cage.

Max Weber is the best-known representative of a tragic sociological perspective originating in Imperial Germany. This book studies five thinkers who contributed to it: Ferdinand Tönnies, Ernst Troeltsch, Weber, Georg Simmel, and Georg Lukács. The first four belonged to the same generation; Lukács, Hungarian-born but a student of Weber and Simmel who wrote for most of his life in German, takes our story to the next generation of social thinkers. Though they differed on many issues, all five shared the idea of society as fate.

For the first half of this century the German sociological tradition became the inheritance mainly of liberals seeking to affirm the necessity (sometimes still tragic, sometimes not) of capitalist society. In recent decades thinkers from the left, too, have discovered an affinity with Tönnies, Weber, and Simmel.[3] And a remarkable outpouring of recent books from a variety of political perspectives has sympathetically reconstructed the thinking of the young Lukács, the pre-Communist aesthete who experienced the tragedy of modern life with extraordinary poignancy.[4] The strong ongoing interest in German sociology seems to be a response to the reaffirmation of capitalism in Western Europe and the United States in the 1980s, a disillusioning aftermath to the student and Eurocommunist movements of earlier decades. Anyone glumly contemplating the fate of our own time may turn back to the pessimism of an earlier era for comfort.

The present book dissents from this emphasis on tragic pessimism in German sociology. To be sure, the tragic pose was there. It belonged to the rhetoric of modernism enunciated by Baudelaire in France and Nietzsche in Germany, both of them in search of a modern heroism to take the place of disappearing aristocratic and religious values and thus overcome the banality of bourgeois society.[5] The sociologists—especially Weber and Simmel, the most unequivocal modernists of our group—made this rhetoric their own. But do we need to keep repeating it? Perhaps a more critical historical perspective would ask what ambiguities it concealed. Even the final pages of *The Protestant Ethic,* with their invocation of the iron cage, do not close off the possibility of transcending modern society's fragmentation.[6] Alongside his determination to affirm modernity, Weber did not conceal his awareness of the earlier values it had shattered and his interest in alternatives to it. The same is true of Tönnies, Troeltsch, and Simmel. All of them longed for a return to a full and beautiful humanity and experienced some moments when they thought they had actually lived to see it. Moreover the meaning of "fate" is problematic. Recognition of it did not always imply withdrawal from politics or loss of belief in the possibility of significant change. As with the Puritan belief in predestination, a serious conviction that impersonal forces ruled the world could lead to action in perceived harmony with those forces. Strong continuities as well as disagreement with his elders carried Lukács from tragic pessimism to revolutionary optimism after 1914. To consider how he could express his revolt against bourgeois society through the idiom of German sociology, we need a more comprehensive view of the sociological tradition.

One fruitful approach to the study of culture hypothesizes that art and thought contain an implicit utopian dimension that internal analysis and contextualization can render explicit.[7] Utopias are imaginative visions of a political order whose realization would revolutionize existing politics and society. As the name implies, they are no place. Their only home is in the mind of their makers. Yet this does not seal them off in a realm of fantasy. Utopia is not synonymous with *Schlaraffenland*, where cooked chickens fly into fools' mouths. Rather, modern utopias include everything from dream states to sober plans for a new society. Their intentions differ too: some criticize society without aiming at any effect on it; some offer regulative ideas; some are revolutionary agendas. They occupy different spatial distances, from island kingdoms separated from existing society by symbolic oceans, to self-stylizations.[8] And they can be situated in different temporal zones. Often projected into an ideal future, utopias can also take the less obvious form of an idealized version of existing society, a kind of map overlay outlining certain features and thereby altering its "real" nature, as in descriptions of a fully competitive capitalist order. All these utopias, island or mainland, future or present, beguile us by mixing novelty with the rediscovery of inherited hopes. Utopia is not simply a negation of the present; it is a resurrection of the past, whose meaning we can only comprehend by overcoming our own fixation on one direction of time and realizing that we, Janus-like, mediate between future and past, discovering in *temps perdu* the gateway to *temps retrouvé*.

The Wilhelmine sociologists made use of a "utopian" approach to the study of culture—but to ironic effect, since they wanted to prove that the utopian impulse of Western Christianity had come to an end. Weber in *The Protestant Ethic* and Troeltsch in *The Social Teachings of the Christian Churches* traced how the Protestant will to realize the Kingdom of God on earth disappeared as religious faith and returned as the irrational habit and iron necessity of capitalism. "Utopian" analysis thus served their tragic vision. Lukács turned their approach to opposite ends. His early studies of nineteenth-century tragedy analyzed the fateful contradictions of bourgeois society in order to discover how the modern tragic hero might surpass them. Utopia changed from the autopsy of a dead civilization into the intimation of a coming one. For German sociology, and for each thinker over a lifetime, the relationship between utopia and reality was uncertain, changing in response to historical experience. Our image of the sociologists begins to alter when we keep in mind that it was there at all, that their thought did not revolve around the single axis of society as fate, but was simultaneously drawn toward fate and utopia.

I have also taken up a more specific thesis of German sociology and turned it back on its makers. Modern secular utopias have been profoundly (though of course not exclusively) informed by religious traditions and motivations. In twentieth-century Central Europe not only Weber, Troeltsch, and Lukács, but also such thinkers as Ernst Bloch, Walter Benjamin, and Karl Mannheim investigated the religious origins of modern utopias with such intensity that one can hardly avoid suspecting some personal relevance to Germany's cultural elite.[9] Indeed at times the debates between revolutionaries and defenders of the status quo look like reruns of older battles between churchmen and chiliasts. To start with the past and impose its patterns on the present is to approach the story from the false entrance, however. The Protestant background was in any case too rich a landscape of local traditions to make such a genealogy more than a search for mythic ancestors. A better starting point is with the subject, in this case the sociologists: as members of a capitalist society, readers of Nietzsche, representatives of a hegemonic Protestant culture, and participants in countercultural waves of interest in German mysticism and Dostoevsky. The

Empire's educated elite had its own significant religious life, which cultural historians have largely ignored.[10] The religious past took on meaning from this starting point. Luther's original idea of anarchic community, heir to apostolic *agape* and medieval German mysticism, exerted a powerful hold even on anti-Lutherans, including all five of our thinkers. They contrasted it to Germany's brittle order and intractable inner divisions at the end of the nineteenth century.

Utopianism and Fatalism as Responses to Fragmentation in Public Life

Comte, Mill, Durkheim, and Spencer interpreted the disorder of their societies as the sign of an age of transition or as free activity compatible with the integration of society's members into an organic unity.[11] The German sociologists disagreed. They considered modern society an articulated order with clearly definable features, but did not simply identify society with the persons inhabiting it. Instead they imagined an antinomy between the private, personal realm of individuals struggling for autonomy and the impersonal social order constraining them. The marketplace, bureaucracy, and social convention reinforced one another in a fateful system imposing fragmentation on individual experience.

On many levels the German Empire offered the sociologists a spectacle of personal fragmentation within impersonal order. The most immediate was politics: three wars of German unification created a German nation-state by 1871, but failed to inspire a corresponding subjective consensus. The most menacing source of disaffection came from the organized working class.[12] During the years its activities were outlawed, from 1878 to 1890, Tönnies conceived and wrote *Gemeinschaft und Gesellschaft,* whose publication in 1887 marked the beginning of the modern German sociological tradition. After 1890 Imperial social policy alternated between paternalism and repression. Tönnies, Troeltsch, Weber, and Simmel viewed these oscillations as left-liberal reformers seeking democratization of the existing political system and acceptance of working-class organizations for the sake of greater national unity. Insight into the structural limits of existing power relations chastened their hopes for change. The immobility of German politics had the opposite effect on Lukács; his revolutionary will fed on frustration. He drove the logic of sociology from fragmentation to a new unity, a dialectical conclusion reached in *History and Class Consciousness,* whose publication in 1923 ends our narrative.

A second kind of fragmentation perceived by the sociologists was cultural. All of them (with the partial exception of Lukács, an assimilated outsider on the eve of World War I) belonged to Germany's *Bildungsbürgertum,* or educated elite, at a moment when education and culture were undergoing fundamental changes. Unity—unified knowledge and a unified sensibility—was the cultural ideal they inherited from the poets and thinkers of the early nineteenth century. By the 1870s, however, the growing specialization of knowledge made it difficult for *Gymnasium* (humanistic high school) and university to provide a universal historical and philosophical outlook.[13] The university system offered a striking example of fragmentation within depersonalized order. Its transformation into the modern "factory of learning," as Adolf von Harnack called it,[14] necessitated a breakdown of the philosophical faculty embracing all the natural and human sciences, and the formation of specialized faculties. Advocates of the neohumanist conception of the university inherited from Wilhelm von Humboldt, the early nineteenth-century Prussian educational reformer, feared the change would close off communication between disciplines and disrupt the unity and direction of German scholarship. Hardly less alarming to cultural conservatives was the invasion of modernist movements such as Symbolism, *Jugendstil,* and Impressionism into the arts in the 1890s. Government cultural officials and members of the *Bildungsbürgertum* generally considered them reflections of social decadence and took steps to stifle them.[15] As for the sociologists, there was a close correlation between their opinions on art and on society. Those who despised modern society saw decadence in its artistic and intellectual expressions, while more accommodating thinkers had greater sympathy with cultural modernism.

Finally, the sociologists were observers of Germany's religious fragmentation. Even though the breakdown of traditional religious communities was inevitable, they blamed one institution in particular for deepening religious disaffection: the Protestant church. Most members of the educated elite came from Protestant families and felt an allegiance to Protestant cultural traditions. But the established Protestant church in Prussia (and most other areas) inspired widespread disgust. Controlled by reactionaries and ridden with confessional and theological conflicts, it seemed to embody the worst divisive traits of the national character.[16] The church fascinated and repelled; thinkers like Troeltsch and Weber, profoundly aware of religion's formative role in German history, blamed Lutheranism for ills of German public life down to their own day. They and others speculated on whether mysticism, socialism, or some other ethos could fill the spiritual void it had left.

One word captured much of the sociologists' discontent with the social divisions of their day: *Gemeinschaft*, first coined as a sociological category by Tönnies. He meant by it a social order bound together by a unity of wills. Family and social institutions naturally created cooperation in a *Gemeinschaft* prior to its members' conscious choice. Tönnies was uncertain in 1887 whether *Gemeinschaft* referred to actual historical example or to an abstract model more or less approximated by empirical social orders. Part of the term's appeal was that it did not separate the two, in the neutral guise of social theory calling up images of pre-modern organic unity. We shall conform to Tönnies's ambiguous usage and permit *Gemeinschaft* to refer to either past precedent or ideal type.[17] The English word "community" has a somewhat different meaning. While it can describe a pre-voluntary *Gemeinschaft*, more often it refers to voluntary associations, as when we speak of ethnic or religious communities in the United States, whose members, unlike those of early modern Europe, are free to join or leave. We shall use "community" in the American sense for either kind of cooperative social order, "traditional community" for historical, involuntary communities.[18]

Fate in Imperial Germany signified the fragmentation of *Gemeinschaft*. Political, cultural, and religious divisions were symptoms of a more fundamental disunity of wills. Instead of affirming one another—instead of forming a general will supporting power, production, knowledge, art, and faith—modern individuals negated one another's existence or combined for limited goals that could not substitute for their lack of general ends. According to the shared vision of German sociology, they participated in a social whole that was supremely efficient at imprisoning the human beings who built it.

Utopia signified renewed voluntaristic unity. The sociologists thought they could see the remnants of an older unity disappearing before their eyes, for until the late nineteenth century most Germans lived in town or rural communities in which personal relations and traditional social status had created a stable social identity.[19] None of them advocated a return to the preindustrial past, for they saw in modern society a fate to comprehend but not control. Whether a new unity could really occur, or would do so in a desirable form, was open to debate. Some saw it as a utopian fantasy, though one still powerfully informing their vision of the present; others saw it as fated to succeed society.

This book's next five chapters follow a dialectical movement from traditional community through modern society to socialism. Tönnies was the most nostalgic for the lost *Gemeinschaft* of the past, though he worked for social reform and looked to the working class for an eventual rebirth of community. Troeltsch self-consciously strove for a synthesis of past and present, rescuable traditions and modern personal autonomy. Weber renounced traditional community and poured skepticism on prophecies of socialism; yet these excluded possibilities gave his work its tragic pathos. Simmel was the most unequivocally modern of the five, the most resistant to the claims of *Gemeinschaft;* yet he, too, strained against modern fragmentation, searching for a missing authenticity and a utopia of social unity. Lukács recapitulated the dialectic of these predecessors, all of whose work he knew; nostalgia for traditional community and affirmation of modern voluntarism entered into his vision of socialism.

Over the course of the book, the temporal locus of the utopias shifts from past, to present, to future. Yet they were too complex for any summary to map their location. None of the sociologists could be entirely identified with one temporal home; each had a center that reached backward and forward in time. To pin down any one thinker's position in isolation from his biographical development is to risk creating an artificially clear schema. The biographical narratives of this book attempt to preserve individual complexities while indicating how the sociologists' shared experiences and mutual encounters shaped a unified discourse.

Interpreting German Sociology

German sociology never formed a school to compare with French sociology under Durkheim's leadership.[20] The makers of German sociology had no master, held chairs in other fields, and contributed irregularly to the nascent discipline.[21] Without institutional or doctrinal boundaries, their activity took the less easily definable form of a movement, with membership a matter of personal choice and retrospective observers' point of view.

Scholars have tried to bring order into the first generation of German sociology from several distinct perspectives. American sociologists have assiduously produced translations and commentaries presenting the German thinkers of a foreign time and place as makers of a new science removed from the vagaries of history. We owe exemplary works of translation to this tradition as well as studies that, originally inspired by German sociology, became important contributions in their own right to social theory. Yet any one perspective has the danger of skewing its subject when it claims to present the whole truth about it, as the scientistic tradition has often done.[22] The American translation of *Gemeinschaft und Gesellschaft* suffers most blatantly from this kind of distortion, but other translations and commentaries also obscure their authors' intentions, bowdlerizing their writings in order to provide American readers with clean, unproblematic social science. Without wishing to slight the considerable achievements of scholars writing in this tradition, I have sometimes found it necessary to provide my own translations and to bring to light aspects of German sociology they would prefer to leave unnoticed.

Chapter 1

Since the end of World War II, a second group of scholars
has reassessed the German sociologists by examining their role
in the German political system. The best-known book in this
tradition is Wolfgang Mommsen's *Max Weber and German Politics*,
but others, too, have analyzed the sociologists' relationship to
German society and state. I have found the attitudes of the
sociologists, and of the educated elite in general, to be more
complex than they are sometimes portrayed. The image of
mandarins in retreat from mass society exaggerates one tendency of an elite still possessing a strong belief in its public responsibilities.[23] I have also not found any clear pattern of
marginalization among the makers of German sociology.[24] To
be sure, one can point to the estrangement of a thinker like
Tönnies, but what is one to make of Troeltsch's professional
success? And how should one account for the fashionableness
of sociology in the Heidelberg professoriate? We need to be
alert to the structural conditions of the sociologists' work without stereotyping their highly complex situations and differentiated responses.

A third group of interpretations has focused on the cultural
significance of German sociology. The sociologists wished to as-
sess the meaning of modern society for the human spirit—how
it created a different human species from the mankind of antiquity, the Middle Ages, and other civilizations; how it degraded or elevated contemporary culture; how it checked or
furthered human dignity for the future.[25] The heritage of authors and traditions providing clues to this assessment is ex-
ceedingly rich. The sociologists' relationship to Kant and Marx
has been discussed for decades; Nietzsche's influence has more
recently attracted attention, as has the role of literature.[26] This
book gives special emphasis to the religious background, a subject that has received little attention compared to philosophy
and literature. Yet it was no less important to a group of thinkers convinced that the shift from a religious to a social framework of meaning was one of the distinctive features of
modernity. To explain how man's social fate had replaced his
religious fate was one of the chief ambitions underlying their
work and remains a powerful, though seldom acknowledged,
source of its enduring interest.

2
Ferdinand Tönnies: In Search of Community

Like the prophet Jeremiah, Ferdinand Tönnies gave birth to a prophetic book against his own will, as if fearing the misunderstanding and hostility his message would arouse. While sitting down in February 1887 to write the preface to *Gemeinschaft und Gesellschaft*, he lamented to his friend, Friedrich Paulsen, "Unfortunately I have to call it a mistake that I've finished it and can't entirely clear you of responsibility for spurring me on. . . . It is a work with a great many shortcomings, though also one that grew out of much meditation. More calm and patience would have resulted in something more genuine and pure."[1] Barely thirty-two when the book appeared in July of the same year, he already had behind him a remarkable intellectual odyssey that had carried him far in time and place from his native Schleswig-Holstein. As he sensed, the book failed to bring to life what he had seen, although one may doubt that waiting longer would have improved it. With its strange terminology and antiquated style, it read like a learned tract from another era.

The reviews justified his anxieties. Most of his critics appreciated his erudition and gift for synthesis. These were internationally praised by Herbert Blunt in the British journal *Mind*, Emile Durkheim in *Revue Philosophique*, and Gustav Schmoller in *Schmollers Jahrbuch*.[2] But his world-historical pessimism and rejection of modern civilization disquieted them. Durkheim reprimanded him for the one-sidedness of his contrast between holistic *Gemeinschaft* and decadent *Gesellschaft*, accusing him of

too much fantasy, too little evidence.[3] Schmoller damned his
book to obscurity: "Who would deny him [Tönnies] his profound feeling for the philosophy of history, his power of psychological observation, his special grasp of things? And yet the
book will leave absolutely no mark. It is the confession of a
lonely thinker. . . ."[4] Even Paulsen, to whom the first edition
was dedicated, publicly took issue with Tönnies's tone of "pessimistic resignation."[5] The established scholarly world of the
1880s was too self-confident to detect anything more than the
ponderings of a North German brooder.

Slowly, *Gemeinschaft und Gesellschaft* found readers. By the
time the second edition appeared in 1912, Tönnies had gained
a respectable place in the German academic world, accompa-
nying Weber and Troeltsch in 1904 to the Louisiana Purchase
Exposition in St. Louis, receiving a regular appointment at the
University of Kiel on the last day of 1908, and serving with
Simmel and Werner Sombart as one of the chairmen of the
German Sociological Society founded in 1909.[6] His new introduction to the second edition noted the steady growth of the
book's reputation since the turn of the century. The reviewers
bore out his observation, this time writing knowledgeable ap-
preciations of a recognized masterpiece.[7]

The contemporary relevance of *Gemeinschaft* went on to over-
whelm the book's place in twentieth-century sociology. Rural
nostalgia turned it into a best-seller going through five more
editions between 1920 and 1926. Its pessimism appealed to the
same kind of audience that read Spengler, with the opposition
between *Gemeinschaft* and *Gesellschaft* turning into one of the
truisms of the era.[8] The Nazis made *Gemeinschaft* an entry in
their racial vocabulary. Tönnies himself was an outspoken anti-
Nazi who joined the Social Democratic Party in April 1930 as
an act of solidarity with the Weimar Republic against the growing threat from the right. The newly installed Nazi regime in
Schleswig-Holstein was a better judge of him than some of his
later critics when it dismissed him without pension from his
professorship in 1933. Nonetheless, an odium of guilt has stuck
to the book.[9] Rene König and Ralf Dahrendorf have indicted it
for the kind of illiberal thinking that led Germany to political
catastrophe.[10] Outside of sociology departments the book's title

is perhaps better known today in the United States, where it still flits ghostlike across the graduate seminar room.

Problematic though it is, *Gemeinschaft und Gesellschaft* remains the beginning of Germany's modern sociological tradition. It was the first work to make *Gemeinschaft* a cardinal concept of sociology and to develop a logical and historical dichotomy between it and modern society. It discovered not just the names but also the psychological counterparts characteristic of German sociology, linking objective social structures to subjective types of feeling and will. Another fundamental contribution was the philosophy of history that so offended the original readers: Tönnies broke with their evolutionary optimism and described *Gesellschaft* as a realm of inauthentic existence.

To found German sociology a generation ahead of his contemporaries was Tönnies's personal misfortune but a boon for the historian, who can observe him grappling with issues later submerged but still potent. Born in 1855, he fully participated in the enthusiasm of 1870–71 over national unification and the subsequent mood of disappointment. His careful documentation of his own intellectual development in publications, letters, and recollections permits a detailed reconstruction of the relationship between Germany's failure to create a national community and his discovery of *Gemeinschaft*.

The Disappointments of Empire

The Fragmented Polity

The Franco-Prussian War, the third and final war of German unification, broke out while Tönnies was a *Gymnasium* student in Husum, a small but prosperous center for cattle trade with England on Schleswig-Holstein's west coast.[11] Even though anti-Prussian sentiment had run high in the two provinces just a few years earlier, the mood had changed to pro-Prussian enthusiasm by 1870.[12] On learning that war had been declared, Tönnies ran home and exclaimed that he wanted to join the army— to which his father replied by slapping him. While others made their way to the battlefront, he stayed home and sang in the local glee club, led by the writer Theodor Storm, "No Finer

Death in the World Than at the Enemy's Hands."[13] After graduating from *Gymnasium* two years later he made his first university choice a patriotic one: Strasbourg, in newly captured Alsace, where he was present on 1 May 1872 to witness the university's opening festivities. Several nights of sleeping in tents in the overcrowded town discouraged him, however, and he left for the University of Jena.[14] Not yet seventeen but a precocious learner, he also joined a fraternity. For the next few years his partying abilities rose while his sense of academic purpose sank. Military service beginning in the fall of 1874 added extra strain; finally, in January 1875, after banging his head during a drinking stunt, he collapsed. For years thereafter he suffered from bad headaches.[15]

In the fall of 1875 he went to study at the University of Berlin with a changed personality: sickly, withdrawn, melancholy. More than just the aftereffects of student debauchery caused his unrelenting hangover: dispiriting changes were taking place in German politics. The Berlin stock market crash of 1873 put an end to two years of national high living and careless speculation, ruining nobles, tradesmen, artisans, and farmers, who responded by turning to antisemitism and agrarian pressure group politics. A year later the percentage of socialist votes more than doubled in the Reichstag elections. Meanwhile Prussia's so-called *Kulturkampf* ("cultural struggle"), aimed at destroying Catholic autonomy and uniting Protestants of all classes, was under way, with neither side winning, but Catholics demonstrating their determination to resist Protestant and official cultural hegemony. The intoxicating effects of military victory gave way to the bleary realization that Germany lacked internal political consensus.[16]

Tönnies was well placed to observe the ill effects of Empire. Although he came from an isolated rural town, his political education had begun early, for his father, a gentleman farmer with real estate and stock market investments, frequently received visitors active in politics. There was plenty of news to overhear during the 1860s, a period when Schleswig-Holstein attracted international attention as cause of the first two wars of unification in 1864 and 1866. Social strife, too, was part of

Tönnies's childhood surroundings. Although it lacked heavy industry, Schleswig-Holstein had a long tradition of popular protest and developed a well-organized labor movement. Kiel, its main port, became a boom town in the mid-1860s, with workers from points south streaming in to its docks and shipyards. Socialist organizers from Hamburg and Altona had little difficulty organizing there and in the surrounding countryside.[17] This was no island of *Gemeinschaft* in a surrounding Imperial *Gesellschaft*. Contemporary class struggle was vivid enough for Tönnies to pay close attention to his school lessons about parallel conflicts in the histories of Greece and Rome.[18]

In Berlin, Tönnies studied Kant in the seminar of a young philosophy teacher who also came from the west coast of Schleswig-Holstein and could understand his growing political disillusionment. Friedrich Paulsen, ten years his senior, stood at the beginning of a successful academic career and stayed in Berlin until his death in 1908.[19] Tönnies left at the end of the winter semester 1875–76 and went to study at the University of Kiel (where he eventually completed his habilitation in 1881 after further wandering from university to university), but visited Paulsen in the capital and corresponded with him. When they first met, Paulsen admired the writings of Lassalle, the great socialist organizer who had died in 1864, while Tönnies was skeptical.[20] Three years later their positions had changed. Paulsen, settling into the complacent conservatism of his later years, received furious letters from Tönnies over the mistreatment of the working class: ". . . In this moral world the starving Chinese eat their children and the factory owners in Germany fire their workers," wrote Tönnies on 27 July 1878, "thanks to thrice-cursed capitalist property rights. . . ."[21] A few weeks before he had denounced the "wretched, scandalous newspaper culture" of the time and looked to the working class for cultural rebirth.[22]

What fired Tönnies's anger was the onset of Bismarck's antisocialist campaign. Two assassination attempts against the emperor in May and June 1878 gave him the excuse he needed to accuse the Social Democrats of subversive activities; the press joined the attack, urging the public to go along with Bismarck's legislative proposal to suppress the labor party, trade unions, and other workers' organizations. The Socialist Law that went into effect on 21 October legalized a police campaign to root out the working-class movement. While most bourgeois onlookers and their liberal political representatives thanked Bismarck for rescuing them from revolution, a few dissenters such as Tönnies looked on with helpless disgust.[23]

Paulsen and Tönnies exemplified diverging responses to the crisis of German liberalism in the 1870s. Paulsen, the son of simple farmers, turned into one of Prussia's professorial apologists and was attracted to the right-wing, antisemitic populism of the former court preacher, Adolf Stöcker. Tönnies was at first the more vehemently antisemitic of the two, but soon shed his prejudice and maintained a critical stance toward the state. When Paulsen sympathized in 1885 with Stöcker's and Adolf Wagner's Christian conservatism, Tönnies replied, "My sympathy for this degenerate species of military-aristocratic conservatism is altogether limited."[24] When Paulsen approved of Bismarck's social welfare legislation during the late 1880s Tönnies remained relentlessly opposed.[25] While Paulsen supported the government policy of excluding socialists from university positions, Tönnies damaged his own chances for a university appointment by lending conspicuous support to a Hamburg dockworkers' strike in 1896 and refusing to promise afterward to keep his opinions private.[26]

In contrast to Paulsen, Tönnies supported populist politics against the state and in the name of universal justice. The hysterical antimodernism of his early letters to Paulsen, private expressions written when he was in his early twenties, gave way to a lifetime of carefully measured, independent, and fearless public political stances. Self-consciously a philosopher and social scientist, who wrote on contemporary issues but only mixed in them directly when extreme circumstances justified it, he took pains to see that his political views matched his high standards of intellectual and ethical probity. Nothing illustrates this more clearly than his correspondence with Paulsen: despite his dependence on him for friendship and contacts with the academic power holders in Berlin, Tönnies went his own way, refusing any compromise with Paulsen's prejudices.

Neohumanism in Decline

Tönnies's teachers in Husum embodied the best spirit of the old-fashioned *Gymnasium* and conveyed their enthusiasm for the most important subjects in the curriculum, Greek and Latin. It did not occur to him on first entering the university to study anything except classical philology.[27] According to the neohumanist precepts laid down by Wilhelm von Humboldt at the beginning of the nineteenth century, moderns could enter the original spirit of antiquity through its languages and experience its culture as a totality, an education preparing them for an equally unified grasp of their own world.[28] Instead of a discipline that would quicken all others, Tönnies encountered an increasingly positivist and specialized profession in which students were supposed to limit themselves to narrow points of textual criticism.[29]

Philosophy, to which he next turned, was no better. Humboldt had expected it to function as the university's unifying discipline. The Philosophical Faculty, as a single administrative body, was supposed to contain all theoretical branches of learning (roughly speaking, the disciplines today comprised by the humanities, social sciences, and natural sciences), to maintain exchange of ideas among its members, and to guarantee the orderly progress of knowledge. By the 1870s the idea of philosophical unity was still officially respected, but the various disciplines were too specialized for universal communication, and their shared faculty only hindered the organization of empirical research.[30] As for philosophy itself, Tönnies encountered the discipline at a low point. The great thinkers of the age of Idealism were gone; the neo-Kantian movement did not attract him. To pursue philosophy as the love of wisdom was to confront the decayed state of humanism in the German university.

No less disturbing was the university's dependence on the state, which, Tönnies wrote to Paulsen in 1881, found independent thinkers too dangerous to tolerate. "If it is smart, the state has to have and further official opinions—freedom of conscience is an anarchic ideal. If we don't think such a state is a fine and good thing, then we can't belong in it."[31] Tönnies was reaching the conclusion that he, unlike his friend, did not in fact belong in it, or at least would not make the slightest compromise to gain a place in it. In 1881 he settled in Schleswig-Holstein in order to lead the pure life of the mind, commuting between Husum and the University of Kiel while carrying out his scholarly projects. The slightest hope of a genuine community of learning was enough to stir his enthusiasm. He wrote seriously to Paulsen about the possibility of establishing a settlement for philosophers in the North German countryside, which, removed from the corruption of modern life, would re-create the atmosphere of Plato's Academy.[32] Excited by a vague possibility of an opening for Paulsen at the University of Göttingen, he declared his readiness to join him there and make it the home of their philosophers' community.[33] He tried to interest Nietzsche's publisher in starting a journal for cultural criticism. Nothing came of these plans.

Tönnies was not alone in noticing the changes taking place in the German university. Nietzsche, too, had lamented the university's lack of genuine philosophy in a lecture series in Basel.[34] Tönnies's own mature views on the modern university became more complex than his youthful complaints to Paulsen might suggest. His dislike of political interference never diminished; years later the need to swear an oath to the Prussian monarchy in order to receive his regular university appointment still troubled him.[35] As for the specialization of modern learning, Tönnies himself became a serious practitioner of empirical and statistical sociology, but believed that sociology had to maintain at least an indirect connection to philosophy. The questions that ultimately interested him had to do with the nature and meaning of modern society. He remained a philosophical sociologist loyal to the early nineteenth-century ideal of the unity of knowledge.

Dialectic of the Enlightenment

In addition to being a social theorist, Tönnies was an original historian of social thought. He was one of his generation's first scholars to recognize the importance of Hobbes as founder of modern social science and one of its most knowledgeable readers of Marx. The list of his readings from the 1870s and 1880s

did not stop here: he was also steeped in Spinoza, Schopen-hauer, Nietzsche, and ninetenth-century ethnology, sociology, and legal history. The historical studies that he wrote from early to late in life comprised a reconstruction of the course of modern social theory, grasping it as a unified movement comparable to the unity of ancient and medieval thought.

This research, a considerable achievement in its own right, also provided historical justification for the theoretical theorems of *Gemeinschaft und Gesellschaft*. Tönnies traced the history of ideas with a sociologist's eye for its relationship to the development of modern society. He followed it on a dialectical path from the unity of the traditional European social order to the atomized dynamic of modern society. The dominant tradition of modern social theory beginning with Hobbes, reflecting the logic of the social forces it analyzed, treated bourgeois self-interest as a universal and necessary law. Comparison with other eras and study of heretical modern thinkers suggested that this was a historically conditioned view of human behavior. A more comprehensive theory would take advantage of certain elements of modern theory, but in order to understand bourgeois society's flaws and the different logic of other social orders, it would have to assimilate prebourgeois methods of thinking, hidden and neglected by the Enlightenment.

Theories of Bourgeois Society: Hobbes and Marx

Paulsen recommended Hobbes to Tönnies at a time when the seventeenth-century English analyst of civil war was almost unknown in Germany. Tönnies bought and read *De Cive* in 1876 and went on to whatever other editions of his writings he could find. The shortage of available texts turned him into a Hobbes scholar; in 1878 he traveled to England in order to examine Hobbes manuscripts in London and Oxford. His research led him to one unknown tract and the original manuscripts of two other works published in corrupt editions. Until 1889—overlapping with his research and writing of *Gemeinschaft und Gesellschaft* until 1887—he prepared critical editions of two of these works as well as historical studies assessing Hobbes's place in modern thought.[36]

Tönnies argued for Hobbes's preeminence as the founder of modern social science. Just as Galileo, Hobbes's contemporary and friend, constructed a mechanistic model of the physical world, so Hobbes treated society, analyzing human beings as mechanical bodies continually in motion, their relationship to one another governed by rational rules. According to Hobbes, the instinct for self-preservation, rooted in biological nature, motivated human action. Natural human appetites made life a continuous struggle for power and wealth, or, from the perspective of the social physicist, a series of collisions between bodies on intersecting paths. This way of looking at things, commented Tönnies, was no less an intellectual revolution than Galilean physics, for it too involved throwing out Scholastic essences and qualities and replacing them with a causal system of analysis. Aristotle and his successors assumed that man was essentially a political animal who fulfilled his natural end by creating a life in common; Hobbes pointed to the brute instinct motivating the human beast. The teleological assumptions of his predecessors, who presupposed that human action tended toward the good or Christian life, gave way to the task of determining individual motives and the means used to realize them.[37]

According to *Leviathan*'s famous argument, political order replaced chaos when human beings agreed to give up their natural freedom and cede power to a sovereign who guaranteed a minimum security of life and property. The state derived from a rational social consensus.[38] In postregicidal England, familiar with the horrors of real civil war and with the catastrophic breakdown of authority in Central Europe during the Thirty Years' War, such a theory could serve as a rationale for royal absolutism. In prerevolutionary Germany it could have the effect of exposing the pseudoconstitutional garb in which Bismarck had clothed the Empire. The Imperial political system rested on contradictions between a *Reichstag* elected by universal suffrage and a *Bundesrat* or federal council elected by the Empire's individual states; between an enlarged Prussia and the rest of the Empire; between the Prussian-German monarch claiming divine authority and a bureaucracy run on rational principles. Designed to keep power in the hands of the monarchy and Prussian ruling class while creating the illusion of popular and rational grounds for legitimacy, these arrangements made an easy target for a critic schooled in Hobbes. Tönnies confided in a letter to Paulsen his plans for replacing them with a rational democratic order. In his ideal state, voters would choose representatives, who in turn would elect higher officials culminating in a council of elders, who would choose a president from their own midst. The minimum voting age would be a philosophical thirty.[39] Whether or not it materialized in the form he proposed, the twenty-three-year-old Tönnies was sure in 1878 that democracy would come: "Monarchy is over with, no matter what it is worth in and of itself. It is stuck together with every half-dead institution and together with them must be buried. No matter what it is intrinsically worth, democracy is the only possible form of government for a future civilized state (*Kulturstaat*)."[40] The Schleswig-Holstein democrat, like his absolutist model Hobbes, abhorred the ramshackleness of existing institutions and believed that society was doomed to disorder unless it worked on principles as logical as a philosophical treatise.

From his Hobbes studies and the trips he made in pursuit of manuscripts and publishers, Tönnies developed a general admiration of English life. Like other middle-class critics of Imperial Germany, including Troeltsch and Weber, he looked to England as the land whose self-confident bourgeoisie had succeeded where Germans had failed, overthrowing absolute monarchy and establishing a modern government. It was not a threatening utopia like France; its revolution was far removed from the present, its culture reassuringly close to one's own. Despite his criticisms of German liberalism, Tönnies did not hesitate to praise its English counterpart, the Utilitarian tradition, which, he stated to the readers of his Hobbes biography, had rescued Hobbes from neglect at the beginning of the nineteenth century.[41]

Tönnies integrated Hobbesian theory and Utilitarianism into a postliberal dialectic. Hobbes, he argued, stood at the beginning of a specific historical development, the dissolving of feudal ties and formation of a capitalist society in England. His theory reflected the logic of a market economy with its competing egos and mechanical means of production.[42] At the end of the bourgeois era, Tönnies confronted a social phenomenon unforeseen by Hobbes, the formation of economic classes, each unified by its rational interests against the rest of society. Hobbes had treated civil society as an aggregate of individuals. This was accurate for its initial phase but did not capture its later regrouping into capital and labor. As their opposing interests took shape, so did Hobbes's nightmare: civil war.

This critique of Hobbes showed the strong influence of Marx, whom Tönnies bravely cited as one of his chief sources in the introduction to *Gemeinschaft und Gesellschaft.*[43] Following Marx's lead Tönnies analyzed the state as an extension of class interests. Either it served as "a general association characteristic of society existing and *simultaneously established* for the purpose of protecting the freedom and property of its subjects . . ."[44]— the state could play the minimum role of guardian of public order assigned to it by liberalism—or it could pretend to be "the social reason which is implied in the concept of a reasonable thinking agent of society"[45]—the actively intervening agent of the public good, historically exemplified by the Prussian state. But in either case, its claims to legitimacy were nothing more than a disguise for class interests. Tönnies affirmed Marx's critique of the state as the instrument of capital and his championship of the working class as the authentic embodiment of the general social interest.[46]

Were this all Tönnies had in mind, his work would have been little more than a gloss on *Capital* enriched by references to Hobbes. But another dimension of his thought led beyond Marx to a new generation's concern with the psychological origins of society. One of Hobbes's great strengths, according to Tönnies, was his penetration to the instinct psychology underlying social behavior. Hobbes argued that the transition from chaos to civil order took place because reason persuaded human beings to sacrifice part of their freedom out of self-interest. Yet the peace resulting from this consensus, the peace of civil society, nurtured an increasingly destructive form of rationality. In the capitalist marketplace the exercise of reason became a continuation of civil war by other means. Over the centuries reason had produced an ever more powerful tech-

nology and accumulated ever greater reserves of power and wealth for purposes of domination. The consequence for his own time, believed Tönnies, was not just the external formation of class society, but also rationalization internalized: heightened knowledge and disposition to regard all social relations as means-end relations furthering one's chances for self-preservation. Hobbes's proto-Enlightenment faith in reason's power to check instinct had ignored the possibility that reason itself might only magnify human beings' power of mutual destruction. The breakdown of the social order at the end of the nineteenth century resulted from an internal contradiction that reliance on reason alone could not correct.[47]

For Tönnies the solution to the contradictions of late nineteenth-century society did not lie in any form of irrationality. The glorification of violence of a Sorel, the emphasis on charismatic leadership of a Max Weber, were alien to him. On the contrary, Tönnies was thoroughly a thinker of the nineteenth century whose writings could later be misused in part because they were so alien to the twentieth. What he proposed was not so much the abandonment of modern rationality as a relativization of it. If capitalism contained a logic of conflict and exploitation, the sociologist might well ask whether a different kind of reason did not correspond to a harmonious and just social order. By leaving the realm of bourgeois society and its contradictions altogether, Tönnies could hope to find the secret of that fraternal feeling that Germany had briefly experienced in 1870.

Theories of Community

In his first semester at Jena, Tönnies noticed an unfamiliar book with an intriguing title: Nietzsche's *The Birth of Tragedy out of the Spirit of Music*.[48] "The student could not make up his mind to buy the little Nietzsche book" he later recalled, "but he found it in the summer vacation of 1873 in his old Husum school library and read it with pleasure, indeed almost with the feeling of a revelation."[49] The greatness of Greek culture, argued Nietzsche, resulted from the tension between its two extremes of Apollonian self-control and Dionysian abandon, as embodied in Aeschylean and Sophoclean tragedy. Inspired by German victory in 1871, Nietzsche's imagination flew from the ancient polis to the modern nation-state. Germany was reliving Greek history, according to Nietzsche, in reverse order: Greece's archaic Dionysian fervor had disintegrated under the critical scrutiny of Socratic reasoning and disappeared amid the intellectualism of Alexandria; Germany's Alexandrian pedantry, by contrast, was just about to yield to a rebirth of the Dionysian. Wagner's music announced the return of the ancient god. Modern Germans could experience their nation's inwardly felt unity in Wagnerian opera just as ancient Greeks had experienced the polis's unity in the theater.

The rebirth of tragedy never came. Tönnies followed approvingly as Nietzsche's mood changed and the former celebrant of Imperial Germany turned into its devastating critic in the *Untimely Observations* of 1873–74. Nietzsche opened the three essays by expressing his fear that military victory had turned into *die Niederlage, ja Extirpation des deutschen Geistes zu Gunsten des deutschen Reiches* ("the defeat, the destruction of German culture for the sake of the German Empire").[50] It is hard to imagine exactly what he expected after unification, but whatever it was, he got the *Bildungsphilister*—the smug middle-class cultural devotee who made a religion out of Beethoven and Goethe without realizing that his worship of them was a negation of genuine culture, substituting past manifestations of the Dionysian for his own experience beyond the concert hall.

During the 1870s and early 1880s Tönnies circled around Nietzsche without ever quite landing, composing imaginary letters to him, visiting his mother in Naumburg, and talking to his publisher.[51] This trailing of his hero reached its climax in the summer of 1883, when he went to spend a few weeks in Switzerland with Lou Salomé and Paul Rée. The couple had just had a falling-out with Nietzsche, Rée's rival for Lou's affection. When Tönnies promptly fell in love with her, she tested his devotion by asking him to visit Nietzsche in the high Alpine village of Sils Maria to arrange a reconciliation. Dutifully trekking off to fulfill his mission, Tönnies sighted his hero several times, but could not work up the nerve to speak to him. This was as close as he ever got. He could have done better with Lou,

who saw him again afterward and later tried unsuccessfully to renew their friendship.[52]

Other thinkers, too, contributed to his conception of a community of wills. The chronological starting point of his thinking was again Hobbes, who, he claimed in an essay of 1881, had exercised an unnoticed but crucial influence on Spinoza.[53] Originally, according to Tönnies, Spinoza's *Ethics* stated that human knowledge of the good led man to will the good—a position asserting the primacy of reason over volition. Halfway through, however, it instead stated that man calls a thing good *because* he wills it—an inversion of the former position asserting the primacy of volition. The inspiration for this voluntarist turn, he argued, came from Spinoza's reading in 1668 of *Leviathan*, from which he borrowed his definition of willing as the act of seeking one's self-preservation.[54] Voluntarism did not, however, necessarily go hand in hand with Hobbesian ego psychology. Spinoza chose to take it in a collective direction, integrating it into a system in which the individual tended to affirm instead of to negate the existence of other wills. In its most perfect state the will of the individual participated in a cosmic totality in which all wills were mutually affirming.

Another important link in Tönnies's voluntarist tradition was Schopenhauer. He appreciated the acerbic, down-to-earth side of Schopenhauer's thinking, his penchant for reducing philosophical problems to plain biology. The will to self-preservation went through sundry forms of self-disguise but at its most elementary was sexual instinct.[55] Tönnies did not show any interest in the life-denying conclusions of Schopenhauer's system— his teaching that the aim of the philosophical life should be the extinction of instinct and with it the extinction of the source of all suffering. Rather he took up the plea of Nietzsche, Schopenhauer's great heir and critic, for a life-affirming pessimism recognizing the suffering but also the creative power inherent in nature. Sexuality and its sublimations did not just set individuals against one another; they could also serve as the source of social solidarity, and this was the possibility Tönnies chose to explore.

Late nineteenth-century ethnography and historical jurisprudence convinced Tönnies that the community eluding him in the present had been the universal reality of the past.[56] The literature was international, as were its sources. Lewis Henry Morgan's work introduced him to the principles of clan organization among American Indians. Bachofen's *Das Mutterrecht* taught him that an era of maternal authority and family organization had preceded the patriarchal, impersonal law of late antiquity. Otto von Gierke unearthed communal legal institutions of the Germanic past. What these scholars, in their different ways, sought to prove was the primacy of the family in premodern social orders. Blood and marriage ties were the fundamental means of patterning social relationships that extended directly and metaphorically into the larger units of tribal and clan organization; matriarchy and patriarchy denoted forms of authority permeating private and public life. All three were conservatives who conducted their research in order to find the sources of social stability, wishing to remind their readers of the fragility of social order and the hidden psychic layers on which it rested, of the need to preserve patriarchy as its ultimate foundation. All came from the law; all criticized at least implicitly the formal, market-oriented individualism of liberal legal thought.[57] Tönnies (like Engels, another admirer of Morgan and Bachofen) spotted the subversive potential of their research.[58] If an era of communities based on the family had preceded capitalist society, then capitalism was historically relativized so that it and the Hobbesian state of nature could be seen as just one stage in the history of man. A new communal era might succeed it.

One of the distinctive features of Tönnies's thought in the 1870s and 1880s was its skill at synthesizing diverging theories. The differences between Hobbes and Spinoza, Marx and Nietzsche, did not compel him to choose one over the other; instead he asked how they belonged together in a comprehensive understanding of the origins of society. Tönnies today has the reputation of a Germanophile thinker whose yearning for community led away from enlightened Western Europe and down the isolated path to disaster. His actual intentions were more nearly the opposite. Few thinkers of his time read and wrote with a more cosmopolitan disregard for national boundaries. Tönnies's fluency in Western European ideas was actually a throwback to the era before 1848 and somewhat out of touch with the late nineteenth century. His historical writings show him at his best. They represent not so much a divergence from the Enlightenment as an attempt to rethink it under new conditions, anticipating the Frankfurt School's self-criticism of enlightened reason.

The Science of Fate: *Gemeinschaft und Gesellschaft*

From 1881 to 1887 Tönnies worked on the manuscript of *Gemeinschaft und Gesellschaft*. He aspired to make his book scientific in the strongest nineteenth-century sense of the word, a contribution to objective knowledge of society comparable to the results of the physicist or biologist. The ambition was not new; he saw himself as deepening the foundations of a science that went back two centuries to Hobbes. Among nineteenth-century social thinkers he had to look no farther than the introduction to *Capital* or the writings of Comte or Spencer for the conviction that social science shared in the general progress of science.[59] Large parts of *Gemeinschaft und Gesellschaft* recapitulated the ideas of his predecessors, just as a work by a writer in any other field would build on the existing store of knowledge. His book would further the progress of a science long in the making.[60]

Tönnies wished to write in a spirit of scientific objectivity, to show the same dispassion toward society as one would toward any other object of knowledge.[61] This intention and the form in which he pursued it, however, were inseparable from the Naturalist mood of the decades in which he conceived his book.[62] Like many contemporaneous writers and artists, he responded to the great social changes of the period by regarding them as forces of nature—overwhelming, mutely transforming, indifferent to human sentiment.[63] Germany's political and cultural crises, from this perspective, were fated events, as inexorable as the decay and death of an organism. To observe society in this way was not to stay neutral toward it; rather, it was a way of reconciling oneself to an unwished destiny by comparing it to natural forces.

The will to scientific objectivity and the urge to criticism jostled uncomfortably in Tönnies's book. He attempted to expunge evolutionary optimism and evolutionary pessimism alike from it. Insight into natural necessity, his supposed aim, had nothing to do with personal sentiments about whether things were getting better or worse. Society's nature and necessity, however, were hardly terms that Tönnies could define unconditioned by his own time and place. *Gemeinschaft und Gesellschaft* contained a tremendous challenge to liberal society's assumptions about the naturalness of possessive individualism and confronted it with a contrary image of man's natural will to a life in common. It predicted that European society, so expansive and successful at the time he wrote, was on its way to decline and fall. Society's fate was a predetermined process of which the social scientist was merely the impersonal chronicler—but the prediction that capitalism, with all its selfishness and injustice, could not survive was also the deepfelt conviction of a social prophet.

The Voluntarist Theory

Tönnies cast *Gemeinschaft und Gesellschaft* in two parts. First came definitions of *Gemeinschaft* and *Gesellschaft* as objective social structures; then came definitions of two corresponding types of will. Ordering the book in this way gave systematic expression to its interest in social psychology. Analysis of objective social structure alone never sufficed to explain a social phenomenon, which required reference to a subjective dimension as well. Tönnies did not deduce one from the other; he did not treat society as an emanation of psychology or vice versa. Instead he considered them as separate but causally interacting. Voluntarism in Tönnies's theory did not signify a psychological reductionism, but simply an insistence that objective description alone yielded one-sided, partial social analysis.

Tönnies's image of *Gemeinschaft* contained an idealized version of medieval Germany. The basic unit of traditional community was the house, a stable, self-sufficient economic unit.[64] Within the house the father exercised authority over wife, children, and servants.[65] Bonds of blood relation, place, and friendship tied individuals to one another and drew houses into the larger units of clan, ethnic group, and people, of village, county, and province.[66] The traditional town, no less than the countryside, was organized on communal lines, its guilds regulating production and trade in harmony with the general needs of collective life.[67] Tönnies made an abrupt transition from this theory of *Gemeinschaft* as stable collective organism to a theory of *Gesellschaft* strongly colored by Marx. Modern society was constituted by commodity exchange. Persons in modern society were isolated individuals who created commodities through wage labor. Contracts and wage labor regulated their relations to one another.[68] Marketplace relations were ubiquitous, turning every individual into a salesman, buying and selling his labor and other commodities.[69] In contrast to localized *Gemeinschaft, Gesellschaft* pushed ever farther outward, encompassing all parts of the globe, dissolving traditional communal relations and creating a universal class of workers who were formally free but oppressed by marketplace conditions.[70]

The *Wesenwille* or essential will of traditional community aimed at maintaining the unity of the social totality. It originated in the longing of mother and child to restore their oneness and persisted in all other communal relations.[71] The members of a *Gemeinschaft* experienced their acts of mutual aid as pleasurable sensations, which, recurring over lifetimes and generations, built up substantive psychological bonds, the equivalent of an organism's physical unity.[72] Tönnies also called the essential will an organic will.[73] He did not mean by this, however, that it was a superpersonal entity floating above the individuals sustained by it. Rather, the attitude of each person made his will organic in the sense that it was intuitively guided by the totality of past experience and directed toward the common good. Nor did Tönnies conceive of the essential will as hostile to reason. It was always capable of verbal articulation in his description of it. Reason functioned as an extension of the essential will, subordinate to it and the activities of the social whole.

The *Kürwille* or arbitrary will of modern society had a status different from that of essential will. It represented a hypertrophy of the intellect, which inverted its natural psychological function. Instead of being determined by the will—and behind

it, by the collective past of the community—the intellect driven
by it looked forward to the future and planned the individual's
advantage over the surrounding members of society.[74] Whereas
essential will affirmed the existence of other persons, arbitrary
will was negative, destroying others to further its self-aggran-
dizement. In contrast to the organic will, which subordinated
the individual to the social whole, the arbitrary will followed
the mechanical logic of means-end relationships, calculating
how to achieve specific, isolated goals without regard for their
larger effect. According to Tönnies, arbitrary will was an illusion, pretender to a sovereignty it could not maintain, for
ultimately it was dependent on the social totality it threw into
disarray.[75]

The transition to *Gesellschaft* was inherent in *Gemeinschaft*, according to Tönnies. Over time, human beings naturally accumulated skill in carrying out tasks, gradually learning to
arrange them into hierarchies of goals. As they did so, intellect
gained ascendancy over the will and apparent freedom from
it.[76] Parallel to this, the craftsman's shop naturally expanded,
intensified its division of labor, and turned into the factory; the
merchant accumulated capital, goods, and power over rural
producers.[77] Commercialization of the social order and intellectualization of man's psyche proceeded apace as subjective and
objective sides of the great transformation.

Despite the seeming simplicity of the monumental building
blocks out of which Tönnies constructed his system—*Gemeinschaft* and *Gesellschaft*, *Wesenwille* and *Kürwille*—it lacked the or-
derliness to which he aspired. The two great social types and
their psychological counterparts were supposed to be ranged
side by side for the reader's inspection, with the author favoring
neither one to the advantage of the other. To put it another
way, Tönnies's method was supposed to be hermeneutic, describing each type from its own perspective.[78] But he proved
unable to resist the opportunity to describe *Gesellschaft* from the
point of view of *Gemeinschaft*, as if the communal world of
the past, defeated by history, at last had a champion to accuse
the modern way of life that had vanquished it. His vindication
of the lost world of *Gemeinschaft* drew on the book's philosophy
of history. Its ultimate perspective on human affairs was an or-

ganic view of things in their cosmic interconnectedness. And this was a communal perspective, which could only treat the conflict and fragmentation of modern society as an interlude of social decay. The two social types were ultimately unequal; one was a state of health, the other a state of social pathology. Of course, Tönnies considered this an "impartial" assessment—nothing more than a statement of truth that modern society was unwilling to hear. But by subscribing to it and making it the book's pervasive message, he climbed to a height of social philosophy from which he could not easily descend. In the form he presented them, the book's categories were not neutral instruments of empirical analysis. Instead they embodied denunciation of one way of life, defense of another. This explains in part why later thinkers, to Tönnies's dismay, made use of the great dichotomy he introduced, but were reluctant to accept it in the systematic form he proposed. They needed to disengage it from his Naturalist philosophy of history in order to penetrate the empirical worlds of the past and present.

The Critique of Natural Right

An entire section of *Gemeinschaft und Gesellschaft*, roughly a third of the book, was a critique of natural right. This was a subject well suited to demonstrating the limitations of modern social theory. Modern natural right as expounded since the seventeenth century contained, in Tönnies's interpretation of it, an implicit defense of bourgeois society. It postulated as natural a social order constituted by abstract, rational individuals who through individual choice and social contract agreed to cooperate. Tönnies came at the end of a century of romantic and conservative criticisms of the unnaturalness of this revolutionary modern natural right, which, argued its opponents, did not correspond to any existing legal order and overturned historically sanctioned legal relationships.[79] Tönnies was not interested in furthering this critique, whose social motives were just as suspect to him as those of natural right theorists; he was not rejecting bourgeois thought only to return to a conservative defense of privilege. Instead he explained the two types of legal thinking, natural right and historical, as reflections of two types

of social orders, *Gemeinschaft* and *Gesellschaft*. Each retained relative validity as natural expression of its kind of volition, *Wesenwille* or *Kürwille*.

Tönnies derived communal law from the natural source of
community, the family. The instinctive attraction of husband
and wife and the development of this primitive bond into fixed
forms of conscience and duty structured all other forms of
communal obligation. Marriage was organized not around individuals, as in modern society, but around the house, whose
members received a fixed place within their own house and related to outsiders as members of other houses.[80] A second
source of communal law was agriculture, which bound together
members of a given generation and tied them to generations
past and future.[81] The rhythms of family and agricultural life
found expression in custom before being formally codified as
law.[82] In the modern world, family law remained the area most
nearly embodying communal principles, while modern natural
law found its most complete expression in contract law, designed to permit universal exchange between formally free persons.[83] One could best observe the tension between the two
kinds of "nature" in property law. On the one hand tradition
sanctioned property as an organic, inalienable extension of the
person—a notion derived from communal law. On the other
hand modern reason found it natural to buy and sell one's
property at will.[84] Tönnies's analysis here did not defend one
kind of law against the other so much as it pointed out the
persistence of both in modern society and their appropriate-
ness to different kinds of social conditions.

More tendentious was Tönnies's discussion of the different
forms of freedom of individual expression in modern society.
Convinced that all true morality was rooted in the settled folk-
ways of *Gemeinschaft,* he did not restrain his disgust toward the
liberties permitted in *Gesellschaft.* Women, delicate creatures of
feeling, belonged in the home; a society that let them leave it
and diminished the differences between the sexes could only be
a decadent society.[85] Intellectuals tended to deny the pious beliefs of their fathers and to replace them with the arbitrary
products of their own reason; the salons in which they ex-
changed ideas were shameless places in which everything was

said for sensation and advantage. The merchant, the most complete embodiment of *Gesellschaft*, was an enemy of the people: homeless, a traveler versed in foreign ways without piety toward his own, adept at using any means to achieve his goals, in all these respects the opposite of the farmer and the artisan.[86]

The thinker who most closely shared Tönnies's critique of modern society was Lukács, for whom too the only authentic order was an affirmative one. The idea that modern natural right stood for a derivative, mechanical idea of nature was not far from his thinking. He called modern society *eine zweite Natur*—"a second nature," artificial and constraining unlike the first.[87] He too sought through his criticisms to divest it of its naturalness and raise his readers' consciousness of its artificiality, which modern man confused with the inevitable order of things. And his work too assailed an enemy of human immediacy already sighted by Tönnies, bourgeois convention. Background, generation, and temperament set the two thinkers apart. Lukács was an assimilated Jewish cosmopolitan of the kind Tönnies implicitly attacked in *Gemeinschaft und Gesellschaft*. Tönnies was in the end a cautious reformer whose politics did not differ greatly from Troeltsch's, Weber's, and Simmel's, while Lukács was a revolutionary determined after 1917 to make his deeds match the radicality of his thought. Yet both of them wished for a return to the kind of natural harmony shattered by modern society. This set them apart from all those modernist thinkers who, whether bourgeois or revolutionary, believed that fragmentation was a lasting and perhaps even desirable feature of modern culture.

From Society to Socialism

"Treatise on Communism and Socialism as Empirical Cultural Forms," ran the subtitle to the first edition of *Gemeinschaft und Gesellschaft*. Tönnies systematically outlined what he meant by "communism": it referred to the archaic and traditional communities he brought together under the name *Gemeinschaft*. "Socialism," however, did not have a corresponding description in his book; certainly *Gesellschaft* in its existing form was the antithesis of a socialist order guided by principles of equality and cooperation. This flawed symmetry pointed to an underlying uncertainty: Tönnies never decided whether socialism was an evolutionary outcome of society or a revolutionary transformation of it.

A great deal speaks for an evolutionary interpretation. There was, first of all, the book's dichotomous organization. *Gemeinschaft* and *Gesellschaft* were its fundamental categories, and all other descriptions and classifications fit into one or the other. For the most part its empirical examples and analysis of natural right adhered to the same plan. "Socialism" became a name for logical tendencies inherent in *Gesellschaft,* such as the internationalization of commerce and science and the dying out of local culture. History then divided into times of *Gemeinschaft* and times of *Gesellschaft.*

A cyclical philosophy of history reinforced this interpretation. Modern Northern Europe was repeating the pattern already completed once by Southern Europe in antiquity. Greece had been its *Gemeinschaft,* the polis a traditional community tied to the surrounding land. Rome had been its *Gesellschaft,* the cosmopolitan city spreading commerce throughout the ancient world. Tönnies compared its extirpation of traditional communities, commercial law, decadent family life, and superficial splendor to the world around him, with the comparison between ancient Rome and modern Berlin perhaps too obvious (and too provocative) to state.[88]

The introduction to the first edition intoned on a note of Nietzschean pessimism, "I see in this [the transition from *Gemeinschaft* to *Gesellschaft*] a connection of facts that is as natural as life and death. I may rejoice in life and bemoan death; joy and sadness disappear beneath insight into divine fate."[89] In this passage Tönnies seemed to regard history with the wisdom distilled by Nietzsche from Greek tragedy: humanity shared the natural cycle of Dionysian oneness (*Gemeinschaft*) and Apollonian individuation (*Gesellschaft*), followed by decay and return to oneness with nature.[90] The social theorist could no more affect the passage of history than the dramatist could halt the tragic hero's death. Dignity lay in accepting nature's course. In contrast to the embittered tone of Tönnies's letters to Paulsen, *Gemeinschaft und Gesellschaft* wore a persona of Hellenic calm, removed from the limits of time and place to an impersonal, philosophical understanding of the passing of community.[91]

This was the book's dominant message, yet it contained revolutionary undercurrents. In his discussion of natural right Tönnies observed that the working class had its own idea of justice that went against the reigning natural right of bourgeois society. This notion came, he believed, from the lingering memories of primitive communism, and the communal impulse in the working class contained the seed of the new, socialist community of the future.[92] Tönnies's analysis of the modern state ascribed a genuinely revolutionary role to the working class: it would inevitably overthrow the state and create a new social order, one qualitatively different from modern society.[93] These remarks suggested that socialism was not simply an extension of *Gesellschaft* and contained the makings of a new community in Tönnies's positive sense, based on mutually affirming wills.

This side of Tönnies's thought stood closer to Marx than to Nietzsche. Society's inevitable development, unfolding like the life of an organism, guaranteed the collapse of capitalism and triumph of socialism. Seen in this light, his images of *Gemeinschaft* were not an inducement to nostalgia so much as a powerful reminder of things that once had been and could return. Though inconsistent with the book's structure, Tönnies's populist solidarity with the working class more nearly expressed the democratic politics he practiced from the 1890s to the 1930s.

The New Gospel

Tönnies shaped his contradictory attitude toward the future out of his lifelong rebellion against Lutheranism. Its religious traditions pervaded his upbringing, for his father was personally pious and his mother came from a prominent family of Holstein church servants.[94] In the best Enlightenment tradition he reacted by becoming militantly anticlerical. One of *Leviathan*'s initial attractions to him may well have been its author's polemic against the meddling of religious authorities in secular government;[95] at any rate, he had a lifelong hostility toward the clergy of his own time. His thinking was consistently and thoroughly materialist, opposed to any notion of transcendent values and insistent that man's psychology was inseparable from his physical condition. Despite all this, *Gemeinschaft* was ultimately something mystical; it referred to an experience of absolute dependence on the cosmic totality. This notion was not without precedent in German religious thought. Even though Tönnies rejected the sacred form of an anarchic community of love, he hoped again and again for its realization as secular utopia.

Tönnies's memoirs played down his struggle to break free of Christianity. The fact, however, that, as he related, he spent much of his first semester at Jena reading the theological tracts he found in the room of an older cousin studying theology suggests that his convictions were by no means settled yet. So does his friendship from the early 1870s to 1876 with a theology student two years older than himself, Carl Franklin Arnold, later professor of church history in Breslau. Arnold's letters from the early 1870s (the first one dated is from 1873) to 1876 reveal the fervid feelings of *agape* that bound them together in their period of intense friendship, mixing expressions of love with attempts to win Tönnies over to the truth of Christianity.[96] Tönnies, reporting to Paulsen in 1887 that he had visited Arnold after a separation of thirteen years, ruefully compared his earlier impressions with his later one: "He is truly a [remarkable] personality, even if not so profound as I supposed back then. But I liked talking to him just as much as before in the silly student days."[97] Perhaps an indirect testimony to the earlier friendship was Tönnies's praise of friendship as mystical community in *Gemeinschaft und Gesellschaft*. "Spiritual friendship," he wrote, was "a kind of invisible place, a mystical city and gathering, vitalized by both an artistic intuition and a creative will." Here, he added—anticipating ideas only fully explored many decades later—community shed its organic, instinctive character and flowed from free choice.[98]

Other enthuasiasms took the place of this first one, some of them hardly less silly, such as his pursuit of Nietzsche and his hopes for creating a community of philosophers. He was also deeply moved by Paul de Lagarde's call for a renewal of authentic German community. Thanking Lagarde for his hospitality when he had visited him in 1881, Tönnies wrote in a letter of

1884, "I hope to experience and take part in it when, one day, an ingathering [*Gemeinde*] forms, which must gather around your *German Writings* as a given center of gravity. But a long period of preparation will be necessary."[99] For a brief time in the 1890s Tönnies thought he had succeeded in finding a community of like-minded contemporaries. The German Ethical Society (inspired by the Anglo-American Ethical Culture movement) provided a gathering place for intellectuals dissatisfied with the traditional churches and synagogues.[100] One of the immediate incentives for founding the German Ethical Society in 1893 was a proposed Prussian school law that would have given the established churches greater influence in public elementary school education. Although the Ethical Society members preferred not to say so too loudly, most of them subscribed to some kind of Naturalist or scientistic world view and were militant opponents of church involvement in public life—especially education, of special concern to the many school teachers in the movement. To Lily Braun, one of the founders, Tönnies wrote in 1892 that for over ten years he had believed the time had come to found communities without superstition (that is, nonreligious communities), in which individuals would work and live together. The Ethical movement, his letter implied, would be this postreligious community.[101] At the Society's first meeting in August 1893 he made proposals to found an international academy of ethics (that would promote ethical research and run a school for all grades of learning from elementary to advanced) and to found family cooperatives that would form the nucleus of the socialism of the future.[102] Nothing came of these proposals. Even worse, in October 1894 the Society refused to pass his resolution to support the eight-hour day and oppose night work.[103] The Society's timidness on social issues offended him, though he stayed on for several more years, making an unsuccessful attempt to have the name changed to "Association for Social Ethics" in 1898.[104]

Tönnies's activity in the Ethical Society led to a curious postscript to his relationship to Nietzsche. When Rudolf Steiner, founder of the Theosophy Society and a Nietzsche devotee, ridiculed the good intentions of the Ethical Society, Tönnies replied with a pamphlet denouncing "Nietzsche nitwits."[105] The early Nietzsche, he wrote, had been "a kind of democrat who still believed in the secret depths of the German popular spirit" and who had attacked David Strauss's religion of culture for a select elite. The later Nietzsche, the prophet of a radically individualized aestheticism and of contempt for the masses, looked very much like Strauss, Tönnies observed. This later Nietzsche appealed to the bad conscience of middle-class aesthetes just as Strauss had done, justifying their otherwise indefensible social privileges. Tönnies asked the younger generation, which was turning Nietzsche into a cult hero, to return to the Nietzsche of *The Birth of Tragedy:* only Dionysian *Gemeinschaft* could inspire a revival of German culture.[106] As late as the early 1890s, Tönnies preserved his longing for the populist *Gemeinschaft* he had discovered in Nietzsche's first book over two decades before.

Was this, then, Tönnies's last word—nostalgia for the cultural program of his own youth, inability to comprehend that of the next generation? Almost, but not quite. Most of his later writings were, in one way or another, commentaries on his masterpiece. He increasingly hid his youthful romanticism, letting the rationalist and positivist components of his thought predominate. His attention turned to empirical and statistical studies aimed at verifying the applicability of *Gemeinschaft und Gesellschaft.*[107] Restrained patriotism and support for social reform characterized his politics.[108] Although he contributed some propaganda during World War I and was particularly angered by England's anti-German propaganda, his belief that modern civilization was in a state of decline gave him some distance from contemporary events and kept his feelings in check.[109]

The final war years jolted loose hopes that shed a final light on the utopian dimension of his thought. He had expected society to decline for centuries before the rebirth of community; defeat, the fall of the monarchy, and revolution accelerated the logic of history beyond anything he had expected. At the end of his autobiographical sketch of 1922, he spoke of a "creed of the holy spirit" that would respect and retain everything valuable in Christianity.[110] The apocalyptic, expressionist mood of the immediate postwar years revived his imaginative vision.

From 1920 to 1925 he carefully composed an essay, never

published, "The New Gospel" (*Die neue Botschaft*).[111] It envisaged a coming new age, the third age of history, reckoned according to the time not of the philosophers or sociologists, but that of the mystics: the age of the Spirit predicted by Joachim of Fiore, succeeding the ages of the Father and the Son. It was to reconcile spirit and matter, overcoming Christian alienation from the world; bring oneness with nature instead of Christian asceticism; bring spiritual freedom instead of dogmatism. Tönnies assimilated into his prophecy many elements of his older Naturalism—indeed, his thinking had in most respects expanded little beyond the horizons of 1887. Capitalism and class struggle were once again the point of departure, *Gemeinschaft* and *Gesellschaft* the categories for comprehending history, a conflict-free community the object of his desire. New was the acknowledged lineage of his hopes, which led from medieval mystics and enthusiasts of the Reformation to his intimation that the hour of fulfillment, when the churches would wither away and humanity would enjoy universal community, was perhaps not so far off.

No one illustrates more clearly than Tönnies the extreme roles that fate and utopia could play in German sociological thinking after 1870. The fatalism of *Gemeinschaft und Gesellschaft* was relentless, carrying humanity on a course as fixed as the movement of the stars. Indeed humanity and fate were linked in Tönnies's Naturalist philosophy, in which the inhabitants of the earth occupied but a tiny corner, without special privilege, in the total order of the cosmos. From past to present events unfolded in their predetermined sequence. Wisdom consisted in comprehending this process without the illusion that one could control it. Tönnies refused to heed his own advice, however, remaining an irrepressible enthusiast for movements ranging from Platonic academies to workers' cooperatives. "The New Gospel" gave voice to his hope of a rebirth of community. This outburst of utopianism remained private speculation, unreconciled with the categories of his public work. Other thinkers would grapple more consciously with the utopian strain in their era to recognize in the yearning for an ideal social order one of the central themes of German sociology.

3

Ernst Troeltsch: From Community to Society

To turn from Tönnies to Ernst Troeltsch is to leave behind a self-willed outsider for one of Imperial Germany's more successful academic insiders. While Tönnies grew middle-aged and the world failed to notice, Troeltsch received an appointment in systematic theology at the University of Bonn in 1892 and moved on two years later, when he was just twenty-nine, to a professorship at Heidelberg. By the late 1890s Troeltsch stood out as the foremost systematic thinker of a brilliant generation of theologians who had studied together at Göttingen. Humorous and self-assured in his personal manner, eloquent and combative as a speaker, Troeltsch eased naturally into the public life of the Empire. From 1909 to 1914 he served as the university's representative to the upper house of parliament in Baden. In 1914 he accepted a chair in philosophy at the University of Berlin, taking up his teaching duties in the capital the following year. From the outbreak of war until his death in 1923 he became a national spokesman for Germany's educated middle class, playing an active role in wartime and postwar politics as a propagandist, publicist, party organizer, and cultural adviser to the Weimar Republic.[1]

Troeltsch, like Tönnies, longed for community. But he did so differently: his vision of it was constructive, not subversive. Although critical of the modern state, he never shared Tönnies's dream of a populist revolt against it. Although he, too, felt flutters of revulsion toward the supposed decadence of modern society and believed national life was lacking in collective spirit, he cherished modern individualism. His utopia was a compromise enriching modern society with elements of traditional community, and he strove again and again to find the right mixture, experimenting until the end of his life in search of it.

Until World War I, when politics and the state rivaled other concerns, the main object of his deliberations was the Protestant church. To many middle-class onlookers, including Troeltsch, the established Protestant church in Prussia had the same authoritarian tone and lifeless workings as secular government. Its official hierarchy regarded spontaneous religious expressions as uncharitably as secular bureaucrats viewed street demonstrations; its orthodox theologians treated deviations from doctrine as if they were acts of *lèse majesté*. Troeltsch turned to sociology for reasons similar to Tönnies's: he wished to circumvent official ideology and recapture the authentic communal will hidden beneath it. *The Social Teachings of the Christian Churches*,[2] Troeltsch's sociological masterpiece, analyzed religious organizations as forms of compromise between two conflicting tendencies: man's inner religious experiences and the demand for brotherhood arising from them, and the selfishness and inequality inherent in human nature. The task of compromise in every age was to create institutions balancing the two, reconciling external social order and inner communal vitality.

Troeltsch's sociology distinguished between tendencies toward community and tendencies toward society. But it separated them in order to synthesize them; its aim was always to explore how the extremes had undergone historical reconciliation. In contrast to Tönnies, Troeltsch never constructed a system of clearly defined opposite types. The idea of compromise guiding his work was a loose one whose constituent parts changed in his youthful theology, his sociology, and his politics. He saw, as Tönnies was constitutionally unable to do, the continuities underlying traditional community and modern society; his sociology made use of religion to grasp the relationship between them, and it did so with an originality and validity unsurpassed by the writings of his more famous friend, Max Weber. Troeltsch's shades of gray were sometimes better approximations of empirical reality than his colleagues' studies in black and white.

The same penchant for compromise marked Troeltsch's political positions. He preferred the muddied complexity of existing society to the logical purity of simplistic ideologies. His mediating temperament had special relevance to the problems of a Germany torn apart by abrupt modernization, caught in the breach between past and present and tempted to blast its way through to a logical resolution of its problems. More than Tönnies or Weber, Troeltsch resisted the pull toward affirmation of one type of social order, community, or society at the expense of the other. Instead he sought out the contribution each could make to Germany's endangered social stability. Troeltsch's readiness for compromise can look plain compared to their uncompromising insistence on principled action in defiance of a compromised world. He did not show how Germany could build a profound community or a heroic society. His social ideal was a realistic mixture of both, providing enough historical landmarks and forms of social integration to keep it intact. This was a modest aim, but, in the course of twentieth-century German history, one requiring its own special qualities of bravery and statesmanship, which Troeltsch did not lack in the last years of his life.

Protestant *Bürgertum* and Bourgeois Society

Augsburg Beginnings

Troeltsch's early years, like Tönnies's are evidence of the strong survival of local traditions in many parts of nineteenth-century Germany. The Troeltsch family had belonged for centuries to the middle-class elite of Augsburg.[3] This old Imperial city was one of Germany's centers of commerce during the sixteenth century, rising with the fortunes of the Fugger banking house. It was also one of the intellectual centers of the Reformation; here Luther met with the Roman emissary, Cardinal Cajetan, in 1518, and here the Augsburg Confession, the central credo of the Lutheran church, came into being in 1530. Although Augsburg belonged to the network of Central European cities that declined after the Thirty Years' War with the shift of trade from inland to the Atlantic, its middle class maintained its self-assurance and control over local institutions. The Troeltsch family at the end of the nineteenth century had lost much of its wealth but still had a mutual benefit society. Ernst Troeltsch's father was a physician who had married a physician's daughter from Nuremberg. Later recalling the scientific atmosphere of the paternal household, he wrote that it was full of "skeletons, anatomical charts, electric machines, botanical books, handbooks of crystals, etc. So it was that from the start I learned to see all historical-cultural problems in the context of a scientific outlook and felt that the relationship of both worlds was a burning theoretical and practical problem."[4] At the time, however, this incipient conflict of values may have mattered less than the fact that the father had a flourishing practice, was well-known and well-liked in the town, could afford to move to a large house in 1867, and seems to have been an affectionate family head toward Ernst and his four younger siblings.[5] There was little incentive to wander from the example of a family that harmoniously blended tradition and openness to the modern world.

Troeltsch later praised his *Gymnasium* for its thorough training in the classics, and recent research has underlined how true he remained to the school's special traditions. The *Gymnasium bei St. Anna* traced its heritage back to the pedagogy of Hieronymus Wolf, librarian and private secretary to Hans Jakob Fugger from 1551 to 1557. Wolf had been a student of Melanchthon, Luther's great ally and assistant, who had systematized the reformer's thought by synthesizing it with classical humanism. Troeltsch proclaimed the school's special tradition of Christian humanism at his graduation ceremony on 6 August 1883, when he was eighteen: "With the aid of religion, the study of antiquity becomes not just idle amusement with beautiful works of poetry, the study of history not just curiosity and entertainment, but the search for truth, for moral truth."[6] This was perhaps a dig at the militant idealization of Greece and Rome that went on at other schools, such as Tönnies's. Though we do not yet know very much about the place of religion in German secondary schooling, education at the *Gymnasium bei St.*

Anna may have stood somewhat apart from the German norm and closer to the Victorian British and American ideal of shaping Christian gentlemen.

From the religious side, too, Troeltsch's Lutheran rationalism was a distinctive feature of his upbringing and certainly differed from Tönnies's experience of jarring contrasts between Lutheran orthodoxy and secular culture. At home, in contrast to the orthodox piety of Tönnies's family, Troeltsch grew up in a mildly religious atmosphere. The minister of the local parish, Julius Hans, who confirmed Troeltsch on 6 April 1879, was a highly educated theologian in the liberal tradition. Friedrich Boeckh, Troeltsch's religion teacher for five years at the *Gymnasium* and a friend of the family, was a religious rationalist.[7] This sweet-tempered religiosity was remarkable in a region soured by confessional conflict. In the early nineteenth century the Bavarian monarchy had denied Protestants internal independence or even the right to constitute a "church"; in response, Lutherans had developed a fierce neoorthodoxy emphasizing personal piety and strict adherence to dogma.[8] This intolerant religiosity only made a negative impression on him, to judge by his disdainful later dismissal of orthodox Lutheran critics of his work.

Confronting Modernity

Troeltsch's higher education began in an almost anachronistic way, one introducing him to the encyclopedic tradition of the premodern university: in 1883–84 he spent two semesters at the Royal Lyceum in Augsburg, a Catholic institution whose main purpose was to provide a general education for priests. His curriculum included courses in philosophy, philology, art history, and physics.[9] He spent the next year at the University of Erlangen, where again his curriculum remained broad and included philosophy and psychology as well as theology.[10] Erlangen was home of a famous faculty of neoorthodox Lutheran theology, and although Troeltsch later spoke of his "cool respect" toward his professors, they gave him a firsthand knowledge of the undiluted confessional tradition.[11] General education continued the next year in Berlin, where he studied history (with Treitschke), art history, and physical anthropology, alongside courses in theology.[12] Altogether, Troeltsch's early course of study confirms his later description of his ambition, similar to Tönnies's, for universal learning.[13] His wanderings from institution to institution and choice of subjects corresponded to the ideal even if he realized it through theology rather than philosophy.

After these years of preparation came three formative semesters at Göttingen from 1886 to 1888. There he encountered one of the most formidable religious thinkers of the nineteenth century, Albrecht Ritschl. Equally gifted as a historian and a systematician, Ritschl wrote with the consciousness of continuing a unified theological tradition reaching back to the Reformation, and indeed beyond, to the early Christian Church Fathers. He hoped his work would provide a normative foundation for the German Empire.[14] When Troeltsch came to Göttingen and heard his lectures on doctrine and on ethics, Ritschl was sixty-four and his life's work virtually complete, with his major works written and his fame at its height. Later, quarrels separated Troeltsch from Ritschl's more faithful disciples; but he continued to acknowledge Ritschl's centrality for his thinking, prefacing *The Social Teachings of the Christian Churches* with words of thanks to Ritschl when it appeared as the first volume of his collected writings in 1912.[15]

The look backward was a critical one, for the unity of Troeltsch's own thought sprang from the completeness with which he confronted Ritschl's. It named two components that fit together to create an overarching system: "a distinct conception of traditional dogma by means of which modern needs and problems were met, and just as decided a conception of the modern intellectual and religious situation, by means of which it seemed possible to accept and carry forward the teaching of tradition, understood in the Ritschlian sense."[16] Ritschl bridged the gap between tradition and modernity, but only, in Troeltsch's view, by ignoring the real nature of the divide separating them. Before beginning his own work of reconstruction, he needed to survey the territory Ritschl had ignored.

In *The Justification and Reconciliation,* his main work, Ritschl shifted the focus of religious conscience from the drama of sin and redemption to the work ethic. Every Christian, according to Ritschl, had been saved from divine judgment through Christ's redemptive work and needed to participate in the life of his Christian community to come to a consciousness of his reconciliation with God. Luther had freed Christianity from its medieval retreat inward in search of signs of grace and redirected it to the public realm. The true Christian life, rediscovered by Luther, was one of service in the world, fulfilled by meeting daily duties toward one's occupation, the family, and the state.[17]

Troeltsch's first book, *Reason and Revelation in Johann Gerhard and Melanchthon*, contradicted Ritschl's equation of Luther and modernity and established a wholly different line of interpretation that later entered into his and Weber's sociology.[18] It argued that Luther was fundamentally unmodern in the distinction he drew between supernatural revelation and natural reason. For Luther the authority of Scripture was absolute; it was the living word of God, the foundation of the church and the Christian life. Reason was completely separate from it and subordinate to it. Luther's successors, Gerhard and Melanchthon, accepted this disjunction as they developed Luther's teachings into an orthodox body of thought. Philosophy (in the broad sense including all the sciences) was the handmaid of theology, and whenever the two were in conflict it submitted to the authority of its mistress without regard to logic or evidence. This relationship was untroubling so long as a naive religious faith was intact. But in the modern era natural science and the historical analysis of scripture had challenged both Scripture's authority and its relationship to nature. The study of nature now revealed its indifference to the claims of theology.[19] Philosophy freed itself from theological considerations, as did the individual sciences; society emerged as a natural realm in its own right, indifferent to religious ethics. All revealed religions confronted an independent secular world, but the disjunction of reason and revelation was more radical in Lutheranism than anywhere else. The very thoroughness of its dualism, originally made in order to assert the sovereignty of theology, now left it helpless in the face of secular realms that had emancipated themselves from it. Troeltsch's book implied that modern theology would have to confront Luther's thoroughgoing unmodernity; only after doing so, and recognizing the fissures inherent in the entire Lutheran tradition, could it begin the work of reconciliation with modernity.

Troeltsch's original interest was the conflict between religion and modern natural science. From the beginning, however, he was sensitive to social issues as well, and here, too, he discerned avoidance of real difficulties in Ritschl's approach.[20] *Instruction in the Christian Religion,* the manual he published for *Gymnasium* students in 1875, preached acceptance of social injustice, loyalty to one's station in life, and obedience to the state as the God-given order of things.[21] As early as his theses for his dissertation defense, Troeltsch hinted at his dissatisfaction by including a brash thesis calling for a new manual of *Gymnasium* religious instruction.[22] His speech of 2 July 1895 to the Learned Society of Protestant Pastors in Baden entitled "The Historical Foundations of Theology in our Century" contained an open critique of Prussian authoritarianism and its effects on religion. In his broad overview of the factors affecting religious life during the nineteenth century, Troeltsch placed special emphasis on Prussia's reliance on the Protestant church as a bastion of counterrevolution since the reign of Frederick William IV (1840–1861). Other problems facing theology, he noted, had been unavoidable—the loss of church control over secondary and higher education, the conflict between religion and science. But the manipulation of the churches to secular ends had been unnecessary and estranged many of those who were interested in genuine religious worship.[23] In conclusion Troeltsch praised the smaller German states, especially Baden, for avoiding interference in the inner life of the church.[24] In contrast to Ritschl's celebration of the modern state, Troeltsch's treatment of it was critical; he assumed that its interests were different from those of religious faith and liked it best when it kept a respectful distance.

An essay of the same year entitled "Religion and Church" pointed the way from a theological to a sociological conception of religion and church.[25] In Ritschl's theological perspective there was no clear difference between them. The modern church was a supernatural institution descended directly from

Christ and the apostles, and the individual had a religious life
only through his membership in it. For Troeltsch, on the other
hand, the church was a worldly institution that had the function
of accommodating religion to the demands of secular authority
and giving it a stability it otherwise lacked. Religion originated
in individual experience, and true religious community had
nothing to do with external organizational structures, but arose
from the spontaneous feelings of individuals for one another.[26]
Troeltsch thus opened the way to a secular analysis of the
church, one that would take a disabused look at its relationship
to secular power politics. Such an analysis would have a liber-
ating effect on religion by calling attention to the harmful influence of the state and the temporal imperfections of the church.
Troeltsch posed the relationship between religion and church
in the form of a paradox rather than a contradiction. To be
sure, religion and church could never exist in uncomplicated
harmony; one followed feeling, the other the rule of an impersonal organization. Yet the tensions between them were not intolerable. If the burden of external organization became too
oppressive, Troeltsch was sure that a new arrangement would
arise and allow greater freedom to man's spirituality.[27]

By the mid-1890s Troeltsch believed that a fundamental an-
tagonism between persons and institutions underlay the tension between religion and church. He viewed the relationship
of church and religion as just one example of a general pattern
of social relations. The source of all authentic life was the inner
experience of the individual. In the theological language of the
time, the individual formed by such an experience was a *Persönlichkeit,* whose values set him above nature and enabled him to
transform it.[28] All societies required organizations, and modern
society, in particular, was made up of organizations that threatened the autonomy of personal experience. Troeltsch did not
hope to end the antinomy of *Persönlichkeit* and society, but
thought that forthright confrontation could at least ameliorate
it. While denying that traditional dogma could meet modern
needs and problems, as Ritschl imagined, he believed that religious tradition in a broader sense, open to critical scrutiny and
contemporary culture, would remain an important source of
education for *Persönlichkeiten.* He criticized Ritschl's conception

of the modern intellectual and religious situation and pointed out the social and political conflicts repressed in Ritschl's theology, but remained confident that *Persönlichkeiten* could penetrate the social and intellectual structures of the modern world and improve them. Even if society was secular, *Persönlichkeit* was still potentially its religious counterpart. This was the promising starting point for an encounter between religion and modernity, in which, in the end, each would receive its due, poised in equilibrium with the other.

In order to understand the theological background of Troeltsch's early turn to a sociological perspective, we need to turn back to Göttingen, where he belonged to a student generation that strove for a more realistic grasp of religion than Ritschl's by situating Christianity in its social and historical context.[29] His closest student friend, Wilhelm Bousset, made it his life's work to trace the Jewish and Hellenic sources of Christianity; unimpeachable on their scholarly merits, his books were scandalous in their historicization of the divinity of Christ and other doctrines, and he had to wait until 1916, just four years before the end of his life, for a full professorship.[30] Troeltsch and Bousset developed their ideas in close exchange with several other students—William Wrede, Alfred Rahlfs, Heinrich Hackmann—who completed their academic work in the late 1880s and early 1890s. The group called itself the "little Göttingen faculty"—a phrase supposedly coined by a contemptuous faculty member and promptly adopted by Troeltsch and his companions.[31]

One of their central interests was a topic charged with political overtones: the historical meaning of the Kingdom of God. Ritschl had not hesitated to identify it with the apostolic church and with present-day society; the Kingdom of God had progressively unfolded in history from the time of the apostles to the present, when Europe's economic productivity signified a transformation of nature into spirit.[32] The "little faculty" wanted to check the accuracy of Ritschl's usage against the original meaning of the phrase in ancient Palestine. One redefinition came from a Göttingen student who finished his studies slightly ahead of Troeltsch: Johannes Weiss, Ritschl's own son-in-law. In 1892 Weiss published a short book entitled *Jesus' Proc-*

lamation of the Kingdom of God, which argued that Jesus had intended something more objective and material than nineteenth-century Protestants usually supposed: "The Kingdom of God as Jesus thought of it," he wrote, "is never something subjective, inward, or spiritual, but is always the objective messianic Kingdom, which usually is pictured as a territory into which one enters, or as a land in which one has a share, or as a treasure which comes down from heaven."[33] Such an "objective messianic Kingdom" had never come; no messiah had abolished the reign of Roman emperors and established the rule of the righteous. Taken to its logical conclusion, Weiss's book would have amounted to a flat denial of Ritschl's equation of Kingdom of God and history. Weiss was devoted to his father-in-law and disavowed any such intention, limiting the impact of his own book.[34] Yet it raised the question of the meaning of the Kingdom of God so pointedly that it continued to trouble Rudolf Bultmann.[35]

In his dissertation defense of 1891 Troeltsch boldly placed Christianity's expectation of the end of history ahead of every other article of faith. Thesis number thirteen read, "To the extent that it is worthwhile at all to systematize the Christian faith (*die christlichen Glaubensvorstellungen*), eschatology must form the midpoint of the relationships."[36] The first phrase, with its "at all" in the middle (*Soweit es sich überhaupt empfiehlt . . .*), suggested a certain skepticism toward the entire enterprise of system building. The second part of the sentence stated the primacy of eschatology, the teaching of final things. Whereas eschatology virtually ceased to matter in Ritschl's system, Troeltsch organized his conception of theology around it with the force of lines drawn toward a single vanishing point. With its demand for a regrouping of systematic theology around this idea, Troeltsch's thesis went beyond the cautious tone of the book Weiss published the following year.

In other respects, however, Troeltsch clung to a less venturesome position than Weiss's. He was upset by the way he thought Weiss had vulgarized Jesus' teaching; in a letter of 23 July 1895 to Bousset, he defended a more spiritualized reading of the Gospels, in which Jesus had only used the promise of his return for pedagogical purposes. Jesus' apocalyptic pronouncements

Weber's and Troeltsch's sociology at a decisive moment.[50] It was one of the first books Weber read in 1902, after a long period of illness and inactivity, and directly shaped the methodology of *The Protestant Ethic,* written over the next three years.[51] Troeltsch wrote a long, complimentary review recommending it to theologians who sought a modern philosophy compatible with their historical and cultural research.[52] Born in 1863, Rickert was almost identical in age with Weber and Troeltsch and shared their cultural outlook, giving philosophical justification to their revolt against Naturalism while retaining the sober spirit of an academic philosopher. Rickert's great achievement for his contemporaries was a critical one; with clarity and precision, he disputed the claim of natural science to be a universal method and created room for an independent method of cultural interpretation. His own conception of such a method, although helpful, was not decisive for them, and we shall see how Weber and Troeltsch went their own ways in establishing their methodologies.

Rickert argued that natural science grasped the world through a process of abstraction, reducing the infinite complexity of the world to manageable proportions by singling out common denominators between objects. By means of abstraction it was able to make general typologies and mathematical equations express laws of universal validity. But the more it abstracted, the less it captured of the world as human beings actually experienced it.[53] Rickert spoke of the historical or (in his earlier work) cultural sciences as the disciplines with a method for grasping the experience of a specific time and place. Their method consisted in relating the object to values, showing its connection to a historical context, and tracing its development over time.[54] Two realms of knowledge, each with its own task, existed side by side. Rickert did not leave the two realms of knowledge completely unreconciled, however. One of the most important points of his book was that natural science and historical science analyzed one and the same world. There was no mysterious human essence that resisted scientific generalization and could only be approached through an intuitive humanistic method.[55] Beyond this, Rickert pointed the way to a synthesis of the two types of knowledge. Natural and historical science were, he noted, ideals that actual scientific disciplines seldom approximated. Most existing forms of knowledge were hybrids.[56] Rickert specifically upheld the possibility of creating sociology as a discipline that would formulate the "natural" side of social life—that is, its general laws—so long as it did not pretend to compete with or supersede historical knowledge.[57] His comments also made it possible to imagine a form of sociology that would combine the methods of the two types of science. On the one hand it would construct a world of general, abstract social forms, interchangeable in different times and places. On the other hand it would specify the values permeating social forms and linking them to historical experience.[58] This was the approach that Troeltsch had already begun to adopt in his writings of the 1890s, with their contrast between religious experience and objective institutions. Rickert showed how such an approach could be systematically broadened out to a comparative sociology of the forms of religious life and their particular spirit in different historical circumstances.

Rickert's reflections contained an important gap that Troeltsch was quick to notice and criticize. According to Rickert, historical science could only make sense out of the chaotic diversity of experience with the aid of values, i.e., outside criteria, apart from the object of research, enabling the researcher to decide what to exclude from his account and what to include and explain. Without values the researcher could not begin to organize his materials; with them he could identify which ones were relevant to his contemporaries and belonged to the history of their culture.[59] Rickert lucidly justified the place of values as a logical condition of cultural interpretation. But in Troeltsch's view he was less successful at determining the nature of their mediation between society and scholarship.[60] His special complaint was that Rickert treated values as if they were entirely unique and analyzed them purely from the standpoint of an immanent historical consciousness. Yet if this were the case, historical comparison would become impossible. One could perhaps argue, as Rickert did, that a culture could understand its own past because it shared common values with it. But Troeltsch argued that Rickert could not account for the fact that researchers studied foreign cultures and not merely applied their values to it, but learned new and foreign values from it. In contrast to Rickert, who derived values from the national community, Troeltsch pushed the problem of values toward a cosmopolitan solution. Values could only be effective by mediating between individual persons and cultures; but they could only mediate if they had a status apart from their particular manifestation. In discovering their common values, individuals and epochs learned how they participated in a higher spiritual community.[61] One aim of Troeltsch's sociology would be to show how such a community of values did emerge from the history of Christianity, despite the multiplicity of its teachings and churches. Even though he was critical of Ritschl's dogmatic idea of a unified Christendom, he was intent on arriving at the same result through the more empirical and inconclusive method of sociology.

The Social Teachings of the Christian Churches

A chance assignment acted as a catalyst on Troeltsch's growing preoccupation with sociology. The *Archiv für Sozialwissenschaft und Sozialpolitik*, the remarkable journal edited by Weber, Werner Sombart, and Eduard Jaffé, asked Troeltsch to review a book by Martin von Nathusius, a theologian at the University of Greifswald, on the Protestant church and contemporary social problems. Nathusius repeated the traditional Lutheran conception of society as a harmony of social orders, each with its God-given tasks; the duty of the church was to proclaim the Gospel of love reconciling each individual to his lot.[62] Troeltsch started writing his review—and the final result, seven years later, was *The Social Teachings of the Christian Churches*. A preliminary version appeared in the *Archiv;* the revised book, published in 1912, came to over a thousand pages.[63] He readily admitted its shortcomings, publishing a separate volume on Augustine to cover one gap, but also took pride in the sustained, epic quality of his effort, whose learning compelled admiration from his critics and whose method gave, he believed, a more realistic picture of Western Christianity than any previous history.[64]

Troeltsch situated his interpretation between the extremes of

dogmatic theology and historical materialism. On the one hand
Nathusius dipped class conflict and all its other problems into
the sacred waters of the church and failed to acknowledge that
modern society had a fundamentally different logic from that
of Christian brotherly love.[65] On the other hand Karl Kautsky
reduced Christianity to either a veil for the interests of the ruling class or a primitive form of proletarian revolt.[66] Troeltsch
was not entirely averse to an ideological interpretation of Christianity, but was careful to mark out points of difference between
Kautsky and himself. Kautsky portrayed Jesus as a social
prophet whose followers formed a communist community until
the upper classes appropriated Christianity and suppressed its
original chiliasm.[67] Troeltsch replied to this interpretation by
excluding social content from Jesus' teaching. In his view the
Gospels offered the promise "of a world entirely controlled by
God, in which all the values of pure spirituality would be recognized and appreciated at their true worth."[68] In contrast to
Nathusius and Kautsky, Troeltsch imagined an enduring interaction between the impulse toward brotherly love and surrounding social conditions. The history of Christianity was the
history of the compromises that took place between the inner
inspiration and the outer conditions of different times and
places.

Troeltsch's analysis worked with a rather mechanical division
between spiritual and material forces in history. One thoughtful critic, the theologian Paul Wernle, argued that such a division was entirely foreign to the mentality of Judaism at the time
of Jesus, and that the Gospels furnished evidence that Jesus
and his early followers did not consistently distinguish between
them.[69] Even in its rather schematic form, however, Troeltsch's
book contained a conception of Christianity that in fact altered
its relationship to society. Troeltsch did not question the fact
that Jesus' spiritual demands had social implications. The Kingdom of God was in its own way a revolutionary idea, one addressed to the poor, critical of the rich, and challenging toward
the social hierarchy and existing property relations.[70] The
promise of a new heaven and earth unleashed explosive fanta-
sies, which could ripple from the lowest to the highest reaches
of society. "What came to light," Troeltsch later wrote of *The*

Social Teachings, "was the dynamic force given by the original utopian-eschatological ideal like a giant spring's source, held in check by the counterforce of profane situations, compromises, new revolutions, side issues. . . ."[71] Even though his own temperament was unenthusiastic and unrevolutionary, Troeltsch recognized the eschatological impulse as an essential ingredient of Christianity and one that had shaped secular civilization until the modern era.

Troeltsch's interpretation was fruitful not in emphasizing the separation between *Innerlichkeit* and outward society, but in discovering how they combined in typical forms of religious organization. The Christian churches and sects took their shape, he argued, from the compromise between eschatology and social conditions. In each great religious age, eschatological enthusiasm reached outward, aspiring to realize the Kingdom of God; held in check by historical circumstances, the original aspirations were folded back into institutions, stable but coiled like springs within the frustrated will of their members. Troeltsch rewrote the history of Christianity as a history of utopianism. The utopian dimension gave his thought an innate drama: sociological categories were never just static classifications, but always vibrated with the struggle of human beings against their social limitations. Every stable form of organization represented a repressed conflict. How the conflict had given way to truce, and how long the truce would last, were questions unanswerable in advance, resolved only by the free play of human aspiration and social conditions in each time and place. The outcome of each past event had to be researched, of each future event to be awaited.

The Social Teachings distinguished two types of religious organization emerging from eschatological disappointment. The church type, the first to appear in history, functioned as an objective, institutional guarantor of salvation (*Heilsanstalt*).[72] According to Troeltsch, Paul created the church in this sense by replacing the original Christian expectation of the Kingdom of God with the mysticism of pagan cults. Christ the Redeemer replaced the historical Jesus; the Lord's Supper became a mystical ritual of union with the risen Christ; baptism became a dying and resurrection; the believer who was baptized and partook of communion became part of an invisible Kingdom of God. By institutionalizing salvation, the church created by Paul removed it from the vagaries of subjective feeling and achievement and turned Christianity into a mass religion bringing spiritual relief to anyone fulfilling the basic requirements for church membership. The church fortified its status as objective bearer of grace by developing a system of dogmas and requiring belief in them as another condition of salvation.[73] In Troeltsch's view, Roman Catholicism had developed the church type to its highest possible degree of articulation in the Middle Ages, when it provided the ethical order for an entire civilization.[74] Even though Troeltsch believed that the traditional church type was incompatible with the conditions of modern society, he admired its capacity to embrace all classes, to channel radicalism into constructive courses, and to establish realistic but elevating standards for secular behavior.[75] In his theological writings Troeltsch opposed the claims of contemporary church leaders, Lutheran as well as Catholic, to be the guardians of absolute, saving truth; but as a sociologist he called attention to the Catholic Church's record as an exemplary shaper of social stability.

The sect, Troeltsch's second sociological type, arose in reaction to the church and made personal enthusiasm and achievement requirements of salvation. Its aim was to remain true to the eschatological spirit of the Gospels and prepare for the imminent coming of the Kingdom of God. The absolute teachings of the Sermon on the Mount were emulated by its members in expectation of Christ's return and rule on earth. Unlike the church, the sect could never be a mass organization, but flourished in small interpersonal groups, set apart from the rest of society by their extraordinary ethical discipline. Troeltsch considered the activism of the sect to be a corrective to the church's tendency toward passive acceptance of grace and moral inertia. But he judged it too narrow and primitive ever to have a formative influence on society. It outran the limits of human nature and ended by compromising or hardening its own principles.[76]

Writing with the problems of modern society in mind, Troeltsch was especially interested in showing how the major

Protestant denominations had structured political attitudes. Lutheranism, he argued, had had a disastrous effect on Germany as a result of its disjunction between the church as realm of grace and the world as realm of sin. Strictly conforming to the church type, promising redemption in return for passive membership, and stressing adherence to ritual and doctrine, Lutheranism channeled eschatology inward and deprived religion of its worldly force.[77] Germany's Protestant middle class liked to imagine an unbroken arch of progress leading from Luther's defiance of Rome to modern freedom of conscience and constitutionalism. Taking issue with this self-serving view, Troeltsch pleaded for a critical revaluation of Luther as the cause of Germany's painful passage to modernity.[78] Within the church, Luther originally tried to leave everything to scripturally inspired spirit; no law except the law of charity should reign within it. When this failed, Luther reacted by handing over disciplinary powers to secular government, without making adequate provisions for the independence of the church. The Lutheran *Landeskirche* or territorial church developed a centralized hierarchy that controlled local parish life and if necessary interfered with it at the bidding of its secular prince. Thus Lutheranism provided an education in ruling-class authoritarianism and popular submissiveness.[79] In his own time, according to Troeltsch, the inheritors of Lutheranism were the reactionary, aristocratic, and agrarian groups in Germany that had the least understanding of democracy, the greatest propensity to use force to solve social conflicts.[80]

For a faith compatible with the modern world, Troeltsch turned to Calvinism. The sociological secret of its success was its blend of church and sect elements. Like a church it administered sacraments, made membership a precondition of salvation, and claimed historical descent from the apostolic church. It had the ambition and means to provide ethical norms for its entire society. But like a sect it sought to transform the world and prepare for the Kingdom of God; its religious and secular leaders held themselves to strenuous standards of achievement and tried to realize them by changing the rest of society.[81] This combination, thought Troeltsch, accounted for Calvinism's peculiar blend of stability and dynamism. In politics the ministers, deacons, teachers, and courts of government constituted a stable elite at the local level, ready to defend its rights against secular government and to punish disobedient parish members. This approximated Troeltsch's political ideal of patrician rule. At the same time he noted that Calvinism had prepared the way for democratic participation by sanctioning revolt of the lower magistrates and instilling respect for the Bible as an impersonal law above men, a precursor of respect for constitutional government.[82] England and America, countries with a predominantly Calvinist religious inheritance, had succeeded in modernizing without political stress. In contrast to Germany they had ruling classes cautiously open to democracy and masses accustomed to independence and worldly activities within the framework of an impersonal legal and political order.[83] Gladstone, who combined religious conscience with democratic social reform, symbolized the strengths of England's Calvinist traditions, while Bismarck, who separated his inner piety from his public policy of social repression, symbolized the flaws of Germany's Lutheranism.[84]

In conclusion, Troeltsch returned to the relationship between Kingdom of God and history. In his panorama of Christian history, church and sect had exhausted their possibilities without realizing it. Catholicism and Lutheranism were, in his view, hopelessly intertwined with medieval social teachings and had lost their capacity to transform the world.[85] The sects of the Reformation had come and gone as short-lived social experiments.[86] Calvinism had been all too successful; it was so compatible with the modern world that it had lost its distinctiveness and ceased to offer a really independent Christian social teaching apart from it.[87] A generation before, Ritschl had demonstrated the continuity of the Kingdom of God from the origins of Christianity to the founding of the German Empire; Troeltsch surveyed the same territory and discovered only a multiplicity of deceptions and disappointments. The Kingdom of God as eschatological transformation of society was as unbelievable to modern minds as speculation about the afterlife.[88]

In Troeltsch's view church and sect had lost their hold on Western civilization. Was he, then, diagnosing the end of Chris-

tianity? Not at all; his ambition was to help reform it. He
believed that since the late Middle Ages a new form of Christianity had been asking for a hearing and had been frustrated
again and again by the power of church and sect. Perhaps his
own time would see the emergence of this free, demythologized
form of Christianity.[89]

For evidence of this religion struggling to be born, Troeltsch
drew attention to the rich religious counterculture of his own
time. Within the official churches there were pastors preaching
mystical and pantheist teachings to their congregations. The
Protestant church took this development so seriously that in
1910 it established an office to examine doctrinal orthodoxy
and in 1911 removed Carl Jatho, a Cologne pastor who had
attracted a large middle-class following, from office.[90] Outside
the churches flourished numerous religious or quasi-religious
movements: Theosophy, Monism, the Nietzsche and Wagner
cults, the Ethical Society, and the revival of interest in medieval
mysticism. Troeltsch often disapproved of the content of these
movements, but he took them as signs of the considerable interest in religion that could not find adequate expression within
the bounds of the established churches. He wrote a bitter denunciation of the proceedings against Jatho, arguing that his
accusers were simply out of touch with the cultural realities of
their day and would drive out of the church many genuinely
spiritual individuals who would be disgusted by such a display
of intolerance.[91] He tried to discriminate carefully among the
nonchurch religious manifestations, opposing the naturalistic
ones espousing an undifferentiated feeling of oneness with nature and encouraging the ones retaining belief in a transcendent, personal deity.[92] Troeltsch shared with these seekers of
different kinds the longing for a mystical community, simple
and spontaneous, free of the dogmatism and hierarchy of the
established churches. Such a community would have to shed
the elitism of fashionable cults of the educated; it would have
to include a clear-cut ethical teaching and not just offer mystical
ecstasy; and it would have to retain its historical connections to
Christianity, its ultimate source.[93] If it met these requirements,
then it could, he thought, become a general form of religious

faith for modern Germany, helping to dispel the nation's inner divisions and creating a spirit of goodwill not limited by region or class.

The Social Teachings traced the history of mysticism as an independent third force apart from church or sect. Mysticism, according to Troeltsch, signified the individual's immediate experience of God and in this general sense was the perennial source of religion, but it assumed different forms in different times and places. The Catholic Church until the late Middle Ages had always managed to channel mysticism into the established order and to overcome any attempts at setting up an independent source of religious authority.[94] Protestantism originated in a mystical movement of a new kind: "There arose a Protestant mysticism which, unlike Catholic mysticism, was not a compensation for ecclesiastical formalism, but which was a conscious, active, and independent principle of religious knowledge, inward experience, and morality."[95] It furthered *Persönlichkeit* through the idea of *unio mystica,* or mystical union with Christ. It did not remain individual or passive, however, but radiated outward, uniting those inspired by its spirit of love and service for others.[96] Calvinism's practical ethics was untouched by it, in contrast to Lutheranism.[97] There was no need for a future Kingdom of God because true redemption consisted in this inward fellowship, available whenever men were willing to seek it. Beneath its hardened orthodox exterior the Lutheran tradition had preserved its affinity with this modern mysticism.[98] Since the end of the eighteenth century Germany's educated elite had deserted the church and rediscovered it, stripping it of its remnants of dogma and turning it into a pure, timeless doctrine. Leibniz, Spinoza, Goethe, Kant, Lessing, Fichte, Schelling, and Hegel had all, according to Troeltsch, drawn on and universalized it. They shared the belief that the divine was implanted in every individual; that cultivation of man's divine essence could lead to a universal, purely spiritual fellowship; and that such a fellowship would supersede the older forms of worship and flourish freely, without the use of external force.[99] Their religious conception had spread so widely that he called it "the secret religion of the educated classes."[100] In one moment of daring or wishful thinking he compared his own age to the beginning of the Reformation, when there had been a similar desiccation of old and ferment of new ideas.[101]

Natural Right and Eschatology

Troeltsch presented his conclusions to the newly founded German Sociological Association (an organization we shall discuss in connection with Max Weber) at its first meeting in 1910, at which he delivered a paper entitled "Stoic Christian Natural Right and Modern Profane Natural Right."[102]

The Social Teachings dealt with natural right as a recurring theme, showing how each of the major churches and sects had developed its doctrine of natural right in response to the exigencies of everyday life.[103] The realm of grace was absolute, and as such remained an unfulfilled promise, never completely able to penetrate secular life; natural right signified the arrangements that a confession accepted as a temporal necessity falling somewhere short of its highest aims, but going beyond the immorality of a wholly un-Christian way of life. In Troeltsch's view, to construct a workable doctrine of natural right was one of the central achievements of a civilization. In it he found historical predecessors of the mean that he sought for his own time.

Troeltsch's speech to the Sociological Association portrayed natural right as a flexible instrument that could legitimize either the existing order or alternatives to it, depending on its formulation and society's needs.[104] Catholicism exemplified a rich, many-sided use of the idea. It borrowed the Stoic notion of a golden age, identified it with the Biblical paradise, and used it as a social model to contrast to the shortcomings of the present. When temporal rulers abused their powers, it could use this aspect of natural right to call them to account. On the other hand it maintained another model of natural law as transformed by man's fall from grace; patriarchy, private property, slavery, and the state were necessary consequences of original sin, and the Church defended them despite their inherent violence and inequity.[105] Calvinism, too, developed a double teaching admired by Troeltsch. Like Catholicism, it unequivocally

affirmed the basic institutions of existing society; but it also expected society to live up to the demands of the decalogue and
developed a doctrine of just rebellion against tyranny.[106] Luther, by contrast, figured as the terrible simplifier of religious
history, who conceived of "nature" (the external realm including politics) as irredeemably corrupt and glorified the princely
use of force to keep man's brutality in check. In Troeltsch's view,
the relationship between utopia and reality broke down in Luther; Christianity lost its transcending impulse and left secular
rulers free to behave unscrupulously without fear of religiously
inspired protest.[107]

Troeltsch traced the modern idea of natural right—the
rights of man of the French and American revolutions—back
to the activist sects and mystical movements of the early modern era. Their stress on the image of God in every individual as
the ultimate source of religious authority survived in revolutionary beliefs about individual dignity and freedom of conscience.[108] Troeltsch was careful, as always, to state that religion
was not the only source of modern natural right and to list natural science, capitalism, and the modern bourgeoisie as other
factors in its formation.[109] The old battle line separating religion and secular modernity, he suggested, should give way to a
more complex landscape with many unnoticed bypaths leading
from one to the other. In calling attention to them, his sociology
was taking up a task of rapprochement: perhaps modernizers
could begin to appreciate their debt to religion, and religious
traditionalists could appreciate their place in modernity.

In the subsequent discussion, Tönnies stood up for the old
battle lines.[110] *Gemeinschaft und Gesellschaft* argued that modern
natural right had arisen as the logical counterpart of bourgeois
individualism and as such expressed the inherent opposition of
modern society to a feudal order not yet overturned in Germany.[111] Troeltsch's views were too repugnant for him even to
begin to grasp them on their own terms. Instead he responded
by reaffirming his allegiance to historical materialism and
sketching the history of religion and natural right as a reflection of class relations. Simmel commented that there was an
ultimate difference between religious and social experience that
Troeltsch had failed to respect.[112] Religion originated in the re-

lationship between individual and God and was therefore by definition an experience prior to every form of social interaction. On the one hand there was the transcendence and absoluteness of religious experience; on the other hand, the immanence and relativity of social interactions. Did a causal connection actually bind one to the other? Troeltsch had tried to demonstrate that it did, but Simmel raised the possibility that the very multiplicity of Christian social teachings, and the compatibility of Christianity with an enormous variety of political ideologies through the ages, canceled out any direct relationship. Perhaps Christianity had always retained its metaphysical otherness in the face of worldly affairs. In this case, it was not really a suitable subject for the kind of sociology Troeltsch had written.[113]

Tönnies and Simmel spoke for varieties of the materialist and spiritualist positions that Troeltsch set out to overcome in *The Social Teachings*—Tönnies treating religion as a projection of material forces, Simmel treating it as free of social influence. Troeltsch and Max Weber, who came to his defense, had no trouble pointing out weaknesses in their critics' arguments. There was often no necessary correspondence between religion and society of the kind Tönnies postulated; for example, as Weber pointed out, one could not predetermine whether Christianity was an urban or a rural phenomenon, or which social setting was more favorable to a specific type of organization, such as the sect.[114] Religion resisted any thoroughgoing reduction of the kind Tönnies proposed. At the same time, one could not encapsulate it in metaphysical isolation as Simmel tried to do, for religious experience was not metaphysical but psychological, and took the specific form of a Catholic, Calvinist, Lutheran, sectarian, or mystical psychology, each with its own formal characteristics and resulting patterns of social action. Weber discussed the Puritan mentality, Troeltsch the mystical tradition, to illustrate the historical specificity of religious experience.[115] Altogether Troeltsch used his sociological types with skill and discretion to trace out the interaction of society and religion and was explicit about his intention of charting unknown territory that only detailed empirical studies could fill in.

In the course of his speech, Troeltsch noted the similarities between Christian eschatology and socialist utopianism; socialism figured as a modern descendant of sectarianism, sharing its expectation of an immanent transformation of existing society and end to injustice. Groups such as the Joachimites, the Hussites, the Münster Anabaptists, and some religious radicals in the English Civil War expressed socialist ideas; and some modern socialists—Troeltsch mentioned only Saint-Simon's affinity for Catholicism—had obvious religious lineages.[116] Within his framework of thinking, the comparison was a deprecatory one. If eschatology rested on illusion, then the secular inheritors of Christian eschatology were living out the illusory and dispensable side of Christianity, waiting for the end of the world instead of developing a realistic compromise between existing society and their ethical ideals. Yet revolutionary-minded thinkers could see the relationship in a different light; perhaps eschatology was the enduring element of Christianity that would survive the decay of its churches and sects and pass over into the historical memory of socialism. Some of the thinkers who entered the university just before World War I would seek a secular fulfillment of religion, a religious deepening of socialism. When they did so, they were able to make use of concepts and problems prepared by their elders. Later we shall see how one of them, Lukács, studied German sociology in order to fuse religion and revolution.

Troeltsch in Politics: The Will to Synthesis

Synthesis *Manquée* at the Protestant Social Congress

The Social Teachings made mention of a forum for discussing just the kind of reconciliation of religious ethics and modern society Troeltsch sought, the Protestant Social Congress (*Evangelisch-Sozialer Kongress*). Since 1890 this collection of theologians, social scientists, pastors, politicians, civil servants, church officials, and other members of the educated middle class had been meeting yearly to discuss Germany's class tensions and other social problems. Originally a joint venture of conservatives and progressives, after 1900 it represented the liberal

Protestant middle class and developed close ties to educational, feminist, and labor reformers. It attracted an influential elite that wished to work with the state to bring about modernization and social integration.[117]

In 1904 Troeltsch gave a speech to the Congress entitled "Christian Ethics and Contemporary Society," his fullest statement of his political views before World War I.[118] It began with a brusque description of how little ethics counted for in Imperial Germany. Pressure group politics, class conflict, and materialism set the tone for public life; a disgusting smugness and contempt for others passed for sophistication. The educated had lost their belief in the idealism of Kant, Fichte, and Hegel and had embraced the cynical political realism of Treitschke and Bismarck.[119] (Troeltsch was criticizing his own youthful views here, for as a student he had been an uncritical admirer of Bismarck and of Treitschke, whom he heard lecture in Berlin.[120]) The state lacked moral ideals and the nation, beneath its jingoist rhetoric, represented nothing more than collective egoism.[121] The genuine normative principles of German public life were the property of different factions. What Troeltsch called the democratic principle, the natural-rights belief in justice and equality, belonged to liberals and Social Democrats.[122] What he called the conservative principle guided the Prussian ruling class's belief in the legitimacy of historical authority.[123] Any proposal for a unified German political ethic would have to make use of these conflicting ideals as expressions of the real social and cultural forces in German society.

With his habitual penchant for synthesis, Troeltsch tried to reconcile their differences. Both were Christian in origin, and their separation was a manifestation of the inner crisis of Christianity itself in the modern world. Social Democracy had secularized the Christian teaching of the essential equality of all souls.[124] Troeltsch accepted the inevitability of this secularization and even valued democratic demands as a counterweight to the otherwise unbearable pressure of Prussian conservatism. But in his view genuine Christianity was other-worldly and antimaterialist; as conservatives knew, it had always learned to live with the imperfections of nature and inequalities in the social order.[125] What disturbed Troeltsch about the conservatives of his own day was not their wealth or their social position, but their lack of respect for the lower social orders. He sought a synthesis bringing together what he thought were the Christian elements of both ideologies, furthering *Persönlichkeit* without upsetting the existing social heirarchy.

Where was the agent to carry out this program of synthesis? The logical choice was the Protestant church—which, however, was failing to fulfill its appointed role. Troeltsch argued that the critical learning of his time made it possible for the church to discard its dogmatism and develop a generalized modern ethics based on the ideals of *Persönlichkeit* and brotherly love; instead it clung to its traditional teachings and harassed the proponents of change. The church could have played the role of mediator above parties, distributing its criticisms evenhandedly among conservatives for their arrogance and socialists for their materialism; instead it contributed to class division by siding with conservatives.[126] The history of the Protestant Social Congress illustrated the narrowness of the church leaders' outlook, for they had withdrawn their support from the organization as soon as it started making the kinds of criticisms Troeltsch had in mind. He was familiar enough with their mentality to know that they were unlikely to make any moves toward reconciliation with Social Democracy.

Troeltsch's listeners remained skeptical about the sincerity of his social conscience and the value of even the cautious hopes he placed on the church. One of his critics was Friedrich Naumann, who as a Christian socialist before 1900 and a secular politician afterward worked to bring about a synthesis of nationalism, social reform, and Protestant values that would appeal to both the middle and working classes. Naumann observed that the Protestant church had always sided with the powerful against democratized *Persönlichkeit,* and doubted that one could expect it to change.[127] Two prominent theologians, Martin Rade (editor of *Die Christliche Welt,* the leading literary organ of liberal Protestants)[128] and Julius Kaftan (a socially conservative Ritschlian and Troeltsch's teacher in Berlin)[129] deplored Troeltsch's dualism of personal dignity and authority and asked how he would really integrate them. Troeltsch was not, Rade suspected, such a friend of democracy as some of his remarks suggested; he was actually in favor of few changes in the authoritarian structure of German society.

Troeltsch had not defined his politics with any precision, leaving unclear his views on such fundamental issues as the three-class voting system in Prussia (in which votes were unequally weighed according to taxable income) and the uncertain legal status of labor unions, two key concerns of middle-class reformers. In his concluding response to his critics, he admitted that his temperament was far more conservative then democratic.[130] Democratic reforms might be useful to correct the aristocratic cast of German society, but in Troeltsch's view they should never go so far as to abolish it. Rather he affirmed the inward nature of culture and morality and their separation from the political realm: "The effects of brute instinct, of the struggle for power and domination in which the state is rooted, remain in my opinion something so irrational and indifferent to the pure idea of *Persönlichkeit* that they can never just furnish the material for it, but always [furnish] the obstacle, too, to the pure idea of *Persönlichkeit*."[131] Troeltsch was unclear about how to overcome the separation of politics and morality, and when pressed rapidly fell back into it. Nonetheless, Troeltsch's analysis did shed light on Germany's competing class ideologies and lack of effective public norms. As he told his critics, he could not resolve the divisions of German society, but could only call attention to their dangerous presence.

Protestantism and Progress in Baden

Troeltsch's hopes for the creation of a progressive Protestant movement looked problematic so long as discussion centered around Prussia, as it implicitly did in his speech of 1904. Yet other regions retained their church and cultural independence after unification and did not always share Prussia's brittle reactionary temper. Baden, home state of Heidelberg, offered a more promising model of religious politics for Troeltsch's way of thinking.[132] The cities of Karlsruhe, Mannheim, Heidelberg, and Pforzheim had a self-confident and largely Protestant middle class that aggressively asserted its cultural hegemony during the nineteenth century.

After mid-century, the politics of German unification fired up the Protestants' sense of collective identity and brought on a long struggle with the rural Catholic majority. In a microcosm of the national mood, Catholics looked south to Austria while Protestants looked north to Prussia for national leadership. During the early 1860s a group of Heidelberg professors founded the Protestant Association (*Protestantenverein*), a lay group that aimed at the creation of a national Protestant church and at unification under Prussian auspices; the group had a wide following in Southwest Germany and disintegrated only after achievement of its main goal in 1871. During the ministry of Julius Jolly from 1868 to 1876 the Karlsruhe bureaucrats fought the first *Kulturkampf*, a campaign emulated in Prussia.[133] After the *Kulturkampf* ended in compromise, the confessional struggle continued in other ways. Protestants dominated the National Liberal Party, which maintained an absolute majority in the parliament's lower house until the late 1890s. The Center Party and SPD (Social Democratic Party) succeeded in breaking the hold of the Protestant *Honoratioren* in parliament when a suffrage reform bill passed in 1904, but even after this happened, confessional animosity remained heated. National Liberals, splinter liberal parties, and Social Democrats formed various coalitions to stave off the combined forces of orthodox Protestants and Catholics gathered respectively in the Conservative and Center parties. Liberal Protestants were an embattled but still powerful elite from then until World War I, their influence guaranteed by their willingness to work with a broad coalition of parties as well as their wealth, status, and control of the bureaucracy.[134]

Troeltsch felt at home with the traditions of Baden's Protestant patriciate and developed his own program for furthering them. He did so by building on the work of a predecessor in systematic theology, Richard Rothe, who taught in Heidelberg from 1837 to 1849 and again from 1854 to 1867.[135] In Rothe's philosophy of history, the time had come to merge Christianity with secular high culture and politics. In the past, churches had been the guardian of a higher morality and had played the role of educator to the secular world; by the nineteenth century the state had fully absorbed its teachings and surpassed it. Individual religious feeling, he thought, should end its estrangement from the state and enter directly into its service. Rothe was a *Vormärz* liberal with faith in constitutional government and enlightened monarchy. It was his idea in 1862 to found the Protestant Association. His vision of sacred and secular history coinciding in the modern state appealed to the pathos of the Protestant *Bildungsbürgertum* in the 1860s, but was outdated by the prosaic realities of German unification after 1870. Thereafter it seemed at best a tribute to Baden's liberal statecraft and the idealism it inspired, at worst an example of the kind of naiveté the Empire's middle class wished to forget.

Troeltsch felt a strong sense of kinship with Rothe and made an important assessment of him when Heidelberg celebrated the centennial of his birth in 1899.[136] Rothe was a radical critic of the church in its existing form, and Troeltsch thought that more than any other predecessor he had seized on and attacked its claims to sacred status. Rothe's demand for the dissolution of the church as sacred institution foreshadowed Troeltsch's own conclusion that the church type had lost its inner validity and outer effectiveness in the modern world. Both thinkers looked forward to the formation of a new kind of church that would no longer dispense grace or defend dogma, but would simply provide an institutional framework for the expression of religious feeling. Both wished for more popular and local participation in the church of the future, but wished to avoid an anarchy of religious individualism. Rothe's attempt to create a national church through the Protestant Association foreshadowed Troeltsch's insistence on the need for a new kind of church that would provide the moral norms for public life, distilling the historical experience of Christianity and applying it to the needs of modern society. It seemed hopeless even to imagine such a church in Prussia—but why not in Baden? Here Protestantism had actually maintained such a strong connection to middle-class politics that it did not seem so hopelessly given over to reactionaries as in the north. And members of the bourgeoisie were readier in Baden than in many other parts of Germany to engage in political dialogue with the working class. If Troeltsch had something of Rothe's misplaced idealism when seen in the harsh light of national experience, it was probably because their shared local experience was exceptionally favorable to a conciliatory religious politics.

How the churches should provide norms for public life became a major issue in Baden politics after the suffrage question was settled in 1904. Centrists and Conservatives wanted to extend church influence as far as possible; liberals and Social Democrats sought to check it. The two coalitions battled over proposals to limit church involvement in elementary education.[137] Since 1876 the Baden elementary schools had been governed by a local board consisting of the mayor, members of the community, and ministers of the two established churches. When the government introduced a general school reform bill in 1906, the secular parties jumped at the chance to challenge the role of the churches. They differed among themselves, however, on what changes should be made. For the Social Democrats, religious instruction was a form of inoculation against their own ideology, and they wished to eliminate it completely as an important step toward separation of church and state. For the National Liberals, religion had to be kept subordinate to reason of state, but they supported some sort of religious instruction as part of the national cultural heritage. In the end, the bill passed without any substantial change in the existing arrangements for a church voice in elementary school education. Feelings ran high on all sides of the education issue, which brought out both the religious and the political differences in German society. Anticlericalists were angered by Catholic attempts (the main object of their attacks) to monitor teachers and classroom; liberals and Social Democrats fell out over their diverging attitude toward religion; orthodox Protestants were alarmed to discover their own public ineffectiveness; Catholics feared a second *Kulturkampf*.[138]

Troeltsch made elementary school religious instruction the subject of his inaugural speech as rector of the University of Heidelberg in 1906.[139] He outlined a solution midway between the extremes of confessionalism and secularism—one close to the proposals of the National Liberals, though motivated by sincere religious belief as well as calculation of state interests. According to Troeltsch, society depended on "strong, deep, and living religion and cannot be separated from it, even if it separates the churches from the state."[140] Skeptical on the one hand toward secular substitutes for religious ethics, he stated, "The only such religion we have, however, is Christianity. It is possible to synthesize it with modern ideas, but not to replace it effectively with ethical-pantheist abstractions."[141] The Ethical Society, Tönnies's choice for such a substitute for Christianity, was in Troeltsch's judgment the kind of ersatz faith that lacked the depth of a real religion and could never instill a binding public ethics. On the other hand Troeltsch wanted to discontinue the traditional teachings of the churches; in his view their dogmas were no better than superstition, and they no longer carried conviction for modern minds. What Troeltsch proposed instead of these traditional and secular alternatives was historical instruction: knowledge of the history of Christianity, presented in such a way that both Catholics and Protestants could agree on its contents, compatible with the standards of modern learning yet maintaining continuity with inherited morality and belief. This general, nonconfessional instruction would encourage students to think of Christianity as one unified body of truth instead of presenting competing doctrines, and it would allow them to worship in their churches or develop their own religious conceptions.[142] Troeltsch's answer to the problem of providing public norms was to turn to the state and to ask it to sponsor a public religion that would dismiss the babble of quarreling ideologues and define the forum in which reasonable citizens shared a common discourse.

Troeltsch made a somewhat similar argument for the creation of a general religious culture in another subject of contemporary debate, the status of the theological faculties. As matters stood, their status was ambiguous; the modern university was a secular institution, yet they taught and examined students preparing for the ministry and church administration. Social Democrats and anticlericalists asked why the theological faculties should be part of universities at all, since they represented a special revelation incompatible with scientific research. Conservatives demanded greater representation on the theological faculties of conservative theologians, who would not lead their flock of students into the paths of modernity and would turn out reliable church servants. To appease them, the ministry of culture in Baden appointed one conservative theologian, Ludwig Lemme, to the otherwise liberal Heidelberg faculty in 1896. Although this was the last appointment of its kind, it permanently put liberals on their guard and made future appointments occasions to fear further setbacks. Intrachurch quarreling detracted from the prestige of the theological faculty and appeared to justify its opponents' complaint that it was the domain of special church interests rather than impartial scholarship. From 1909 to 1914, Troeltsch served as the University of Heidelberg's representative to the upper house of Baden's parliament and had a chance to defend its membership in the university and Heidelberg's particular cast as a liberal stronghold. He replied to his critics that the existing theological faculties were "an essential means of conservative progress, attempting to reconcile the church's religious strength and warmth with science's enormous transformation of modern thinking. They lead to a relative unity of cultural life without a loss of badly needed confidence in ideals."[143] Theology—that is, Protestant theology, since Troeltsch thought Catholics too beholden to the authority of tradition to make contributions to this synthesis—would provide the "relative unity of cultural life" that was presently missing, discovering that impartial and nondogmatic history of Christianity that could be taught in the schools. Troeltsch had long maintained that such a synthesis of religion and contemporary learning was the perennial task of theology. Here as in *The Social Teachings* he spoke as a sociologist concerned with the functional stability of his society and convinced that religion was necessary in order to maintain it.

1914 and After

Troeltsch continued to seek the functional unity of German society under the changing circumstances of world war, revolution, and republic. At the outbreak of the war Troeltsch shared in the tremendous feeling of unity that overcame most Germans and made them feel that their differences had at last receded, that the divisions of class, confession, and region disappeared in the face of the common danger.[144] Troeltsch became a busy propagandist, seeking to enhance his countrymen's sense of common purpose by contributing to the "Ideas of 1914," according to which the nation was undergoing a rebirth comparable to Prussia's experience in the Wars of Liberation from Napoleon a century ago.[145] He used the dichotomy of community and society to describe the transformation:

Our spirit reawakened, easily bringing together everyone despite all confessions and theories. Simultaneously that sophistication died that separates culture from the people and from the masses, impurifying everything. To be sure, this opposition belongs to the development of society and the state everywhere. It is, in the words of one of our most thoughtful sociologists, the separation of the abstract, rationalized, and subjective society from the great unified community of blood and instinct, ethos and symbol. This division had become deeper and deeper among us. Above all, it had had the most terrible aesthetic, artistic, and intellectual effects. All certainties turned into problems, all moral and historical traditions into prejudices, all objects into possibilities, all knowledge into sensation. . . . Then came the war, and with it, the revelation of what was common to all.[146]

What a reversal of the laws of social evolution! For years Troeltsch had accepted Germany's transition from community to society, making his judicious suggestions to hinder its worst effects. He himself had been among the foremost thinkers accused of turning certainties into problems and traditions into prejudices. The war came as an unexpected deliverance—indeed, as such a complete surprise that it put new words into his mouth. Perverting Tönnies's ideas, he turned the contrast between *Gemeinschaft* and *Gesellschaft* into a justification of Germany's wartime machine. Never particularly sympathetic toward Prussia, he now exulted in its traditions of duty and discipline; overcoming his previous distance toward the German idea of the state, he now made defense of it against the British and French a sacred calling; never a special friend of the military, he now praised it for instilling a sense of collective responsibility in the masses. The war at first seemed to solve the problems of modern society by eliminating them, bringing about a complete, and welcome, regression to *Gemeinschaft.*[147]

Troeltsch's initial enthusiasm for the war faded quickly. By the end of 1914 he was already worried by hypernationalism in Germany and the breakdown of the European cultural community. Over the course of 1917, he and other members of the moderate educated elite—Max Weber, Adolf von Harnack, Hans Delbrück, Friedrich Naumann, Friedrich Meinecke—were aware that the monarchy and army were rapidly losing public confidence and that democratic electoral reforms in Prussia and cooperation with labor were necessary in order to prevent the collapse of the Empire.[148] From then until his death in 1923, Troeltsch worked incessantly to preserve the stability of the social order and to fend off attacks from the left and right. Germany's need for a unified political center was the underlying principle of his politics as the war came to a disastrous end. He gazed on the events of 1918 to 1922—the end of the war, the abortive revolution, the dissolution of the monarchy, the Versailles peace, the creation of the Weimar Republic, the Kapp Putsch, the economic disorders of the early Weimar years—with stoic detachment, determined to confront misfortune and find the forces of order amid chaos.[149] Shedding his briefly acquired sympathies, he dissected the political irresponsibility of Prussia's military leaders, who had obstructed parliament and chancellor and had inflamed class hatred until it exploded in civil war.[150] He recognized that little help for healing class divisions would come from his own social stratum, the academically educated, which leaned to the radical right.[151] His hopes for the stability of the Weimar Republic rested with his old opponents, the Center Party and the Social Democrats. Ideological labels did not distract him from seeing that these parties alone could guarantee the unity of the state and a rational foreign policy.[152]

Troeltsch's mood during the postwar years was despondent.[153] His political observations emphasized the fragility of the new republic and registered every new danger to it, apprehensive of a slide into complete chaos in Germany. The assassination of Walter Rathenau in 1922 came as a terrible confirmation of the radical right's readiness to destroy the democratic center.[154] His main intellectual effort of the postwar period, *The Problem of Historicism,* remained a vast unfinished meditation on the collapse of Western values, ransacking the past for a stable intellectual order to guide the present.[155] The

formlessness and inconclusiveness of his ruminations testified
to his failure to find the elements of a final synthesis.

And yet the pieces of German history eventually fell into
place along the' lines he wished. In his final years he assessed
more realistically than most liberal or left-wing observers the
evils brewing on the radical right. What he could not foresee
was the reconstruction of German society after 1945, in which,
as he hoped, usable elements of the past took their place alongside an efficient capitalist economy. This was particularly true
with regard to religion: in postwar West Germany the established churches came into their own as democratic religious organizations and institutionalized guarantors of public norms.[156]
The Protestant churches maintained a balance between independence from the state and cooperation with it; critical theology predominated in the universities. Few members of German
society had strong religious beliefs, but most welcomed a religious establishment providing a strong reminder of historical
continuity and adding legitimacy to a young democracy. The
churches did not offer anything like the mystical community
that was Troeltsch's occasional hope; instead they embodied the
spirit of compromise. His search for synthesis pointed the way
to the prosaic realities of the late twentieth century, when a judicious blend of tradition and modernity, and a willingness on
the part of all classes to live without absolutes, would bring West
Germany functional stability.

4
Max Weber: The Allegory of Society

One of the first readers of *The Protestant Ethic and the Spirit of Capitalism* was Tönnies. A terse notebook entry, dated November 1904, records his judgment after the essay's first part appeared: "clings to superficialities" (am äusserlichen klebend).[1] From Tönnies's point of view, Weber was probably "superficial" because he ignored the organic will of *Gemeinschaft*, the reality underlying all social relationships, traditional or modern. Instead Weber limited his discussion to the social psychology formed by religious creeds. This psychology fell into typical patterns that Weber attempted to explain, but never referred back to anything like the deeper level of *Wesenwille* that Tönnies claimed to have discovered. Weber was, in fact, one of the great opponents of organic theories of community. He admired *Gemeinschaft und Gesellschaft* and found the two terms of its title useful for describing traditional and modern social orders, but did so in a way that polemically excluded Tönnies's belief in a substantive will as the true life of a human community.[2]

With Troeltsch the relationship gets more complicated. To start again from *The Protestant Ethic:* Troeltsch influenced the essay; learned from it; complemented it with his own sociology of religion. The house they shared on the Neckar may symbolize their friendship. The familiar image can overstate it too, however, and closer inspection reveals strong contrasts. Like Troeltsch, Weber understood modernity by measuring it against the eschatological expectations of Christian tradition. But he rejected Troeltsch's hope that the idea of a Christian community could somehow extend into modern society. Capitalism, for Weber, had shattered the possibility of such a normative community and compelled moderns to ask what kind of dignified existence was possible within the confines of secular society.[3]

Weber shared these thinkers' preoccupation with the problem of Germany's inner unity. The breakup of the liberal movement in the 1870s and 1880s and the failure of social reform in the 1890s deeply impressed on him the lack of consensus underlying Imperial politics. He became a more resolute opponent than Tönnies or Troeltsch, however, of nostalgia for earlier forms of *Gemeinschaft*. Though not without sympathy for the value of past communities, Weber thought that yearning for them could only distract his contemporaries from the task of creating a distinctively modern culture. In place of *Gemeinschaft* he imagined a nation of heroic individualists, unified by common political experiences and strengthened by imperial expansion, economic competition, and the struggle for world cultural hegemony. Allegiance to these tasks would, he hoped, be compatible with self-interest yet fill modern society with a transcending sense of purpose.

Weber's modern heroism had one of its models in a distinctly Protestant idea of *Persönlichkeit*. For Weber, who hated liberal utililtarianism and socialist materialism alike for reducing man to the status of a hedonistic creature, *Persönlichkeit* signified something radically different from both—the individual who acted on purely individual values transcending sensuous existence. He upheld this notion of human dignity throughout his adult life: in his politics of the 1890s; in *The Protestant Ethic*, which discovered its historical forerunner in seventeenth-century Puritanism; and in the methodology and conceptual structure of his later sociology. Modern society isolated the individual from collective sources of meaning. Just this circumstance, however, gave modernity its special dignity, compelling the individual who wished to be anything at all to find his values within himself and challenging him to realize them in an otherwise meaningless world. From the very bleakness of the modern condition Weber fashioned a dramatic conflict between *Persönlichkeit* and society worthy of its Protestant ancestors.[4]

Protestantism and Postliberal Politics

Even though Weber's reputation rests mainly on his writings from after the turn of the century, his early work has received attention for its own considerable merits and for the ways it foreshadowed his later achievements.[5] Yet for the most part recent scholarship has shied away from discussing Weber's early religious involvements. Marianne Weber's biography of her husband bears witness to how important these were, even if she herself, religious in a way that he was not, had a natural interest in emphasizing them; they permeated both his family and his friendships and public activities in the 1890s. Perhaps Weber's interpreters fear that remembering this side of his life somehow diminishes his stature as a hard-headed social scientist and analyst of power politics. One could more legitimately argue, however, that by playing down his religious involvements they have given us a partial view of his politics as well. The following pages try to redress this, not by substituting a one-sided religious interpretation for a one-sided political one, but by asking how the two sides fit together, with Weber's attachment to certain Protestant traditions giving him critical distance from liberal ideology.

The Limits of Liberalism

In contrast to Tönnies and Troeltsch, Weber grew up in a political household. More than that, it was a household at the center of liberal party politics in Germany, in which from earliest childhood he could form impressions of German liberalism's strengths and weaknesses. His father, Max Weber senior, was a lawyer and politician who moved with his family in 1869 to Charlottenburg, the fashionable suburb of Berlin to take a seat in the City Council. As a prominent member of the National Liberal Party (who later held Reichstag and Prussian Landtag seats as well) he entertained leading politicians and such professors as Dilthey, Treitschke, and Mommsen. The elder Weber made his name as a technician, supervising building projects in the City Council and serving as a budget specialist in the Landtag. As fissures deepened in the liberal movement during the

1860s, he sided with the advocates of *Realpolitik*, who placed political unification and big business interests ahead of fidelity to the classical liberal principles of constitutional government and laissez-faire economics.[6]

Born in 1864, the younger Max Weber seems to have accepted (or at least to have avoided openly challenging) his father's political ideas. Soon after leaving for the University of Heidelberg in 1882, however, his political thinking began to change. His encounter with his uncle, the historian Hermann Baumgarten, stimulated his doubts about the wisdom of leading liberal policymakers. During his first semester Weber formed a close friendship with his cousin Otto Baumgarten, Hermann's son, and for the Pentecost holiday went with him to Strasbourg. A year of draft duty in Strasbourg starting in the fall of 1883 gave him opportunities to visit the Baumgarten family and continue the dialogue begun with his uncle the year before.

By the time Weber met him, Baumgarten had turned from a founder of the National Liberal Party into one of its most dyspeptic critics. Made professor of history and literature in Karlsruhe at age thirty-six in 1861, he had access to Baden's political elite through Julius Jolly, his brother-in-law, and also became friendly with Treitschke, then teaching in Freiburg. On the eve of the war of 1866 he wrote a polemical pamphlet entitled *German Liberalism: A Self-Criticism* to persuade fellow liberals to throw their support behind Bismarck. Accusing the German middle class of congenital political immaturity, he advised it to accept aristocratic leadership, making the fateful observation that "the bourgeois is born to work, but not to rule, and the statesman's essential task is to rule."[7] Prussian unification fulfilled his longing for an end to political division, but not for noble public deeds. His anger over Bismarckian demagogy and National Liberal opportunism later erupted in a polemic against the second volume of Treitschke's *German History in the Nineteenth Century* (1883), which in his view epitomized the Empire's vainglorious nationalism. The controversy over his review, which overlapped with Weber's year in Strasbourg, alienated him from his former liberal compatriots and increased his despondency.[8]

Baumgarten's criticisms of German liberalism from the 1860s and 1870s contained themes that reappeared decades later in *The Protestant Ethic*. He and his nephew agreed that the German middle class had demonstrated its unfitness for political leadership, failing to seize power and adulating Bismarck as a result of character flaws deeply embedded in its history. At the very beginning of his self-criticism of 1866 Baumgarten suggested the source of the middle class's immaturity: its Lutheranism, which turned it into a class of idealists unable to come to terms with the mundane realities of politics. Weber pursued a similar line of thought in *The Protestant Ethic*, contrasting the unworldly, Lutheran idealism of his compatriots with the Calvinist-trained realism of the English. Weber's analysis differed in many respects from his uncle's, but belonged together with it as an effort to confront the disappointments of German liberalism in the late nineteenth century. The years between their writings only added to the need for critical reflection.

In 1884, the year Weber returned to Berlin, the breakup of the liberal movement became irreversible. The National Liberal Party turned farther to the right, preferring cooperation with the two conservative parties and Bismarck to renewed alliance with its former left-liberal allies. As for the left-liberals, they patched up their own differences and formed a unified party only to suffer a major setback in the elections of that year. He expressed his fear in a letter of April to his uncle that liberalism would be split for the foreseeable future between "schematic fanatical demagogues on the one hand and blind Bismarckians on the other."[9] Though it exaggerated the left's dogmatism and the right's cynicism, his judgment was not far off the mark. The left-liberals doggedly upheld their free-trade, civil libertarian, and parliamentary principles, but were reluctant to develop a social program to meet the needs of social groups hurt by capitalism, while National Liberals settled into their new role as parliamentary representative of business interests. The two factions remained divided and never again set the tone for national politics as they had done in the early 1870s.

In the same letter Weber reported that he had found a groups of friends who were free of liberalism's legalistic approach to social issues and instead sought active state intervention. What accounted for their fresh program, he implied, was their professional training as economists and reformers, not class or confessional partisanship.[10] Weber would not have had to look far if he had simply sought a group that paid attention to the need for social reform and sought government intervention. Even the National Liberals were ready to support protective tariffs and welfare measures to satisfy Bismarck and the conservative parties, and the Social Democrats and the Center Party, too, had programs for state regulation of Germany's economy and society. But each of these parties sought to use the state to the advantage of its own constituencies. Weber expressed a widespread feeling in educated circles that liberalism had failed in its original ambition to speak for the national interest, leaving those who wished to adhere to this ideal politically homeless. During the 1880s he was only able to share this sentiment with isolated groups of friends and colleagues, while the social issues they wished to address remained off the public agenda. Not for long, however: in just a few years the repressive atmosphere of German politics would briefly dissolve, putting him and other young social scientists in the vanguard of a movement to win workers back to middle-class values.

A Protestant Ethic

Weber's maternal religious background provided him with an initial standpoint for rejecting the utilitarian outlook he associated with nineteenth-century liberalism. Helene Weber, his mother, belonged through her mother to a patrician Huguenot family, the Souchays; the founder of their branch, Jean Daniel Souchay, was pastor of the French Reform parish in Frankfurt am Main.[11] Helene's father was a pensioned civil servant who settled with his family in Heidelberg, where he enjoyed a close friendship with the liberal historian Gervinus. She and her sister Ida (later Hermann Baumgarten's wife) absorbed both their mother's stern Calvinist morality and Heidelberg's broadminded, antidogmatic theology. When Weber began his studies in Heidelberg, Otto Baumgarten, who was then finishing his studies in theology, introduced him to the special religious atmosphere of the Southwest. He and Otto read and criticized books together; they attended religious services whose liturgy and sermons sounded amusingly fanciful, if not irreverent, to Weber's Prussian ears; and through Otto he met other interesting and open-minded theology students. In addition he visited his uncle, Adolf Hausrath, a theology professor in Heidelberg and an embittered liberal, who had helped found the Protestant Association and spent his later years in melancholy retreat, chronicling the lives of Jolly, Rothe, and other heroes of the liberal movement.[12] Heidelberg exposed Weber to a kind of Protestantism fundamentally different from what he had known in Berlin. Then and later he had nothing but bitter words for Prussian Protestantism, with its deadly ceremoniousness and compromising pact with the Prussian aristocracy.[13] By contrast, Protestantism in the Southwest had a self-critical spirit and close ties to the region's urban patriciate. The encounter with it deepened his interest in religion and exposed him to a Protestantism of the middle class.

Weber's youthful attitude toward religion in several ways anticipated his mature treatment of it. In March 1884 he wrote to his younger brother Alfred (the later sociologist) to instruct him on the significance of his confirmation. After declaring that all the great deeds, laws, states, and science of civilization had developed under the influence of Christianity, he discussed the pervasiveness of its effects in their own time:

So it has come about that today everything that we summarize under the name of 'our culture' rests above all else on Christianity, that today in the contrivances and ordinances of the whole of human society, in its forms of thought and action, everything depends with it and on it, indeed so much that we ourselves don't always notice it at all and are no longer conscious of the fact that we are influenced by the Christian religion in all that we do and think. Christianity is the common bond tying us to all peoples and human beings on the same level as we; even the very persons among us who do not call themselves or claim to be Christians, and want to have nothing to do with Christianity, have nonetheless assimilated the basic tenets of Christianity and act according to its teachings.[14]

To a remarkable degree (especially for someone schooled no less than Tönnies in the *Gymnasium* neohumanist tradition) Weber ignored Greece and Rome, instead giving Christianity all the credit for creating and maintaining modern civilization. To insist on the permeation of Christianity into the motives of "the very persons among us who do not call themselves or claim to be Christians" went beyond the kind of truisms to be expected in a letter of his kind and indicate that Weber was already thinking of modern secular culture as an extension of its religious predecessor. The continuities between religious and secular culture would, of course, be one of the main themes of *The Protestant Ethic*.

In July of the same year he wrote to his mother that he was reading a small volume of essays by William Ellery Channing.[15] They were a gift from Ida that he continued reading with his mother after his return to Berlin. For the first time in years, he stated, "something religious has had more than an objective interest for me." Channing was one of the Boston founders of Unitarianism; with his antitrinitarianism, rejection of the doctrine of man's innate depravity, and enthusiasm for social reform, he was an important figure in the transition from Calvinist orthodoxy to Transcendentalism.[16] Weber found his theoretical principles naive, but admired the practical consequences he drew from them and the idealism emanating from his belief in "the infinite worth of the individual human soul." It was especially significant that Weber should react with such unaccustomed enthusiasm to a representative of New England Calvinism who came at the moment of its secularization, for this was just the kind of phenomenon that interested him in *The Protestant Ethic*. Weber was already dismissive toward rationales for religious belief; what mattered to him was its practical effect. In his later scholarship he would always show impatience with attempts to explain the origins of religion, whether with the aim of justifying or attacking it, and concentrate as he did here and in his letter to his brother on its significance for the believer and his world.

At twenty Weber had already begun to value religion as a practical attitude, a psychology that created a distinctive external pattern of behavior. Much reflection lay between his youthful likes and dislikes and his mature analyses of the relation between religion and public activity. Yet a clear continuity led from one to the other. Neither the externalized religiosity of doctrine, ritual, and institutions nor the internalized religiosity of mysticism ever held any personal attraction for him. But he eagerly affirmed Channing's individualism, which had the virtues of simplicity and of being anchored in an imperative to moral activism. Later he would respond in a similar vein to individuals who seemed to embody such a *Persönlichkeit* ideal, not hesitating to criticize whatever he found naive in their beliefs, but forgiving this so long as he sensed an underlying ideal conviction and the will to test it.

Protestant Social Reform

Bismarck's dismissal marked 1890 as a year of new beginnings in German politics. Members of the middle class with an interest in social reform had good reason to hope for change for the better: William II wanted to try out a conciliatory policy toward the working class in place of repression and deposed the chancellor partly in order to have a chance to lead the nation back to social unity. The parliamentary defeat of the Socialist Law in January restored legitimacy to the activities of the Social Democratic Party and made thinkable for the first time in twelve years a dialogue between socialists and middle-class reformers. When William made a speech in March announcing a coming era of social harmony, he added further legitimation to reformers' aspirations. They could now try out a role that had been denied to them for years by Bismarck's hostility and the breakup of the liberal movement, that of mediator between the working class and the state.

This fresh start in domestic politics (matched by William's determination to set Germany's foreign policy on a so-called new course of his own making) overlapped with Weber's first forays into public life. Living for the most part in Berlin during the second half of the 1880s and early 1890s, he was well placed to make incisive observations on political events in the capital, as he did in his letters to Hermann Baumgarten. At the same time, his studies in law and economics were preparing him to make proposals on the direction German policy should take at home and abroad to accommodate its burgeoning capitalist economy. These prescriptions were too complex for any single label to do them justice. Certainly he was a passionate nationalist who sought industrialization of Germany and imperial expansion in the name of national greatness. But this description says little about the content of his politics, which went beyond advocacy of power politics for its own sake. Another important part of his political vision was his secularized Protestant idealism. He repudiated any kind of confessional politics, which would have been partisan rather than a program for national unity, and any ethical treatment of politics, which in his view merely obscured the objective conditions of political action. Instead he took over from Protestantism an ideal of individuals free to shape their own destiny amid adverse conditions; Germany, in his imagination, should become a modern industrial nation made up of proud and self-reliant *Persönlichkeiten*, driven by more than just the pursuit of material goods. He expressed this ideal most outspokenly in the Protestant social movement of the 1890s.

Weber was among the visitors to the first conference of the Protestant Social Congress in May 1890. We have already encountered the Congress as the forum of Troeltsch's 1904 speech on ethics and politics. The organization's early history brought together a wide range of church groups, from the orthodox to the free-thinking and left-wing, in an attempt to unite for the common cause of social reform.[17] William II's speech in March created excitement among these church servants and lay Protestants longing for an end to the Prussian church's policy of indifference toward workers' welfare. At a time when pastors were beginning to seek out dialogue with workers anyway, the church hierarchy followed up William's speech with a declaration encouraging pastors to address workers' needs, even paying respect to their material well-being as a condition of their spiritual life. The Protestant Social Congress was to serve as the center of a new, church-sponsored social movement, whose ultimate boundaries, which might range from charity to political activism, were left undefined. Stoecker gave the initial impetus toward founding the Congress, but liberal and left-leaning church members responded to his call to participate. By the time the May conference opened, secular professors, politicians, civil servants, and teachers had got involved, so that a fair sample of Germany's educated elite was represented.

At the yearly Congress meetings of the 1890s Weber could meet a number of individuals who remained important for him then and later. Several of its members exemplified the kinds of Protestant thought and action that he admired. Otto Baumgarten got deeply involved with the Protestant social movement, for several years editing a journal, *Evangelisch-Soziale Zeitfragen*, with assistance from Max Weber, who defended Otto's social activities to his father. From 1912 to 1921 he served as president of the Protestant Social Congress.[18] Another Congress leader respected by Weber was Adolf von Harnack, who served as Congress president from 1903 to 1911. At the time of its first meeting Harnack was already a well-known public figure and the most prominent spokesman for the anti-Stoecker forces in the organization. His *History of Dogma* argued that dogma—a term encompassing doctrine, ritual, and institution as repositories of the sacred—represented a Hellenic incrustation over the authentic message of the Gospels.[19] The essence of Christianity was a direct encounter of *Persönlichkeiten*. The dogmatic forms evolved to satisfy Hellenistic intellectuals only covered over this authentic personal life, offering in its place a rationally hardened guarantee of salvation. By opposing the inward life of *Persönlichkeit* to the external encumberments of institutionalization and intellectualization, Harnack anticipated important tendencies in Weber's thought. His argument that the seemingly lifeless formulations of church doctrine actually sheltered prior experience was close to Weber's later understanding of the relationship between doctrine and experience in *The Protestant Ethic*, and his belief that intellectuals' need for meaning had shaped religious history foreshadowed a thesis of Weber's later sociology of religion.

Another active Congress member in the 1890s, Rudolf Sohm, was one source of Weber's famous concept of charisma.[20] Professor of church law at the University of Leipzig, Sohm contended from a radical Lutheran perspective that secular government should get completely out of the church's internal life. As in the apostolic church, those inspired by the holy spirit should provide leadership: charisma, spontaneous and imme-

diate, should prevail. One feature of Sohm's thought that probably made it attractive to Weber was its antinomy of the
external realm of force, legal and rational, and the internal
realm of the spirit, forever foreign to systematization.[21] Sohm
maintained that charismatic authority had actually regulated
the internal life of the early church and, in a reconstituted
modern church, could do so again. With far greater insistence
than Harnack, he distinguished *ratio*—to use Weber's later vocabulary—from charisma. From such thinkers Weber could
derive considerable authority for viewing the history of Christianity as a force field organized around irreconcilable
opposites.

Weber may have begun his lifelong friendship with Friedrich
Naumann at the Congress in the early 1890s.[22] The son of a
Saxon pastor, Naumann at the time wished to bring workers
back into the church, but also to learn from Social Democracy's
chiliastic ambitions of this-worldly change. In a review of 1894
for *Die Christliche Welt* Weber distanced himself from Naumann's socialism. "We bourgeois," as he called himself and his
readers, had an appreciation of private property absent from
Naumann's writings. This was his rhetorical tack for swinging
around to the side of his readers and leading them to an appreciation of Naumann's real strength, "his significant and original
Persönlichkeit."[23] Weber was right to see the *Persönlichkeit* as prior
to Naumann's professions of socialism. By the turn of the century the socialism had evaporated and Naumann had become a
political spokesman for the educated elite and its cultural individualism. Under Weber's tutelage he learned to envisage politics as a contest between the dictates of power and of ideals.
Wisdom in the modern world consisted in recognizing the brutality of power while furthering the idealism that was, after all,
Germany's special glory. He preached imperialism abroad, social conscience and nationalism at home. Naumann was respected, though not widely followed. His attempt in the late
1890s to create a combined working-class and middle-class political party, the National Social Union (which Weber regarded
from the beginning as a quixotic venture) ended in failure, and
his political gifts never found an adequate outlet in public life.[24]
To Weber, Naumann exemplified the politician with a calling,

who tested his convictions against the limits of the possible and held to them through decades of disappointment.[25]

While these educated Protestants tried to tug German politics in their own direction during the 1890s, oceanic forces were carrying it away. Convinced of the superiority of their values and fearful of the creation of a mass society that dispensed with them, they vied to create a Protestant alternative to the business, Catholic, working-class, and rural blocs that increasingly dominated the public struggle for wealth and power. Although shaped by other involvements as well, Weber's politics matured during the decade in which he experienced the defeat of their program. At the Congress of 1894 he delivered a speech that plunged the organization into a crisis from which it barely recovered. The story surrounding it reveals much about the specifically Protestant element in his political expectations.

The subject of this controversy was the great estates east of the Elbe River, the homes of Prussia's Junker landowners. In the internationalized grain market of the late nineteenth century they could not compete with overseas imports and faced economic disaster. To protect their interests the Conservative Party formed an alliance with the National Liberals, a combination violating ideology on both sides but working to their mutual advantage as they traded tariff concessions for industry and agriculture. Weber had a chance to observe the agrarian crisis firsthand while on draft duty near Posen in 1888. Two years later the Social Policy Association (*Verein für Sozialpolitik*) decided to sponsor an inquiry into rural economic conditions in Germany. Founded in 1872 to promote state intervention and oppose liberal laissez-faire policies, this prestigious organization counted many of the leading social scientists of the era among its members and attracted wide public attention with its debates and detailed empirical reports.[26] In early 1892, Weber, one of six young researchers involved in the project, agreed to write on the East Elbian region. Between the spring and fall of 1892 he completed his analysis, working from questionnaires filled out by employers. *The Condition of Rural Workers in East Elbian Germany* masterfully described the great estates' transformation from traditional to modern economic units. The personal relationships and common economic interests binding peasant to master were in a state of decay, for the landlords were abandoning paternalistic care and turning into capitalists who preferred the cheap labor of Polish migrants, leaving the German laborers, with their higher standard of living, to migrate to the cities or overseas. The analysis combined a fine grasp of local conditions with a larger theme, the transforming effects of capitalism on an entire way of life.

Weber's report was the most important part of the Association study and won praise from conservative, liberal, and socialist critics. Both liberals and Social Democrats, however, ·attacked the study's one-sided reliance on information from employers.[27] Interested in getting closer to the workers' thinking, Weber agreed to take part in a second study sponsored by the Protestant Social Congress, which sent out questionnaires to rural pastors, who in turn were supposed to interview workers.[28] He worked together with Paul Göhre, a pastor and fiery activist who had disguised himself as a factory worker for three months and in 1891 published a book about his experiences.[29] Weber was deeply impressed by Göhre's *Persönlichkeit* and defended his book from conservative attack.[30] Troeltsch later judged their friendship (which did not outlast the decade) to have been uniquely warm, an exception to the reserve Weber otherwise maintained toward even his closest acquaintances outside his family.[31]

At the Congress of 1894 Weber spoke on East Elbia, Göhre on the rest of Germany. They called on the government to break up the Junkers' estates and sell off the land to German laborers. This would stem migration, curb the need for Polish laborers, and create a stable Eastern economy in place of the decaying one. Their proposal was in the national interest—but it came at an intolerable political cost, since it would have undermined the existence of the Junkers.

A comparison of their speeches brings out the radically individualist nature of Weber's thinking. Göhre acted out of ethical convicton:

Sirs, I belong to none of the political parties. I am only a Protestant socialist [*evangelisch-sozial*]. That is, I am serious about applying the moral ideas of Christianity not only to the personal life of the individual, but—this is the colossal progress, this is the beginning of the new era for the history of Christianity—also to the great area of public life and especially its economic structure.[32]

Christianity contained a community ethics, Göhre believed, that could criticize the injustices of capitalism. Most Congress members shared this belief, even if they differed widely on what that ethics should be. Göhre expressed a widely felt sentiment when he stated that a new era was approaching in which Christianity would enter public life as never before. Conservatives like Stoecker, liberal Protestants like Harnack, and radicals like Naumann agreed that Lutheranism's long-standing indifference to things of this world was a grave historical error that had to be revised if they wished to regain the loyalty of the working class. They had assembled in the Protestant Social Congress to work out a new social ethics for the church, and Göhre's speech, though provocative, was in keeping with this aim.

Weber disagreed. Ethical norms were no longer possible, he told his listeners; capitalism had shattered the personal relations on which they depended. He spoke as a bourgeois interested in furthering individualism by giving workers a piece of land on which they could be masters of their own destiny. The individualism he wished to further had to do with workers' *Persönlichkeiten*, not their egos; their inner autonomy, not their happiness. *"We do not busy ourselves with social policy to create human happiness,"* he told the Congress, adding later, "That which to us appears *worthy* in man, his sense of responsibility to himself, the deep impulse upward toward the spiritual and moral goods of mankind—that is what we want to preserve and support, even when it confronts us in its most primitive form."[33] Weber's *Persönlichkeit* ideal was secular, for the individual's responsibility was to himself, not his fellow human beings or God. But in secular form it remained true to a Protestant cultural pattern, affirming "the spiritual and moral goods of mankind" and their superiority over external conditions. What intrigued Weber about the pastors' reports on the workers was that they discovered a primitive *Persönlichkeit* ideal. A longing for freedom from vestigial feudal bonds, according to their observations, motivated the rural workers. Weber hoped to build on that impulse, and to do so before they were enticed by what he considered to be the new bondage of socialism, by giving them land. Unlike Göhre, who tried to make a case for the profitability of small holdings in the East, Weber emphasized that the new arrangement would not be economically superior to the old; its justification was purely cultural. Although Weber is sometimes portrayed as the most secular and pragmatic of modern social thinkers, this proposal revealed a more complex approach to contemporary society placing the calculation of social forces in the service of *Persönlichkeit.*

The Weber-Göhre speeches created a national political scandal. At the Congress session itself Adolf Wagner came to the defense of the Junkers.[34] This did not spare the organization accusations of revolutionary agitation in the National Liberal and Conservative press.[35] The press attacks in turn foreshadowed the beginning of a new period of political repression. In December 1894, Hohenlohe, the new imperial chancellor, brought the Subversion Bill (*Umsturzvorlage*) before the Reichstag. It proposed up to two years imprisonment or a fine of up to six hundred marks for public criticism of religion, the monarchy, marriage, the family, or property.[36] A combined Social Democratic and liberal majority defeated the proposal, but not before its proponents used the debate to denounce subversive activities within the middle class. Speaking for the Conservatives, the Freiherr von Stumm, a Saarland industrial magnate who epitomized the fusing of feudal attitudes and big business, singled out Naumann for his socialist sympathies.[37] In the Prussian legislative house another Conservative, Zedlitz-Neukirch, listed the Protestant Social Congress among the forces breaking ground for Social Democracy.[38] The reformers replied with declarations in *Die Christliche Welt* and the Congress newsletter.[39] But they could not stop the government from favoring the alliance of industrial and agricultural capitalism. Weber's call for a breakup of Junker estates turned out to be the prelude to Junker political resurgence and a breakup of the social reform movement.

Weber's work on rural labor established his reputation as

economist and led to the offer of a chair in economics at the University of Freiburg, which he assumed in 1894. His Inaugural Address of the following year summed up his youthful political perspective, though in a more pessimistic vein than in preceding years. His description of the life-and-death struggle between Germans and Poles in the East underlined the German workers' "primitive idealism" and culminated once again in the demand for dividing up the Junker estates.[40] For Weber the East Elbian crisis illustrated a larger point about economics: the values orienting its policy prescriptions should be not utilitarian theorems about the greatest happiness for the greatest number, but the national interest. As in his speech to the Protestant Social Congress, he glorified hardship as the path to the values that made national life worth living. This time, however, he turned his attention to the German middle class, asking whether it was prepared to accept the burdens of political responsibility. His answer was doubtful. Unification, the fulfillment of millennial hopes, had left it apolitical and complacent; instead of overthrowing aristocratic leadership it yearned for the coming of a new Caesar. The speech concluded with a call to live up to the historical responsibilities of the present, mingled with anxiety that the present was condemned to post-millennial disappointment.

The reactionary political atmosphere of the second half of the 1890s filled Weber with foreboding.[41] Instead of developing a distinctive middle-class ethos, the sons of Germany's industrial and educated elite were imitating the aristocratic attitudes they learned in fraternities and the reserve officer corps. If this refeudalization continued, he feared, potential entrepreneurs would pick up their social superiors' disdain for business and retreat into the gentlemanly life-style of the urban rentier and the country lord. At the Protestant Social Congress of 1897 he excoriated the economist Karl Oldenberg's nostalgia for the culture of preindustrial Prussia and pleaded once again for a proud and self-sufficient middle class.[42]

Meanwhile Weber's private life was approaching a crisis. For years he had worked at a demonic pace, doing double degrees and double examinations in law and economics while loading on extra assignments like the rural labor reports. Neither his marriage to Marianne Schnitger in the fall of 1893 nor their move to Freiburg the next year changed his work habits. The marriage remained unconsummated, a problem with precedents in Helene Weber's family. Another trial, too, was reaching a breaking point. While living at home during the 1880s and early 1890s Weber had watched his father's petty tyranny over his mother and her growing estrangement from him. A month after a quarrel between father and son in July 1897, the elder Max Weber died, the breach unreconciled. Finally, Weber had a nervous collapse in May 1898. He became unable to work or sleep, dependent on rest, travel, and whatever cures the doctors could propose. From then until 1903 he published little and, with starts and stops, withdrew from teaching.[43]

During the early 1890s Weber fought for his religious and class culture of individual dignity as an alternative to utilitarian liberalism and a rival to working-class socialism and aristocratic conservatism. By mid-decade however, he could see that any hope for political realization of his ideal had become problematic: even the middle class ran after the foreign gods of the Prussian aristocracy instead of defending its own cultural inheritance. After recovering from illness he made it his task to seek out the origins of Germany's flawed political culture, his imagination reaching back to the Reformation to grasp the middle class's failure to live up to its historical calling at the end of the nineteenth century.

The Protestant Ethic as Cultural Criticism

Few scholarly works have ever aroused more controversy than Weber's essay of 1904–05, *The Protestant Ethic and the Spirit of Capitalism*.[44] Criticisms came almost at once from German critics, and Weber swelled the footnotes of the second edition, prepared in 1919, with replies to Werner Sombart, Lujo Brentano, Felix Rachfahl, and H. Karl Fischer. After World War I, discussion spread to England, America, and the rest of the world, attracting orthodox defenders, uncomprehending opponents, modifications, extensions, and attempts at proof or disproof. It is not easy to pin down Weber's claims even after so much discussion, for the work contains not one argument, but several.

It wavers between asserting that certain Protestant attitudes were decisive in causing the breakthrough to modern capitalism and that they merely provided it with a compatible ethos; it starts by inquiring into the origins of capitalism, but broadens out into a study of modern culture. The historical actors who played a causal role in the formation of capitalism also, in Weber's view, prefigured the cultural constellation of modern Germany, Western Europe, and America. Within his narrative about economic history he hid an allegory about Germany in his own day. *The Protestant Ethic* at this level grappled with the political setbacks Weber had experienced, distilling his insights into the conflict between his personal values and the actual nature of German public life.

A Tragic Calling

In 1896 Weber moved from Freiburg to Heidelberg, where he assumed the chair in economics in the fall. The university had not undergone major expansion since his student days: enrollment in the philosophical faculty went from 167 in 1880–81 to 169 in 1895–96, and the number of chairs in the philosophical-historical section went from 10 in 1880 to 14 in 1900.[45] His was the only economics professorship, and on arriving he found no separate library or teaching facilities.[46] Some of his former professors were still teaching, and he and his wife found the social atmosphere among the older generation (including dinner by candlelight in darkened rooms on sunny summer days) intolerably stuffy.[47] The university was just about to undergo modernization and renewal, however, and they could already discover a few friends among the younger professors. One was Troeltsch; we have already seen how his relaxed personality was a welcome presence in their house at a time of tremendous inner stress in their lives.[48] Another was a member of the law faculty, Georg Jellinek, whose monograph *The Declaration of Human and Civil Rights* included the thesis, provocative for Weber's views on the secularization of religious culture, that the American conception of natural rights derived from the Puritan belief in a covenant between the religious community and God. Such colleagues, as well as familial memories and the

Catholic-Protestant confessional mixture of the surrounding region, made Heidelberg a rich setting for Weber's interest in the sociology of religion.[49]

Heidelberg had the additional advantage of lying outside the Prussian university system. At the time of his Freiburg appointment, Weber had to resist a compromising job offer from Althoff. The minister of culture was anxious to keep him and tried to arrange for a professorship in Berlin in 1893, but at the cost of political favors from his father, who was sitting on the Prussian Landtag's subcommittee for the cultural budget; at the same time Althoff tried to dissuade the Baden authorities from hiring him in Freiburg. These tactics deeply offended Weber, who regarded them as samples of the authoritarian style taught by Bismarck. Heidelberg was only a shade less provincial than Freiburg, but offered better conditions for professional dignity than did more prestigious positions under Althoff's purview.[50]

Weber's deteriorating health soon tested the discretion of Baden's cultural bureaucrats and his Heidelberg colleagues. When his difficulties began a year and a half after the move, the demands of his calling placed an itolerable strain on his nerves. Repeated attempts to resume it ended in relapse. At one point (probably in early 1903) Marianne Weber wrote to Helene,

Max's state of health fluctuates from one day to the next. . . . In the meantime he has again expressed himself about what torments him most. It is always the same thing: the psychological pressure of the 'unworthy situation' in which he draws a salary and will not be able to accomplish anything in the foreseeable future, combined with the feeling that to all of us—you, me, and everyone—only a person with a *calling* [*Berufsmensch*] counts fully.[51]

Later the same year he decided to resign and received the title of *Honorarprofessor*, carrying an adjunct status, instead of his full professorship or *Ordinarius*. The break was great enough for him to feel cut off from his former social standing. The man who had been an exemplary careerist, meeting every expectation during his rapid rise upward, found himself thrust to the edge of his profession.[52]

At the moment he gave up his external calling, he regained

his ability to write. A methodological essay completed in the summer of 1903, "Roscher's Historical Method," still demanded torturous exertion, but after this came a triumphant outpouring. In July he agreed to join Edgar Jaffé and Werner Sombart as an editor of the *Archiv für Sozialwissenschaft und Sozialpolitik.* Weber's manifesto for the journal, "The Objectivity of Knowledge in the Social Sciences and Social Policy," completed in early 1904, sketched out some of his most important contributions to the methodology of the social sciences, including his concept of the ideal type. Another contribution to the *Archiv* was *The Protestant Ethic,* written and published in two parts. According to Marianne Weber, her husband began the first part in the second half of 1903 and completed it by the time he left with a group of German professors including Tönnies and Troeltsch at the end of August 1904 to take part in one of the international congresses at the Louisiana Purchase Exposition in St. Louis. After returning to Germany at the end of 1904 he wrote the second part within three months, finishing it at the end of March. It appeared in the *Archiv* approximately June 1905.[53]

The Critique of Utilitarianism

The famous essay began almost casually. There was a widespread affinity between prosperity and Protestantism: some meager statistics from Baden bore this out, as did anecdotes from Western Europe and the United States. To account for it, Weber went on to argue that certain denominations, collectively called ascetic Protestantism, inculcated a spirit peculiarly compatible with capitalism. The source of this compatibility was the ascetic Protestant idea of the calling, the belief that unremitting work in the world was a form of service to God. Although discovered by Luther, the idea of the calling did not significantly alter the behavior of Lutherans, which remained profoundly traditional. Instead the Protestant ethic—the calling in its revolutionary form—took hold in Calvinist churches and in sectarian groups, such as Quakers and Baptists. In seventeenth-century England, ascetic Protestants injected their work habits into the nascent market economy; the perfect fit between inner culture and outer conditions was a unique historical event destroying traditional limitations on capitalism and resulting in a modern economy and society. Once established, capitalism no longer required its inner spirit. Weber concluded by depicting the disappearance of the vestiges of the spirit of capitalism in his own era, even in its Anglo-American home, an event leaving behind a soulless society enslaved to capitalism.

Weber's first critics had little difficulty pointing out the tenuousness of the links between ascetic Protestantism and capitalism. Capitalism flourished during the early modern era in such Catholic regions as Northern Italy, the Rhineland, and Flanders. One could argue that Calvinists became capitalists because they were a persecuted minority, as was the case for the French Huguenots, or because their religious beliefs turned into an ideological justification for their business practice. Objective historical trends, such as the decay of feudalism, the growth of cities, the discovery of the New World, and the influx of precious metals, further explained the emergence of capitalism without an additional religious hypothesis.[54]

Weber anticipated these objections and offered counterarguments in the first edition of the essay. The external conditions of modern capitalism could not account for the systematic and diligent pursuit of economic goals distinguishing it from earlier merchant societies.[55] Werner Sombart had recently singled out rationalization as capitalism's defining characteristic. Weber agreed but demanded that the term be made historically specific.[56] The economy of Renaissance Florence was relatively modern; but, Weber argued, a glance at the Florentine merchants' way of thinking revealed a premodern outlook that acted as a brake on their business practices and would never have created the economic dynamism of a truly modern capitalist economy.[57] For evidence of a contrary kind Weber turned to Ben Franklin: living in the relatively primitive conditions of eighteenth-century Pennsylvania, writing as a craftsman who had learned his trade in traditional artisan shops, he preached a pure doctrine of capital accumulation, translating time, morality, and every waking activity into equations for money-making.[58] Just this ethos was lacking in Florence and its counterparts in premodern Europe, Asia, and the ancient world. To understand the difference, the historian had to go beyond classification of external features and seek out capitalism's spirit.

Less explicitly Weber subverted one of his critics' fundamental assumptions about human motivation. All of them took for granted that greed was an adequate explanation of the acquisitive behavior of the first modern capitalists. Weber ingenuously adopted the narrative viewpoint implied by this assumption, that of the utilitarian who expected human behavior to satisfy sensuous or other egoistic motives. Consistently applied, the utilitarian viewpoint led to a paradox. In its formative years, capitalism compelled endless accumulation and postponement of gratification. The person who met the utilitarian's expectation was the traditional merchant who balanced production and consumption, while the modern capitalist with his one-sided devotion to production was by purely this-worldly standards irrational. What was so striking about Franklin's advice, wrote Weber, was "the thought of the *individual's duty* toward the increase in his capital, an interest assumed to be an end in itself (*Selbstzweck*)."[59] The next page returned to the strangely unutilitarian strain in Franklin's sermon on wealth:

But above all, the "summum bonum" of this [Franklin's] 'ethic' is: the gain of money and ever more money, with the strictest avoidance of all simple pleasure. It is so entirely removed from all eudaemonist or hedonist viewpoints, so purely conceived as end in itself, that it appears as something entirely transcendent and completely irrational, at least in relationship to the 'happiness' or 'use' of the isolated individual. Man is subordinated to gain as his life's end; gain is no longer subordinated to man as the means to the end of satisfying his life's needs. For simple feeling this is a completely meaningless reversal of the 'natural' order (as we would say) of things; but just the same, quite obviously it is unconditionally a main motive of capitalism to the same extent as it is foreign to the person not touched by it.[60]

Utilitarianism, the classic philosophy of nineteenth-century liberal capitalism, had, according to Weber, forgotten the original motive of its own activity. His audience might think it pursued happiness; but he drew it around to the realization that historically it had worshipped an unknown god, something he called "entirely transcendent and completely irrational." The spirit of capitalism, at first sight something completely banal, turned out to conceal a mystery. Was capitalism rational? Only in a limited, economic sense. As soon as one sought a more comprehensive understanding, it became a human anomaly, irrational to any visitor from another civilization. The insider, too, the capitalist who endlessly pursued profit, would be hard put to justify his own behavior.

Weber's rhetoric at this point closely resembled that of Marx. According to the chapter on money in the first volume of *Capital*, "The wealth-gatherer . . . sacrifices the desire of his flesh to his gold fetish. He takes seriously the Gospel of denial. . . . Hard work, thrift, and stinginess make up his cardinal virtues; buy much, sell little, the sum of his political economy."[61] As the mocking description noted, the capitalist sacrificed the benefits of this world to a "gold fetish" in a bizarre imitation of religious asceticism. There was also a deeper similarity in the logic of the two analyses: central to the structure of Marx's thought was its critique of capitalism as an inversion of the natural relationship between means and ends, creating a perverse enslavement of human beings to their own means of production.[62] This was precisely the relationship that Weber accused the utilitarian of failing to notice. He stressed the strangeness of Franklin's advice, his language seemingly echoing *Capital:* for "simple feeling," endless pursuit of wealth violated the natural order of things.

Despite these similarities, Marx's materialist approach to the problem more nearly resembled the utilitarian's. For Marx, the capitalist's behavior was simply an unleashing of the age-old motive of avarice to the point where it developed its own upside-down logic. He compared the capitalist to the misers ridiculed by Shakespeare and medieval literature, and he found a philosophical predecessor of his own analysis in Aristotle, who distinguished between economics, the satisfaction of needs, and chrematistics, the accumulation of wealth for its own sake. The chrematistic behavior that was a marginal phenomenon of civilizations past had become the dominant pattern of behavior in modern capitalism.[63] Weber wished to call this whole way of thinking about capitalism into question; the capitalist's behavior completely escaped this-worldly categories.

It was not a repetition on a larger scale of traditional greed, but contained novel qualities of discipline and devotion. What set the modern capitalist apart was not that he wanted money, as the traditional miser did, but that he worked to satisfy a higher law. The psychological condition for the possibility of capitalism was a nonmaterialist value. The historian of capitalism had to abandon his utilitarian or materialist viewpoint if he wished to discover this value and understand how it transcended earthly commodities while multiplying their production.

Lutherans, Calvinists, and Other Contemporaries

All Weber's rhetorical skill could not persuade his critics to see the problem of motivation from his point of view. As in later debates over his book, some readers intuitively found the argument compelling, while others rejected it as irrelevant. In one of his exasperated responses, Weber tried to make plain the contemporary relevance of his work:

. . . Puritanism reveals the great inner tensions and conflicts between 'calling' (*Beruf*), 'life' (as we like to call it today), 'ethic,' in a stage of particular agreement that has never before or since existed in the same way. It happened precisely in an area in which the traditions of antiquity and the Middle Ages went other ways. Today we live in the midst of renewed tensions in this area, which—far beyond the sphere I have chosen—is turning into a cultural problem of the first order in a fashion known only to our 'bourgeois' (*bürgerlich*) world.[64]

It was the conflict between capitalism and middle-class values at the beginning of the twentieth century that had led Weber back to his study of Puritanism three centuries before. The German middle class's attitude toward capitalism and the society it had brought into being was, he feared, one of chronic discontent. The revolt of upper middle-class youth against reason, bureaucracy, and bourgeois convention endangered Germany's ability to compete with America and England in the world market. Their calling or occupation demanded narrow expertise, but their 'ethic' or criterion for conduct was just the opposite— an insistence on experiencing life as an undivided totality. Even though Weber was unable to fulfill his own calling as university professor, broke the bounds of specialization in his own work, and took a sympathetic interest in the countercultural students who gravitated to him, he affirmed capitalism and its calling as contemporary necessities.

With its "lesser ascetic penetration of life,"[65] Lutheranism shaped personalities more natural and spontaneous but also more prone to hysterical outbursts in modern politics than Anglo-Saxon *Persönlichkeit* would ever permit.[66] Hence the English and Americans could have their great men—Gladstone was Weber's example—but maintained an inwardly freer attitude toward them, avoiding naive feelings of duty or thankfulness toward them.[67] Bismarck, on the other hand, had reactivated Germany's Lutheran tendency toward awe of one's superior. The contrasting religious psychologies explained the problem that had preoccupied Weber since his youth of Germany's political immaturity. It had deeper roots than any reform measure could reach, extending back into the psychology formed by Luther and his successors. The politics of personal community, in which feelings always crisscrossed power relations, resulted in an abdication of critical judgment in the modern Empire.

Weber's Puritans were at the farthest remove from organic *Gemeinschaft;* every natural bond between them was pulverized and reshaped into a rational relationship. Each Puritan was supposedly a radically individuated being whose place and participation in the social order were calculated. *Gemeinschaft* and *Gesellschaft* did not even admit the possibility of a smoothly running society of this kind, calling on Hobbes and Marx as analysts of the chaos that would ensue from a social order constituted by self-determined individuality by struggling against the others. Troeltsch's *Social Teachings* contained a different interpretation of the Puritan experience, one stressing the balance between individual and community in its social organization, in contrast to the individuation perceived by Weber, who argued that Puritans worked together so efficiently because they obeyed an impersonal set of moral injunctions. They functioned with the collective force of a machine only through the complete elimination of communal feeling.

This Puritan synthesis of inner calling and impersonal moral code, individual motivation and collective purpose, was irretrievable. Germany's character was formed; Weber was not turning to Calvinism to reform it. Even in the classic lands of Puritanism, the old-fashioned Protestant ethic was disappearing. What took its place was utilitarianism: as the transcendent motive of Puritan activity disappeared, it became a purely worldly habit of acquisition, insistently asking after use as the measure of all things. Utilitarianism, however, was precisely the shallow philosophy that Weber had set out to criticize, seeking in the Protestant past a spiritual dignity lacking in contemporary bourgeois individualism. Weber's quest into the past was a useless triumph. He had found the spirituality he sought, but could not bring it into the present. All he could do was measure the ironic distance between past and present, reminding those who cared to listen that such a spirituality had once existed.

Weber's interest in cultural diagnosis makes sense of one feature of *The Protestant Ethic* that would otherwise seem out of place, the prominence of Lutheranism. Catholicism would have been the logical partner for comparison with Calvinism if his problem had simply been to explain the historical origins of capitalism. To be sure, Weber did not entirely neglect Catholicism and made plausible observations about its place in his typology. But only Lutheranism received a chapter of its own, from which we learn primarily that its idea of the calling was a false start. And Lutheranism, not Catholicism, served as Weber's great contrast to the psychology of Calvinism. All this had little to do with the formation of capitalism in England, but fit in well with Weber's preoccupation with Germany's negative attitude toward capitalism. From this perspective Lutherans and Calvinists were allegorical figures, stand-ins for the Germans and Anglo-Americans of his own time.[68]

Weber's Calvinists were radical individualists whose rigorous belief in predestination eliminated every possibility of redeeming community: neither sermon, sacrament, church, nor any other means could alter one's eternal fate.[69] For the successor generations lacking the intuitive self-confidence of Calvin and his immediate followers, argued Weber, the strain was unbearable. They found solitary reassurance in the accumulation of works in the world—the systematic, self-denying kind of behavior that led to capital formation.[70] By contrast Lutheranism, in

Weber's description, had the effect of breaking down individuality and creating a community of feeling. Its *unio mystica*, mystical union of the individual with Christ, afforded relief from anxiety over salvation for the Lutheran believer, as did affective community with one's fellow believers.[71] Instead of demanding constant diligence from the individual as proof at every instant that he was one of God's elect, Lutheranism alternated between lax moral standards and periodic floods of communal exaltation.[72]

This drastic contrast between Calvinist individualism and Lutheran communitarianism distorted the chief interpretations Weber himself drew on for his portrait of the two confessional psychologies. The most important of these was *Vergleichende Darstellung des lutherischen und reformierten Lehrbegriffs* by Matthias Schneckenburger, a mid-nineteenth-century theologian who systematically analyzed the psychology underlying Lutheran and Calvinist doctrine.[73] Weber generously acknowledged Schneckenburger's work as the backbone of his own.[74] Indeed one can already find the main outlines of the social scientist's contrasts between dynamic, activist Calvinism and contemplative, passive Lutheranism in the theologian's study. But Schneckenburger did not make a dichotomy between individualism on the one hand and communitarianism on the other; in important respects Lutheranism was the more isolating, Calvinism the more community-oriented faith.[75] Weber was in this respect far less differentiated than his model. Even more striking was Weber's use of *Puritans and Anglicans* by Edward Dowden. Weber cited Dowden's portrait of John Bunyan out of context as crucial proof of Puritan solitude when in fact Dowden wished to point out the formation of a Puritan human community.[76] Finally, Weber ignored one of the most distinctive tenets of Anglo-American Calvinism, its covenant theology. This doctrine addressed precisely the kind of psychological anxiety that interested Weber; it relieved the individual's fear of damnation by reassuring him that his community shared a special covenant with God guaranteeing each of its members a chance of salvation.[77] Even though Jellinek and Troeltsch stressed the cultural importance of covenant theology, Weber ignored this extremely inconvenient historical reality, which would have required severe qualification of his image of Puritan isolation.

Another puzzling feature of Weber's theory was its implicit assumption of generational change. Calvinists and Lutherans went from intuitive certainty to characteristic types of relief from anxiety. But how, when individual anxiety takes place on an individual scale? Weber's point here was that a psychological transformation could affect large numbers of people in unison when religious faith was involved.[78] What in Weber's story shaped the collective Calvinist work ethic and the Lutheran community of feeling, the shift from the original, elevating faith to the routinized, worldly behavior succeeding it?

There are only hints of an answer, not a satisfactory solution, on this crucial point, and the best guide comes not in Weber's analysis of ascetic Protestantism, but in his account of Luther's discovery of the idea of the calling. Luther, Weber reminds us, began the Reformation with the apostolic community's expectation that the Kingdom of Heaven was at hand. Now if this was so, then things of this world mattered little, and Paul could advise everyone to remain in the station in which God's "call" had reached him and to continue working as before. As a result of his eschatological expectations, Luther shared this Pauline indifference toward work in the initial years of the Reformation. But the public conflicts of the 1520s caused a profound revision of his views:

After the struggles with the 'enthusiasts' [*Schwärmgeister*] and the Peasant Wars, the objective historical order, in which the individual is set in his place by God, for Luther becomes more and more the direct emanation of divine will. Henceforth the stronger and stronger emphasis on the role of Providence even in the individual events of life grows into a conception of fate ['*Schickungs'-Gedanke*] of a traditionalist hue: as a matter of principle the individual should *stay* in the station and calling in which God has set him and keep his earthly efforts within the limits of this given situation in life.[79]

Religious enthusiasm and social rebellion provoked Luther to acquiesce in physical force and sanctification of secular authority. Weber shared Troeltsch's view that his social teachings sanctioned extreme conservatism. Beyond this he drew out another implication: Luther's valuation of work, formerly indifferent, rose as his eschatological expectations diminished. With the perspective of a long secular future opening up, work became a substitute for collective salvation, a way for the individual to enjoy the Kingdom of God in the world. The Lutheran, according to Weber, passively conformed to the God-given order of things. For German culture this resulted in the formation of a passive idea of fate. His *Schickung*, the circumstances into which he was sent, became his *Schicksal* or fate, accepted as an externally imposed burden.

Weber did not explain the falling off of Calvinism's original, intuitive confidence in one's salvation and the corresponding rise of anxiety and the work ethic. One sentence made the transition: "The elect therefore are and remain God's *in*visible church. [It is] naturally (*naturgemäss*) quite otherwise for the epigones—already Theodor Beza—and above all for the broad stratum of ordinary human beings (*Alltagsmenschen*)."[80] At this crucial historical moment, Weber left collective self-confidence and its diminishment to nature. Yet a plausible historical explanation was at hand. Weber did not explore the possibility that the English Civil War with all its social and political turmoil was responsible for a shift comparable to the one he pointed out for Luther from immediate expectation of the Kingdom of God as a collective, public event to the private idea of the calling even though he did view it as the decisive battle for modernity, with the aristocratic cavaliers and Puritan roundheads confronting one another as if members of radically different races.[81] The Puritan victors, no less than Lutherans, were imbued with a notion of fate that they applied to their economic activity. Theirs was not a passive *Schickung*, however, but a destiny calling them to ceaseless transformation of society and nature. Perhaps their victory in the Civil War confirmed their belief that personal election and public fate coincided, and their compromises after victory, fears of lower-class enthusiasm, and loss of national leadership contributed to their eventual turn from collective action to the work ethic. Richard Baxter, Weber's main source of evidence for the formation of the work ethic, was, Weber neglected to mention, a political moderate of the Restoration era.

Weber rediscovered in the Protestant past the political experience of his own time. The German middle class had gone from world-historical expectation before 1848 to world-historical disappointment afterward; it had endured political failure in 1848 and went on to watch its aristocratic enemy, Bismarck, complete its historical mission of unifying Germany. No one was more conscious of this political defeat than Weber, who during the 1890s had summoned his fellow bourgeois to take pride in their class identity and strive once again for national leadership. Work, the private and personal creation of meaning, only took on central importance for a class or civilization that had lost its power to shape a public destiny. This was the historical lesson, derived from the disappointments of national unification, that underlay Weber's sociology of a "natural" routinization of political and religious movements.

Persönlichkeit and Society

At the end of *The Protestant Ethic* Weber outlined a program for testing the essay's thesis by tracing the history of asceticism from its beginnings in medieval monasticism to its end in utilitarianism. Numerous other projects distracted him in the decade and a half after he completed *The Protestant Ethic*. He continued to write methodological essays as he had done since 1902, usually in polemical response to the views of others; together these add up to a thick volume and a powerful defense of his neo-Kantian conception of the social sciences. *Economy and Society,* published posthumously, contains much of Weber's sociology in its chapters on methodology, authority, politics, the city, charisma, law, economics, and religion. A third major research area, his essays on the world religions examining the economic ethics of China, India, and ancient Judaism, appeared in the *Archiv für Sozialwissenschaft und Sozialpolitik* from 1915 to 1921. These essays brought Weber back to the themes of *The Protestant Ethic.* He worked on them and on uncompleted studies of Islam and early Christianity from 1911 until the time of his death in 1920.

The scope of Weber's research broadened, but one of his underlying interests remained the meaning and destiny of *Persönlichkeit.* His methodological essays defined its place in the pursuit of scholarly truth. *Economy and Society* described the logic by which social organizations guaranteed their own persistence and resisted the intrusion of personal expression. The essays on the world religions placed Puritan *Persönlichkeit* in comparative perspective, contrasting it with non-Western personality types and its ancient Jewish ancestor. These writings assembled the pieces of a modern drama. *Persönlichkeit,* more isolated and individuated than ever before in history, faced a harsh and unyielding modern society. Modern society, as a result of its very barrenness, necessitated a modern heroism more self-reliant than any that had ever gone before. Two terms of his later thought mark the polar extremes of this drama: value-freedom, the methodological principle Weber deduced from a world devoid of inherent meaning, and charisma, Weber's name for the quality distinguishing *Persönlichkeit* at its purest and most effective. Weber's use of these two terms illustrates the dramatic unity of his later work and his continued fashioning of it out of his Protestant culture.

Value-Freedom in the German Sociological Association

In his methodological writings as elsewhere Weber polemicized against his contemporaries' longing for community and explored the dimensions of a radically individuated modernity. This critique took the methodological form of the distinction between facts and values. On neo-Kantian methodological principle, the world had no inherent order; research structured it through either the generalizing method of natural science or the particularizing method of historical or cultural science.[82] As a criterion for selecting facts and making order out of the world, historians and social scientists made use of values derived from the subjective interests of one's own culture. This value-*related* enterprise admitted that the researcher's values were a matter of personal conviction, not absolutes guaranteed by a superhistorical authority. Research guilty of value-judgments, on the other hand, naively projected its values onto the object of knowledge and supposed that they were part of it. The value-judgment thus committed could take several forms. One was the ontological error of imputing substantive reality to the State, the Proletariat, or some other entity, instead of regarding it as a construction informed by one's own, value-related perspective on it. Another was the teleological error of imputing necessity to the end of history.[83] One might believe in the inevitability of bourgeois enlightenment or proletarian revolution, but belief was something fundamentally different from supposing that history was inevitably moving toward fulfillment of such an end. A value-judgment was tantamount to a wish for an illusory community: in the ontological error, to wishing for the reality of one's favored collective entity; in the teleological error, to wishing for the unity of generations past, present, and future. Weber's value-free social scientist gave up the comforts of community for the dignity of individuation. He lost the illusion that God or history was guarantor of his values in exchange for the knowledge that all deities reside within the human breast.

Weber tended to regard value-judgments as quasi-religious errors, injections of inherited expectations into a modern world barren of any promise of fulfilling them. He specifically attacked the ontological errors of German conservatives as warmed-over Lutheranism: their belief in the metaphysical reality of the State or *Volk* rested on the religious supposition that God emanated into history by breathing life into these collective entities, unfolding His spirit through their world-historical development.[84] The same was true for thinkers who worshipped the great man in history: they were the latest candidates for the Lutheran *unio mystica*, secretly possessed of the belief that God entered history through the vessel of a chosen individual.[85]

From this perspective the meetings of the Social Policy Association were extremely dissatisfying. Its reports had the authority of academic science, but also served as propaganda, influencing public policymakers and appealing to Prussia's paternalistic traditions as the valid set of values for judging the national interest. When the economist Eugen von Philippovich identified "productivity" with "popular welfare" at the Association's 1909 meeting in Vienna, Weber and Sombart objected that he had inserted an unacknowledged value-judgment into his definition. A conflict broke out over the place of values in the social sciences, culminating in an argument between Weber and Schmoller at a closed session of the Association in January 1914.[86]

In the winter of 1909–10 Weber began exploring the possibility of a sociological society dedicated to value-freedom, an idea he first shared with Simmel and Sombart during a visit to Berlin.[87] After follow-up trips to Berlin and Leipzig he got annoyed by the unwillingness of others to cooperate as they should—"By now I have finally gathered at least a few of those people who are indispensable for the Sociological Society. But we shall not make any progress; it is enough to make a man despair. Nobody wants to sacrifice any of his time and work and interests, and as for acting, they don't do a thing!"[88] Despite his complaints the organization quickly got under way with Tönnies, Simmel, and Sombart collectively serving as chair while Weber took the title of treasurer.

The German Sociological Society held its first conference 19–22 October 1910 in Frankfurt am Main. As Weber later remarked, it provided a meeting place mainly for untitled academics; the older generation that dominated the Social Policy Association stayed away, depriving the new venture of access to established financial and institutional resources.[89] The conference met in the Academy for Social and Commercial Sciences, a technical school founded by Wilhelm Merton, a Frankfurt industrialist whose English Jewish family had migrated to Germany in the mid-nineteenth century.[90] He contributed time and money to the Institute for Social Welfare (*Institut für Gemeinwohl*), the journal, *Soziale Praxis,* and the Society for Social Reform (*Gesellschaft für Sozialreform*), all of which tried to build a broad coalition of working-class and middle-class reformers.[91] Merton had tried to recruit Weber in the mid-1890s for the Institute, which now provided part of the funding for Weber's pet research project on the sociology of the modern press.[92] Weber hoped at first that private philanthropy could free sociology from financial dependence on the state and—presumably—guarantee its freedom from the kind of state paternalistic ideology that pervaded the Social Policy Association.[93] The Society's first statute included a statement of its commitment to value-freedom: "It [the Society] gives all scientific orientations and methods of sociology equal space and rejects the representation of any practical (ethical, religious, political, aesthetic, etc.) aims."[94] Thus value-free social science found its first home in an organization with an elective affinity to left-liberal capitalism.

Weber's business report, overstepping the bounds of business, elaborated:

The Society is not 'above parties' just in the sense of trying to do justice to everyone, to understand everyone. It does not wish to draw the beloved 'middle line' between different parties' points of view, between political, social activist, ethical, aesthetic or other valuations of whatever kind. Rather, it has nothing at all to do with stances of this kind; it is simply disengaged from parties as such.[95]

Thus Weber proposed a postnormative society in miniature: secularized, pluralized, regulated by respect for values as *Privatsache* and by adherence to a neutral scientific method. To draw the middle line was the error of groups like the Protestant Social Congress and the Social Policy Association; what they created was not a clear path but confusion, distorting facts with values and diluting values to accommodate everyone's view of the facts. Weber's radical alternative depended on voluntary self-censorship, with all the participants practicing an ascetic willingness to keep their prior assumptions and practical interests to themselves. With his program of value-freedom in force, the Society tested the limits of neutral empirical research in two senses: the degree of actual willingness of the members to stick to the rules, and the degree to which scientific discussion could claim to exclude values without logical contradiction.

In their different ways the two opening presentations reaffirmed the value-freedom statute, at least indirectly. Simmel's evening address on the "Sociology of Sociability" opened the conference by analyzing the modern conditions that gave value-freedom its significance. Business for the sake of business—the logic of capitalism analyzed in *The Protestant Ethic*—was but one of many autonomous realms in modern society. Simmel provided the Society with a playful example of another: sociability, originally a means to some other, practical end, could become an autonomous form, serving no end other than itself, the free play of being sociable.[96] The task of the sociologist was to grasp its formal structure. Simmel's demonstration of sociological method could strike observers as unserious, but it concealed a serious point: the injunction not to judge one realm of modern society by the laws of another. With its fragmentation of the social totality, modernity only yielded its inner logic to the observer willing to recognize the limits of his own standpoint and ready to accept the foreign laws of neighboring realms.

Tönnies opened the first morning session by recognizing the fragmentation of modernity and drawing out its consequences in a fashion remarkably compatible with Simmel's and Weber's conclusions.[97] Empirical sociology, he told his listeners, had to step back from aspirations to universality and respect the line separating it from speculative knowledge. Tönnies also insisted on a point left unclear by Weber: that there was room for a philosophical branch of sociology as well. He had revised his earlier conjunction of speculative and empirical knowledge, but only to make an analytical distinction between two kinds of learning, not to deny the legitimacy of one of them altogether. This enabled him to work together with Weber in the Society and to respect value-freedom; but it also raised the question of how one would eventually house philosophical discussion alongside empirical knowledge—and whether one was not creating a rebellious outcast by ignoring values altogether for the moment.[98]

Some speakers satisfied Weber's conception of value-freedom. For example Sombart, speaking on technology and culture, accused Marxism of technological determinism and argued for a view of technology as one of the conditions of social action.[99] Troeltsch's speech on natural right, too, relativized Marx; it recognized the interaction of religion and class but upheld the ultimate causal heteronomy of religion.[100] These speeches brought out another feature of value-free social science: its causal pluralism. To subscribe to a monocausal view of history would lead to teleological assertions about the future; causal plurality guaranteed the irreducible complexity of history, the impossibility of making any assertion about its future

direction that could not be amended by reference to a counter-
vailing causal sequence.

Throughout the proceedings Weber was continually irritated
by speakers and discussion participants who injected their
world views into the discussion. Their interventions sometimes
crossed so theatrically into the dread realm of value-judgment
that they seemed like blasphemous clowns planted to arouse his
wrath. The liberal economist Gerhard von Schulze-Gaevernitz
rebuked Sombart for avoiding judgments about the value of
technology;[101] in response to the racial theorist Alfred Ploetz's
speech, the Viennese sociologist Rudolf Goldscheid pleaded for
the necessity of values to define the "fit" and "unfit" members
of society.[102] To bring the group back to order, Simmel opened
Troeltsch's afternoon session on the second day with a solemn
injunction from the Society's governing committee to the audience not to make value-judgments by applauding![103] Even this
act of censorship was not enough to keep the proceedings
value-free. Hermann Kantorowicz, the afternoon speaker on
the third day, used the podium to propagandize for the "free
law" movement (which stood for greater recognition of judges'
independent decision-making powers and would have enlarged
their application of sociological findings in reaching decisions).[104] With anarchistic gusto, he declared the value-freedom
statute to be suspended; his subject was a metasociological one,
the theory of jurisprudence, in which value-judgments were
unavoidable.[105] Tönnies, who was presiding, tried to call the
discussion to order during the debate, and Weber scolded and
argued, but to no avail as other participants took up the case
for value-judgments in the sociology of law.[106] Weber pointed
to Troeltsch's speech of the day before as a model of value-free
discourse despite the subject-matter's nearness to the speaker's
values and declared it shameful should the Society have to admit that the only value-free discussion partner was a theologian. He left the meeting in disgust over the "salon des refusés"
he had organized, his patience worn out by the participants'
sense of self-importance. They had failed to live up to the sociological requirement of the Sociological Society as he conceived it, the will to value-freedom.[107]

Weber's letters to Tönnies after the meeting reveal what a

frustrating event it had been for both of them. Tönnies was rueful about losing control of the session on the sociology of law and wondered if his conduct had been "ethical" enough. Weber assured him that he did not personally blame him, but that his overly "ethical," humorless manner had offended many of those present. The session, Weber told him, had cost the organization dearly. His hopes of founding a legal section, his chances of getting a contribution of 10,000 marks from an unnamed Academy had gone from excellent to almost nil. Weber was already beginning to wish he could drop his responsibilities for the organization as a whole and concentrate on the projects that really interested him, such as the study of the press.[108]

In Weber's view the chief function of the Society ought to have been to sponsor research carried out by specialized committees.[109] The Society's second conference, held 20–22 October 1912 in Berlin, justified his fear that another conference on general themes would only produce generalities, not the kind of real advances in empirical knowledge that would overcome official suspicion and qualify it for university status.[110] Even the better papers were disappointing. One notable example, Alfred Weber's evening address entitled "The Sociological Concept of Culture," navigated uncertainly between the individual and the general, culture and civilization, intellect and feeling, the biological and the spiritual: marshy oppositions hardly firmed up by the underlying notion of the conflict between personal life and the abstract forms of modern civilization.[111] The rest of the conference focused on aspects of a single theme, the concept of nationality. While some of the papers were respectable, none demonstrated how sociology offered a novel means for empirical social analysis.

The breaches of value-freedom were as egregious at the second conference as at the first. One of the speakers, Paul Barth, was author of a sociological work in the Comtean-Spencerean evolutionary tradition, *The Philosophy of History as Sociology* (1897).[112] His talk entitled "The Sociological Significance of Nationalities" began with an unprovocative description of instances of national consciousness from antiquity onward, but culminated in the question of whether a national or international state was preferable. Off went the alarm bells of the guardians of value-freedom. Sombart, who was chairing the session, interrupted Barth and reminded him of the prohibition against value-judgments. When Barth tried to continue, Weber cried out, "It is strictly forbidden. You are not allowed to make value-judgments!"[113] An embarassed pause followed; then the floor was opened up for discussion. First Tönnies added his warning against value-judgments, after which Weber continued his fit of rage:

This is perhaps the last sociology conference I will take part in. But as long as I take part I will see to it that the separation between discussion of *practical* questions and the treatment of *theoretical* problems cultivated here is strictly observed, that separation which brought about the branching off of the Sociological Society from the Social Policy Association.[114]

Still not satisfied, he insisted once again at the end of the discussion on the complete avoidance of value-judgments and told the gathering that his continued membership depended on it. His motive for founding the organization had been to create a forum for value-free scholarship, and such flouting of it was rapidly wearing out his patience.[115]

The line between theory and practice was not so clear-cut even in Weber's own thinking, however. Alfred Ploetz's speech, "The Concepts of Race and Society," at the first conference outlined the ideology of Social Darwinism in a form that by Weber's standards clearly contained value-judgments.[116] Social biology, according to Ploetz, studied the processes of natural selection within a race and its struggle against its neighbors for survival. Ploetz treated race as a metaphysical unity, ascribed an evolutionary logic to its historical development, and assumed that its physiologically stronger members were the fitter members worthy of survival. Weber delivered an impressive array of counterarguments: he disagreed with Ploetz's assertion that the Christian principle of love of neighbor had traditionally regulated social behavior; considered Ploetz's assumption that social prosperity depended on racial prosperity completely unproven; called the whole racial vocabulary mystical and unscientific; explained how Negro-white relations in the United States could be explained entirely in social categories, without recourse to racial ones; disputed Ploetz's definition of society as a living being and asserted that it was constituted by the social action of individuals; and concluded that racial biologists had not yet proved a single thesis.[117] This was not an attack on racial biology as such, however. Weber had gone to some trouble to secure Ploetz's participation in the Society and went out of his way the next day to reassure him that he was welcome in it.[118] Correcting the impression left by newspaper reports of the proceedings, he emphasized the importance of racial biology for sociology and reaffirmed the Society's plan to found a social biology section.

Racial theory was on the agenda of the 1912 conference, but this time was taken up by an opponent, the economist Franz Oppenheimer.[119] Whereas Weber at both conferences limited his remarks to empirical rebuttal, Oppenheimer seized the methodological and ideological issues at the root of racial theory, satirizing the "Teutschtümler" and their "Germano-manie," criticizing their evidence for identifying language and racial community, reciting the negative results of attempts to measure racial physiognomy, attacking the scientific preten-sions of neoromantics who identified race with an "Aryan" or "Jewish" soul, and emphasizing the primacy of social milieu in the formation of individual character. He concluded that racial theory was nothing more than a class ideology, "the typical legitimating group ideology of the ruling upper class."[120] Ac-cording to the gleeful report in the *Vossische Zeitung,* "His [Op-penheimer's] arguments were so on the mark and effective that a number of those he accurately characterized as Germano-maniacs, whether of Gobineau's, Woltmann's, or Chamberlain's persuasion, left the room in loud protest."[121]

A powerful advocate stayed behind to make their case. Som-bart, who had been on the radical left in the 1890s and passed through a left-liberal phase, was rapidly moving toward the radical right.[122] In 1911 he created a sensation with a series of antisemitic public lectures collected into a pamphlet, *The Future of the Jews.*[123] The same year he published *The Jews and Economic Life,* an attack on Weber and an exposé of Jewish responsibility for the evils of capitalism.[124] In the rhetoric of value-free sci-ence Sombart purported to discover Jewish influence wherever capitalism was taking shape, whether in international trade, colonialism, the early modern state, the circulation of paper money, or—*contra* Weber—the spirit of capitalism. Weber's Puritans, according to Sombart, were quasi-Jews who had taken over their essential doctrines from Judaism.

In his discussion of Oppenheimer's paper, Sombart recommended a more objective attitude to the Jewish speaker. He demonstrated his own dispassionate approach by naming three questions ignored by Oppenheimer and requiring investigation before one could reach a judgment of racial theory: whether heredity could innately qualify persons for certain activities, whether psychological or physical qualities could be collective, and how similarities took shape within a social group. In his estimation one had at least to be grateful to racial theory for freeing science from the tyranny of historical materialism—a one-sided perspective that still distorted Oppenheimer's views.[125]

Weber followed with a devastating dismissal of empirical proofs of racial theory.[126] He himself, he told his audience, had tried to measure racial influence on the productivity of different workers and had not found any way to isolate specifically racial differences from other qualities. Where laboratory hypotheses failed, historical speculation could only abound in errors, foggy concepts, and unverifiable or contradictory assertions. Racial theorists argued that the depletion of Roman soldiers caused the Roman Empire's downfall—yet once assimilated into its culture, "barbarians" became the most "Roman" emperors. They sought traces of race in art—yet Weber had found similarities between Greek and Chinese music. They spoke of the upper classes as a race, yet monogamous marriage had taken hold and guaranteed pedigree only late in history. They spoke of a natural boundary between Germany and the East when none existed; they spoke of a Yankee race when it was the American educational principle of self-reliance (*Selbstverwaltung*) that unified a diverse population and shaped the distinctive American character. To make racial theories worthy of discussion at all, two things were needed: exact measurable differences of inherited response to stimuli and proof that these qualities made a difference for cultural causality. And the results so far: "Not a single fact of this kind has yet been found."[127]

Weber left the German Sociological Society after the 1912 conference. Marianne Weber quotes him as writing at the time (probably 1912 or 1913), "Will these gentlemen [i.e., the ones who disregard the value-freedom statute], not *one* of whom can stifle the impulse (for that's just it!) to bother me with his subjective 'valuations,' all infinitely uninteresting to me, kindly stay in their own circle. I am sick and tired of appearing time and again as a Don Quixote of an allegedly unfeasible principle and of provoking embarassing 'scenes.'"[128]

The Society survived his departure, however, and actually continued to grow for the next two years along the lines of specialized scientific research that he had lain down for it. A statistical section was formed, as he himself announced to the second conference in 1912.[129] In 1913 and 1914 the Society began agitating for the creation of university chairs in sociology, drafting a petition and sending it to sixty-three faculties and institutions of higher learning and five hundred and sixty professors in June 1914.[130] In the summer of 1914 the Society also signed an agreement with the Institut Solvay, a private sociological institute in Belgium, for creation of a joint newsletter.[131] The Society was beginning to play the role of an effective public advocate for sociology in Germany; what cut short its work was not its internal disagreements, but the war. In December the Society's directors decided to put its treasury at the disposal of German propaganda efforts for neutral countries.[132] The Society voluntarily dissolved, reorganizing and resuming its work only after the war. Thus Weber's experiment, with its dedication to separating theory and practice, ended with a grotesque disavowal of his intention; it capitulated to that mobilization of the spirit that was the special contribution of German professors to the wartime community of 1914.

Weber's experience in the Sociological Association brought out some of the difficulties underlying his notion of value-freedom. Value-freedom was supposed to enable *Persönlichkeiten* to choose their own values, without censorship by any authority. Science could never validate values, but values had the indispensable function of leading to significant hypotheses for science to test. From his point of view the organization was a failure because its members did not understand the difference between empirical science and self-expression that he had tried to formulate in the value-freedom tenet; he thought they degraded both by trying to dignify their convictions with the name of science. Certainly this was true of some of the speakers, who unintentionally demonstrated why sociology had the reputation of a dilettante's pursuit and why Weber hoped to steer it sharply away from cultural criticism onto a course of quiet collective research. Yet the two meetings also revealed how quickly value-freedom turned into a form of censorship in its own right. The discussions of racism revealed this most pointedly. Left to value-free discussion, they became a charade in which racial theory received respectability by being discussed without inquiry into its motives. Ploetz was an amateurish defender of his cause, but Sombart showed how effectively the airing of social resentments could take place in the name of value-free science. Weber's conception of value-free discussion took for granted a consensus of values: not merely about the value of empirical science (a point Weber himself recognized), but also about human dignity. Where that consensus was lacking, as in prewar Germany, rational discussion required articulation of underlying differences. Weber could not see how deeply his own conception of scholarship was embedded in inherited, culturally specific values. The most profound loss to science did not come from the immaturity of the members of the Sociological Association who annoyed Weber, but from Weber's own failure to distinguish between racial ideology and science, an issue that did not disappear from Germany or its refounded sociological association after 1918. One could only "understand" racial theory by erasing Weber's line between facts and values, drawn to preserve the pure interiority of post-Protestant *Persönlichkeit*.

Charisma and the Modern Calling

The notion of charisma illustrates Weber's abiding concern with the form of individuality historically derived from ascetic Protestantism. Borrowed from theology, it belonged to a constellation of concepts giving his sociology its power and co-hesiveness. He developed it from 1911 on, just as he was begin-ning his research on *Economy and Society* and on the essays on the world religions, which he conducted simultaneously over the next decade.[133] Weber defined it as a quality marking out an individual as endowed in the perception of others with supernatural or at least exceptional powers. The charismatic individual disrupted the everyday world (*Alltag*), creating a sit-uation in which old customs or rules could end and new ones could begin.[134] In politics it applied to the Germanic chieftan and the modern demagogue, to the dictator and the democrat, so long as they enjoyed their followers' unconditional trust and could act contrary to their normal expectations. In its parallel religious usage it applied to anyone from the tribal magician to the prophet and reformer who commanded similar awe for possession of transcendent powers. The religious charismatic, too, could abolish the old order and promulgate a new one.

Weber divorced the pure notion of charisma from any com-munal origin or continuation. Its appearance could not be ex-plained; it was not a product of class, tradition, or any other collective source. Weber called it irrational, or entirely specific to the person with the conviction of being called to carry out a divine or higher mission. Whatever the content of this mission, its uniqueness created conflict with the existing social order, which the authentic charismatic leader defied in order to real-ize his appointed end.[135]

A charismatic movement could transform the existing social order, but only at the cost of its original spirit. The Christian churches exemplified how charisma lost its revolutionary force and turned into ideology. The most extreme example of this, according to Weber, was the Catholic Church, with its teaching that the priest's office, not his character, guaranteed the sanctity of his acts—just the opposite of the charismatic church, whose leaders were individuals filled with the Holy Spirit.[136] Luther-anism, too, had turned its founder's idea of a charismatic church regulated by scriptural inspiration into a hierarchy, or divinely sanctioned bureaucracy. In *Economy and Society* as in *The Protestant Ethic*, the two churches stifled individualism, though by different means: in the earlier work by shaping a traditionalist psychology, in the later work by making individual spontaneity submit to their rational design. In either case, their promise of community was incompatible with Weber's conception of individual human dignity.

Ascetic Protestantism's relationship to charisma became somewhat less consistent with the earlier argument. The aim of *The Protestant Ethic* was of course to define the *spirit* of capitalism. *Economy and Society* contrasted charisma and rationalization so sharply that such a spirit was hardly thinkable. On the one hand Weber recognized a special relationship between ascetic Protestantism and authentic, personal charisma, returning to examples from *The Protestant Ethic*—Gladstone's popularity as a man of conscience, America's celebration of the self-made man and contempt for bureaucracy—as evidence of this. On the other hand Weber virtually limited charisma to the original leader and his followers.[137] By this definition, the privileged moment of a collective Puritan spirit was impossible; ascetic discipline was already a substitute for the charisma of Calvin, an instance of rationalizing *Ungeist* succeeding the founders' spontaneous calling. Either order or charisma: the schema did not allow them to mix. In this respect Weber actually intensified the conflict between authentic individuality and social order to the point where brief charismatic outbursts turned society on its head only to be set aright and routed by the cunning of *ratio*.

The essays on the world religions could almost be called a comparative history of *Persönlichkeit*. Hindu society was so deeply embedded in traditionalism and in the organic rhythms of life that it gave Weber new standards of collective sluggishness, its caste ethic and passive acceptance of Karma surpassing even the Lutheran calling.[138] Buddhism took another phenomenon first observed in Lutheranism to a new extreme: salvation through union with the sacred. The Buddha was an "exemplary" prophet who showed how to retreat from this world, in contrast to the "ethical" prophetic tradition of the West, which issued an impersonal command to transform it. As for the Chinese educated elite, seemingly so secular and "modern," Weber treated it as an Eastern case of utilitarianism. Precisely its worldliness, its interest in long life and cautious enjoyment of earthly pleasures, was antithetical to anything like Puritan self-denial. For Weber the mandarin was the epitome of the bureaucratic conformist who always bent to his surroundings and the opposite of *Persönlichkeit* fearlessly transforming man and nature in the name of a higher law.[139]

The great historical contrast to all these Eastern types was the Hebrew prophets. They received their calling in isolation, Weber emphasized, and in a form preserving their individuality: not mystical vision, not orgiastic bliss, but an aural message went out to them and required a response. Their calling set them apart from their contemporaries, who persecuted them for the ill tidings they brought. Unlike magicians and priests, they did not pursue their calling for economic gain—their own or anyone else's—but out of inner necessity. *The Protestant Ethic* had already noticed the Puritans' affinity with the Old Testament. In his essay on ancient Judaism, Weber argued that the Old Testament contained the origin of the Western tradition culminating in the Puritans. The prophets were the first exemplars of the Western idea of inwardly formed, outwardly oriented *Persönlichkeit*.[140]

Charisma and *Persönlichkeit* resonate as complementary concepts in Weber's essays "Science as a Calling" and "Politics as a Calling."[141] He delivered them in 1918 and January 1919, respectively, facing—or at least, to judge by the published essays, expecting—a student audience filled with pacifists, anarchists, and socialists in search of *Gemeinschaft* and inclined to view him with suspicion as spokesman for a discredited, older generation.[142] Sensing this hostility, he wrote almost in the voice of a debater, anticipating his critics while boldly pronouncing his own allegiances.

Charisma characterized both the scholar and the politician with a calling. The original scholar, the one who did more than just mechanically reproduce the results of others, worked from an intuitive insight; the politician who was more than just a careerist pursued an original vision. They enjoyed a gift analogous to Puritan election, which no amount of labor and no force of will could conjure. For the scholar Weber compared it to *mania*, Plato's name for the divine madness of the poets. This

much of Weber's speech may have appealed to the Expressionist mood of his listeners. But he circumscribed it with a quasi-
Puritan discipline setting it apart from their cult of feeling.
Their favorite word, Weber told them, was *Persönlichkeit*, but
what *they* meant by this was nothing but a sensation (*Erlebnis*), a
momentary rush of exaltation.

His generation had a truer understanding of it as fidelity over
time to one's innermost values. The extreme rationalization of
the modern world set the stage for extreme heroism. Those
who really wished to prove their personal charisma had to test
it in an impersonal world: the scholar in the modern factory of
learning, the politician amid the bureaucratic machine. The
Puritan virtue of constancy turned the individual into a *Persönlichkeit* who risked his earthly welfare as the instrument of transcending beliefs. Of course these beliefs were no longer
determined by collective norms; in value-free modernity, each
person had to discover and follow his own deity. Wherever one
found it, the calling imposed a discipline as ascetic as its religious predecessor; it still followed values that were in the world,
but not of it.

This modern calling embraced and transformed the idea of
fate. Modern society imposed a fateful set of conditions on
thought and action. It condemned the scholar to expertise in a
tiny specialty instead of the encyclopedic knowledge of earlier
eras. It confronted the politician with a world in which ethics
and responsible political decisions followed separate, often
irreconcilable laws. Yet nothing was farther from Weber's thinking than *sich-schicken-lassen*, the resignation he accused Lutheranism of adopting in the face of a fateful world. *Schicksal* could
take on a second meaning as something not just external to the
individual, but also the destiny driving him from within. This
destiny might fail in its test with the world—and Weber, the
observer of the cunning of *ratio*, impressed on his audience the
real hazards of attempting to fulfill one's calling. The moments
when it worked, when outer conditions and inner calling came
together, were as rare as that Puritan predestination that permitted the elect to serve as providential instruments. One
worked for such moments without knowing when they would
manifest themselves like grace. By thus developing the idea of

fate, Weber transcended fatalism and affirmed the openness of historical experience. He broached a possibility of spontaneous, creative action that Lukács could broaden in search of a revolutionary ending to history.

5
Georg Simmel: From Society to Utopia

Berlin was an indispensable condition of Simmel's work. He once remarked to his son, "Perhaps I would have achieved something of value in another city; but the particular achievement that I have produced in these decades is unquestionably bound to the Berlin milieu."[1] In the family lore, even his birthplace suited him to the role of quintessential Berliner, for in 1858 his parents lived at the corner of Friedrichstrasse and Leipzigerstrasse, one of the city's most bustling intersections.[2] After attending the Werder Gymnasium in the heart of the city, he enrolled at the University of Berlin, completing his dissertation in 1881 and his habilitation in 1884–85.[3] For the next three decades the city of his formative years became the setting of his fate. Students crowded into his lectures, and his reputation spread around the world. But he waited in vain for a full professorship while jealousy and antisemitism barred the way to advancement in the German university system. Excluded from the Empire's official culture, he formed his own elite counterculture. Rilke and the playwright Paul Ernst came to hear him; Lukács and Ernst Bloch joined the private seminar at his house; he corresponded with Bergson and visited Rodin. His acceptance of an offer from Strasbourg in 1914 led to an unhappy anticlimax: the prestige of an academic chair came at the cost of proximity to friends and followers, and he spent his last four years regretting the exile from his native city.[4]

Simmel studied Berlin from the viewpoint of a thoroughgoing modernist. Aware of his contemporaries' complaints against modern fragmentation, and not entirely unsympathetic to them, he nonetheless tried to reveal how modern society, as epitomized by Berlin, contained its own stable forms of social unity. In part his attitude resembled Weber's: both thinkers accepted social *forms* as inevitable constraints on human activity. Unlike Weber, however, with his view of society as an empty cage, Simmel discovered novel modernist *values*. Society threatened certain kinds of individuality while furthering others; the modern fate could call forth a modernist heroism. His sociology balanced the gains and losses.

So far we have treated Simmel as a bourgeois and modernist without regret for *Gemeinschaft* lost. Certainly this captures one side of his personality, and even more, of the persona he projected for his contemporaries and later critics. This Simmel is so useful that we should have to invent him if he had not existed. And indeed, to some extent we have. Simmel was too alive to all the cultural eddies of his own time not to try to think through the relationship of fragmented modernity to a larger whole. The place where he did so most consistently was in his sociology and philosophy of religion. Here, in essays on religion and in scattered remarks in his major writings, he asked how the fragmented and isolated phenomena of modernity were redeemed by their participation in a present or future totality. Simmel's commitment to modernity conflicted with a will to utopian transcendence of it.

The Modern Fate

Simmel attempted to reconcile individual and society with the aid of a regulative principle borrowed from Kant: interaction (*Wechselwirkung*). The *Critique of Pure Reason* introduced it as the third of three "Analogies of Experience," or principles regulating judgments about the empirical world. Despite the heterogeneity of all substances and our perception of them at different instants, argued Kant, we must assume for the purposes of knowledge that they are interrelated parts of a single world. The principle of interaction presupposed this unity by stating that at any given instant, all substances were in a state of mutual causal influence.[5] Simmel turned this principle to the purposes of social science. It allowed him to maintain the paradox that members of society were distinct from one another yet interrelated, individual yet parts of a unified totality.[6]

Wechselwirkungen were accelerating at a dizzying rate in Imperial Berlin as it underwent its rapid transformation in the late nineteenth and early twentieth century from provincial capital to world metropolis.[7] Simmel tried to calm his contemporaries' nerves by explaining the logic underlying the seeming chaos they experienced. Modern society, he repeated in seemingly infinite variations, shaped personal identities out of social relationships and social relationships out of isolated persons. The individual occupied a middle zone, never wholly himself, never absorbed in a community. Social boundaries often limited one's chances for finding meaning—and created opportunities; the ambiguous effects of social constraint always tantalized Simmel's imagination. He attempted to be a modernist without illusions, neither celebrating nor condemning the modern condition, but instead undertaking the invaluable, unrewarding task of structuring it for an audience suspicious of whatever he had to say. His sociology demanded bipolar thinking, a discipline designed to initiate his readers into the complexities of the world around them. To a degree unthinkable for Tönnies and Troeltsch, and more problematic for Weber, he linked fate and freedom to the impersonal structure and chances for personal expression of the metropolis.

Social Liberalism

In contrast to Tönnies, Troeltsch, and Weber, Simmel never got involved in a movement or institution forcing him to take an open stance on public issues. Nonetheless, before the turn of the century his writings were fully sensitive to the crosscurrents of working-class activism, social reform, and reactionary government policy. Like his fellow sociologists, he was not satisfied by any of the existing parties and tried to judge the social conflicts of their time from a neutral standpoint. *Wechselwirkung* served as his principle for systematically relativizing the claims of liberals and Social Democrats, making each side yield something to the demands of the other. Social liberalism, the name he gave to the mediating economics of his friend Ignaz Jastrow, aptly describes his own political perspective.[8]

Some of Simmel's articles from the 1890s read like evidence of *parti pris* for one side or the other. Occasionally he polemicized against middle-class resistance to workers' demands, as in one article criticizing individual freedom as an outdated dogma and maintaining that the workers' right to organize (one of the chief concerns of social reformers, who supported it to teach workers self-reliance and draw them into peaceable relations with the state) would further the interests of the social whole by creating a *Wechselwirkung* between labor and business.[9] Another article attacked members of the bourgeoisie who looked down on the class struggle as a struggle for mere material things and could not see that ending hunger signified a first step toward raising the cultural level of the German working class.[10] On the other hand he twitted socialists for their dogmatism. Resentment, not the abstract ideal of justice they claimed as their own, spurred their demands for equality. Even if they succeeded in eliminating existing class differences, socialists would never achieve equality, for the remaining residual differences would loom larger and excite just as much envy.[11]

Simmel wrote several pieces balancing his opposition to dogmatic individualism and dogmatic socialism. His review of Gustave le Bon's *Psychology of the Crowd,* whose denigration of the masses he found superficial and stupid, lamented the tragic polarization of contemporary thought into individualism and democratic socialism as mutually exclusive alternatives.[12] Elsewhere he tried to reconcile their conflicting demands. Reporting on a Berlin Women's Congress in 1896, he compared the motives and goals of the socialists (who refused to attend) and the middle-class feminists. The socialist women's movement had arisen from too little protection of working-class women, exposing them to exploitation at work; the middle-class movement had arisen from too much protection, imprisoning them at home. The socialists pointed to their party program as the solution to the oppression of women; the middle-class feminists had a different set of economic, legal, and cultural proposals. Yet Simmel saw an underlying common ground: both middle-class and working-class women were victims of technical progress, and general conditions had changed more rapidly than individuals and groups could adjust to. He concluded, "Our only purpose was to show that the middle-class and proletarian women's question, despite or because of their seeming divergence, are nonetheless only two sides of the same overall economic and ethical structure as the center from which the problems have become more acute on both sides and from whose development alone, therefore, their solution may be expected."[13] Another article focused on the limits of structural change, in this case for improving public hygiene. Hygiene was, first of all, a social issue; individual charity could not remove the causes of illness in modern society. A radical might conclude that revolution was the most logical form of social medicine, since one must eliminate all the conditions contributing to the ill health of society, which were ultimately systemic in nature. Simmel replied to this imaginary opponent that the causes of the problem were general, yet the solution could only be partial and specific. Social reform had to work gradually, approaching a never entirely realizable ideal.[14]

Many members of the German public would have agreed. Middle-class reformers, educators, feminists, Center politicians, enlightened civil servants, and revisionist Social Democrats—all tried to further structural reforms leaving capitalism intact while creating minimum conditions of social welfare. Tönnies, Troeltsch, and Weber envisioned a similar program. Despite their theoretical differences (and, as we shall see, their fierce objections to Simmel's sociology), in practice they shared his sympathy with a social-minded liberalism.

On Social Differentiation

On Social Differentiation, Simmel's first book-length work of sociology, published in 1890, had a split character. Its title hinted at its positivist inheritance: from Spencer it took over differentiation and integration as the fundamental pattern of social evolution.[15] Primitive communities, according to Simmel, lacked internal articulation and relied on external force to band their members together, stifling personal identity by pressing them into a collective mold.[16] The growing differentiation of higher societies made individuals more distant (leaving more room for individuation) yet more interrelated.[17] The slim volume's five chapters illustrated some of the typical patterns of differentiation: the movement from collective to individual responsibility; the formation of heterogeneous groups; the correlation of social stratification and personality; the overlapping of different social circles; specialization and the resulting social conservation of energy. Integration and individuation reinforced one another in an infinite evolutionary progression.

At the same time, the book was a modernist manifesto. Its introduction dissolved all certainties in a flux of *Wechselwirkungen*. The soul was a religious dogma; science had replaced it with an individual who was a sum of heterogeneous parts.[18] "Society" was a conservative social prejudice; the word referred not to a real thing but to a function, a set of elements in a dynamic state of mutual influence.[19] Neither one had lasting shape, for society had only emerged over time from primitive inchoate disorder, and in doing so had created the individual. Whoever sought the certainties of *Gemeinschaft* would find none here: "Law, morality, religion, and language do not emanate from an inward, closed unity. Rather, social unities that are externally in contact with one another form these contents and forms through inherent suitability, need, and force, and only this causes or rather signifies their unity."[20] Simmel delighted in showing how simple truths gave way to ironies under modern conditions. All that was solid melted into air; the ceaseless flux of modernity took on a new solidity.[21]

One of his shocked readers was Tönnies. From his rural isolation in Husum he wrote Paulsen on the last day of 1890: "Do you know G. Simmel? I received his book, *On Social Differentiation*, to review from the *Jahrbücher für Nationalökonomie und Statistik*, which I quickly did. The book is solid, but from the study of an urbanite."[22] His respect for Simmel's talent hardly checked his indignation over his moral shortcomings. The book's second chapter on collective responsibility struck him as an especially offensive example of civilized decadence. Modern society, it argued, emancipated egoism, but avoided anarchy by creating impersonal forms of order, sociologically binding on all members of society. In a complex society even the criminal had to make use of the general forms of law, morality, and communication in order to achieve his ends; and in making use of them he necessarily strengthened them. This, wrote Simmel, was the social "tax" that modern society demanded of its members and that grew higher over time.[23] Tönnies took a darker view of emancipation from communal constraints:" . . . The author may be right to view in this an increase in refinement and value—from the one side; from the other side one can note and find described here the spread of *lack of character*, making the *whole* impotent in good as in evil, and of refined egoism. . . ."[24] As for the notion of the criminal's social tax, he wrote, "Well, yes: as taxpayers we are all equal—and no longer *need* any inner relationship because we yield the forced or conventional tribute. But what is 'morality' if we no longer have any inner relationship to it?"[25] Writing from "the other side"— that is, from the rural, traditional side—he viewed Simmel as a kind of modern Socrates who unsettled established norms with his ever-probing dialectic. Even the respectful obituary he wrote twenty-eight years later, long after his *völkisch* tendencies had diminished, could not understand the constructive side of Simmel's thought and continued to view it as a failure for its inability to grasp the essential communal unities of social life.[26]

On Social Differentiation outlined many of Simmel's lasting ideas. It explicitly made *Wechselwirkung* the regulative principle of his sociology and acknowledged Kant as his philosophical master, identified many of the mechanisms of modernization he would contine to explore in years to come, and subscribed to a radically anti-metaphysical relativism that pervaded his later aesthetics and social thinking. His hostility toward *Gemein-schaft*, too, remained firm until 1914. Simmel defended the avant-garde post he had staked out in this first sociological work. His provocative rhetoric later diminished, however. The charge of decadence, which others besides Tönnies made, added to his enemies' reasons for denying him a university chair—they could point to him as the embodiment of the analytical, destructive Jewish intellectual—and made him underline his "constructive" intentions. Furthermore, his insight into modernity's dark side deepened. Without giving up his allegiance to it, Simmel confronted the new forms of dependence it created.

The Philosophy of Money

In 1899 Simmel presented a paper to Gustav Schmoller's seminar at the University of Berlin entitled "The Psychology of Money."[27] This was the germ of what grew to be the large book published eleven years later as *The Philosophy of Money*. Dated 1900, it breathed the spirit of the new century. Streaming through banking, the stock exchange, real estate speculation, marriages between noble and bourgeois, a glittering parvenu class, and business-labor conflicts, money intoxicated a society without the metropolitan traditions of a Paris or London. To write a *philosophy* of money was a startling enterprise; the very phrase implied a union between filthy lucre and unsullied contemplation.[28] Simmel's preface declared his intention of bringing them together, deriving from the surface level of economic affairs a plumb line leading to ultimate values. His philosophy would be an act of salvation—as he expressed the secularized theological intention of his work—rescuing money from its repulsiveness and demonstrating how it permeated the entire range of modern culture.[29] Hegel had once asked philosophers to teach reconciliation with the present.[30] His apology for the Prussian state was a tame undertaking, however, compared with this attempt to teach one's contemporaries to be at home with their money-ridden society.

Like three other important works of sociology that we have examined—*Gemeinschaft und Gesellschaft, The Social Teachings of the Christian Churches,* and *The Protestant Ethic*—Simmel's book contained a critique of historical materialism. It had an especially close connection to *The Protestant Ethic* as one of the first books Weber read while recovering from his illness and preparing to write the latter.[31] Remarkable passages anticipate Weber's concerns, such as a discussion of Franciscan poverty hinting at the idea of inner-worldly asceticism developed by Weber for Puritanism.[32] A closer comparison reveals similarities and striking differences in their analyses of capitalism's origins.

Both Weber and Simmel aimed at relativizing historical materialism in such a way as to limit its validity and demonstrate the equal validity of other approaches. When *The Protestant Ethic* concluded

But it is, of course, not my aim to substitute for a one-sided materialistic an equally one-sided spiritualistic causal interpretation of culture and of history. Each is equally possible, but each, if it does not serve as the preparation, but as the conclusion of an investigation, accomplishes equally little in the interest of historical truth.[33]

it echoed the spirit of *The Philosophy of Money*'s preface:

The attempt is made to construct a new storey beneath historical materialism such that the explanatory value of the incorporation of economic life into the causes of intellectual culture is preserved, while these economic forms themselves are recognized as the result of more profound valuations and currents of psychological or even metaphysical pre-conditions. For the practice of cognition this must develop in infinite reciprocity.[34]

Their methods of demonstrating alternatives to Marx's materialism sharply differed, however. Weber's was causal, linking predestination, Puritan anxiety, ceaseless work, and capital accumulation in strictly sequential order. A materialist counter-sequence would in theory be neither more nor less valid, for the empirical researcher could only follow out one sequence at a time: each was, as Weber wrote in the passage just cited, equally possible. Simmel's *Wechselwirkungen* mixed what Weber held apart. His interactions showed how economy influenced society *and* society simultaneously influenced economy. The first or "analytical" part of *The Philosophy of Money* gave priority to the social and psychological forces causing the formation of a money economy, while the second or "synthetic" part considered how money, once established as a dynamic totality in social circulation, conditioned society.[35] In practice the two parts of the book interpenetrated far more than this plan suggests; at any instant either entity could affect the other, so that one could hardly point to discrete causes and effects. Simmel underlined this message in a chapter that sketched a world view corresponding to this reciprocity of things and ideas: he explicitly left open the question of whether relativism had made possible the growth of a money economy or had been created by it.[36] Both were the case in a world of mutual conditioning.

In an unfinished and (in their lifetimes) unpublished critique, Weber objected to Simmel's method, which he accused of drifting into uncontrolled analogies. Everything might interact with everything else in a universally interrelated cosmos. According to Weber, this explained why—aside from invidious personal motives—Simmel's ventures into foreign disciplines stirred up so much resentment; he broke down their specific logic and replaced it with the free play of imagination. Despite his admiration for Simmel's genius, Weber shared his colleagues' skepticism toward *Wechselwirkungen* without limits.[37] In retrospect, one can make the observation that their methods served different purposes. *The Protestant Ethic* inquired into the historical genesis of capitalism, its causal narrative unfolding through time the paradox of a religion based on faith becoming an ethic based on work. *The Philosophy of Money* examined capitalism as a functioning system and largely ignored the entrepreneur and skilled worker who were Weber's chief actors. Instead it focused on another figure largely ignored by Weber: the consumer. The central paradox of Simmel's book had to do not with the original motivation behind the habits of accumulation and work, but with the consumer psychology of securely established capitalism. The consumer oscillated between desiring and not having things, and having but destroying ("consuming") the object of his desire.[38] The ever greater complexity of modern society required that he go through ever longer sequences of means in order to reach his end, ever greater frustration for ephemeral satisfaction of wishes. How could he enjoy himself in a world of ceaseless waiting? Consumer society's solution, according to Simmel, was that money, originally a means to acquire goods, became in itself the ultimate good, granting the satisfaction of knowing one could convert it into any other commodity. The place of means and ends was inverted: commodities seemed abstract and substanceless, money the concrete and immediate source of pleasure.

Once he had established this psychology of consumerism, Simmel could make an assessment of modernity more positive than Weber's. The money economy did not merely compel the individual to work at the cost of traditional values; it created immanent values to replace the old. Whatever its dilemmas, they were self-contained and not derived from comparison with the past. Whereas Weber contrasted present fragmentation with the fullness of ancient Athens,[39] Simmel refused to concede the superiority of the polis to the metropolis. Accustomed to the concreteness and stability of an agrarian economy, the Greeks developed an aversion to the unpredictable, disruptive aspects of their own society, shutting out the glimmerings of an emerging world and looking away, according to Simmel, to an illusory realm of static ideas. The all-pervasive modern money economy had taught the denizens of the metropolis, by contrast, to discern the unity of a world in which nothing was definable in itself and everything rested on its relations to the other parts of a complex totality.[40] In Simmel's interpretation the passage from tradition to modernity brought about a new synthesis as rich and satisfying as the old.[41] Dissatisfaction with the insubstantiality of modernity, he noted near the end of *The Philosophy of Money,* was stimulating fresh efforts to comprehend it in the arts, styles, and religious life of his time.[42] In contrast to *The Protestant Ethic,* with its displacement of meaning to the Puritan past, *The Philosophy of Money* treated alienation as a side effect of modernization. Simmel eased his contemporaries' reconciliation with the present not by tracing society's origins, as Weber did, but by revealing its immanent significance.

Sociology

Tönnies considered Hobbes the founder of modern social science precisely because *Leviathan,* rejecting Aristotelian teleology and Christian theology, gave primacy to the animal appetites underlying social behavior. He organized his own social theory, too, around two antiidealist models, the organism for *Gemeinschaft* and the machine for *Gesellschaft.* Troeltsch and Weber wrote in a different spirit; idealism mattered as it could not in Tönnies's materialist sociology. Yet personal idealism collided with impersonal social structures; church and sect conditioned religious genius, bureaucracy obstructed political leadership. Society followed an intrinsic logic of self-preservation that individual initiative could modify but never entirely redeem. All three shared the insight that society had become a second nature, as Lukács and Adorno later called it:[43] a mindless collectivity motivated by animal instinct, maintained by mechanical rules, and aimed toward commodity production.

Simmel confronted this second nature with extreme sensitivity to the conflicting trends of his age. No one more deeply imbibed the vitality of German modernism after 1890 or hoped more fervently for cultural renaissance. He enjoyed a sense of spring thaw far removed from the unmitigated disappointment of a cultural pessimist like Tönnies after the turn of the century. Optimism, however, overlapped with the awareness of a new menace to individualism in Germany. A corporate social order, dominated by banks, bureaucracy, trade unions, and mass parties and interest groups, was taking the place of anarchic late nineteenth-century capitalism. After the turn of the century left-liberals began debating how they could best prevent the individual's personal and professional calling from disappearing. *Sociology*, Simmel's last major contribution to the discipline, appeared in 1908, just when social reformers were openly worrying that the welfare measures they had fought for were contributing to the "new feudalism" of a bureaucratized German society.[44] The book mingled Simmel's anxiety toward mass society with his continued belief in its openness to personal autonomy.

As in his earlier writings, *Wechselwirkungen* wove actions into larger social units. Instinct initiated the simple interactions between individuals; these interactions took on a life of their own, apart from the motivations of individuals, and became the fixed patterns constituting society.[45] Small group interactions, social hierarchies, institutions, and mechanisms of social evolution hardened into social forms, compelling the individuals entering into them to act out preordained roles. Sociology was to analyze these forms in strict separation from their contents.[46] Their historical origins were irrelevant, the persons filling them were accidents of time and place, and their proclaimed ends were ideology.

Simmel was not a social technician intent on classifying these social forms for their own sake; in *Sociology* he sought to capture the confrontation between *Persönlichkeit* and society. This drama was organized according to rules he called the three a prioris of sociology: first, the a priori of socialization—every individual conformed to a social type; second, the a priori of individuality—socialization was never complete, the individual always retaining at least a marginal personal identity apart from it; third, the a priori of society's unity—each individual retained his uniqueness yet belonged, with all the others, to a functional totality.[47] In Simmel's sociology individuals oscillated between extremes of individuation and socialization, nearing one pole only to rebound toward the other.

Old themes and new played out the possibilities of freedom and fate, self-expression and socialization. Simmel asked how the quantitative determination of the group affected the qualities of personal life; how the simple fact of numbers in miniature groups (the pair, the triad) and the relative size of social configurations (the small group, the large group) conditioned the individual's inner life and outward actions.[48] The secret, subject of another chapter, yielded its social-psychological function to Simmel's microscopic scrutiny. Apart from its ostensible purpose, the secret reinforced the individual's sense of otherness, giving him a secure personal possession apart from his social surroundings. On the other hand the secret society, treated in the same chapter, had ambiguous effects, either reinforcing its members' individuality or—when its members became mere means to its collective ends—violating their personal integrity.[49] *Sociology* also showed sensitivity to marginal figures like the poor and the stranger,[50] victims of the social majority whose perceptions imprisoned them in an externally formed identity. One of Simmel's most influential chapters, much admired by liberal theorists, affirmed the social functions of conflict, which apparently destroyed social unity, but could actually reinforce it by engendering rules according to which both parties acted out their interests.[51] Finally, as in *On Social Differentiation* Simmel assessed society through the telescope of grand theory. One chapter on the overlapping of social groups and another on the widening of the group and the formation of individuality argued once again that society's increasingly complex forms of interaction permitted ever greater possibilities of individuation.[52]

Did society further individuality or frustrate it? Simmel's ambivalence was too great to permit anything less than a complex answer, always requiring correction from the other side. Certainly, however, *Sociology* announced the end of *human* history and replaced it with a natural history beyond significant intervention. Natural metaphors dominated its vision of society: the introduction compared social forms to the ideal forms of geometry, *Wechselwirkungen* to the cells functioning as elementary units of an organism.[53] Although Simmel considered these images crutches, aids to be thrown away as soon as the reader had got used to the unfamiliar terrain of the sociologist, the biological imperative of self-preservation remained society's logic, production and social stability its goals. No one argued more strongly than Simmel for the absence of any physical or psychological medium of *Gemeinschaft*. Yet subtle, innumerable interactions linked the individual to the social whole, often working against his will to further the life of the modern Leviathan.

Whereas *Sociology*, for all its ambivalence, tended to affirm the modern condition, some of Simmel's other writings of the same period recoiled from it as the modern fate. History was heightening the tension between individual and society. As man created objective cultural forms—moral, scientific, artistic— they accumulated and weighed ever more heavily on succeeding generations. Each of these spheres separated from the others, developing its own techniques and combining them according to its own rules. The individual born into the modern era faced these finished forms unable to master the logic of more than a fraction of them and unable to make them part of his personal development, or subjective culture. He experienced objective culture as a realm of things, products of the human spirit that had lost their humanity and confronted him with deadening objectivity, bearing down with overwhelming force on the tiny realm of inward, individual feeling. This was the tragedy of modern culture, imprisoning civilization in the capital of its own intelligence, just as, in Marx, economic capital made it the slave of physical production.[54]

Simmel's discussion of the tragedy of modern culture articulated a theme taken up by his student Lukács, who drove his ambiguities to clear conclusions. Simmel treated society as second nature; Lukács would make the comparison more explicit and consider it synonymous with humanity's loss of its collective soul, its reduction to a rubble of things in need of redemption. In the a priori structure of Simmel's sociology human beings communicated indirectly, by means of signs; Lukács would seek to replace the distance between self and other with an immediate relationship between souls. Simmel analyzed the autonomous realms of modern culture and asked how they interacted to form a mediated unity; Lukács condemned their fragmentation as the intellectual reflection of bourgeois society's disarray. Simmel's "tragedy" was inalterable; Lukács's was a prophetic drama pointing the way from the reification of human relationships to the humanization of everything. Lukács, in his obituary of his former teacher, would dismiss him by calling him the greatest transitional figure of modern philosophy;[55] Simmel insisted that modernity offered no exit from a transitory existence, even though he himself was not entirely immune to longing for the wholeness of a new *Gemeinschaft*.

Sociological Aestheticism

Around the turn of the century Simmel's thought underwent a subtle transformation. The positivist and Social Darwinist assumptions of a work like *On Social Differentiation* retreated, and he ceased writing about social issues. Students who knew him between 1900 and World War I thought of him as a disinterested aesthete, largely detached from contemporary social and political conflicts.[56] Although this was not quite true—he did not shed his earlier views so much as he added new ones—his thought did undergo an unmistakable aestheticization. There was remarkable continuity in Simmel's conception of society as the forms of interaction from his earliest to his latest works, but he increasingly turned his attention from the forms to the personal refinement they could stimulate. Simmel came to intellectual maturity with the appearance of modernism in Germany: at first attracted to the dominant Naturalism of the 1870s and

1880s, he became a devotee of Symbolism and Impressionism as they spread from France in the following decade. Aestheticism and sociology became the partners of a harmonious *Wechselwirkung,* with sociology explaining the conditions of modernist art and values, modernism revealing the meaning of society.

Nietzsche and the Ideal of Distinction

The Philosophy of Money carefully balanced the possibilities of degradation and elevation in its chapters on the monetary conditioning of human values. Prostitution was the one extreme: the selling of one's most intimate and personal possession, the reduction of a human, social being to a biological means, symbol of money's power to violate moral and spiritual as well as sexual integrity. The money economy by nature prostituted every private, personal quality and turned it into a quantity for exchange.[57] Nature did not necessarily take its course, however. The threat of violation could provoke an absolute determination to preserve one's personal dignity. Simmel called this attitude *Vornehmheit,* the ideal of distinction. The word referred literally to separation from a crowd and was traditionally a synonym for nobility of persons or objects.[58] Simmel argued that the modern ideal of distinction was an absolutely new value brought into existence by the challenge to personal values of the money economy. With his habitual sensitivity to the subtleties of interaction, he sketched the ideal of distinction as a blend of difference and discretion: on the one hand it consisted in emphasizing one's incomparability in a commodity society; on the other hand, in an avoidance of conspicuousness, which would draw one back into social circulation.[59]

The ideal of distinction came from *Beyond Good and Evil.* Nietzsche began the section of the book titled *was ist vornehm?*

Every enhancement of the type 'man' has so far been the work of an aristocratic society—and it will be so again and again—a society that believes in the long ladder of an order of rank and differences in value between man and man, and that needs slavery in some sense or other. Without that *pathos of distance* which grows out of the ingrained difference between strata—when the ruling caste constantly looks

afar and looks down upon subjects and instruments and just as constantly practices obedience and command, keeping down and keeping at a distance—that other, more mysterious pathos could not have
grown up either—the craving for an ever new widening of distances
within the soul itself, the development of ever higher, rarer, more
remote, further-stretching, more comprehensive states—in brief,
simply the enhancement of the type 'man,' the continual 'self-
overcoming of man,' to use a moral formula in a supra-moral sense.[60]

Distance—one of the central categories of Simmel's sociology,
which singled it out as a sign of growing social complexity—
was the social condition for the possibility of *Vornehmheit*. According to Nietzsche, the attitude required distance in a double
sense: with respect to the social hierarchy, which the person of
distinction viewed from above, thus becoming aware of his own
superior value; and with respect to his own soul, which he
viewed from afar in a continual striving for self-transcendence.
Vornehmheit could not have been further removed from *The
Birth of Tragedy*'s merging of wills in a homogeneous unity. It
represented the later Nietzsche whose repudiation of feeling
for others Tönnies could not abide. Simmel in 1897 disputed
Tönnies's portrayal of Nietzsche in *The Nietzsche Cult* as an im-
moralist, arguing that Nietzsche had criticized traditional morality in order to make way for a superior morality.[61] Their
conflicting moralities vied for the inheritance of the great im-
moralist: Tönnies's notion of the rational welfare of the whole
versus Simmel's devotion to impersonal individual discipline.
The early and late Nietzsche served as advocate for their conflicting ideals of *Gemeinschaft* and *Gesellschaft*.

In *Schopenhauer and Nietzsche*—the book he considered his
chief work, he confessed to Troeltsch[62]—Simmel singled out
Vornehmheit as the central value of Nietzsche's philosophy.[63] According to Simmel it signified "a formal attitude . . . in which a
decisive individual and a decisive objectivity came together in a
characteristic way."[64] When this happened, the inner psychological disposition of the individual lost its arbitrariness, the outer
world it influenced lost its naturalness; subjectivity took on the
objectivity of an inner law, while objectivity took on a humanly
imposed design. This was a sublimation of fate similar to what
we have seen in Weber and will encounter again in Lukács: so-

ciety's objective order turned into the condition of freedom as soon as man's inner nature was in harmony with it.

The ideal of distinction extended the general process of differentiation that Simmel observed for society and culture to the inner realm of the psyche, which, no less than science or law or institutions, became separated from its surroundings and autonomous. Its "law" was a unique style realizing a unique individual potential. The person of distinction was possessed by a sense of the absolute worth of his soul without regard for the world and was ready to sacrifice everything to remain true to himself. His distinction supposedly asserted his independence from society. Yet paradoxically it shared modern society's impersonality. If impersonality signified the stifling effect of institutions and conventions on individual idiosyncracies, *Vornehmheit*'s inner law, too, eradicated every spontaneous impulse in the name of an artificial order. Absolute personal autonomy offset the social order only by internalizing its logic, creating, to be sure, a style setting the bearer apart, but doing so only through a pattern of radical repression. This was the price one paid for turning the modern fate into a personal destiny.

Simmel's person of distinction bore a certain resemblance to Weberian *Persönlichkeit*. Even Nietzsche pointed out the Protestant origins of the ideal of distinction: "What is noble (*vornehm*)? . . . It is not the works, it is the faith that is decisive here, that determines the order of rank—to take up again an ancient religious formula in a new and more profound sense. . . ."[65] The new and secular superiority of the person of distinction resounded with Calvinist *certitudo salutis*. Weber was a close reader of Simmel's monograph on Schopenhauer and Nietzsche, published a year after *The Protestant Ethic*, and his marginal notes emphatically agreed with Simmel's insistence that what a person was, not what he did, made him *vornehm*. Next to Simmel's observation, "If noble natures matter for what they are, common [natures] for what they do . . . ," Weber noted: "*Bismarck! Napoleon!*" After Simmel continued, "Society cares only about what the individual does," Weber added, "*Sehr richtig. Cf. Bismarckism*"[66]—a reference, it would seem, to the popular adulation celebrating Bismarck's outward successes but ignoring his inner nobility and deserting him when his political fortunes waned. Simmel for his part compared *Vornehmheit* to a secular state of grace in which the individual had a quasi-Calvinist belief in the absolute value of his personality.[67] The person of distinction worked in the world, but not for the world. He abhorred *social* conscience and acted only out of loyalty to the higher discipline, the calling, imposed from within, relentlessly bearing the suffering imposed by this secular path of the cross.

The very names of their ideals remind us that, despite their points of affinity, Simmel's was more compatible with modernity, Weber's more rooted in religious tradition. *Persönlichkeit* had real ties to liberal Protestantism that Weber did not hesitate to acknowledge, and charisma had ancient Christian associations. However much Weber formalized their meaning, they looked back to the past. Every reappearance of charismatic *Persönlichkeit* only had the ironic effect of accelerating the process of rationalization and creating still more unlikely circumstances for its survival. *Vornehmheit* was a neologism. Its inner autonomy reproduced the larger logic of modern society, whose impersonality and rationality it internalized. The person of distinction could never have existed in a traditional community; he needed the modern separation of man from man for his individuation. Not that Simmel failed to perceive the dangers to human dignity preoccupying Weber; he too avoided naive celebration of modernity, balancing *Vornehmheit* against prostitution, and emphasizing the harsh asceticism required by true obedience to inner necessity. These considerations ultimately added interest to the modern condition; they reminded readers that they faced a real choice between heroism and degradation.

Stefan George

In 1897 Simmel met a poet who seemed—one may observe in retrospect—to embody the ideal of distinction: Stefan George. George's reputation was just beginning to grow, and Simmel was one of the first to recognize his greatness. Over the next decade and a half he became to the world of letters what Simmel became to the world of thought: one of the most influential teachers of avant-garde academic youth. George's poetry, his translations, the journals he edited or oversaw, and the work of his disciples established a new canon for German literature. No less important, he was one of the first cult heroes of the twentieth century, an artist who encouraged the kind of personal adulation later showered on film stars and politicians. Simmel's years of friendship with the poet came at just the time when he was giving mature expression to his sociology. Simmel's essays on George and his letters to him—an exceptional trove, spared the destruction that befell Simmel's private papers and make his biography for the most part rather shadowy—illuminate in some detail the personal milieu behind the ideal of distinction.[68]

Simmel met George through Sabine and Reinhold Lepsius, friends whom he had known since their school days, when he had befriended Sabine's older brother Harald at the Werder Gymnasium and became a frequent guest at her parents' dinner table. His marriage to Gertrud Kinel, Sabine's closest girlfriend, in 1890, and the marriage of Sabine and Reinhold in 1892, drew the two couples into a tight-knit circle of personal friendship and intellectual exchange, especially since the two men shared a penchant for learned analysis of art. One memorable evening in November 1897 Simmel was part of a select company (Rilke and Lou Salomé were among the other guests) invited to hear Stefan George read from his new book, *The Year of the Soul*.[69] During the next year the poet began visiting the Simmel's home, making an afternoon tea or evening with them a regular part of his stays in Berlin.[70]

Twenty-nine when they first met, George had already perfected his pose as poet-seer. His craggy features and carefully controlled gestures conveyed a forbidding air to outsiders. But he could also flatter new acquaintances with his warmth and directness. His esotericism was not original—he had the example of Mallarmé—but he quickly became his own master, adopting a personal idiom that enthralled even the supercilious Berliners. George often brought along students or other young friends on his visits to the Simmel home, several times choosing the poet-scholar Friedrich Gundolf as his escort. A passage from one of Simmel's letters says more about his special feelings toward the poet than about any unkind feelings toward Gundolf: "I must openly admit: the incomparable, utterly rarified, wholly personal tone that the three of us share in our evenings together could never be attained in the presence of a fourth person, even one so likable as Gundolf."[71] Poet and thinker came from completely dissimilar backgrounds: in contrast to the assimilated Berlin Jewish philosopher, George was the son of a well-to-do Rhineland wine merchant and never lost his feel for small-town Catholic culture or his peasant ancestry. What brought them together was their shared estrangement from Germany's official high culture. These two supremely cultivated members of the two marginalized religious groups felt that they belonged to their society's true elite, one based not on birth, but on talent and shared sensibility.

Simmel wrote three essays on George. The first two contained important insights into his notion of modern individuality, for they interpreted the autonomy of modern poetry such as George's—its creation of a hermetic realm with the seal of *l'art pour l'art*—as an expression of modernist *Persönlichkeit* in general. The earliest essay, written in 1898, distinguished between two sources of art: the natural ego, which produced mere outbursts of emotion, and the higher self finding objectification in artistic form. The former had dominated the German lyric tradition until the end of the nineteenth century; the latter was the source of modernist art such as George's.[72] Simmel deepened the same line of interpretation three years later in an essay on George's newly published book of verse, *The Tapestry of Life*, celebrating the poet as the exemplary meaning-maker who found the symbolic forms to order an otherwise chaotic world. His soul or higher self had the synthetic function of fusing the fragments of experience into a unified whole in which each element had its necessary place and interacted with all the others.[73] Simmel could hardly have dreamed up a better sample of poetic imagination for his purposes than *The Tapestry of Life*. As the the title suggested, it wove the world into a beautiful and exquisitely arranged design. In the "Prelude," the part exciting Simmel's highest praise, a muselike angel visited the poet and renewed his creativity after a period of spiritual exhaustion. This angel was not a visitor from another world, but mirrored the poet; it symbolized that higher inner self overcoming disordered reality. A strict plan governed the rest of the book, which was built out of three sections, each containing four times twenty-four quatrains. The metric strictness of the poetry excluded flights of fancy, placing feeling under the watch of constant reflection. A powerful vision of the good life animated this formal unity. The poet rejected the extremes of vulgar sensuality and Christian asceticism and aimed at a rebirth of aesthetic culture in Germany, one nurtured on Attic and Weimar ideals of measure and clarity.[74] The call to a higher life; the quest for the source of it within oneself; a haughty distance toward society as a result of this turn inward—these were the themes that held together George's brilliant *Jugendstil* tapestry. Simmel stood in awe of the poet who worked the ideal of distinction into modern images rivaling the perfection of classical art.

Each of the sociologists we have so far examined had an ideal forum to substitute for Germany's existing culture. Tönnies dreamed of a philospher's commune, Troeltsch of a revitalized church community, Weber of a value-free sociological association. Simmel, too, had his cultural ideal, which we know about from a letter he wrote to George in February 1903. He invited the poet to join a club that was to serve as Berlin's artistic center and attached a three-page manifesto. "You can see from the enclosure what it is about—an enterprise that I have joined because I hope it will turn into a cultural center such as we bitterly need; for it grows clearer every day that we live among barbarians."[75] William II and Prussia's cultural bureaucrats may have been among the "barbarians" Simmel had in mind. They not only kept talented scholars such as himself on the margins of the university but tried to force their own bad taste in the arts on the general public. Since 1899 Max Liebermann and the other leaders of the Berlin Secession had turned their backs on the official, state-affiliated salon and put together their own exhibition bringing Impressionist, Symbolist, and *Jugendstil* paintings to public view. They fought a successful war against the antimodernist taste of officialdom by running their organization from the top down, opening their show only to the better modernist artists. By 1903 the Secession was widely recognized as an arbiter of the new art and had no trouble attracting customers. It also proved that despite the prestige attached to official approval in Germany, modernist culture could break through the incrustations of tradition.[76]

The manifesto of the proposed club declared its makers' intention of broadening the principles of the Secession by extending them from painting to other arts. A clubhouse would include rooms available for exhibitions, lectures, recitations, and artistic displays of every kind, and the exhibitions of the Secession would be transferred to its building. The composition of the club's executive committee vouched for its closeness to its model. Max Liebermann, the painter Ludwig von Hofmann, and the museum director and art critic Count Harry Kessler were all prominent Secession members. The only newcomer on the executive committee of the venture was Simmel. To display culture was only a secondary consideration, however. The primary aim was as follows:

The *inner* aims of the association should permit intellectually motivated personalities to come close to one another in a natural, clublike atmosphere. One hears the complaint everywhere that neither professional relations nor informal contacts in Berlin have created a "society" in the sense that one existed here at the beginning of the nineteenth century—a most highly cultivated circle that feels itself to be the bearer of a unified general culture above all individual differences. The club should be a center for the formation of such a culture and an influence on public opinion in the interest of the higher things in life (*in den Interessen geistigen Lebens*). It should be a source of the productivity that consists not in books and works, but in the intercourse of refined personalities; for despite its ephemeral character, neither the culture of Athens nor of Florence, of Weimar nor of Paris, would be thinkable without it. In place of the gradual organic growth of a refined atmosphere or the happy accident that significant individuals come together, modern life, here as elsewhere, must try to find a substitute in institutions and conscious support.[77]

Here was a recipe taken from Simmel's sociology! Culture grew from individual interactions that crystallized into artistic forms; but the fragmented conditions of life in modern Berlin no longer permitted such contacts to arise naturally as in traditional towns, including Berlin itself at the beginning of the nineteenth century. Where nature failed, reform would take its place—with the unusual twist that in this case it was elite members of society who felt impoverished.

George was not enticed. His reply violently repudiated the whole plan. In May the poet told Sabine Lepsius he had thought of breaking with Simmel over it.[78] Simmel salvaged the friendship only by pleading that it would be improper to start such a club without letting George decide for himself whether to take part.[79]

Why did George react so harshly? In Simmel's own language, he had failed to reckon with the poet's *Vornehmheit*. The club was conceived as a pluralistic meeting place for all kinds of modernists. The actively participating individuals named by Simmel in his letter of 24 February—the art historian Heinrich Wölfflin, the composer Richard Strauss, the museum director Alfred Lichtwark, and the artists Max Klinger and Henry van de Velde—represented a broad spectrum of German culture.[80] He wrote in his original letter to George, "Now, we were of the opinion that the greatest magnanimity as to paths and styles must be united with the greatest stature as to the purity and independence of artistic will."[81] Such a venture called for the attitude of peers in an aristocratic republic—the independence to go one's own way, the openness to let others go theirs. But George's temperament was strictly monarchical. In 1903 he was in the midst of reshaping his personal relationships, leaving behind the youthful friends who were accustomed to treating him as an equal and gathering young disciples who revered him as teacher-prophet and addressed him as master.[82]

George's next book, *The Seventh Ring*, announced in 1907 his evolution from aesthete to prophet. It honored the boy-god Maximin (based on a real youth George had briefly known before his death at age sixteen), incarnation of a neo-Hellenic ideal of physical and spiritual beauty. At the same time the George circle had become a conspicuous feature of the German cultural landscape. Its members were few, but with a great poet at its center and gifted and wealthy acolytes, it enjoyed a vogue among Germans in search of cultural renaissance.[83]

Simmel was not among them. His review of *The Seventh Ring* in 1909 discreetly ignored the Maximin experience and spoke about the kind of author who could turn it into a cosmic myth to be proffered as authentic revelation. "George's poetic soul sings only of itself, not the world, not the world above. When things outside his personal experience get expressed in his verse, such as a historical or other object—then it has the effect of a foreign body, the incoherent intrusion of a world that is not and cannot become his own."[84] George claimed to put his poetry in the service of prophecy, but Simmel returned it to the realm of fantasy. He now realized that he had misjudged its point all along. George's higher self had always been a human ego swollen to epic proportions.

What finished off the friendship was not George's excursion into boy-worship, but his circle's increasingly blatant misogyny. The poet admonished Gertrud Simmel in 1911 for upholding the Protestant principle of personal autonomy that was corrupting the modern world. When she asked for a chance to discuss this with him, he replied by sending the third volume of the *Jahrbuch für die geistige Bewegung,* whose introduction by Gundolf and Friedrich Wolters polemicized against Protestantism, progress, individualism, and emancipated women. Indignant over the behavior of the master and his minions, she wrote George demanding an apology. Meanwhile Rickert, also one of the poet's early academic admirers, wrote a letter to Georg Simmel expressing his shock over the *Jahrbuch* and asking whether he could not intervene to bring the poet back to his senses. Simmel darkly replied that he had made an attempt, but that personal relationships within the circle were involved that he could not hope to affect. The professors had earlier excused, and even admired, George's tyrannical behavior, which Simmel had interpreted as a manifestation of the higher, inner freedom of the artist. Now he discovered that the poet's wilfulness was not limited to the aesthetic realm, but included demands for personal obeisance and plans for political domination.[85]

Just when Simmel's friendship with the poet was fading, Max Weber met him several times in Heidelberg, one of the regular stopping points on George's wanderings (he had no fixed residence, but went from place to place like the medieval emperors) and an epicenter of the George circle. Friendly with Gundolf, by then professor of German in Heidelberg, and an admirer of George's verse, Weber met the poet several times between 1910 and 1912.[86] Like Simmel, Weber found him charming, but this time poet and thinker confronted each other from the beginning as intellectual opposites.[87] Weber scrutinized George as an example of the charismatic leader, attempting with his band of followers to found a new religious order. George's circle regarded Weber as the epitome of the rationalized intellectual, his critical spirit the antithesis of *Gemeinschaft*.[88]

Weber's and Simmel's encounters with Stefan George reveal some of the similarities and differences in their attitudes toward modernity. Weber considered the poet and his followers a quixotic group, intriguing but ultimately a collection of bored children of the upper middle class, parodying the founding of a real religious order. They confirmed his skepticism about the emergence of charisma in modern society through their very inability to distinguish their cult for the privileged from a genuine revolutionary movement. For Simmel, George had a more constructive significance. From the beginning their personalities were clearly different; Simmel embodied the urban spirit despised by George, while George's cultic *Vornehmheit* demanded extraordinary tolerance from Simmel. What George represented, however, was important enough for him to overlook a great deal of foolishness; the poet was his connection to a new, living culture, a deliverance from the dreariness of the 1870s and 1880s. George's very rebellion against modern society demonstrated its vitality; his anti-urban poetry could never have been written without the stimulus of the metropolis. The poet who for Weber represented a magnificent folly was for Simmel a source of rejuvenation, proof that modernity was shaping a new culture to replace the old.

The End of the World

Simmel's relationship to utopianism was—like most things about him—a complicated matter. He did not like to prettify society; his interactive method was a steady caution against doing so, with its endless pairing of opposites, its refusal to dissolve society's good and bad aspects in a dialectical synthesis.

And yet he was modern society's great advocate, constantly squaring off against traditionalists and attempting to press its claims to cultural superiority. Hence it is not entirely surprising that he tried to show how modern society was—if not a utopia—a social order guided by a utopian ideal. And he did this by challenging tradition at the source, arguing that society could be viewed as secular fulfillment of the Kingdom of God. By opening up this perspective on an ideal future, he took issue with contrasts of the kind Weber made between the meaningfulness of the past and the spiritual void of the present.

That Simmel developed a secularized theology seems at odds with the fact that his "objective culture" was Jewish. Friends and enemies alike commented on his Jewish mannerisms, appearance, and speech. Comments about his Jewish attributes were indistinguishable from insinuations about his uprooted urbanity. His Jewishness contributed to his exclusion from Baden's and Prussia's universities. We need to beware, however, against too readily accepting the prejudices of his contemporaries. His "subjective culture" was Protestant, and he and his family went to great lengths to win social recognition of this choice. Simmel was the baptized child of baptized parents; a liberal Protestant theologian, Hans von Soden, presided over his wedding to Gertrud Kinel, a Prussian Protestant.[89] Simmel considered Judaism spiritually inferior to Christianity and expected it to dissolve completely in modern European civilization—which meant, in his view, the secularized Protestant civilization of his contemporaries. Even though he had no use for religion as church or credo, he thoroughly shared the prejudices of other secularized *Kulturprotestanten*.

In 1899 Simmel lectured on the philosophy of religion, a course he repeated several times in years to come.[90] Around the same time he began writing a series of essays on the same subject. Just when his sociology was coming to fruition—in the period marked by the publication of *The Philosophy of Money* in 1900 and *Sociology* in 1908—he sketched the *Wechselwirkung* between society and secularized Protestantism, in which society furthered Protestant individualism and Protestantism provided the ideal of social unity.

Simmel's religious writings introduced a utopian strain into his thinking by envisioning the ultimate end toward which society was tending. This utopia had the function of indicating the direction of social evolution and drawing attention to certain features of society that might otherwise remain invisible. Above all it clarified the nature of society's unity, difficult to see amid the social conflicts of Wilhelmine Germany, but never far from Simmel's concerns. It was nowhere perfectly realized—yet everywhere inherent in society's logic and destined to increase over time.

The objective direction of Simmel's thought could not satisfy his own longing for social unity, however. Always, even when he most strongly affirmed it, Simmel confronted modernity ambivalently. Whereas Weber's thought leaned backward, and could only affirm modernity with regrets for the lost wholeness of an earlier era, Simmel's leaned forward in time, and could only affirm it by arguing that its appearance of fragmentation belied an underlying tendency toward greater unity.

Utopia as Secularized Kingdom of God

Religion intrigued Simmel as a psychological and sociological category—as a way of defining one's relationship to self and society.[91] An antimetaphysical thinker, Simmel was skeptical toward the religious believer's faith that he communicated with a transcendent deity. He thought of experiences of the sacred as a valid psychological reality, however, which could not be "disproved" because they were a given fact of existence alongside ethical, aesthetic, and scientific perceptions.[92] The sociological critic was less concerned with the validity of religious claims than with understanding how religion helped constitute society and gave clues to its meaning. For Simmel, as for Tönnies (and Comte and Durkheim—the thesis was hardly original or limited to Germany) the experience of the sacred arose from the individual's perception of social unity and feeling of oneness with it. The majesty, love, and other attributes of God could all be translated back into such feelings as dependence on society and enjoyment of *fraternité* with it. The decline of religion in modern times, in this analysis, symptomized modern society's lack of self-conscious unity; Comte was only the most dramatic case of a sociologist who proposed a cure in the form of a religion of society, which in his case would actually provide a complete cult based on Catholicism. Other sociologists, even if they lacked the sublime madness to offer a complete secular substitute, agreed that the sociologist had the ethical task of healing modern society by discovering the means of achieving unity.

More than Tönnies or the French sociologists, Simmel insisted that this unity could only work if it satisfied those needs of the individual that were a distinctive feature of modernity. Modern man faced the unprecedented spiritual frustrations of a technological society in which immediate gratification gave way to longer and longer sequences of means-end relationships.[93] In *The Philosophy of Money*, as we have seen, one modern solution was to regard money, the ultimate means, as an end in itself. Another solution was the *Vornehmheit* ideal; the individual concentrated on the discipline of perfecting his higher self and subordinated all his social relationships to it. Simmel's essay "The Soul's Salvation" suggested that the traditional Christian notion of salvation could be translated into something resembling the modern *Vornehmheitsideal*. In Simmel's decidedly Protestant understanding, the soul was wholly unique and had no institutional or communal setting to guide its spiritual way. Traditional Christianity had imagined a path to God; its modern successor was a path to one's higher self. Modern salvation was achieved when a person's being formed a unified whole, radiating a consistent personal style from an unseen central point. Simmel was making a call for peaceful cultural anarchy in which freely interacting individuals would not hinder one another's self-realization. In contrast to the aristocratic tone of his discussions of Nietzsche's *Vornehmheitsideal*, this one was broadly democratic, defending Christianity from Nietzsche's attacks on it as the religion of weaklings, arguing that Christianity had always been as demanding and as absolute in its power to individuate as its modern successor ideal.[94]

Simmel's monograph on religion for his friend Martin Buber's series, *Die Gesellschaft*, modernized the other pole of religious feeling in his conception of it, the individual's relationship to an all-embracing totality. The relationships traditionally projected into heaven, he argued, had their actual counterpart in interpersonal relationships. Faith in God was analogous to faith in the motives of others, without which society could not be constituted. Each person confronted the other members of his society as an ultimately unknowable Other; interactions could not take place without some measure of mutual trust. The believer's feeling of being part of a cosmic totality, symbolized by the church as universal community, had its counterpart in the secular individual's participation in society as totality. For Simmel this comparison was not so much a degradation of organized religion as an elevation of society. If man's dependence on society inspired awe and his role in a division of labor inspired a sense of harmony, if the religiosity projected into another world actually belonged in this one, then society deserved to be the modern object of religious reverence.[95]

Simmel took this notion of an incipient religion of society seriously enough to distinguish further between two forms it could take. One was pantheism, which he polemicized against as the longing for an undifferentiated *Gemeinschaft* absorbing humanity in an all-embracing feeling of brotherhood. Like socialism, according to Simmel, pantheism defeated its own purpose; the willing self, which sought to overcome its isolation in absolute identity with others, would cease to exist if it merged completely with them. Simmel described pantheism and socialism as limiting cases in which a valid impulse was taken to an absurd extreme.[96] His alternative was a secularized Christian one: a state of social identity-in-difference that translated the Christian principle of love into the logic of modern society. "Love is everywhere the struggle of separate beings against their separation, which can never be victorious and whose victory would turn its sense into nonsense. Love's charm is as inexhaustible as this secret contradiction of all love: only to be possible in duality and yet to wish to destroy duality. This is the inner life with which it longs to make the deepest union a still more inward, still deeper one."[97] Modern society conformed to this ideal in uniting all its members in a totality of *Wechselwirkungen* in which each individual existed apart from yet for the others. Society was, in Simmel's paradoxical phrase, a vitalized pantheism,[98] each part of it self-determined yet woven through its very activity into social relations.

Perhaps Simmel's most remarkable experiment in secular theology appeared in *Sociology*, which concluded by synthesizing individual and social unity into the higher whole that Simmel proclaimed to be society's utopian end. Each individual would realize his inmost potential in a unique role in the world—that is, he would fulfill his calling.[99] By allowing every individual to do so, society would approach a state of universal freedom, embracing all souls as the church had tried to do— hence it would be a secular realization of the Kingdom of God.[100] One of Simmel's most penetrating critics has criticized Simmel's sketch of this utopia at the end of *Sociology* as an example of the aestheticism behind his writings, which diverted attention from the real conflicts between individual self-determination and a society reducing individuals to disposable bearers of social functions.[101] While the charge of aestheticism is partly right—we have seen the powerful hold of Stefan George on his thinking—to criticize Simmel's utopian ideal this way misses the point. Simmel clearly stated that his closing remarks about society as Kingdom of God were a speculative vision, not society's existing shape or necessary future. In an important sense, the utopian conclusion actually offered a critical perspective on contemporary society. It marked the point where Simmel aspired to move beyond the confines of existing society, where he looked forward to a transcendence of its inner divisions, where the dialectical rhythm of German sociology strained—still in incipient form—from society to a unity transcending it.

Apocalypse 1914

Troeltsch was among the many contemporaries fascinated by Simmel. He was one of the most vocal leaders of the effort to bring Simmel to Heidelberg in 1908 and again in 1915.[102] His writings repeatedly called attention to the significance of Simmel's work, as when he praised him in 1911 for giving sociology "an exact scientific meaning as a social-psychological science of the forms and laws of the relations back and forth between individual and society" and emphasized his influence on *The Social Teachings*.[103] Simmel's modernism seemed to him a sign of the sickness of the age, however; *The Problem of Historicism* called Simmel "a child and darling of modernity with all its terrible diseases and weaknesses."[104] Simmel was a relativist and Troeltsch, for all his historicism, sought substantive truths. His most penetrating formulation of the ultimate differences in their viewpoints came in a prewar encyclopedia article, "Eschatology," in which he contrasted Simmel's refusal to acknowledge any other-wordly, transcendent realm, his complete collapsing of religious categories into this-worldly, social ones, with his own belief that all relativizations were ultimately dependent on religious truth.[105] He found Simmel's secularism threatening precisely because it made such thoroughgoing use of religion to "redeem" the modern world.

Simmel's reaction to the outbreak of war in 1914 revealed that Troeltsch and like-minded contemporaries had profoundly misjudged him, failing to sense his deep-seated longing to throw off the burden of modernity's "objective culture" and experience a new authenticity. As the nation mobilized for total war he abandoned his previous diffidence and did what he could to further Germany's emerging *Gemeinschaft*. The mechanical divisions of the recent past, the private dilemmas preoccupying the cultural elite, disappeared before the collective tasks of the present. Simmel experienced a sense of collective oneness previously denied to him: "One of the greatest gains of this great time," he told a Strasbourg audience in November 1914, "is that the mechanical division between those two (individual and collective life) disappears, so that once again we feel the *organic* character of our being."[106] All the carefully balanced antinomies of modernity suddenly collapsed as Simmel abandoned his previous distance from mass society. Division of labor meant stultifying difference instead of invigorating differentiation—as he could see for the first time now that war had helped overcome its damaging effects and restored the nation's primal oneness.[107] Endemic obsession with money now signified corrosive vice instead of a natural social pattern; Simmel maintained that the war had done Germany a great service by impoverishing the middle classes and restoring their sense of life's basic needs.[108] The strain of social division proved too great for even Germany's most skilful defender of modernity when he saw a chance for the full assimilation into national life denied to him under prewar conditions.

Initial exultance gave way to a more confused mood. As early as March 1915 Simmel asked whether anything would survive of the European cultural fraternity that had once transcended national boundaries—a question he could only answer uncertainly.[109] His hopes for a renewal of German culture gave way to growing fears that the war would destroy the values of the prewar world. And in fact the war turned into a terrible confirmation of his prewar analyses: even the most concerted national wish for *Gemeinschaft* could not escape the natural divisions of modern society, which only deepened under the impact of war. Simmel died in 1920 with the conflict unresolved between the "subjective culture" of his own soul, with its longing for a deeper form of unity than modern society could offer, and his intellectual formulations.[110]

Simmel's oscillation between *Gemeinschaft* and *Gesellschaft* at the end of his life does not lessen the interest of his prewar modernism. It does, though, encourage skepticism toward social scientists from Simmel's time to our own who wish to persuade us that alienation is a fantasy of left-wing ideologues.[111] Simmel exemplifies how deeply it may be implanted even in the heart of its most urbane opponent. Even he could not live completely in the present, tolerant of its tensions and indifferent to hopes for the future derived from the past. His sudden discovery of *Gemeinschaft* in 1914 hearkened back to the unfinished work of 1871. It looked forward to a utopia that his students Lukács and Bloch would identify with socialism.

6
Georg Lukács: Community Reborn

Georg Lukács, Hungarian by birth, was closely involved in his native country's history until his death in 1971. And yet, he belonged to German culture too.[1] Before World War I he became one of those wanderers who, not unlike American émigrés from the other side of the globe, felt attracted from their homes on the European periphery to the older centers of European civilization. Born to a prominent Hungarian Jewish banker and his Austrian wife in 1885, after the turn of the century he almost intuitively strove to go beyond the spiritual and geographic limits of his home.[2] His first book, *History of Modern Drama,* surveyed the dramatic literature of Germany, France, Britain, and Scandanavia as well as that of Hungary; the books that followed, *Soul and Form* and *Theory of the Novel,* ranged from Western Europe to Russia. Lukács strove for a last judgment of the European civilization which nineteenth-century commerce had created and twentieth-century warfare would nearly destroy. At the center of this apocalyptic order was Germany: German literature since Goethe as the chief record of bourgeois striving for personal fulfillment, and German sociology as the theoretical guide to the relationship between self and society. His foreign birth did not hinder Lukács's participation in the German world of learning on the eve of its cataclysm.

The dialectic of German sociology, the movement from community to society to socialism, found its completion in his work. In its end was its beginning. Both Lukács and Tönnies were communitarians, though with opposite teleological accents. Traditional community was the one authentic stage of history for the young Tönnies; society appeared as loss, socialism as faintly delineated hope. Lukács, on the other hand, regarded traditional community as an admirable memory. Going beyond Tönnies, he learned from Simmel and Weber to penetrate society's inner logic and to search for an authentic life transcending its routines. After testing its limits under their tutelage, he was determined to surpass it, to press forward from society to socialism.

In a deeper sense, too, Lukács attempted to surpass his teachers' thinking. All of them were preoccupied with the irretrievable loss of the past, the dissolution and death of community. For them human history was tragic because the evolution from *Gemeinschaft* to *Gesellschaft* liquidated what had preceded modern society. The young Lukács comprehended the movement of history in a different, dialectical sense, in which the past was conserved in the present. "Aber nicht das Leben, das sich vor dem Tode scheut und von der Verwüstung rein bewahrt, sondern das ihn erträgt und in ihm sich erhält, ist das Leben des Geistes. Er gewinnt seine Wahrheit nur, indem er in der absoluten Zerrissenheit sich selbst findet."[3] Lukács viewed history as a movement of death and resurrection, in which the decay of a community evoked its highest intellectual and artistic forms of expression, and the decay of society was the condition for a new community of freely cooperating individuals. His critique of their tragic philosophy of history and discovery of a life of the spirit torn asunder within capitalism was an achievement that would survive his own later development into an apologist for Stalinism. Lukács rediscovered the unity that each living generation creates by shaping a new future out of historical memory. His friends and successors—one thinks of such different thinkers as Walter Benjamin, Ernst Bloch, and the Karl Mannheim of *Ideology and Utopia*—could draw inspiration from this lesson of his early thinking without imitating the decline into propaganda of his later writing.

Lukács's own early development imitated the labor of history, with successive *Aufhebungen* transcending yet conserving its earlier stages. He found himself only after successive transformations. And yet, at the end, he had not left behind his earlier identities so much as he absorbed them into the position he finally took for truth. This applies above all to the religious impulse underlying his restless experimentation. He sought an absolute community transcending the isolation and conventionality of bourgeois existence. His final communism completely rejected Christian other-worldliness, yet remained more than anything else a faith that he had merged with the universal, redeeming community of human history.

Community and Crisis

How is culture possible? Under what conditions did it flourish in the past, and do those conditions still hold good in the present? As a young man Lukács assumed that there was no authentic culture in modern Europe, but at most the striving toward one. Inherited art and thought memorialized the cultures that once were; he and other seekers looked in vain for the epic, philosophy, and drama of their time. His early writings tried to sort out an existential riddle, to understand the decline condemning the present to stunted productivity. He turned to sociology for a systematic grasp of modern society and clarity about its inability to bring forth an authentic culture, hoping it would teach him the hidden logic leading beyond the present to a rebirth of great art and thought, symbols of a revitalized society.

His first lessons in sociology were practical. In 1904 the nineteen-year-old Lukács and his friends Laszlo Bánóczi and Marcell Benedek decided to found an avant-garde theater in Budapest, the Thalia Society, and won a gifted young director to their enterprise, Sándor Hevesi, who was as disgusted as they with the provinciality of theater life in the Hungarian capital. They looked abroad for other examples of successful avant-garde theater, in Germany to Otto Brahm's Freie Bühne, which had introduced Gerhard Hauptmann to the Berlin public. The Thalia Society did not have a specific program; it sought simply to bring the best of nineteenth-century drama to the Budapest stage, especially plays exploring the weaknesses of bourgeois morality. After February 1906, when Bánóczi agreed to a request to organize a series of performances for workers, the police harassed the Thalia Society, forcing it to move from place to place until it dissolved two years later after Hevesi left to head Hungary's National Theater. In the four years of its existence the Society was remarkably successful in modernizing the taste of its public, introducing Hebbel, Ibsen, Strindberg, and Hauptmann to Hungary. It came to an end not just because of outside interference, but because its offerings had gained such wide acceptance, encouraging established theaters to play them too.[4]

Lukács spent much of the time of the theater's activity outside Budapest, depending on Bánóczi and Hevesi to keep him in touch by mail with the problems of balancing the repertoire and finding suitable performance halls. In August 1906, Bánóczi wrote to alert Lukács to a competition close to his interests: "The Kisfaludy Society is awarding a prize for the following question (among other things): the main tendencies of dramatic literature in the last quarter of the past century. Deadline October 31, 1907. I wonder what excuses you will find now. Five seasons lie between now and then, which you will spend abroad concerned with the theme anyway. There is no escape."[5] The letter reached Lukács in Berlin, where he had gone to study with Simmel. Despite its untraditional approach of applying sociological categories to literature, his essay found favor with the judges of a society representing the official literary establishment in Hungary; in January 1908 Bernát Alexander, professor of philosophy at the University of Budapest, sent a letter congratulating him on winning the competition.[6] Afterward Lukács expanded his entry and turned it into the two-volume *History of Modern Drama,* completed in December 1909. With the exception of one fragment, it remained untranslated into German (or any other Western language) until 1981 and did not receive the kind of attention accorded to his other books. Only recently have Lukács's biographers raised it to its rightful place as one of his most remarkable works—one of the first, and still one of the most successful, attempts at a sociology of literature.[7]

Lukács's study was an attempt to outline the social conditions for the emergence of great drama. Taking Attic and Elizabethan drama as the classic past exemplars of the genre, he argued that traditional drama had had a communal audience, content, and form.[8] His conception of community accorded with Tönnies's notion of an organic human unity manifest in a common will. The traditional theatrical audience represented the life of the entire community and for this reason had a different function from that of the modern audience, responding not as an atomized collection of individuals, but as the bearer of a common will that interacted as one will with the playwright and actors, each side inspiring the other. Such an audience sought something more profound than just amusement. It came to share a religious mood that Lukács named *Feierlichkeit*, the spirit of holidays in the original sense of the word, mixing merriment with participation in a transcendent order. The theater both entertained and taught.[9] The spectators gathered to enjoy the spectacle of their own society, its essential life compressed by the formal requirements of the stage. Drama did not just mirror society; Lukács abhorred contemporary Marxist critics (especially Karl Kautsky) who interpreted it thus, as if there were no essential difference between art and life, and dramatic art could simply be read as a document of social realities.[10] Dramatic art differed from life by shaping the essential elements of its audience's existence into a form. This form revealed something latent but hidden in the empirical social order, its collective meaning and destiny, or in Lukács's word, its fate.[11] The evolution of a human conflict in the play and—already decisive for Lukács's judgment of individual works, as it would remain in his later aesthetics and politics—the resolution of this conflict concentrated in a microcosm the fundamental ethical paradoxes of the community and its most deeply held beliefs about how these paradoxes fit into the human and divine order of things. Such a dramatic culture could only arise from a harmony in which the artist drew on the norms of his audience for his plot, while the audience intuitively recognized his representation of fate as its own.[12]

Modern drama according to this conception was a paradoxical enterprise, for it aimed at creating a dramatic form in the absence of community. Since the French Revolution the audience had been made up of bourgeois individuals. Bourgeois playwrights tried to dramatize the typical fate of their audience as the fate of isolated individuals, each at odds with the rest of society.[13] Could great drama emerge from this novel situation? Lukács argued that since the late eighteenth century all attempts to create great drama had ended in disappointment. The German classical drama of Lessing, Schiller, and Goethe had understood that its task was to reach a national audience, but had never succeeded in doing so, instead retreating into theater for an elite. It had upheld the inner nobility of traditional drama, but at the cost of its vitality; it had drawn heroes and heroines, but only as abstractions from the past; it had a teaching, but lacked spectacle.[14] At the other extreme, the French social drama (*Tendenzdrama*) of the mid-nineteenth century achieved popular success, but only by succumbing to the taste of its audience, the Parisian bourgeoisie, and affirming the righteousness of its conventional morality. Its lack of inner meaning required meaningless plots whose rapid change of scenes entertained its onlookers without ever forcing their values to a crisis.[15] Every other attempt at a modern drama, argued Lukács, fell somewhere between these extremes of pedagogy and pandering.

And yet, Lukács did not rule out the possibility of creating a comprehensive drama of modern individualism. He discovered an opportunity for the bourgeois era by generalizing about the historical moment when great drama came into being: "The dramatic era is, in short, the heroic era of the disintegration of a class. It is the era in which a class (the dominant mass in the drama's public), represented by its people, its heroic types and talents, perceives the tragic decline of its typical experiences in events symbolizing its whole life."[16] Drama did not capture the life of a community; it *resurrected* it at the moment of its extinction. As an example of this process Lukács pointed to Shakespearean drama, representing the values of the declining English nobility.[17] The mere fact of decline, to be sure, did not make up for the modern lack of a cohesive theater public with shared norms. Lukács thought the lack of such an audience had flawed the work of Hebbel and Ibsen, who lost touch with their society and created artificial conflicts when they tried to express heroic values through a high degree of formal closure, while Naturalism gave up any principle of formal unity in order to stay close to the surface of modern life.[18] Still, the day of great drama might be approaching. Lukács speculated that if the eighteenth- and nineteenth-century bourgeoisie had failed so far to create great drama, this was in part because it was still a rising class and could not comprehend its fate as a rounded totality; it awaited the moment when it could see its history from beginning to end. Mixing doomsaying and prophecy, he descried the first stirrings of great drama.[19]

Just when he was completing the drama book, Lukács also wrote an essay that illustrates how his conception of community compared with Tönnies's. "The Middle-Class Way of Life and L'art pour L'art: Theodor Storm," written in the fall of 1909, studied Tönnies's friend and mentor in their Schleswig-Holstein setting.[20] Lukács shared their belief that an older and preferable way of life, which had vanished from Europe's metropolises, survived a generation longer in its towns and villages. In the rolling North German plains, where sea, earth, and sky merged in their shifting shades of gray, every human being and every event maintained its original oneness with nature. Lukács marveled at the subtle beauty of this landscape: at first sight so monotonous, on closer examination such a rich harmony of elements.[21] He praised Storm as a writer who out of a living tradition created his preferred form of narrative, the novella, differing from the short story or novel in its unbroken relationship to the folk tale. The novella typically relied on a narrator who told a wondrous incident drawn from popular memory. Storm used the novella in just this way to capture the essential experience of his region, which his art concentrated into a miniature, self-enclosed totality, an achievement beyond the reach of writers from more modern and hence fragmented backgrounds.[22]

Both Tönnies and Lukács found Storm's way of life as significant as his work—or rather, they were both impressed by a life and work that were inseparable. Storm reminded them of a traditional German craftsman, who perfected his art over the unhurried course of a lifetime; and he did so not in isolation from his surroundings, but in keeping with his duties as husband, father, judge, and local patriot.[23] But Lukács penetrated more deeply to the idea at the heart of this image: work as the rhythm governing the interactions of the community. What characterized craft work was "the rule of order over mood, of the lasting over the momentary, of quiet work over genius fed by sensations. Its most profound consequence, perhaps, is that such dedication can vanquish egotistical solitude."[24] According to this prettified view of the preindustrial *Bürger* world, each townsman did his work not in competition but in time with others, according to a shared, inwardly regulated pace. Lukács pointed to Storm's work as an authentic example of the craftsmanship resulting from such a shared tempo. It suited his purposes especially because Storm was not a major talent and had not triumphed through the force of a singular personality; on the contrary, he demonstrated how persistence and steady receptiveness could lead to the mastery that he attained at the end of his life. This art, argued Lukács, was no different from any other form of work in a traditional community, and for just this reason it ripened to a perfection denied to modern artists, with their reliance on momentary inspiration.[25] Lukács's emphasis on the phenomenon of work foreshadowed a central theme of *History and Class Consciousness,* in which the fragmentation of modern work would determine the fragmentation of modern bourgeois consciousness and the proletariat would strive for a return to a holistic form of work comparable to unalienated craftsmanship.

Lukács's evaluation of Storm reveals another important difference between him and Tönnies. Tönnies had no higher and no other aesthetics than the one represented by Storm: art as imaginative synthesis of the normal life of the community. Lukács, on the other hand, set limits to Storm's achievement, assigning it to a lower aesthetic order than great drama or its prose counterpart, great epic. Storm had managed to do his work by self-consciously closing himself off from the modern world and avoiding confrontation with its effects on the traditional world he described. For this reason, his characters accepted disaster as a natural event, one that temporarily broke in on them without ever shattering them; they bore up under it until the rhythm of community resumed its normal course.[26] Although this was a precious remembrance of the strengths of community, it failed to illuminate the nature of traditional life in all its fullness, as it was in fact revealed by its breakup at the end of the nineteenth century. Lukács's essay looked to Thomas Mann's *Buddenbrooks* as a work in which the mood of decay had pervaded the old German burgher world and therefore permitted it to become monumental once more.[27] Lukács criticized Storm according to the aesthetic maxim of his drama book: great art did not merely represent the life of its community, but resurrected it. By distinguishing, as Tönnies did not, between the biological and social shell and the form transcending them, Lukács could carry his analysis of authentic culture beyond the death of community and trace the symbols of its estrangement in society.

Modern Tragedy

"The basic philosophy of the drama book," remarked Lukács in 1971, "is Simmel's philosophy."[28] Chronology supports the accuracy of this recollection; Lukács wrote the *History of Modern Drama* during the period demarcated by his study with Simmel in Berlin in 1906–07 and again in 1909–10.[29] And in fact his central analytic categories closely resemble Simmel's. The coming crisis that he predicted for the modern era was the crisis of the bourgeois individual in conflict with objective culture. "It is," he wrote of the modern consciousness of history, "the problem of the established world that—even if its inadequacy is recognized—purely through its existence is capable of the most far-reaching, indeed victorious resistance. It is identical with the potential energy of things, the problem of the power of what has been inherited."[30] Like Simmel, he argued that the products of man's own activity had replaced nature as the hindrance to authentic culture. He analyzed the fragmented relationship between stage and audience along the lines laid down in *The Philosophy of Money:* the intellectualized theatergoer of the modern metropolis had trouble responding to what he saw because he was too used to abstract conceptualizations, too far removed from the symbols that drama had traditionally relied on for its concrete, sensuous storytelling.[31] Yet in an ironic turn worthy of Simmel, he maintained that this same intellectualization of modern life provided modern drama with the materials of its own myth. In place of the traditional dependence on other persons, modern society had created a new form of bondage, the impersonal entrapment of modern man in the sociological laws of his society. The ethical form of these laws was bourgeois convention, a set of rules having nothing to do with the happiness of the individual. Ibsen occupied a high place in Lukács's canon of modern playwrights because he had attempted to make drama out of the bourgeois rebel's frustration with the abstract constraints of modern life. His heroes strove against the objective circumstances constituting the modern fate.[32]

Lukács accepted Simmel's notion of modern culture as the modern fate, but drew opposite conclusions from it. Simmel viewed it as irreversible and found a saving grace within it: *Vornehmheit*. Secrecy, silence, inwardness, and distance were the means to create a distinguished demeanor and to establish a balance between subjective and objective culture. For Lukács, on the other hand, the only meaningful culture was one manifest in the objective world, and he criticized *Vornehmheit* as an unheroic retreat from the struggle for self-realization:

The new life has no pathos. This means that everything elevated and everything tragic withdraws itself. . . . *Vornehmheit*, too, becomes passive. He who is *vornehm* does not hurt the other, but silently walks by the person who hurts him. Silence, the dismissal of all noise with a quiet gesture, is *vornehm;* so is keeping tragedies secret, the deepest contents of the soul, held at a distance from human beings and things human.[33]

Lukács argued that in drama, the presence of *Vornehmheit* as the protagonist's chief trait was a sign of artistic failure. The playwright had not tested him against his circumstances and brought out his inner qualities; instead he had created an uneven contest in which the external world was necessarily superior to its victim. Whereas Simmel was resigned to objective culture as an irreversible fate, Lukács relativized it as an episode in the history of the bourgeoisie. The very completeness of its present victory stirred him to challenge its legitimacy. *History of Modern Drama* asserted, as *History and Class Consciousness* would do too, that the totality of contemporary submission to objective forces created the conditions for regaining control over one's destiny. Moreover, a dynamic conception of time already entered into Lukács's work and set it apart from Simmel's. Lukács's utopia of transformed human relationships, of a world beyond bourgeois isolation and convention, affected past and present, impelling the tragic hero to challenge society's objective culture, whereas Simmel's utopia of a future like the present only more so, allowing each person room for private fulfillment within a fragmented whole, was static, leaving past and present unaffected while retreating inward into an ever more private sphere. At the same time, Lukács was still Simmel's student enough to think of tragedy primarily as an aesthetic problem removed from politics. His book was a plea for changed artistic consciousness. The irremediable barrenness of the external world would fill modern playwrights with a dramatic vision of the greatest possible intensity, inspiring a final, hopeless duel of fate and character.[34]

Cultivation of sensibility attracted Lukács when it seemed to contain potential for movement back into the world. His interest in the movement from withdrawal to activism distinguished his interpretation of Stefan George from Simmel's. "The New Solitude and Its Poetry: Stefan George" defended George on formal grounds closely resembling the arguments for the autonomy of the modern artist used by Simmel. Lukács, too, addressed the complaint that George's poetry was too cold to be lyrical by deriving the so-called coldness from the conditions of modern artistic productivity.[35] The modern artist no longer inherited living cultural forms of the kind still available to a traditionalist such as Storm. For the lyric poet, this meant that the folk song materials still usable in early nineteenth-century Germany had lost their vitality, resulting in the loss of the common culture that had functioned as a spontaneous medium of understanding between artist and audience. The modern lyric poet was on his own; he was alone with his feelings, cut off from any community, and he had to find his own themes and forms of expression. It was this socially imposed self-reliance that made George's poetry aloof and esoteric, not an arbitrary choice made by the poet.[36] Lukács followed Simmel's lead to this extent, analyzing George in terms of the sociology of modern culture. But Lukács was aware of George's urge, imperceptible to Simmel, to overcome his isolation and rejoin a community. George was a wanderer; his poems of companionship, friendship, and love, Lukács noted, repeatedly led to awareness of human beings' isolation. The search did not end in resignation like Simmel's, however. It continued: "the great search, along a thousand paths, in every solitude, in all the arts, the search for human beings like ourselves, for a communion with simpler, more primitive, unspoilt beings."[37] Despite its turn inward, George's poetry contained a tension projecting it ever outward again. For this reason Lukács could admire it as the lyric, psychological accompaniment to the same kind of conflict between individual and society that great drama should enact.

Lukács restlessly experimented with different approaches to the conflict between alienated soul and social form, becoming dissatisfied with each in turn for failing to bring the conflict to a resolution. "On the Path to Great Drama," the climactic chapter of *History of Modern Drama,* hinted that such a resolution might be in the making in the theater of his time.[38] A year later Lukács was bolder: "The Metaphysics of Tragedy: Paul Ernst" offered his vision of a fully realized modern tragedy. The method of the essay seemed superficially to disavow that of the book, for it no longer defined the sociological conditions of tragedy, but attempted to distill its "metaphysical" essence. In fact the two works were complementary; Lukács could dispense with explicit sociological discussion because his book had already prepared an introduction to the metaphysics of the essay. What interested him in the essay was not a timeless artistic genre, but the essence of *modern* tragedy.

Traditional tragedy, as we have seen, reasserted the norms of its community, which were upheld in the moment of their extinction by the hero. The modern tragedy discussed in the essay had the different aim of upholding the inner life of an individual surrounded by a lifeless world, a world of objects and of human beings whom he experienced as objects. It challenged him either to assert himself or to be reduced to one more object. Silence and misunderstanding typified his relationship to this world, since the logic of his inner being was utterly foreign to everything around him. The hero ultimately sacrificed his life rather than submit to the conventions enforcing the lifelessness of ordinary life.[39]

How could modern drama have an audience? Traditional drama was based on a community of artist and audience, but modern drama in Lukács's definition lacked a community and with it any medium of communication between the hero's values and his bourgeois onlookers' conventions. Just as meaningful dialogue between hero and ordinary characters became impossible under the conditions of modern tragedy, so the hero's words could no longer reach beyond the end of the stage. Lukács's resolution of this conflict was a metaphysical leap: "A drama is a play about man and his fate—a play in which God is the spectator."[40] Where human community failed, a superhuman one remained. This was a solution Lukács could not have proposed within the bounds of his drama book, structured as it was around the relationship between artist and audience. Lukács had to abandon his sociological method for metaphysics in order to carry out the argument of the essay.

In this metaphysical context the idea of a resurrection of values recurred with a clarified function. The twilight of the bourgeois era confronted the individual with a desacralized world that frustrated all his efforts to realize his values. What he then discovered was that if there was no way for him to make his values intelligible or substantial within the world, he had to catapult them out of it and into the next. His physical death signified not defeat by fate, but transcendence of it and obedience to a higher logic. By choosing how his life would end he gave it a definitive form that it would not have had in the natural course of events. Suicide bore witness to values otherwise beyond expression.[41]

History of Modern Drama pointed to Paul Ernst as the playwright whose works most nearly approximated the idea of modern tragedy. "The Metaphysics of Tragedy" argued that Ernst had actually realized the tragic idea in his play *Brunhild*: "*Brunhild* is the first success granted to Paul Ernst as a writer of tragedies. . . . *Brunhild* is his first real action, the first steel cast without any dross, a work that has faults but no flaws."[42] Lukács met Ernst in Weimar in June 1910 and probably wrote the essay later the same summer.[43] Their meetings and letters continued until after World War I, well beyond the time when political events had placed them on opposite ends of the ideological spectrum.[44] How highly Lukács regarded Ernst in the initial years of their friendship emerges from his answer in 1913 to a request from a French journal editor to give his judgment of contemporary German culture. In general Lukács had a low opinion of the contemporary literary scene, which he accused of lacking a unified style. Nonetheless there were hopeful signs of a growing desire for genuine culture: for systematic philosophy, for religious renewal, and for community. So far there were only signs and promises, not deeds. He named one exception: "The only deed which in this respect may be called a deed is the life's work of Paul Ernst. . . . His tragedies are made as if a German culture were once again present, a culture which had gathered the entire essential past and—precisely for that reason—pointed to the essential future."[45] Lukács did not think Ernst's work was superior to that of his contemporaries on its intrinsic artistic merits; what made it so important was that it stood for the will to authentic culture. By restoring the broken links of time, it showed what a culture should be, even if such a culture did not yet exist.

Ernst exemplified to an extreme degree the revolt against materialism of German culture around the turn of the century. The son of a Harz miner, he had started his university studies as a theology student. Then he became attracted to Marxism, schooling himself in the social sciences and making his living writing journalism on social issues and on theater. In the late 1890s he tried his hand at writing Naturalist one-act plays about Wilhelmine society. These experiments stopped after a trip to Italy in 1900 that opened his eyes to the severe beauty of pre-Renaissance and Renaissance art, especially Giotto (whose art became a favorite of Lukács, too, after a trip to Italy). On returning to Germany Ernst discarded Naturalism for an ascetic Neoclassical style. In 1903 he started writing Neoclassical plays; in 1904 he and a circle of like-minded friends founded a theater in Düsseldorf to realize their dramatic ideal. By 1906 the theater closed, and a journal planned by the group never appeared.[46]

Ernst did not abandon his Neoclassicism, however, and the cultural orientation he discovered during these years profoundly affected Lukács. His essay of 1904, "The Possibility of Classic Tragedy," outlined the conception of tragedy that Lukács enriched in his essay of 1910. Ernst defined tragedy as the crux of two necessities: "At the point of intersection stands the tragic hero, and both necessities appear to him as his inner struggle, which he must fight. He develops his highest power in this task by following the one necessity and being destroyed by the other."[47] For Ernst as for Lukács, the two necessities in question were suggested by the tragic logic of contemporary social relationships. Ernst had met Simmel in the late 1890s and adopted his conception of modern society as a state of conflict between the money economy and the individual.[48] He wrote of the relationships created by the money economy in his essay of 1904: "But these relationships are neither created for the goals of the individual, nor do they obey a rational design. They develop according to their own laws: for the individual they are a blind fate."[49] Too estranged from his contemporaries to consider them worthy of tragic treatment, he turned to legendary and historical heroes of the past—in particular, the Germanic past—for worthy dramatic subjects.

Lukács thought *Brunhild* realized his conception of modern tragedy through its rigorous contrast of human and superhuman love. At the beginning of the play, Günther, king of the Niebelungen tribe, has used deceit in order to marry the warrior-goddess Brunhild. The man who has really subdued her at the behest of the king and deserves her love is the young blond hero, Siegfried. Siegfried's wife, Chriemhild, sister of the king, is as weak-spirited as her brother; afraid to lose Siegfried, and aware of the latent love between him and Brunhild, she reveals the secret. By then Brunhild realizes that Siegfried, not the king, is her predestined lover. But as a representative of Germanic womanhood, she places loyalty to her husband's family above everything else and arranges for Siegfried's murder in order to save the honor of the Niebelungen. Making her way to the bier where he is dying, she sings a final love duet with him before taking her own life.[50]

Lukács praised the play for its elimination of every superfluity and reduction of the plot to Sophoclean purity. The king and his sister wanted to fulfill petty personal ambitions—and lived. The two lovers were obedient to a higher law—and died. Their death was tragic, but tragic as the privilege of greatness. Siegfried remained faithful to his lord, Brunhild to her husband, and both of them to one another in the moment of their death.[51] Lukács understood her tragic guilt neither in its classical sense as atonement for trespassing bounds set by the gods nor in its Christian sense as moral error, but rather as *affirmation* of one's fate. "Guilt" lost its reproving connotation and became another name for the decision to choose authentic life.[52] The interpretation was highly forced; Brunhild's betrayal of her lover actually placed family convention *above* the higher law of divinely ordained love. Whatever its shortcomings as elucidation of Ernst's play, however, Lukács's essay clearly conveyed his own hatred of the existing world and his admiration for even the most suicidal determination to destroy it.

As early as 1910, a gulf separated Ernst from his former mentor. Simmel did not appreciate Neoclassicism; in reply to a manifesto for a proposed Berlin theater that Ernst sent him, Simmel wrote, ". . . If the deduction is made that the time for 'great drama' as expression of the forces of the present has come, I see no connection that then justifies taking up Corneille and Gozzi. . . . According to my knowledge of the Berlin public, it is pointless to wish to attrach it with Tell and Mirra, with Turandot and Cid. These things bore us, even when they are acted as consummately as possible." Two years later Simmel wrote to Ernst that his real gift lay in psychological portrayal in the Naturalist style he had abandoned, not in the abstract types filling his tragedies.[53] Ernst apparently avoided a confrontation with Simmel at the time. During the war, however, he was still discussing the "Simmel problem" with Lukács. After Simmel refused to contribute to a Festschrift for him, he commented, "I believe that Simmel's problem, which we have often spoken about, is the problem of the clever person who lacks instincts. He has no roots; so he shot up astonishingly in his early years, and in the years when he should have broadened out, the strength was not there."[54] This proved to be far from accurate, since Simmel only reached intellectual maturity around the turn of the century and remained productive until his death. Lukács's obituary of Simmel in 1918 more insightfully defined the "problem" from his and Ernst's perspective as having to do with the meaning of form. Simmel, he wrote, was "unquestionably the most significant and most interesting transitional figure in all modern philosophy . . . he was a great source of inspiration, but neither a great teacher, nor—and this at once leads us closer to the center of his being—did he bring anything to a conclusion. . . . He is the true philosopher of Impressionism."[55] The philosopher whose name had drawn him from Budapest to Berlin was not a great "teacher" because he offered no doctrine such as Lukács sought; he did not bring anything to a conclusion because his numerous books taught readers not to expect a world without ambiguities; he was an "Impressionist" because he resisted authoritarian certainties. Simmel strove to balance subjective and objective culture, individual autonomy and social convention, and to develop the logic of their interactions. These antinomies provided Lukács with a problematic constellation of forces—hence Simmel's significance as transitional figure—which he pushed in the direction of explosive contradictions.

Even at the time he wrote "The Metaphysics of Tragedy," Lukács could not treat *Brunhild* as more than a provisional solution to the dilemmas of modern society. It perfectly realized the tragic ethic, but at the cost of life—not the hero's own life, but the life of the world. Lukács was too much the militant critic of modern society to rest content with a spectacle of departure from it. And he was not wholly unaware of the barrenness of *Brunhild,* which he could excuse as the cost of one dramatic experiment, but could not impose on the whole future development of modern drama.[56] His essay turned to Ernst's histories as one possible alternative to the limitations of tragedy. Pope Gregory VII and Emperor Henry IV, the heroes of Ernst's play *Canossa,* attempt to follow absolute ethics, Gregory that of the saint, Henry that of the worldly ruler. They suffer ironic fates in the course of the play: in order to keep the support of the nobility, Gregory must betray the poor, while Henry must humble himself in the snow at Canossa in order to keep his kingdom. Lukács used the play to show how death took on a figurative meaning within society. Unlike the heroes of tragedy, who died a literal death in fulfillment of their fate, historical heroes survived broken and estranged, sacrificing their inner purity in order to be effective in the world.[57] If there was a solution to the problem of realizing authentic life in history, Lukács did not yet see it, and he criticized Ernst's historical plays to the extent that they failed to offer one. Yet his turn to the histories was a significant step: it marked his determination to go beyond the fatal logic of tragic individualism in search of an integration of individual and society within history. And it foreshadowed the vision of death and rebirth within history in *History and Class Consciousness*.

Beyond Tragic Sociology

The German Intellectuals

Until 1912, Lukács's home was Hungary despite his dissatisfaction with Hungarian intellectual life and frequent stays abroad; in that year he decided to try to settle in Germany. Private calamities contributed to his readiness to migrate westward. In December 1907 he had met a young Hungarian artist, Irma Seidler, at the home of Cecil Polanyi. They soon fell in love and traveled to Florence together, but within a year Lukács withdrew from the relationship, fearing that marriage would limit his development by interfering with his dedication to his work. After their separation Irma married a businessman, and Lukács kept loosely in touch with her, showing concern as the marriage fell apart, but still satisfied that he had disposed of their romance in their mutual best interest. The news of her suicide in May 1911 filled him with the belief that his behavior had been correct by conventional standards, but in a deeper moral sense had contributed to the catastrophe.[58] A second disturbing loss came a half year later: the death of his friend Leo Popper. A gifted critic and musician, Popper had done much to shape Lukács's aesthetic canon, with its reaction against "formless" Impressionism and Naturalism. Popper was also the sole confidant to Lukács's relationship with Irma and had accompanied them on their trip to Italy.[59] *Soul and Form*, its first chapter written as an open letter to Popper and its dedication in the German edition going to Irma, had grown out of his encounters with them.[60] After Popper's death of tuberculosis in October, Lukács felt that no close attachments tied him to Budapest.[61]

Although Lukács was in touch with leading intellectual circles of the capital, they were for the most part too "unmetaphysical" for him to feel at home with them. The journal *Huszadik Század*, edited by Ozskár Jászi, had a positivist orientation; *Nyugat*, a leading literary organ, was too "impressionistic" to satisfy Lukács's taste. Neither *History of Modern Drama* nor *Soul and Form* brought Lukács public acclaim. Together with the journalist Lajos Fülep he decided to edit a new journal, *A Szellem* (*Mind* or *Spirit*). Others associated with it, such as Béla Bálazs and Karl Mannheim, were, like Lukács, Simmel students. Fülep described himself and the other members of the *A Szellem* circle as "quite simply . . . seekers of a spiritual outlook on the world and of a spiritual life of a higher order."[62] Two issues came out in 1911. Metaphysical and mystical contributions predominated, including translations from Plotinus, G. K. Chesterton ("The Paradoxes of Christianity," from *Orthodoxy*), Meister Eckhart, and Hegel, as well as Lukács's "Metaphysics of Tragedy." The journal lacked an audience, and no more issues appeared. Another setback in the same year made it clear that he would have trouble pursuing an academic career at the University of Budapest: in May, his application to write a *Habilitationsschrift* was turned down. Antisemitism had risen dramatically in Hungary since the turn of the century, and the country's Magyar elite was no longer interested in allowing Jews to rise to positions of prominence, as it had been in his father's time. Georg Lukács, who had attended a Protestant secondary school and until recently had never paid much attention to his Jewish ancestry, no longer qualified for membership in the national community.[63]

At a moment of personal and professional difficulties in Hungary, Lukács was encouraged by Ernst Bloch, whom he had met in Simmel's seminar in early 1910, to come to Heidelberg, where he would find something of the great philosophy and new German culture he was seeking.[64] The same age as

Lukács, Bloch was a philosophical prodigy who as a schoolboy in Ludwigshafen had educated himself in philosophy by reading through the palace library of neighboring Mannheim. As a university student he absorbed the multitudinous neoromantic and neoidealist currents of the time while already showing the intellectual independence he would continue to display for the rest of his life.[65] Bloch's dissertation of 1909 cricitized Rickert for limiting philosophy to either abstract classification or recording inherited cultural developments, with no room for grasping lived experience. Looking to Bergson, Neitzsche, and Simmel as its prophets, he hinted at a coming philosophy that would develop the categories to grasp the present as mystical instant, the future as latent presence.[66] Lukács later remarked that Bloch showed him how to philosophize as if no one had ever philosophized before, just as Aristotle and Hegel had done in their time.[67] One can also see Bloch's example as having a more specific value for Lukács's orientation: Bloch's nascent philosophy of the *Noch-Nicht-Sein,* the unrealized but immanent future, corresponded to his own repudiation of Simmel's treatment of the past as a dead weight upon the present. Both of them sought a mystical experience of the present that would somehow transform the material of history and redeem the authentic life hidden within it.

Lukács arrived in Heidelberg to enroll for his *Habilitation* in May 1912. Within a few months, he could savor something of the esteem he had missed in Budapest. Simmel helped him with introductions, as did Emmy Lederer-Seidler, Irma's sister, who had married the economist Emil Lederer and turned their home into a center of Heidelberg cultural life.[68] *Logos,* the philosophy journal that included Rickert, Simmel, Troeltsch, and Max Weber on its editorial board, had published "Metaphysics of Tragedy" the preceding year and made his name familiar to its readers.[69] Emil Lask, Rickert's outstanding student and a teacher in Heidelberg, wrote in June to thank him for a copy of *Soul and Form;* they soon developed a warm friendship.[70] Troeltsch, too, wrote an appreciative note about *Soul and Form.* By August his father, who was still unhappy about his son's move to Germany, had to admit that "you are right when you think that in Heidelberg you would meet with greater interest and warmer sympathy. . . ."[71] Having made his entrance into Heidelberg's leading philosophical circles, he could set to work on the studies leading toward an academic appointment.

One of the professors taking a friendly interest in Lukács was Max Weber, who made an unsuccessful attempt to speak to the Heidelberg philosopher Wilhelm Windelband about Lukács as a *Habilitation* candidate and promised to get in touch with Rickert in the fall.[72] Lukács became a welcome guest at the Webers' Sunday salon, where according to Marianne Weber he and Gundolf were among the few personalities strong enough to offset her husband and form an independent center of attention.[73] A shared dislike of romantic sensationalism drew them together. In one of their first conversations Lukács impressed Weber by telling about the aesthetics he was planning to write. Kant, he said, had asserted that aesthetic judgment was the essence of the aesthetic. But, he continued, aesthetic judgment enjoyed no such priority; the priority belonged to the work itself. "There are works of art; how are they possible?" was how he posed the issue to Weber.[74] This was the opposite of the cult of feeling against which Weber had polemicized since the turn of the century; instead of investigating subjective response, Lukács placed extreme emphasis on the objectivity of aesthetic value. Weber esteemed the formulation enough to quote it later in "Science as a Calling" as a model of aesthetic method for neoromantic German youth to take to heart.[75]

We can further compare Lukács and Weber by going back to Lukács's essay on Storm, which showed strong affinities with *The Protestant Ethic*. Lukács's contrast between the burgher and bourgeois work ethic resembled Weber's comparison of Lutheran and Calvinist. For both of them traditional work was integrated into a cosmic totality of meaning, whereas modern work was a fragmented individual activity. But Lukács, unlike Weber, denied the possibility of a spiritual modern calling:

Life becomes *bürgerlich* in the first place through the *Bürger's* calling; but in the life of the former [the *bourgeois*] is there at all a calling? A single glance shows that this is impossible. It shows that the *Bürger*-like regularity and order of such a life are just masks hiding the most arbitrary and anarchistic preoccupation with one's own ego. Only in the most superficial superficialities, with romantic irony and conscious stylization, does it conform to the outward forms of its mortal enemy.[76]

This critique of bourgeois work allowed no possibility of a heroic Calvinist ethic such as Weber described. Work was either traditional and part of a communal rhythm or modern, isolated, and meaningless. A third possibility did not exist for him as it did for Weber, who agreed that modern work had become meaningless, but looked back to a privileged moment when it had been individuated yet linked to a spiritual end. Lukács introduced an important metaphor with no parallel in Weber to make his point by calling the outward discipline of the bourgeois a "mask" hiding inward disorder. This turned the entirety of modern existence into a realm of the inauthentic, an artificial, formalized form imposed on the soul in search of a home. Those who felt no tension with this world, who thought that they were following a calling, were merely mirroring the outward anarchy of modernity.

Despite their obvious differences (or perhaps because they enjoyed differing within a shared discourse) Lukács and Weber had formed a warm friendship by 1914. The subsequent years of war and revolution severely tested it, yet their admiration for one another persisted—a remarkable testimony to the human qualities of two imperious thinkers. Weber's response to the outbreak of war was more measured than that of many other professors. From the beginning he was skeptical about Germany's chances of victory and worried about the clumsiness of German diplomacy, the strength of the Allied coalition, and the devastating economic effects that would ensue from a long war.[77] Nonetheless, he too was caught up in the nationalist fervor momentarily uniting the country. In October he wrote to Tönnies, "This war is great and wonderful despite all its horrors. It is worth experiencing; it would be even more worthwhile to take part in it, but unfortunately they can't use me in the field, as they could have if it had been fought at the right time, twenty-five years ago."[78] His intimations of the coming defeat only heightened his attachment to the war as a heroic experience. The war figured in his correspondence and public pronouncements as a struggle for German cultural supremacy over English convention, Russian barbarism, and French rhetoric.[79] His longing for *Gemeinschaft* overpowered whatever doubts he had about the rationality of the war.

Lukács later described his initial reaction: "My own deeply personal attitude was one of vehement, global, and, especially at the beginning, scarcely articulate rejection of the war and especially of enthusiasm for the war. I recall a conversation with Frau Marianne Weber in the late autumn of 1914. She wanted to challenge my attitude by telling me of individual, concrete acts of heroism. My only reply was, 'The better the worse!'"[80] Simmel's comments to Marianne Weber documented the gulf separating the nationalist professors from their Hungarian disciple:

The unforgettable thing about this time is that at last, at last for once the demand of the day and the demand of the Idea are one and the same. That can only be understood 'intuitively,' or rather, in actual experience. If Lukács does not have this experience, it cannot be demonstrated to him. In that case, of course, he is entirely consistent in seeing 'militarism' in all this; but for us it is the liberation from all militarism because it loses its self-sufficiency (which it threatens to take on precisely in peacetime) and becomes a form and means to an elevation of all life.[81]

An uncompleted essay (intended for publication in the *Archiv für Sozialwissenschaft und Sozialpolitik*) analyzed just this kind of reaction of the German "intellectuals" to the war. In Lukács's assessment theirs was "an utterly general, spontaneous enthusiasm that lacked any clear or positive content."[82] He defined it in negative terms: as an expression of relief from the over-strained individualism of the German intellectuals before the war, which not only separated the intellectuals collectively from other groups, but isolated every authentic *Persönlichkeit* from all others. Isolation had abruptly given way to the jubilant expectation of a new, brotherly community. Lukács thought of this not just as a patriotic experience, but as a quasi-religious one. Simmel and Weber, who had diagnosed the isolation of modern man, provided the analytical categories now turned on them. Their temporary enjoyment of community brought about his loss of one. While these two affirmers of modern isolation basked in *Gemeinschaft*, Lukács, the seeker of community and guest from a wartime ally, declared himself an outsider.

Lukács's relationship to German culture underwent a rapid revaluation in 1914–15. On the eve of the war he had been making the traditions of middle-class German culture his own, working his way through the problematic of individual and society along lines laid down by Simmel and Weber. To be sure, he had always been a rebellious student of their work, but he had taken the tragedy of the modern condition as his starting point. Now he questioned the starting point, analyzing German culture in a new tone of disillusionment.

What "Germany" stood for emerged with remarkable clarity in Lukács's correspondence with Paul Ernst. According to Ernst the *Gemeinschaft* of 1914 had the peculiarity that the national community ws inseparable from the state. The true, inner Prussian conquest of Germany was taking place now that all Germans looked to the state as the highest realization of their nationality.[83] The new community was religious, thought Ernst, with the wartime state as the new German god, the ultimate outward realization of Germany's inner spirituality. He did not hesitate to identify it with the Third Age of Joachim of Fiore, the *drittes Reich* signifying the end of world history. Each individual fulfilled his *Persönlichkeit* in the state, the state realized its members' higher destiny. This was the conclusion to the promise of German philosophy, the idea of freedom become concrete in the world.[84] Lukács argued the opposite: the German worship of the state since Hegel was the "mortal sin" of German philosophy.[85] Its victory signified the collapse of freedom, for the state, as an objective structure, could only serve as an instrument, never as a substitute for direct human relationships. Their positions were strikingly similar to the ones taken up by Paulsen and Tönnies in the 1880s. Ernst, like Paulsen, put populism in the service of the state, while Lukács, like Tönnies, considered this the worst possible perversion of authentic community. The issues involved had taken on heightened urgency, however, under wartime conditions. Lukács feared that German victory over the Allies would result in the creation of a bureaucratic socialist regime, integrating the individual into a monstrous collective machinery.[86] On the other hand he shared the wartime belief of Ernst and thinkers like Weber, Troeltsch, and Simmel that whereas Germany's soul was endangered, the

West had no soul. If there was any hope of salvation, it had to come from elsewhere.[87]

Lukács made his journey from Central Europe to the East in a project begun shortly after the outbreak of war, the first part of which he published as *Theory of the Novel*. It analyzed the novel as the typical art form of bourgeois civilization, the pathological record of an "age of absolute sinfulness."[88] His critique of German culture culminated in an analysis of Goethe's novel, *Wilhelm Meister's Years of Apprenticeship*. Wilhelm Meister's apprenticeship begins in the theater; after years of wandering and adventure, he learns that the theater is not his true calling, but does find wisdom, friendship, and happiness, completed by his marriage to a noblewoman. For Lukács, *Wilhelm Meister* illustrated the paradoxes inherent in the novel as the literary genre that tried to show how modern man could realize his inner potentiality in a society made up of institutions and conventions devoid of meaning. Goethe balanced character and plot so that "a reconciliation between interiority and reality, although problematic, is nevertheless possible; that it has to be sought in hard struggles and dangerous adventures, yet is ultimately possible to achieve."[89] The hero can partly permeate society with his intentions, partly not; his education is a long process of uncertainty and struggle, of adventures, with no certain outcome, as he attempts to find an earthly home.[90] Lukács conceded the supreme tact of Goethe's handling of the balance between individual and society. But in his wartime mood of disgust toward bourgeois civilization, he accused Goethe of failing to bring the novel to a satisfactory conclusion and argued that this failure revealed the fundamental flaw of its bourgeois outlook. The novel only comes to a happy ending when Wilhelm is initiated into an order of freemasonlike friends who have secretly been guiding his education. ". . . The miraculous," commented Lukács, "becomes a mystification without hidden meaning, a strongly emphasized narrative element without real importance, a playful ornament without decorative grace."[91] Goethe's supposed retreat from realism to fantasy signified for Lukács the middle class's inability to give a cohesive literary account of its way of life, and all later novels, in his view, would fall short of this first experiment.[92] Actually, what Lukács objected to was not Goethe's fantasy, but his realistic belief that man always had to accept historical limitations and conventions as the condition of freedom. For Lukács, this was bourgeois ideology; the only acceptable "ending" was a world of completely dissolved personal boundaries and immediate *Gemeinschaft.*

This critique of the bourgeois hero was, by implication at least, an attack on Simmel as well. One of Simmel's most important essays examined the adventurer as an archetypal figure of modern society, who like *Wilhelm Meister* opened his life to the hazards of freedom. The adventurer might be destroyed by external circumstances—yet he felt guided by a cosmic destiny and like a gambler accepted the risk of failure in order to prove that he was actually at one with the total order of things. Precisely this element of gamble was reprehensible to Lukács; he sought a transparent world in which the meaning of things was evident on the surface of things.

Even before the war Lukács had discovered an alternative to German culture. In April 1911 he had written to Irma Seidler of his longing for solitude and dissatisfaction with the limits of communication between friends. But he had just encountered a different kind of life in the fiction of Dostoevsky: "For a long time I thought life consisted in this lack of inward harmony. Today I no longer believe that. To put it simply: read Dostoevsky and you will see what I mean. Now I see life as sharply and clearly as literature—and can't stand the form of life to which my whole psychological disposition condemns me."[93] After her death, he wrote an essay (which he showed to Marianne Weber before publishing) entitled "On the Poverty of Spirit," distinguishing a "first ethic" of conventions and a "second ethic" of saintliness. In the first ethic each individual had a limited set of obligations toward others, which could be defined by a general commandment, and could have a good conscience so long as he or she carried out the obligations imposed by that commandment. Such a commandment led to harmonious relationships between human beings who knew one another externally, each person regarding others as objective phenomena in a causally regulated world. Personal communication took place by means of external signs, from which one deduced the presence of other subjects; but this indirectly relayed intelligence did not change their status as objects.[94] As opposed to this first ethic, the saintly second ethic belonged to a chosen few with the calling to realize "goodness." Their behavior did not depend on a reading of signs because they had the power to see immediately into the soul of others and know their spiritual needs. Instead of performing duties limited by law, they served others. Their actions ignored the causal laws governing ordinary behavior. They did not calculate motives and consequences; they might cause disaster; they left consequences to God. The good flourished "beyond tragedy," which conformed to the logic of cause and effect; its masters were "gnostics of the deed" acting out of a visionary knowledge of a higher order; their works manifested "the descent of the Kingdom of God down to earth"; their life was "the true life, the vital life (*das lebendige Leben*)." The gnostics of goodness lived out the fanatical will to save someone even if this meant, in conventional terms, immorality. To do good was "to stay pure in sin, deceit, and horror (*Grausamkeit*)."[95]

Lukács's correspondence with Paul Ernst identified the ethic of convention with German culture. As for the second ethic, he saw the first prophetic signs of its realization in Russia.[96] Ernst recorded one of their conversations in a semifictional retelling: "It seemed to him [Lukács] that there was now the possibility of a higher development of mankind in the Russian Idea, and it would be the most terrible tragedy of the war if this development were cut off. Its beginnings were in its imaginative works, in Tolstoy and Dostoevsky."[97] *Theory of the Novel* concluded by turning to the Russian writers' vision of a postbourgeois world. Tolstoy, according to Lukács, looked beyond the novel with the help of insights won from the remnants of organic community in Russia. He criticized Tolstoy as he did all representatives of traditional community for nostalgia and dismissed his attempt at a return to the soil as artificial and unworkable.[98] The community of the future would be a social community among human beings, not a community binding man to nature. The real prophet of the new community appeared in the book's final paragraph: "It is in the words of Dostoevsky that this new world, remote from any struggle against what actually exists, is drawn for the first time simply as a seen reality."[99] After asking whether the new world would be born or would be crushed by the sterile power of the existing world, the essay abruptly broke off.[100]

Lukács originally planned *Theory of the Novel* as the introduction to a book on Dostoevsky. Recent scholarship has reconstructed Lukács's plan for the rest from extensive notes and outlines.[101] Lukács believed that Dostoevsky radically eliminated objective structures as determinants of his characters' behavior. Normal social etiquette dissolved in the criminal and marginal milieus of his stories, leaving men and women to act out their destinies in direct confrontation with one another. The Western hero was an adventurer who learned about his individual soul by running up against the objective resistance of other persons and things. Dostoevsky's characters discovered through dialogue that their essential self was their community with others, and through others with God.[102]

Lukács's social and aesthetic critique of Western civilization was ultimately a *religious* critique that aspired to a new form of religious community. His notes contrasted the German idea of the individual soul in direct relationship to God and isolated in the world with the Russian idea of the soul in a divinely inspired community.[103] This opposition in turn fit into the larger pattern of two types of Christian civilization: the triumph of the objective spirit in the Western church and state versus the authentic Christianity of the Sermon on the Mount, preserved in Eastern Orthodoxy. The institutionalized guardian of grace erected by Paul and Augustine was in Lukács's eyes the embodiment of depravity, the cunning victory of Satan, for it placed spirituality in the service of power and gave the institutional bearer of power religious sanction.[104] The ethical code of this church was Lukács's first ethic, a minimum of correct behavior as the condition for salvation. Lukács argued that Luther had deepened the depravity by extending religious sanction from church to state, turning the state itself into a churchlike institution with metaphysical sanction, in which man fulfilled his ethical nature through objectively defined service.[105] By contrast, the authentic ethic of Jesus was the same as Lukács's second ethic, whose imperative was not the performance of abstract duty, but of concrete good deeds.

Lukács's religious critique of Western civilization resembled Troeltsch's in *The Social Teachings*. This was no accident, since he knew Troeltsch's work and had sent him a copy of *Soul and Form*. Troeltsch's reply in August 1912 praised Lukács's striving toward a new cultural unity amid the decaying forms of their time (he found the chapter on Storm particularly novel and convincing).[106] Lukács included a summary and analysis of *The Social Teachings* in his Dostoevsky notes. His critique of Catholicism closely followed Troeltsch's views on objectification of the sacred in general and his dislike of Catholicism in particular. His view that Luther represented a deepening rather than a break with Catholicism's objective spirit was the same as Troeltsch's. To seek a mystical community beyond church and sect, too, was to follow Troeltsch's prescription. Where Lukács differed was in seeking the cultural source of that mysticism outside Central Europe. While Troeltsch developed a new insistence on Germany's spiritual mission, Lukács abandoned it for Dostoevsky's vision of a non-Western idea of community. He considered Dostoevsky's fiction the prophecy of a new age: just as German literature a century earlier had intuitively imagined the bourgeois world systematized in German Idealism, argued Lukács, so Dostoevsky visualized a coming spiritual reality awaiting its philosopher.[107]

The Dostoevsky project caused considerable strain in Lukács's relationship to Weber, who convinced a journal editor to publish *Theory of the Novel* intact, but expressed alarm over Lukács's sudden abandonment of his aesthetics manuscript for the Dostoevsky project. Because this sudden change in plans seemed to throw doubt on Lukács's willingness to write a work of systematic philosophy, Weber wrote that he "hated this work and hate[s] it still."[108] The project's contents as well as its significance for his academic future disturbed Weber, as Lukács knew; after Weber had objected to the "metaphysical beginning," Lukács expressed his hope that the second, more empirical part would make a better impression on him.[109] Yet if the second part's method was more concrete, its message was a complete inversion of Weber's outlook, for while Lukács had moved spiritually from the West to Russia, Weber had studied the Eastern alternative only to reaffirm his loyalty to the West.

Fascination with Russian politics and culture was not foreign
to Weber, who learned the language in order to be able to follow the revolutionary events of 1905 in the Russian press.[110] He
linked the politics of Russia's radical democrats to their peculiar
religiosity in an essay of 1906: "The absolute repudiation of the
'ethic of success' in the political sphere signifies here: only the
unconditional ethical commandment has any validity as a guide
to positive action; there is only the possibility of the struggle for
right *or* holy self-denial."[111] Weber's "ethic of success" and "unconditional ethical commandment" corresponded to Lukács's
first and second ethics, but with reverse value judgments, for
although he respected the sincerity of ethical absolutists such
as the Russian democrats, he abhorred the practical consequences of their political behavior. "Politics as a Calling" singled
out Dostoevsky's heroes as representatives of the saintly second
ethic he termed *Gesinnungsethik* ("ethic of conviction") and contrasted to *Verantwortungsethik* ("ethic of responsibility").[112] In
contrast to the Dostoevskian politics of irresponsibility, the politics of responsibility only took an absolute leap of conviction
after going through the discipline of weighing the consequences of one's actions. The mature politician, wrote Weber,
"acts by following an ethic of responsibility and somewhere he
reaches the point where he says: 'Here I stand; I can do no
other.'"[113] Thus Weber not only rejected Dostoevsky, but
turned for expression of his political ethic to Luther, a source
now most alien to Lukács. And while Lukács turned East in
hope of salvation—first religious, later political—from the
West, Weber's political thinking became profoundly anti-
Russian as his belief grew that the land hunger of the peasants,
the nationalism of the upper classes, and the government's
need for external successes would push Russia's armies toward
German soil.[114]

After returning to Budapest in 1915 to undergo examination
for military service (he was declared unfit and given a job in the
censorship office), Lukács became the leader of an intellectual
gathering called the Sunday Circle. Its members paid scant attention to contemporary politics and viewed the crisis of contemporary civilization primarily as cultural and spiritual.[115]

Some of Lukács's friends were therefore surprised when the former aesthete accepted Bela Kun's invitation in late 1918 to join the Communist Party.[116] Doing so meant accepting an invitation to break with the dilemmas of bourgeois culture and act on the kind of messianic politics he had been discussing in his correspondence with Paul Ernst. Between December 1918 and February 1919, he took part in public discussions organized by the Party at the University of Budapest, joined the editorial staff of its journal, *Internationale*, and became a member of the Central Committee's subcommittee for students and working youth.[117] After Bela Kun came to power as leader of the Hungarian Commune on 21 March, Lukács was appointed Deputy People's Commissar of Culture and Educational Affairs, involved in creating a new theater, reorganizing the educational system, and setting up public support of writers.[118] By July, a mixture of internal opposition and Western pressure toppled the Kun government. Admiral Horthy, Kun's counter-revolutionary successor, imprisoned and killed thousands of its supporters, and Lukács spent two months in hiding before fleeing to Vienna.

During and after the revolution, Lukács went through a brief period of adherence to unmitigated *Gesinnungsethik*. The political pieces published in May 1919 as *Tactics and Ethics* regarded the working class's collective will as a flame that could fuse ethics and activity, means and ends, socialism and organization, as long as its leaders allowed it to flare up in all its natural purity. Even after the collapse of the Hungarian revolution Lukács refused to tolerate limits on activism, in 1921 supporting a controversial strike by German miners in Saxony that had faint prospects for success but seemed desirable to him as a demonstration of revolutionary ardor. He justified the strike even after its calamitous failure in March, but found himself in the minority at the July meeting of the Comintern. This marked the end of the period in which ethics took absolute priority over tactics.[119] The dying down of revolutionary movement throughout Europe confronted him in history with a problem he had often addressed in literature: the victory of external forms over life.

History and Class Consciousness

History and Class Consciousness, completed by Lukács in Vienna at the end of 1922, attempted to rethink the sociological and ethical categories of his previous work and arrive at a synthesis that could comprehend this post-revolutionary situation. In one sense, it represented a beginning; Lukács argued as a Marxist working his way through the Hegelian foundations of Marx's thought. But it also documented continuities with his sociological training, incorporating the historical movement adumbrated in their work from *Gemeinschaft* to *Gesellschaft* and beyond to a reborn socialist community.

"Reification and the Consciousness of the Proletariat," the book's central essay, gave the name reification to the deadened forms of human activity in bourgeois society. The transformation of living relationships into hardened things had its origins in the structure of the commodity as defined by Marx. During the evolution from the simplest isolated exchanges to a market economy, the human activity underlying production disappeared and natural economic laws seemed to take its place. In the early stages of capitalism it was the objects of production and exchange that took on this appearance of naturalness. In the advanced stages of capitalism, such as Lukács believed his own time had reached, reification pervaded every aspect of culture. Lukács analyzed the historical emergence of reification within the sociological schema: as part of the transition from community to society, in which the organic relationship between worker and product broke down and was replaced by a partial, mechanical relationship of isolated individuals. As in his essay on Storm, Lukács argued that the relationship between craftsman and artifact that had once united all the members of the community into a whole disintegrated under the impact of capitalism.[120] The qualitative, traditional process of production got broken down into discrete, quantifiable parts that the capitalist could measure and synthesize according to plan. This Weberian rationalization of the economy destroyed the worker's will and turned him into a mechanical instrument, a passive being, who, according to Lukács, faced a world of mechanical processes, indifferent to his wishes and impervious to his intervention.[121]

Lukács could find many of the insights for his theory of reification in the writings of Simmel and Weber. His footnotes acknowledged his ample use of Weber's ideas, and he specifically mentioned Simmel's *The Philosophy of Money* as a phenomenology of reified society.[122] But the two bourgeois sociologists believed that objective culture or bureaucratization, the conceptual forerunners of reification, would eventuate in either a heroic individualism or irreversible despiritualization of modern man. Simmel pointed to *Vornehmheit* and Weber to charisma as sources of creativity that might endure, while in their more pessimistic moods, Simmel feared an imbalance of objective over subjective culture, Weber the prospect of total bureaucratization. Both conceived of *Persönlichkeit* as a constantly diminishing inner space. Lukács imagined the relationship between individual and society differently. There was no private space left for preserving a last remnant of pure *Persönlichkeit*, for reification had no subjective limits. Indeed German sociology itself, he argued, documented how completely reification pervaded bourgeois consciousness before the war, mesmerizing its makers into seeing the humanly fabricated world as a sociological fate, which they could grasp only through a process of abstraction removed from the specific, historical, qualitative dimension of social relationships.[123] Bourgeois science reproduced the general logic of bourgeois society in accepting the given order of things and manipulating it to one's particular advantage.

Lukács tried to transcend the conflict between individual autonomy and social laws by turning from middle-class thought to the consciousness of the proletariat. The worker could not maintain the illusion of freedom within the existing social system because his subjectivity had been so radically estranged. He *was* a commodity. "Thus for the worker the reified character of the immediate manifestations of capitalist society receives the most extreme definition possible. . . . But this very fact forces him to surpass the immediacy of his condition."[124] At this point, the process of emancipation began. With the other members of his class and the party embodying its most advanced consciousness, he would begin to comprehend his situation in a historical development that the working class's own labor had brought into existence. The very moment of absolute denial of his humanity was the first stage of seeing his own activity beneath the seeming impermeability of bourgeois society.

Inconspicuous, half-hidden, yet a powerful presence from Lukács's past—the quest for *das Leben* inspired the essay. Lukács announced it in the first paragraph while writing about the centrality of commodity-structure to Marx's analysis of capitalism: the commodity problem, he wrote, had to be seen not as an isolated problem, or the central problem of economics as an isolated discipline, "but appears as the central, structural problem of capitalist society in all its life expressions (*Lebensäusserungen*)."[125] Elsewhere Lukács spoke of the inability of Kantian (read: bourgeois) reason to fill its purely formal definition of freedom *mit lebendigem Leben* (a phrase going back to "On the Poverty of Spirit"),[126] of the intensive objectification of life in capitalist society,[127] and of the revolutionary promise of transcendence of reification not just in thought but also in the vital forms of society (*Lebensformen der Gesellschaft*).[128] So long, Lukács argued, as a class still maintained a small inner measure of freedom, as the bourgeoisie did, it could ignore its own alienation. Only the poor in spirit could redeem society. The proletariat was the revolutionary class of history as the crucified class of history, transcending all preceding social relationships because it had lost its life in them.

We can only read this against Lukács's stated intentions, for *History and Class Consciousness* tried to bury Lukács's religious past. Christianity, he argued, polarized the human condition, dividing it between spiritual inwardness and immobile material reality. Either its social ethic left things of this world untouched and in the hands of secular authority, or it selected a chosen few for sainthood while leaving the rest of mankind without means of redemption.[129] This disavowal of religion put him sharply at odds with Ernst Bloch, who also made a commitment to Marxism and political revolution during the war, but tried to synthesize these allegiances with romantic and mystical speculation. In *Geist der Utopie*, first published in 1918, Bloch expressed this marriage of materialism and idealism in Expressionist dithyrambs diverging in style no less than in substance from the *Neue Sachlichkeit* of Lukács's prose. Like Lukács, Bloch seized on the revolutionary will as the mainspring of the revolutionary process, but in contrast to Lukács, he argued that this will originated outside society, drawing on the same transcendent source as the faith of all the revolutionary heretics, world-storming chiliasts, and mystical messiahs of Judeo-Christian history.[130] *Thomas Münzer*, published in 1921, held up the Reformation heretic as the great German exemplar of this will to build a new Jerusalem on earth, a countertradition to the conservative tradition of Luther and a spiritual ancestor of the Revolution of 1918–19.[131] Another significant difference between the two men was that Bloch, like Lukács, felt attracted to Russian messianism, but at this time did not lose sight of Western democratic values. His political journalism of 1917–18 affirmed the ideals of the French Revolution as a living inheritance, applauded Wilson's program for self-determination of European nationalities, and welcomed American help to defeat German militarism.[132] Both Bloch and Lukács wished to unite the utopian hopes of the past with political revolution, but Bloch thought that this could be done with real attention to the strands of living history that would enter into and be preserved in it.

History and Class Consciousness belittled Bloch's Münzer as a hapless enthusiast whose example was useless for the present because it lacked the dialectical method that alone could transform the external word.[133] Bloch replied in a masterful review of Lukác's book that repudiated its idea of society as immanent totality: "Beyond just the social conquest of still-hidden social man, the artistic, religious, metaphysical conquest of the secret transcendental man belongs to the thought of man's Being, of a *new* depth dimension of Being."[134] With these words Bloch put his finger on the irremediable flaw in Lukács's intention: by reducing human beings to an immanent set of social relations, he violated their complexity. Yet as Bloch added, Lukács did not stay within his self-set social limits.[135] The moment of revolt, when the proletariat arose to create a human world, remained a mystery, spontaneous and free within a totally determined world. Lukács's insistence on the absolute reification of the proletariat unconsciously acknowledged that its redemption originated beyond the world of things. By finding its truth in the moment of its absolute alienation, Lukács conveyed an unabated longing for transcendence of man's social condition: the hope that accompanied German sociology throughout its history and reached its purest expression in his work.

Epilogue: The Politics of German Sociology

Lukács was almost immediately dissatisfied with the utopianism of *History and Class Consciousness* and turned toward resolute acceptance of the limits that fate, in the form of history, sets to human endeavor. His essays of the later twenties and his biography of the young Hegel affirmed the wisdom he himself had condemned just a few years before of learning to live within fixed historical conditions. After embracing one extreme possibility of the sociological tradition, he rediscovered the other. Nor was this the end of his story. To the end of his life he alternated between loyalty to the Soviet system and messianic belief in the imminence of authentic socialism.

Critics of the German sociological tradition can point to Lukács as the extreme example of its rejection of the conditionality of day-to-day political life. The charge is not wholly unjustified. One can multiply the examples of negation, distance, and critique in the sociologists' attitude toward parliamentary politics before 1914. Tönnies displayed anarchic impatience with the grubbiness of Imperial politics in the 1870s and 1880s; Troeltsch tried to formulate a Christian politics that would transcend existing party divisions; after the 1890s Weber wrote little on domestic politics, and his conception of charismatic leadership was a radical departure from the wearying business of consensus building in Germany; Simmel's thought underwent a striking aestheticization after the turn of the century; Lukács repudiated the entire existing political order. *Gemeinschaft* would seem to have provided them with a prepolitical utopia, a merging of wills that they could never expect to materialize but nonetheless used to criticize the Wilhelmine state. At crucial moments their behavior bore out this critique, as when Troeltsch, Weber, and Simmel celebrated a magical realization of *Gemeinschaft* after the outbreak of World War I, Lukács after the outbreak of the Hungarian Revolution.

Yet we need to beware of identifying the sociologists' behavior at these crucial moments too completely with their theorizing. Hard-headed politicians and thinkers of different political perspectives shared the illusion of *Gemeinschaft* in 1914, and experienced revolutionaries were no better able than Lukács to foresee the limits of revolution. Dissatisfaction with the fragmentation of modern society was a widespread feeling in prewar Europe; the sociologists struggled to analyze it in ways that would deepen their grasp of contemporary politics. None of them completely absented himself from politics before the war, and each seized the opportunities for meaningful action that came his way. If the existing political parties did not satisfy them, they found other ways of participating in Wilhelmine public life, such as Tönnies's involvement in the Ethical Society, Troeltsch's in university and church affairs, and Weber's reports on the Russian Revolution of 1904–05. After 1914, all of them plunged into wartime and postwar politics. They wrote and acted with acute sensitivity to the limits imposed by social structures and the conditionality of political action, usually raising the level of political discourse in Germany when they contributed to it.

Interpreters do them another kind of injustice in praising them for neutral descriptions of modern society while ignoring their speculations on possible alternatives to it. Weber scholars have been especially tempted to do so, but apologists for Lukács, too, beginning with the later Lukács himself, have presented his early development as a search for scientific objectivity that ended in his adherence to Marxism. To treat them in this way is to ignore the visionary daring that deserves our attention precisely because they tested it against empirical social conditions. Of course, they and the other sociologists expressed their hopes cautiously, and we need to listen closely to hear them. Often hidden, these tended to surface in association with a preferred religious tradition: for Tönnies, the "Third Age" of Joachim; for Troeltsch and Simmel, German mysticism; for Weber, the voluntary associational life of ascetic Protestantism;

for Lukács, Russian mysticism. A common aspiration was not entirely absent from these highly distinct and personal choices. All were aware that *Gemeinschaft* in the past had imposed external bonds of a kind that none wished for humanity's future. A community compatible with human dignity would have to be a community of freely interacting individuals. Tönnies believed this no less than Troeltsch and Simmel, Lukács no less than Weber.

Differences remain. This book's utopias do not culminate in a final image of Utopia. What they yield is not that ultimate synthesis of positions that eludes intellectuals like the philosopher's stone, but a language for criticizing society. Utopias are experiments. Playthings of the imagination, they become deadly when they lose all their playfulness; good places, they remain no place because they change the moment we attempt to translate them into reality; expressions of a will to change, they harden into plans for domination when they lose their tentativeness. At its best, German sociology used them to test society's limits for the sake of an uncertain future. That is more realistic than any purely tragic perspective, since history, unlike theater, has no predetermined parts and no script for an ending.

Abbreviations

Arch. f. Sozialwiss. = *Archiv für Sozialwissenschaft und Sozialpolitik.*

Ästhetik und Soziologie = Hannes Böhringer and Karlfried Gründer, eds., *Ästhetik und Soziologie um die Jahrhundertwende. Georg Simmel* (Frankfurt am Main, 1976).

Biography = Marianne Weber, *Max Weber: A Biography* (1926; New York, 1975).

Briefwechsel = Olaf Klose, E. G. Jacoby, and Irma Fischer, eds., *Ferdinand Tönnies-Friedrich Paulsen. Briefwechsel 1876–1908* (Kiel, 1961).

Buch des Dankes = Kurt Gassen and Michael Landmann, eds., *Buch des Dankes an Georg Simmel. Briefe, Erinnerungen, Bibliographie. Zu seinem 100. Geburtstag am 1. März 1958* (Berlin, 1958).

Community and Society = Ferdinand Tönnies, *Community and Society (Gemeinschaft und Gesellschaft)*, transl. Charles P. Loomis (1887; New York, 1963).

Correspondence = Georg Lukács, *Selected Correspondence 1902–1920*, ed. Judith Marcus and Zoltán Tar (New York, 1986).

DGS Akten = Akten der Deutschen Gesellschaft für Soziologie, Tönnies-Nachlass, Schleswig-Holsteinische Landesbibliothek.

Dokumente einer Freundschaft = Karl August Kutzbach, ed., *Paul Ernst und Georg Lukács. Dokumente einer Freundschaft* (Emsdetten, 1974).

Dramengeschichte = Georg Lukács, *Entwicklungsgeschichte des modernen Dramas,* ed. Frank Benseler (1911; Darmstadt und Neuwied, 1981).

Economy and Society = Max Weber, *Economy and Society,* ed. Guenther Roth and Claus Wittich (1921; New York, 1968).

From Max Weber = Max Weber, *From Max Weber: Essays in Sociology,* ed. Hans Gerth and C. Wright Mills (New York, 1958).

Gemeinschaft und Gesellschaft = Ferdinand Tönnies, *Gemeinschaft und Gesellschaft. Grundbegriffe der reinen Soziologie* (1887; Darmstadt, 1979).

Gesammelte Schriften I–IV = Ernst Troeltsch, *Gesammelte Schriften,* vol. I: *Die Soziallehren der christlichen Kirchen und Gruppen* (Tübingen, 1912); vol. II: *Zur religiösen Lage, Religionsphilosophie und Ethik* (Tübingen, 1913); vol. III: *Der Historismus und seine Probleme. Erstes Buch: Das logische Problem der Geschichtsphilosophie* (Tübingen, 1922); vol IV: *Aufsätze zur Geistesgeschichte und Religionssoziologie,* ed. Hans Baron (Tübingen, 1925).

Individuum und Freiheit = Georg Simmel, *Das Individuum und die Freiheit. Essais* (Berlin, 1984).

KZSS = *Kölner Zeitschrift für Soziologie und Sozialpsychologie.*

Lebenserinnerungen = Ferdinand Tönnies, "Lebenserinnerungen aus dem Jahre 1935 an Kindheit, Schulzeit, Studium und erste Dozentenzeit (1855–1894)," ed. Rainer Polley, in *Zeitschrift der Gesellschaft für Schleswig-Holsteinische Geschichte* CV (1980), 187–227.

Max Weber and German Politics = Wolfgang Mommsen, *Max Weber and German Politics, 1870–1920* (1959, 1974; Chicago and London, 1984).

Philosophische Kultur = Georg Simmel, *Philosophische Kultur. Über das Abenteuer, die Geschlechter und die Krise der Moderne— Gesammelte Essais* (1911; Berlin, 1983).

The Philosophy of Money = Georg Simmel, *The Philosophy of Money,* transl. Tom Bottomore and David Frisby (1900; London, Henley and Boston, 1978).

Protestant Ethic = Max Weber, *The Protestant Ethic and the Spirit of Capitalism*, transl. Talcott Parsons (New York, 1958).

Prot. Ethik = Max Weber, *Die protestantische Ethik I. Eine Aufsatzsammlung*, ed. Johannes Winckelmann (Gütersloh, 1981).

Prot. Ethik 1904 = Max Weber, "Die protestantische Ethik und der 'Geist' des Kapitalismus. I. Das Problem," in *Arch. f. Sozialwiss.* XX (1904), 1–54.

Prot. Ethik 1905 = Max Weber, "Die protestantische Ethik und der 'Geist' des Kapitalismus. II. Die Berufsidee des Asketischen Protestantismus," in *Arch. f. Sozialwiss.* XXI (1905), 1–110.

Prot. Ethik Kritiken = Max Weber, *Die protestantische Ethik II. Kritiken und Antikritiken* (Gütersloh, 1981).

Religion and Industrial Society = Harry Liebersohn, *Religion and Industrial Society: The Protestant Social Congress in Wilhelmine Germany* (Transactions of the American Philosophical Society LXXVI/6, Philadelphia, 1986).

Selbstdarstellung = Ferdinand Tönnies, "Selbstdarstellung," in *Die Philosophie der Gegenwart in Selbstdarstellungen*, ed. Raymund Schmidt, vol. III (Leipzig, 1922), 199–236.

Simmel: Sociologist and European = Peter Lawrence, ed., *Georg Simmel: Sociologist and European* (Sunbury-on-Thames, 1976).

Soziologie = Georg Simmel, *Soziologie. Untersuchungen über die Formen der Vergesellschaftung* (1908; Berlin, 1968).

Theory of the Novel = Georg Lukács, *The Theory of the Novel: A Historico-Philosophical Essay on the Forms of Great Epic Literature*, transl. Anna Bostock (1920; Cambridge, Mass., 1971).

Tönnies Papers = Ferdinand Tönnies Nachlass, Schleswig-Holsteinische Landesbibliothek, Kiel.

Troeltsch-Bousset = "Ernst Troeltsch. Briefe aus der Heidelberger Zeit an Wilhelm Bousset 1894–1914," ed. Erika Dinkler-von Schubert, in *Heidelberger Jahrbücher* XX (1976), 19–52.

Über soziale Differenzierung = Georg Simmel, *Über soziale Differenzierung. Soziologische und Psychologische Untersuchungen* (1966; Leipzig, 1890).

200

Abbreviations

Verh. DGS I and II = *Verhandlungen des deutschen Soziologentages*
I (19.–22. Oktober 1910, Frankfurt am Main) and II (20.–22.
Oktober 1912, Berlin) (1969, Frankfurt am Main).

Werk und Person = Eduard Baumgarten, ed., *Max Weber. Werk
und Person* (Tübingen, 1964).

Notes

Chapter 1

1. *Protestant Ethic*, 181. I have added the italics to make the translation conform to Weber's original text. I have also corrected Parsons's erroneous placing of the first quotation mark behind the word "saint." Cf. *Prot. Ethik*, 188.

2. *Protestant Ethic*, 181.

3. For some recent perspectives on fate and tragedy in German sociology, see Kurt Lenk, "Das tragische Bewusstsein in der deutschen Soziologie," in KZSS XVI (1964), 257–287; Herbert Marcuse, "Industrialization and Capitalism," and the ensuing debate, in Otto Stammer, ed., *Max Weber and Sociology Today*, especially the remarks by Benjamin Nelson, 161–171, and Marcuse's reply, 186; Arthur Mitzman, *The Iron Cage: An Historical Interpretation of Max Weber* (New York, 1969); Mitzman, *Sociology and Estrangement: Three Sociologists of Imperial Germany* (New York, 1973); Geoffrey Hawthorn, *Enlightenment and Despair: A History of Sociology* (Cambridge and New York, 1976), 175–190; Bryan S. Turner, *For Weber: Essays on the Sociology of Fate* (Boston, London and Henley, 1981); Reinhard Bendix, *Force, Fate, and Freedom: On Historical Sociology* (Berkeley, 1984); and the editors' introduction to *Max Weber's Political Sociology: A Pessimistic Vision of a Rationalized World*, ed. Ronald M. Glassman and Vatro Murvar (Westport, Conn., and London, England, 1984), 3–11.

4. See Michael Löwy, *Georg Lukács—from Romanticism to Bolshevism* (London, 1979); Andrew Arato and Paul Breines, *The Young Lukács and the Origins of Western Marxism* (New York, 1979); Lee Congdon, *The Young Lukács* (Chapel Hill, 1983); and Mary Gluck, *Georg Lukács and His Generation 1900–1918* (Cambridge, Mass., 1985).

5. Cf. Raymond Williams, *Modern Tragedy* (Stanford, 1966), 38–42; and T. J. Clark, *The Painting of Modern Life: Paris in the Art of Manet and His Followers* (New York, 1984), 15.

6. *Protestant Ethic*, 182.

7. Cf. Karl Mannheim, *Ideology and Utopia: An Introduction to the Sociology of Knowledge* (New York, 1936). Colin Loader, *The Intellectual Development of Karl Mannheim* (Cambridge and New York, 1985), pays special attention to the place of utopia in Mannheim's thought and contains a rich discussion of his relationship to Wilhelmine sociology. See also David Kettler, Volker Meja, and Nico Stehr, *Karl Mannheim* (New York, 1984). On

Mannheim's Hungarian background and early relationship to Lukács, see Gluck, *Georg Lukács and His Generation;* and Éva Karádi and Erzsébet Vezér, eds., *Georg Lukács, Karl Mannheim und der Sonntagskreis* (Frankfurt am Main, 1985).

8. On the spatial localization of early modern utopias, see Wilhelm Vosskamp, "Einleitung," in *Utopieforschung. Interdisziplinäre Studien zur neuzeitlichen Utopie* vol. I (Frankfurt am Main, 1985), 5–7.

9. Cf. Walter Benjamin, "Goethes Wahlverwandtschaften," in *Gesammelte Schriften* vol. I/ 1 (1924–25; Frankfurt am Main, 1974), 123–201; idem, *The Origins of German Tragic Drama* (1928; London, 1977); idem, "Theses on the Philosophy of History" (1940), in *Illuminations,* ed. Hannah Arendt (New York, 1969), 253–264; Ernst Bloch, *Geist der Utopie* (1918; Frankfurt am Main, 1971); and idem, *Thomas Münzer als Theologe der Revolution* (1921; Frankfurt am Main, 1969).
  A parallel case has long been argued, and recently reasserted, for the influence of Protestantism on American social thought. Cf. Arthur J. Vidich and Stanford M. Lyman, *American Sociology: Worldly Rejections of Religion and Their Directions* (New Haven, 1985); and Bruce Kuklick, *Churchmen and Philosophers: From Jonathan Edwards to John Dewey* (New Haven, 1985).

10. Art historians, however, have noted the religious and occult influences on Expressionism and the Bauhaus. See Rose-Carol Washton Long, "Expressionism, Abstraction, and the Search for Utopia in Germany," in *The Spiritual in Art: Abstract Painting, 1890–1985* exh. cat. (Los Angeles, 1986), 201–217.

11. John Stuart Mill's *Autobiography* (1873; Boston, 1969) uses the phrase "age of transition" in a well-known passage praising Saint-Simon's and Comte's philosophy of history. Cf. Frank Manuel, *The Prophets of Paris* (Cambridge, Mass., 1962), 274–287, on Comte's search for sociological order. On Spencer see David Wiltshire, *The Social and Political Thought of Herbert Spencer* (Oxford and New York, 1978), 235–242. Steve Fenton, Robert Reiner, and Ian Hamnett's *Durkheim and Modern Sociology* (Cambridge and New York, 1984), includes a thoughtful evaluation of Durkheim's evolutionary optimism in *The Division of Labor* and how it was modified in his later work.

12. On the separation of the working-class movement from the middle-class state, see Werner Conze and Dieter Groh, *Die Arbeiterbewegung in der nationalen Bewegung. Die deutsche Sozialdemokratie vor, während, und nach der Reichsgründung* (Stuttgart, 1966).

13. See Fritz K. Ringer, *The Decline of the German Mandarins: The German Academic Community, 1890–1933* (Cambridge, Mass., 1969); James C. Albisetti, *Secondary School Reform in Imperial Germany* (Princeton, 1983); Charles E. McClelland, *State, Society and University in Germany, 1700–1914* (Cambridge and New York, 1980); Werner Conze and Jürgen Kocka, eds., *Bildungsbürgertum im 19. Jahrhundert. Bildungssystem und Professionalisierung in internationalen Vergleichen* (Stuttgart, 1984); and the excellent monograph by Reinhard Riese, *Die Hochschule auf dem Wege zum wissenschaftlichen Grossbetrieb. Die Universität Heidelberg und das badische Hochschulwesen, 1860–1914* (Stuttgart, 1977).

14. Quoted in Riese, *Die Hochschule auf dem Wege zum wissenschaftlichen Grossbetrieb,* 13.

15. See Peter Paret, *The Berlin Secession: Modernism and Its Enemies in Imperial Germany* (Cambridge, Mass., 1980); and Peter Jelavich, *Munich and Theatrical Modernism: Politics, Playwriting, and Performance, 1890–1914* (Cambridge, Mass., 1985).

16. Most works dealing with the history of the Protestant church concentrate on the minority of Germans sympathetic to it. John E. Groh, *Nineteenth-Century German Prot-*

estantism: The Church as Social Model (Washington, D.C., 1982), is a knowledgeable and unusually critical survey of the church's troubled relationship to modern society.

17. Gerald L. Soliday, *A Community in Conflict: Frankfurt Society in the Seventeenth and Early Eighteenth Centuries* (Hanover, N.H., 1974), offers a subtle analysis of how much oppression and conflict are compatible with "community." While Tönnies's concept of *Gemeinschaft* had great pioneering value, it contains an irreducible streak of romanticism and does not do justice to the complexity of historical European communities. See Manfred Riedel's trenchant critique, "Gemeinschaft, Gesellschaft," in *Geschichtliche Grundbegriffe. Historisches Lexikon zur politisch-sozialen Sprache in Deutschland*, vol. II, ed. Otto Brunner, Werner Conze, and Reinhart Koselleck (Stuttgart, 1975), 801–832.

18. Tönnies's usage of *Gesellschaft* was equally ambiguous: it referred either to an ideal type or to historical instances of a voluntary, contractual social order. "Society" is an adequate translation but will occasionally have to serve as the generic term as well when "social order," covering both *Gemeinschaft* and *Gesellschaft*, is too ungainly. "Modern society" will refer to historical instances of *Gesellschaft*.

19. See Mack Walker, *German Home Towns* (Ithaca and London, 1971), ch. 12.

20. See Terry N. Clark, *Prophets and Patrons: The French University and the Emergence of the Social Sciences* (Cambridge, 1973); and Philippe Besnard, ed., *The Sociological Domain: The Durkheimians and the Founding of French Sociology* (Cambridge and New York, 1983).

21. Some of the more important books on German sociology are cited in n.3. From the older literature, Raymond Aron, *German Sociology*, transl. Mary and Thomas Bottomore (1936; New York, 1979), is still rewarding reading. Dirk Käsler, *Die frühe deutsche Soziologie 1909 bis 1934 und ihre Entstehungs-Milieus. Eine wissenschaftssoziologische Untersuchung* (Opladen, 1984), surveys the literature on the subject and attempts to quantify the history of German sociology. Käsler, ed., *Klassiker des soziologischen Denkens.* 2 vols. (Munich, 1976), and Wolf Lepenies, ed., *Geschichte der Soziologie. Studien zur kognitiven, sozialen und historischen Identität einer Disziplin*, 4 vols. (Frankfurt am Main, 1981), contain valuable contributions on German sociology and its counterparts elsewhere in Europe and America. On the empirical tradition, see Anthony Oberschall, *Empirical Social Research in Germany, 1848–1914* (New York, 1965). On German sociology after 1918, see M. Rainer Lepsius, ed., *Soziologie in Deutschland und Österreich 1918–1945. Materialien zur Entwicklung, Emigration und Wirkungsgeschichte* (Opladen, 1981).

22. The two most important examples are Talcott Parsons, *The Structure of Social Action: A Study in Social Theory with Special Reference to a Recent Group of European Writers* (New York, 1968), and Parsons's edition of *The Protestant Ethic.* Parsons canonized Weber's work for American social science only by dehistoricizing and imposing deadening restrictions on interpretation of it. For two critiques by sociologists, see Robert W. Friedrichs, *A Sociology of Sociology* (New York, 1970), and Alvin W. Gouldner, *The Coming Crisis of Western Sociology* (New York and London, 1970).

23. Cf. Ringer, *Decline of the German Mandarins.*

24. Cf. Arthur Mitzman, *Sociology and Estrangement: Three Sociologists of Imperial Germany* (New York, 1973).

25. Wilhelm Hennis has made this point for Max Weber in *Max Webers Fragestellung. Studien zur Biographie des Werks* (Tübingen, 1987), ch. 1—translated as "Max Weber's 'Central Question,'" in *Economy and Society* XII (1983), 135–180.

26. Wolf Lepenies, *Die drei Kulturen. Soziologie zwischen Literatur und Wissenschaft* (Munich and Vienna, 1985), merits special mention for its portrayal of how sociology and literature have carried on a semiillicit, mutually enriching commerce since Comte invented the science of society, a chapter in the history of smuggled ideas he follows through France, England, and Germany. Less persuasive is Lepenies's belief that sociology represents the party of progress, in conflict with another party of reaction during the nineteenth and twentieth centuries. Comte's attraction to Catholicism, John Stuart Mill's to Romanticism, and Weber's to Puritanism are evidence of a more complex relationship to the past. The spiritual impoverishment of modern society, not its self-sufficiency, attracted them to forms of ritual, poetry, and religion at odds with the nineteenth century's utilitarian culture.

Chapter 2

1. Tönnies to Paulsen, 21 Feb. 1887, in *Briefwechsel*, 230.

2. Herbert Blunt in *Mind* L (1888), 143; Emile Durkheim in *Revue Philosophique* XXVII (1889), 416–422, transl. in Werner J. Cahnman, ed., *Ferdinand Tönnies: A New Evaluation—Essays and Documents* (Leiden, 1973), 240–247; and Gustav Schmoller in *Schmollers Jahrbuch* XII (1888), 327–329. See also Friedrich Paulsen in *Vierteljahrsschrift für wissenschaftliche Philosophie* XII (1888), 111–119; Ludwig Gumplowicz in *Deutsche Literaturzeitung* IX (1888), 132–140; and Rudolf Stammler, review reprinted in *Rechtsphilosophische Abhandlungen und Vorträge*, vol. I (Aalen 1970), 43–48.

3. Durkheim, review in *Revue Philosophique*, 421–422.

4. Schmoller, review in *Schm. Jahrb.*, 329.

5. Paulsen, review in *Viert. f. wiss. Phil.*, 117.

6. For biographical details see E. G. Jacoby, *Die moderne Gesellschaft im sozialwissenschaftlichen Denken von Ferdinand Tönnies. Eine biographische Einführung* (Stuttgart, 1971), 29–114, as well as Lebenserinnerungen and Selbstdarstellung. For a biographical interpretation in English complementing the one offered here, see Mitzman, *Sociology and Estrangement*, part II.

7. See the reviews by K. Marcard in *Die Hilfe* XLIV (1912), 700–701; Eduard Rosenbaum in *Schmollers Jahrbuch* XXXVIII (1914), 445–492; Cay von Brockdorff in *Schulblatt für die Herzogtümer Braunschweig und Anhalt* XXV (1912), 765–768; Wilhelm Metzger in *Weltwirtschaftliches Archiv* II (1913), 184–187; anonymous in *Revue de métaphysique et de morale*, May 1914; [?] Baltzer in *Mecklenburger Tageblatt*, 23 May 1912, Beilage zu Nr. 118; and "D." [Adolf Damaschke?] in *Bodenreform* XXIV (1913), 255–256.

8. Cf. Tönnies's introductions to the later editions of the book in *Gemeinschaft und Gesellschaft*, xxv–xlvi. There are also good discussions of the book's reception in Alfred Bellebaum, "Ferdinand Tönnies," in Dirk Käsler, ed., *Klassiker des soziologischen Denkens*, vol. I: *Von Comte bis Durkheim* (Munich, 1976), 261–264; Norbert Blüm, *Willenslehre und Soziallehre bei Ferdinand Tönnies. Ein Beitrag zum Verständnis von 'Gemeinschaft und Gesellschaft'* (Bonn, 1967), 23–31; and René König, "Die Begriffe Gemeinschaft und Gesellschaft bei Ferdinand Tönnies," in KZSS VII (1955), 348–420. See also the discussion of Tönnies's influence on American sociology in John C. McKinney and Charles P.

Loomis, "The Application of Gemeinschaft and Gesellschaft as Related to Other Typologies," in *Community and Society*, 12–29.

9. On Tönnies and Nazism, see Werner J. Cahnman and Franziska Tönnies Heberle, "Tönnies and National Socialism: Two Documents and a Commentary," in Cahnman, ed., *Ferdinand Tönnies: A New Evaluation*, 284–290; and Horst Rode and Ekkehard Kluge, "Ferdinand Tönnies' Verhältnis zu Nationalsozialismus und Faschismus," in Lars Clausen and Franz Urban Pappi, *Ankunft bei Tönnies. Soziologische Beiträge zum 125. Geburtstag von Ferdinand Tönnies* (Kiel, 1981), 250–274.

10. René König, "Die Begriffe Gemeinschaft und Gesellschaft bei Ferdinand Tönnies," 348–420; and Ralf Dahrendorf, *Society and Democracy in Germany* (New York, 1967), 127–131.

11. The Schleswig-Holstein economy stagnated under Danish rule in the eighteenth and early nineteenth centuries, but by Tönnies's lifetime its ports and cattle trade made it moderately prosperous. See Otto Brandt, Wilhelm Kluver and Herbert Jankuhn, *Die Geschichte Schleswig-Holsteins. Ein Grundriss* (Kiel, 1976), 280ff.; Friedrich Kleyser, *Kleine Kieler Wirtschaftsgeschichte von 1242 bis 1945* (Kiel, 1969), 43ff.; and Jürgen Brockstedt "Frühindustrialisierung in den Herzogtümern Schleswig und Holstein. Ein Überblick," in Brockstedt, ed., *Frühindustrialisierung in Schleswig-Holstein, anderen norddeutschen Ländern und Dänemark* (Neumünster, 1983), 19–77.

12. Brandt, *Geschichte Schleswig-Holsteins*, 274ff.

13. Lebenserinnerungen, 203–204, 206.

14. Ibid., 210.

15. Ibid., 217.

16. On the change in political climate, see Hans Rosenberg, *Grosse Depression und Bismarckzeit. Wirtschaftsablauf, Gesellschaft und Politik in Mitteleuropa* (Berlin, 1967); Peter G. J. Pulzer, *The Rise of Political Anti-Semitism in Germany and Austria* (New York, 1964); and Paul W. Massing, *Rehearsal for Destruction: A Study of Political Anti-Semitism in Imperial Germany* (New York, 1949).

17. On social conflict in Schleswig-Holstein, see Gerd Calleson, "Die Arbeiterbewegung in Nordschleswig 1872–1878—Hauptzüge ihrer Entwicklung," in *Zeitschrift der Gesellschaft für Schleswig-Holsteinische Geschichte* C (1975), 193–216; Heinz Volkmar Regling, *Die Anfänge des Sozialismus in Schleswig-Holstein* (Neumünster, 1965); and Gunter Trautmann, "Liberalismus, Arbeiterbewegung und Staat in Hamburg und Schleswig-Holstein, 1862–1869," in *Archiv für Sozialgeschichte* XV (1975), 51–110.

18. Lebenserinnerungen, 190–191.

19. See Paulsen, *An Autobiography*, ed. Theodor Lorenz (New York, 1938).

20. Ibid., 248; and Selbstdarstellung, 206.

21. Tönnies to Paulsen, 21 July 1878, in *Briefwechsel*, 33.

22. Ibid., 9 July 1878, 29.

23. Cf. Heinrich August Winkler, "Vom linken zum rechten Nationalismus. Der deutsche Liberalismus in der Krise von 1878/79," in *Geschichte und Gesellschaft* IV (1978), 5–28.

24. Tönnies to Paulsen, 18 July 1885, in *Briefwechsel*, 218.

25. Paulsen, *Autobiography*, 329.

26. Paulsen to Tönnies, 2 Aug. 1898, in *Briefwechsel*, 330–331; and Tönnies to Paulsen, 12 Aug. 1898, ibid., 331. Paulsen's social philosophy defined the state as an outgrowth of the popular will: "The state is the organization of a people into a sovereign unity of will, power, and law. Its task is to further the vital interests of the people abroad and to maintain peace at home. It is also responsible for maintaining and increasing material and ideal welfare, so far as these may be left to the free activity of the individual without danger for the self-preservation of the whole"—Paulsen, *System der Ethik. Mit einem Umriss der Staats- und Gesellschaftslehre* (1889; Stuttgart and Berlin, 1913), 544–545. Cf. Tönnies's analysis of a conflict of interest between society and the state, discussed below, 22.

27. Cf. Selbstdarstellung, 202.

28. Cf. Wilhelm von Humboldt, *Werke*, vol. IV, *Schriften zur Politik und zum Bildungswesen*, ed. Andreas Flitner and Klaus Giel (Stuttgart, 1964). On Humboldt, see Peter Berglar, *Wilhelm von Humboldt in Selbstzeugnissen und Bilddokumente* (Reinbek bei Hamburg, 1970); Clemens Menze, *Die Bildungsreform Wilhelm von Humboldts* (Hannover, 1975); and Paul R. Sweet, *Wilhelm von Humboldt: A Biography*, vol. II (Columbus, Ohio, 1978), 54ff.

29. Cf. Selbstdarstellung, 202–207.

30. On the Philosophical Faculty and the organization of the university system, see the works cited above, 202, n.13.

31. Tönnies to Paulsen, 2 June 1882, in *Briefwechsel*, 158–159.

32. Tönnies to Paulsen, 21 Oct. 1880, in *Briefwechsel*, 94–95; ibid., 27 March 1881, 120–121; and undated letter (between 15 March 1889 and 4 May 1889, probably never sent), 265–266. Cf. Paulsen, *Autobiography*, 329–330.

33. Tönnies to Paulsen, 11 Nov. 1882, in Tönnies Papers Cb54.51, typed copy.

34. Friedrich Nietzsche, "Über die Zukunft unserer Bildungsanstalten. Sechs öffentliche Vorträge" (1872), in *Werke. Kritische Gesamtausgabe*, vol. III/2, *Nachgelassene Schriften 1870–1873*, ed. Giorgio Colli and Mazzino Montinari (Berlin and New York, 1973), 133–244.

35. Selbstdarstellung, 216.

36. The critical editions: Thomas Hobbes, *The Elements of Law Natural and Politic* (1650; London, 1889); and Thomas Hobbes, *Behemoth or the Long Parliament* (London, 1889).

37. See Tönnies, "Anmerkungen über die Philosophie des Hobbes," in *Vierteljahrsschrift für wissenschaftliche Philosophie* III (1879), 453–466; ibid., IV (1880), 55–74, 428–453; ibid., V (1881), 186–204; and idem, *Hobbes. Leben und Lehre* (Stuttgart, 1896). A selection of Tönnies's shorter studies in early modern thought has been collected as *Studien zur Philosophie und Gesellschaftslehre im 17. Jahrhundert*, ed. E. G. Jacoby (Stuttgart-Bad Cannstatt, 1975).

38. Hobbes, *Leviathan*, ed. C. B. Macpherson (1651; Middlesex and New York, 1968).

39. Tönnies to Paulsen, 9 July 1878, *Briefwechsel*, 31.

40. Ibid., 29 Sept. 1878, 46.

41. Tönnies, *Hobbes*, 219. On Tönnies's relationship to England, see Jacoby, *Die moderne Gesellschaft*, 18ff.; Tönnies to Paulsen, 6 July 1897, in *Briefwechsel*, 325; Tönnies, "Ethische Betrachtungen," in *Ethische Kultur* III (1895), 218; and idem, "Politische Stimmungen und Richtungen in England," in *Das freie Wort* VI (1906), 337–343.

42. Idem, *Hobbes*, 88–89.

43. *Gemeinschaft und Gesellschaft*, xxiii.

44. *Community and Society*, 216. Translation altered to conform to the original.

45. Ibid., 217.

46. Cf. ibid., 218.

47. Cf. Tönnies, *Hobbes*, 156–198.

48. Nietzsche, *The Birth of Tragedy* (1872) and *The Genealogy of Morals*, transl. Francis Golffing (Garden City, New York, 1956). Cf. *Selbstdarstellung*, 203. On Tönnies's relationship to Nietzsche, see Jürgen Zander, "Ferdinand Tönnies und Friedrich Nietzsche. Mit einem Exkurs: Nietzsches 'Geburt der Tragödie' als Impuls zu Tönnies' 'Gemeinschaft und Gesellschaft,'" in Clausen and Pappi, *Ankunft bei Tönnies*, 185–227.

49. *Selbstdarstellung*, 203.

50. Nietzsche, *Unzeitgemässe Betrachtungen*, in *Werke. Kritische Gesamtausgabe*, III/1, 155–156.

51. *Selbstdarstellung*, 214; Tönnies to Paulsen, 29 Feb./1 March 1880, *Briefwechsel*, 74–75.

52. Rudolph Binion, *Frau Lou: Nietzsche's Wayward Disciple* (Princeton, 1968), 115–118, 133, 143.

53. Tönnies, "Studie zur Kritik des Spinoza," in *Vierteljahrsschrift für wissenschaftliche Philosophie* VII (1883), 158–183; and ibid., "Studie zur Entwicklungsgeschichte des Spinoza," 334–364.

54. "Studie zur Kritik des Spinoza," 164–165.

55. Cf. Blüm, *Willenslehre und Soziallehre bei Ferdinand Tönnies*, 40ff.

56. For the influence of the ethnological and legal literature on Tönnies, see *Gemeinschaft und Gesellschaft*, xxiii.

57. On Maine, see George Feaver, *From Status to Contract: A Biography of Sir Henry Maine, 1822–1888* (London, 1969). On Bachofen, see Karl Meuli, "Nachwort," in Johann Jakob Bachofen, *Gesammelte Werke* vol. III, *Das Mutterrecht* (Basel, 1948–1967), 1011–1079. On Morgan, see Bernhard J. Stern, *Lewis Henry Morgan: Social Evolutionist* (New York, 1967); and Carl Resek, *Lewis Henry Morgan: American Scholar* (Chicago, 1960). On

Gierke, see Erik Wolf, *Grosse Rechtsdenker der deutschen Geistesgeschichte* (Tübingen, 1963), 669–712; Ernst-Wolfgang Böckenförde, *Die deutsche verfassungsgeschichtliche Forschung im 19. Jahrhundert. Zeitgebundene Fragestellungen und Leitbilder* (Berlin, 1961), 147–176; and Albert Janssen, *Otto von Gierkes Methode der geschichtlichen Rechtswissenschaft. Studien zu den Wegen und Formen seines juristischen Denkens* (Göttingen, Frankfurt, Zurich, 1974).

58. Cf. Friedrich Engels, *The Origin of the Family, Private Property and the State: In the Light of the Researches of Lewis H. Morgan* (1884; New York, 1942). Tönnies later visited Engels and corresponded with him. See the letter from Engels to Tönnies, 24 Jan. 1895, in Marx and Engels, *Werke* vol. XXXIX (Berlin, 1968), 394–396.

59. On the influence of all three, see *Gemeinschaft und Gesellschaft,* xxii–xxiii.

60. Ibid., xxi.

61. Ibid.

62. Tönnies was especially influenced by Theodor Storm. I have dealt with their relationship in the chapter on Lukács, below, 165–167. Cf. Rolf Fechner, ed., *Der Dichter und der Soziologe. Zum Verhältnis zwischen Theodor Storm und Ferdinand Tönnies. Referate der Arbeitstagung im November 1984 in Husum* (Ferdinand-Tönnies-Arbeitsstelle an der Universität Hamburg, Materialien Bd. 2, 1985).

63. On Naturalism in German art and thought, see Richard Hamann and Jost Hermand, *Naturalismus* (Munich, 1972).

64. *Community and Society,* 53.

65. Ibid., 44, 53–54.

66. Ibid., 50, 57–59.

67. Ibid., 50, 62–64.

68. Ibid., 64–76.

69. Ibid., 76–78.

70. Ibid., 78–80, 100–102.

71. Ibid., 37–38.

72. Ibid., 40.

73. Ibid., 135–136, 139–140.

74. Ibid., 103–104, 125–126.

75. Ibid., 128–134.

76. Ibid., 120–121.

77. Ibid., 87–89.

78. On the tension between partisanship and hermeneutics in Tönnies's thought, see Cornelius Bickel, "Ferdinand Tönnies. Soziologie zwischen geschichtsphilosophischem

'Pessimismus', wissenschaftlicher Ratio und sozialethischem 'Optimismus,'" in Sven Papcke, ed., *Ordnung und Theorie. Beiträge zur Geschichte der Soziologie in Deutschland* (Darmstadt, 1986), 307–334.

79. On the historical school of jurisprudence, see Ernst-Wolfgang Böckenförde, "Die Historische Rechtsschule und das Problem der Geschichtlichkeit des Rechts," in Böckenförde et al., *Collegium Philosophicum. Studien. Joachim Ritter zum 60. Geburtstag* (Basel and Stuttgart, 1965), 9–36; Rudolf Gmür, *Savigny und die Entwicklung der Rechtswissenschaft* (Münster, 1962); and E. Rothacker, "Savigny, Grimm, Ranke. Ein Beitrag zur Frage nach dem Zusammenhang der historischen Schule," *Historische Zeitschrift* CXXVIII (1923), 415ff.

80. *Gemeinschaft und Gesellschaft*, 176–177. The explicit references to the idea of the house disappear in Loomis's translation. Cf. *Community and Society*, 197–198.

81. *Community and Society*, 206–207.

82. Ibid., 207–208.

83. Ibid., 178.

84. Ibid., 178–181.

85. Ibid., 151–156, 162–166.

86. Ibid., 161–162, 168–169. Loomis unaccountably translates "salon" as "society." Cf. *Gemeinschaft und Gesellschaft*, 134–135.

87. Cf. the discussion of *zweite Natur* below, 137.

88. *Community and Society*, 202–205, 234–235.

89. *Gemeinschaft und Gesellschaft*, xxiii.

90. Cf. Zander, "Ferdinand Tönnies und Friedrich Nietzsche," 185–227.

91. *Community and Society*, 235.

92. Ibid., 205.

93. Ibid., 218.

94. Cf. Lebenserinnerungen, 193–194; Selbstdarstellung, 199; Tönnies to Paulsen, 25 May 1878, *Briefwechsel*, 24; and Friedrich Hoffmann, "Ferdinand Tönnies im Gedenken seiner heimatlichen Verbundenheit zu seinem 100. Geburtstag," in *Zeitschrift der Gesellschaft für Schleswig-Holsteinische Geschichte* LXXIX (1955), 303.

95. On this aspect of Hobbes's thought, see J. G. A. Pocock, "Time, History and Eschatology in the Thought of Thomas Hobbes," in idem, *Politics, Language and Time: Essays on Political Thought and History* (New York, 1971), 148–201.

96. The correspondence preserved in the Tönnies Papers Cb54.56 includes forty-three items from Arnold to Tönnies. On Arnold, see the entry in *Wer Ist's* IX, ed. Herrmann Degener (Berlin, 1928), 35, and Selbstdarstellung, 203–204.

97. Tönnies to Paulsen, 22 Oct. 1887, in Tönnies Papers Cb54.51, typed copy.

98. *Gemeinschaft und Gesellschaft*, 13. Loomis's translation of this passage is one of his more mediocre efforts. His translates *eine mystische Stadt und Versammlung* as "an invisible scene or meeting." *Community and Society*, 43.

99. Tönnies to Paul de Lagarde, 8 January 1884, in Lagarde Nachlass, Niedersächsische Staats- und Universitätsbibliothek, Göttingen.

100. On the Ethical Society, see Hermann Lübbe, *Politische Philosophie in Deutschland. Studien zu ihrer Geschichte* (Basel and Stuttgart, 1963), 127ff. Lily Braun, *Gesammelte Werke*, vol. II, *Memoiren eines Sozialisten* (Berlin-Grunewald, n.d.), 430ff., contains a fictionalized account of the Ethical movement, with Tönnies portrayed as Professor Tondern, 516ff. Tönnies wrote a short account of the movement's history and aims, "Die ethische Bewegung," in *Die Umschau* III (1899), 842–845. Some members of the London Ethical Society, the model for the German branch of the movement, had a Monist world view resembling Tönnies's. Cf. John Henry Muirhead, *Reflections by a Journeyman in Philosophy in the Movements of Thought and Practice in His Time*, ed. John W. Harvey (London, 1942), 87. See also Melvin Richter, *The Politics of Conscience: T. H. Green and his Age* (London, 1964), 119–121.

101. Tönnies to Lily Braun (*née* von Kretschmar, at that time still married to her first husband, Georg von Gizycki), 30 Oct. 1892, in Tönnies Papers Cb54.51.

102. *Ethische Kultur* I (1893), 287, 295–297.

103. Ibid. II (1894), 335–336.

104. Selbstdarstellung, 219.

105. Tönnies, *Ethische Cultur und ihr Geleite: [in der "Zukunft" und in der "Gegenwart"]. 1. Nietzsche-Narren 2. Wölfe in Fuchspelzen [2 Kirchenzeitungen]* (Berlin, 1893). See also Tönnies's reply to his critics, "In Sachen der 'Ethischen Cultur,'" *Burschenschaftliche Blätter* (1893), 126–127.

106. Tönnies, *Ethische Cultur und ihr Geleite*, 13–24.

107. See the selections in Ferdinand Tönnies, *On Sociology: Pure, Applied and Empirical. Selected Writings*, ed. Werner J. Cahnman and Rudolf Heberle (Chicago and London, 1971). Tönnies's empirical studies are discussed in Alfred Bellebaum, *Das soziologische System von Ferdinand Tönnies unter besonderer Berücksichtigung seiner soziographischen Untersuchungen* (Meisenheim an der Glan, 1966); and Anthony Oberschall, "The Empirical Sociology of Tönnies," in Cahnman, *Tönnies: A New Evaluation*, 160–180.

108. See, for example, Tönnies, "Die Zerrütung der liberalen Partei in England," in *Das freie Wort* I (1901), 289–292; "Political Parties in Germany," in *The Independent Review* III (1904), 365–381; "Der Massenstreik in ethischer Beleuchtung," in *Das freie Wort* V (1905), 537–543; "Zum Verständnis des politischen Parteiwesens," in *Das freie Wort* V (1906), 752–759; "Französisch-deutsche Beziehungen. Ein Vorwort zur Haager Konferenz," ibid. VII (1907), 121–129; "Politische Stimmungen und Richtungen in England," ibid. VI (1906), 337–343; "Ethik und Sozialismus," in *Arch. f. Sozialwiss.* XXVI (1908), 56–95, and XXIX (1909), 895–930; "Die Gleichheit des Wahlrechts," in *Das freie Wort* VIII (1908), 165–169; "Das Reichstagswahlrecht für Preussen?" in *Das freie Wort* VII (1907), 492–497; and "Die Weltlage," in *Das freie Wort* VII (1908), 286–288.

109. Tönnies, *Warlike England as Seen by Herself* (New York, 1915); "Marokko und der Weltkrieg," in *Neue Rundschau* XXVI (1915), 1540–1546; "Der Friede," in *Ethische Kultur* XXIII (1915), 25–27; "Der Wiederbeginn geistiger Gemeinschaftsarbeit zwi-

schen den Völkern," in *Ethische Kultur* XXIII (1915), 105–106; "Frohmut und Ernst in der Kriegszeit," in *Ethische Kultur* XXIV (1916), 81–82; "Machtgedanken," in *Neue Rundschau* XXVII (1916), 261–265; "Boz-Dickens," in *Ethische Kultur* XXV (1917), 5–7; *Germany's War Guilt Disproved, Russia's Responsibility as Instigator of the Great War Established by Documentary Evidence of the Year 1914* (Amsterdam and Rotterdam, 1919); and *Der Zarismus und seine Bundesgenossen, 1914. Neue Beiträge zur Kriegsschuldfrage* (Berlin, 1922).

110. Selbstdarstellung, 35–36.

111. Tönnies Papers, Cb54.34/39. For historical background, see Gunter Scholz, "Drittes Reich. Begriffsgeschichte mit Blick auf Blochs Originalgeschichte," in *Bloch-Almanach* II (1982), 19–38.

Chapter 3

1. For biographical details, see Troeltsch, "Meine Bücher," in *Die Philosophie der Gegenwart in Selbstdarstellungen* vol. II, ed. Raymund Schmidt, (Leipzig, 1923), 165–182 (reprinted in Troeltsch, *Gesammelte Schriften* IV, 3–18); Albert Dietrich, "Ernst Troeltsch," in *Deutsches Biographisches Jahrbuch*, ed. Verbände der Deutschen Akademien, vol. V [1923] (Berlin and Leipzig, 1930), 348–368; Walter Köhler, *Ernst Troeltsch* (Tübingen, 1941); and *Troeltsch-Studien. Untersuchungen zur Biographie und Werkgeschichte. Mit den unveröffentlichten Promotionsthesen der "Kleinen Göttinger Fakultät" 1888–1893*, ed. Horst Renz and Friedrich Wilhelm Graf (Gütersloh, 1982).

2. Troeltsch published a first version of the work, "Die Soziallehren der christlichen Kirchen," in *Arch. f. Sozialwiss*. XXVI (1908), 1–55, 292–342, 649–692; XXVII (1908), 1–72, 317–348; XXVIII (1909), 1–71, 387–416, 621–653; XXIX (1909), 1–49, 381–416; XXX (1910), 30–65, 666–720. He greatly expanded and altered these essays for the final version published as *Gesammelte Schriften* vol. I. I have cited throughout from the English translation, *The Social Teaching of the Christian Churches*, transl. Olive Wyon, 2 vols. (New York, 1931). The otherwise conscientious translator makes the error of translating "Soziallehren" in the singular as "teaching" when one of Troeltsch's basic arguments is that there is a plurality of Christian social teachings. Hence I refer to the work hereafter by the short title *Social Teachings*.

3. On the history of Troeltsch's family, see Horst Renz, "Augsburger Jahre. Grundlagen der geistigen Entwicklung von Ernst Troeltsch," in *Troeltsch-Studien*, 13ff.; and Troeltsch's description of his family history in Troeltsch, *Briefe an Friedrich von Hügel 1901–1923*, ed. Karl-Ernst Apfelbacher and Peter Neuner (Paderborn, 1974), letter of 4 September 1913, 99–100.

4. Troeltsch, "Meine Bucher," 165–166.

5. Renz, "Augsburger Jahre," 15ff.

6. Ibid., 24.

7. Ibid., 25–27.

8. See G. Pfeiffer, "Bayern: Evangelische Kirche," in *Die Religion in Geschichte und Gegenwart*, third ed. vol. I (Tübingen, 1957–1965), 939–947; and Ernst Rudolf Huber and Wolfgang Huber, eds., *Staat und Kirche im 19. und 20. Jahrhundert. Dokumente zur Ge-*

schichte des deutschen Staatskirchenrechts, vol. I: *Staat und Kirche vom Ausgang des alten Reichs bis zum Vorabend der bürgerlichen Revolution* (Berlin, 1973), 653–662.

9. Horst Renz, "Troeltschs Theologiestudium," in *Troeltsch-Studien*, 49, 53–54.

10. Ibid., 49–51, 54.

11. Ibid., 54. On the Erlangen School see H. Grass, "Erlanger Schule," in *Die Religion in Geschichte und Gegenwart*, vol. II, 566–568. Troeltsch wrote of his and his friend Wilhelm Bousset's attitude toward the Erlangen theology professors, "We had cool respect toward the gentlemen and felt them to be ancient monuments from the time of the German Confederation, left over from the conflict between Neo-Pietism and Enlightenment." Troeltsch, "Die 'kleine Göttinger Fakultät' von 1890," in *Die Christliche Welt* XXXIV (1920), 282. He remarked elsewhere, however, that he had got a thorough acquaintance of contemporary Lutheranism from the "superb" (*vortrefflich*) Erlangen theologians; *Gesammelte Schriften* II, viii.

12. Renz, "Troeltschs Theologiestudium," 51.

13. Troeltsch, "Meine Bücher," 166.

14. On Ritschl, see Hermann Timm, *Theorie und Praxis in der Theologie Albrecht Ritschls und Wilhelm Herrmanns. Ein Beitrag zur Entwicklungsgeschichte des Kulturprotestantismus* (Gütersloh, 1967); Otto Ritschl, *Albrecht Ritschls Leben*, 2 vols. (Freiburg, 1892–1896); Rolf Schaefer, *Ritschl. Grundlinien eines fast verschollenen dogmatischen Systems* (Tübingen, 1968); David L. Mueller, *An Introduction to the Theology of Albrecht Ritschl* (Philadelphia, 1969); and Philip Hefner, *Faith and the Vitalities of History: A Theological Study Based on the Work of Albrecht Ritschl* (New York, 1966).

15. On Troeltsch and the Ritschlians, see Johannes Rathje, *Die Welt des freien Protestantismus. Ein Beitrag zur deutsch-evangelischen Geistesgeschichte dargestellt am Leben und Werk von Martin Rade* (Stuttgart, 1952), 71ff., 89ff., 94, 106–107; Troeltsch's prefatory remarks on Ritschl are in *Social Teachings*, 19–20. See also Troeltsch's comments in "Rückblick auf ein halbes Jahrhundert der theologischen Wissenschaft" (1909), in *Gesammelte Schriften* II, 207ff.; "Die theologische und religiöse Lage der Gegenwart" (1903), ibid., 13; and the preface, ibid., viii.

16. *Social Teachings*, 19.

17. Albrecht Ritschl, *Die christliche Lehre von der Rechtfertigung und Versöhnung* 6 vols. (Bonn, 1870–1874). Ritschl summarized his system in "Instruction in the Christian Religion" (1875), included in Ritschl, *Three Essays*, ed. Philip Hefner (Philadelphia, 1972), 221–291.

18. Troeltsch, *Vernunft und Offenbarung bei Johannes Gerhard und Melanchthon. Untersuchung zur Geschichte der altprotestantischen Theologie* (Göttingen, 1891).

19. Recent German theologians have qualified Troeltsch's judgment, but credit it with a considerable measure of truth for Lutheran orthodoxy, if not for Luther himself. See Ulrich Duchrow, Wolfgang Huber, and Louis Reith, *Umdeutungen der Zweireichenlehre Luthers im 19. Jahrhundert* (Gütersloh, 1975), 15, 67. Cf. Ahti Hakamies, "Der Begriff 'Eigengesetzlichkeit' in der heutigen Theologie und seine historischen Wurzeln," in *Studia Theologica* XXIV (1970), 122, which criticizes Troeltsch for not distinguishing adequately between Luther and Lutheranism.

20. On Ritschl's political evolution, see the sketch in Hefner's introduction to Ritschl, *Three Essays*, 3ff.

21. Ritschl, "Instruction in the Christian Religion." This translation is taken from the third edition of 1886, with important variations from the first edition indicated in the footnotes.

22. The defense took place on 14 February 1891. The theses are reprinted in *Troeltsch-Studien*, 299–300; the thesis calling for a new instruction manual is number seventeen, 300. I have relied on the analysis of this thesis and its context in Friedrich Wilhelm Graf, "Der 'Systematiker' der 'Kleinen Göttinger Fakultät.' Ernst Troeltschs Promotionsthesen und ihr Göttinger Kontext," in *Troeltsch-Studien*, 274–279.

23. Troeltsch, *Die historischen Grundlagen der Theologie unseres Jahrhunderts* (Karlsruhe, 1895), 25.

24. Ibid.

25. Troeltsch, "Religion und Kirche," in *Preussische Jahrbücher* LXXXI (1895), 215–249. Troeltsch made substantial changes in the version of the essay printed in *Gesammelte Schriften* II, 146–182.

26. Ibid., 219ff.

27. Ibid., 247–248.

28. On *Persönlichkeit*, see *Religion and Industrial Society*, ch. 6.

29. On Troeltsch's relationship to his Göttingen friends and teachers, see Graf, "Der 'Systematiker' der 'Kleinen Göttinger Fakultät,'" 235ff., 279–290; and Graf, "Licentiatus theologiae und Habilitation," also in *Troeltsch-Studien*, 78–102.

30. On Bousset, see Anthonie F. Verheule, *Wilhelm Bousset. Leben und Werk. Ein theologiegeschichtlicher Versuch* (Amsterdam, 1973). Some of the correspondence is published in Troeltsch-Bousset. After Bousset's death, Troeltsch recalled their friendship in "Kleine Göttinger Fakultät."

31. Cf. Troeltsch, "Kleine Göttinger Fakultät"; and Graf, "Licentiatus theologiae und Habilitation," 83.

32. See Timm, *Theorie und Praxis*, 73ff.

33. Johannes Weiss, *Jesus' Proclamation of the Kingdom of God*, ed. R. H. Hiers and D. L. Holland (1892; Philadelphia, 1971), 133.

34. Cf. Graf, "Der 'Systematiker' der 'Kleinen Göttinger Fakultät,'" 259–265, which emphasizes Weiss's diffidence and sharply distinguishes his position from Troeltsch's consistent emphasis on the centrality of eschatology.

35. See Hiers's and Holland's introduction to Weiss, *Jesus' Proclamation of the Kingdom of God*, 24ff.

36. *Troeltsch-Studien*, 300; cf. Graf's interpretation, 263–264.

37. Troeltsch-Bousset, 23 July 1895, 28–29.

38. Ibid., 5 August 1898, 35.

39. Ibid., 12 October 1894, 24–25.

40. Ibid.

41. Ibid. See also the biographies of Merx by O. A. Ernst in *Badische Biographien* VI. Teil (1901–1910), ed. A. Krieger and K. Obser (Heidelberg, 1935), 44–56; and Oskar Herrigel, "Zum Gedächtnis von Adalbert Merx," in *Protestantische Monatshefte* XIV (1910), 41–50, 89–103. On Hausrath, see Karl Bauer, *Adolf Hausrath. Leben und Zeit* (Heidelberg, 1933). See also the remarks below in connection with his nephew, Max Weber, 84.

42. On Bassermann, see Otto Frommel, "Heinrich Bassermann," in *Badische Biographien* VI. Teil (1901–1910), 525–527; on Holsten, see W. Hess, "Carl Holsten," in *Allgemeine deutsche Biographie* L (1905), 450–454; and Adolf Hausrath, *Carl Holsten. Worte der Erinnerung* (Heidelberg, 1897). In general, see Hausrath, *Geschichte der theologischen Fakultät zu Heidelberg im 19. Jahrhundert* (Heidelberg, 1901).

43. Troeltsch-Bousset, 5 August 1898, 32–33.

44. On Heidelberg as cultural milieu, see Richard Benz, *Heidelberg. Schicksal und Geist* (Sigmaringen, 1975), 451–454; and Helene Tompert, *Lebensformen und Denkweisen der akademischen Welt Heidelbergs im wilhelminischen Zeitalter vornehmlich im Spiegel zeitgenössischer Selbstzeugnisse* (Lübeck and Hamburg, 1969).

45. *Biography*, 227–228.

46. Troeltsch, "Meine Bücher," 173. See also Troeltsch's obituary of 20 June 1920 for Weber reprinted in idem., *Deutscher Geist und Westeuropa. Gesammelte kulturphilosophische Aufsätze und Reden*, ed. Hans Baron (Tübingen, 1925), 247–252.

47. Cf. *Biography*, 279–280, 449.

48. Troeltsch stressed the independence of his own research and the continuity of his interests from the time of his dissertation in *Social Teachings*, 987. He noted that he drew a sharper line than did Weber between Calvin's original teachings and the later spirit of capitalism—ibid., 894; cf. Troeltsch, *Die Bedeutung des Protestantismus für die Entstehung der modernen Welt* (1906; revised 2nd ed., Munich, 1911), 69, in which Troeltsch called for more stress on the difference between Western and Central European political and economic conditions as an explanation for the difference between the Calvinist and Lutheran work ethics. Troeltsch, the theologian, was more anxious than Weber, the social scientist, to make the spiritual lineage of modern society an indirect one.

Both Weber and Troeltsch protested when a critic attacked their works together: see Weber, "Antikritisches zum 'Geist' des Kapitalismus" (1910), and Troeltsch, "Die Kulturbedeutung des Calvinismus" (1910), in *Prot. Ethik Kritiken*, 149–151 and 188–199, respectively.

49. On Weber and Rickert in Freiburg, see *Biography*, 203–206.

50. Heinrich Rickert, *Die Grenzen der naturwissenschaftlichen Begriffsbildung* (1896–1902; Tübingen, 1902).

51. *Biography*, 260, 311.

52. Troeltsch, "Moderne Geschichtsphilosophie," in *Theologische Rundschau* VI (1903), 3–28, 57–72, 103–117. See also the following reviews for Troeltsch's views around the turn of the century on the philosophy of the social sciences: review of Paul Barth, *Die Philosophie der Geschichte als Sociologie* I. Teil: *Einleitung und kritische Übersicht* (1897), in *Theologische Literaturzeitung* XXIII (1898), 398–401; review of Rickert, *Kulturwissenschaft und Naturwissenschaft* (1898), in *Theologische Literaturzeitung* XXIV (1899), 375–377; review of Paulsen, *Kant der Philosoph des Protestantismus* (1899), in *Deutsche Literaturzeitung* XXI (1900), 157–161; and review of Otto Ritschl, *Die Causalbetrachtung in den Geisteswissenschaften* (1901), in *Theologische Literaturzeitung* XXVII (1902), 387–389. For Troeltsch's later judgment of Rickert, see his review of Rickert, *Kulturwissenschaft und Naturwissenschaft* (2nd ed., 1910), in *Theologische Literaturzeitung* XXXVIII (1913), 440; review of Fritz Münch, *Erlebnis und Geltung. Eine systematische Untersuchung zur Transzendentalphilosophie als Weltanschauung* (1913), in *Theologische Literaturzeitung* XXII (1915), 470–472; review of Rickert, *Wilhelm Windelband* (1915), in *Theologische Literaturzeitung* XLI (1916), 469–471; discussion of Rickert in *Gesammelte Schriften* III, 119–122, 150–158, 221–242, 559–565, 568, 570, and passim; and review of "Die Geisteswissenschaften und der Streit um Rickert. Aus Anlass von Erich Becher, Geisteswissenschaften und Naturwissenschaften. Untersuchungen zur Theorie und Einteilung der Realwissenschaften," in *Schmollers Jahrbuch* XLVI (1922), 35–64.

53. See especially Rickert's discussion of how scientific concepts are abstract common denominators, how science does not represent things but makes laws, and how it eliminates the individual character of experience, in *Die Grenzen der naturwissenschaftlichen Begriffsbildung*, 53, 97–98, 236 (respectively).

54. Ibid., 307–308.

55. Ibid., ch. 2—especially the critique of Dilthey, 188–189.

56. Ibid., 266ff.

57. Ibid., 294.

58. Rickert's student Emil Lask outlined such a synthetic science, combining the methods of the natural and historical sciences, in *Fichtes Idealismus und die Geschichte* (Tübingen, 1902), 249ff. See Troeltsch's review of Lask in *Theologische Literaturzeitung* XXVIII (1903), 244–251; see also his review of Maria Raich, *Fichte. Seine Ethik und seine Stellung zu dem Problem des Individualismus* (1905), in *Göttingische gelehrte Anzeigen* CLXVIII (1906), 680–682.

59. Rickert, *Die Grenzen der naturwissenschaftlichen Begriffsbildung*, 571ff.

60. Troeltsch, "Moderne Geschichtsphilosophie," 110ff.

61. Ibid., 115. Cf. Rickert's argument that values issued forth from a community and that the nation was the most important of all human communities in *Die Grenzen der naturwissenschaftlichen Begriffsbildung*, 573, 720–721.

62. Martin von Nathusius, *Die Mitarbeit der Kirche an der Lösung der sozialen Frage. Auf Grund einer kurzgefassten Volkswirtschaftslehre und eines Systems der christlichen Gesellschaftslehre (Sozialethik)* (Leipzig, 1897).

63. See n.2.

64. Troeltsch, "Meine Bücher," 173–174. For reviews see Friedrich Loofs in *Deutsche Literaturzeitung* XXXIV (1913), 2885–2893; Walter Köhler in *Historische Zeitschrift* CXIV

(1915), 598–605; Tönnies in *Theologische Literaturzeitung* XXXIX (1914), 8–12, reprinted in Tönnies, *Soziologische Studien und Kritiken* vol. III (Jena, 1929), 432–438; Gottfried Traub in *Die Christliche Welt* XXVIII (1914), 339–346; and Paul Wernle, *Zeitschrift für Theologie und Kirche* XXII (1912), 329–368, and XXIII (1913), 18–80.

65. *Social Teachings*, 26–27.

66. Ibid., 28.

67. Ibid., 165–166. Troeltsch was criticizing Kautsky's description of early Christianity, entitled "Der urchristliche Kommunismus," in Eduard Bernstein et al., *Die Geschichte des Sozialismus in Einzeldarstellungen*, vol. I (Stuttgart, 1895), 16–35.

68. *Social Teachings*, 40. See also Troeltsch's critique of Kautsky's class interpretation of Luther, ibid., 821.

69. Wernle, review in *Zeitschrift für Theologie und Kirche*, 331ff.

70. Cf. *Social Teachings*, 39, where Troeltsch on the one hand argued that Christianity was not the product of a class struggle, but on the other hand that Jesus addressed himself primarily to the oppressed.

71. Troeltsch, "Meine Bücher," 9–10. See also Troeltsch's comments on the eschatological dynamic of Christianity in "Religion, Wirtschaft und Gesellschaft" (1913), in *Gesammelte Schriften* IV, 32–33; and in his review of Bruno Archibald-Fuchs, *Der Geist der bürgerlich-kapitalistischen Gesellschaft* (1915), in *Gesammelte Schriften* IV, 782.

72. Cf. Troeltsch's summary definition of the church type in *Social Teachings*, 993. See also *Die Bedeutung des Protestantismus*, 20; and Troeltsch, *Religiöser Individualismus und Kirche* (Karlsruhe, 1911), 6–10.

73. *Social Teachings*, 69–71, 89–96.

74. Ibid., 203.

75. See the history of medieval Catholicism, ibid., especially 306–313, for Catholicism's incompatibility with modern society.

76. Ibid., 331–343, 996.

77. On Luther's eschatology, ibid., 487–488; for some of Troeltsch's many descriptions of Lutheran acceptance of the world, ibid., 474, 509, 606.

78. In addition to the entire discussion of Lutheranism, ibid., see Troeltsch, *Bedeutung des Protestantismus*, 13, attacking the glorification of Luther as a protomodern man in Hegel, Ritschl, and Treitschke. Here Troeltsch saw Luther's outward effects as being uniformly harmful. But in the end he honored Luther as author of Germany's inward principle of *Persönlichkeit* and asked his listeners to uphold this sacred heritage despite the unfavorable conditions of the modern world. *Bedeutung des Protestantismus*, 65–66.

79. On Luther's disappointment with purely spiritual church government, see *Social Teachings*, 490ff.; on the relationship between Lutheranism and secular government, ibid., 561–575.

80. Ibid., 575–576.

81. The Calvinist principle synthesizing church and sect was the notion of the sanctified community: the Calvinist leaders regarded the public order as a theocracy in which they were responsible for upholding pure moral standards—ibid., 590–592. Troeltsch argued that Calvinism had rediscovered the Jewish idea of the chosen people, which he defended as a vital locus of practical religion transcending the weaknesses of church and sect—ibid., 601, 618. In the larger setting of his book, this rediscovery was the beginning of the end of Christianity's hitherto existing historical forms. For when primitive Christianity broke off from Judaism, the church, according to Troeltsch, took shape to replace the outward life of the Jewish nation, substituting the mystical *corpus christi* for the concrete life of the people—ibid., 89–90. When the Calvinists turned their energies away from the church and systematically redirected them toward the nation, they began a process that ended, in Troeltsch's view, with the complete merging of Calvinism with the modern secular world, as one could observe in England and America—ibid., 576–578, 1012.

Troeltsch's emphasis on the idea of the sanctified community in Calvinism is, I believe, his fundamental point of disagreement with Max Weber's interpretation. Cf. below, 104–105.

82. On the role of Scripture in church government, ibid., 592; on just revolt, ibid., 651; see also the description of the blend of authoritarian and democratic elements, ibid., 619.

83. Ibid., 577–578, 649, 675–676, 688–689. See also Troeltsch's article, "Calvinismus und Luthertum. Überblick" (1909), in *Gesammelte Schriften* IV, 254–261.

84. *Social Teachings*, 675–676, 858.

85. Ibid., 1011–1012.

86. Ibid., 1011.

87. More systematically than Weber was able to do, Troeltsch nonetheless emphasized the difference between old-fashioned Calvinism and its modern successor. He was able to contrast the mixture of communal (church) and social (sect) elements in old-fashioned Calvinism with the radical individualism of modern American society. For Weber, on the other hand, the church elements of Calvinism had always been superficial and had never—even in Calvin and the first generation of believers—defined its underlying psychology. Its later individualism came as an unmasking of the psychological character it had always had.

88. Troeltsch hinted at the end of eschatology in the final paragraph of *Social Teachings*, 1013. He made his case more explicitly in the encyclopedia article, "Eschatologie: IV. Dogmatisch," in *Die Religion in Geschichte und Gegenwart*, 1st ed. vol. II (1910), 622–632. Troeltsch was well aware that in arguing religious eschatology had come to an end, he was implying that the history of Christianity had entered a crisis, since its absolute values were predicated on the belief in a future day of judgment, which would rectify the injustices and clarify the uncertainties of secular history. His article took as its point of departure a critique of Simmel, whose *The Philosophy of Money* he saw as the expression of a relativistic modern philosophy that accepted the collapse of religious values resulting from the end of eschatology. Cf. the discussion of Troeltsch and Simmel below, 157.

89. *Social Teachings*, 729ff.

90. See Wolfgang Huber, "Die Schwierigkeit evangelischer Lehrbeanstandung. Eine historische Erinnerung aus aktuellem Anlass," *Evangelische Theologie* XL (1980), 517–536.

91. Troeltsch, "Gewissensfreiheit (Bei Anlass des Falles Jatho. Aus 'Christliche Welt'" (1911), in *Gesammelte Schriften* II, 134–145. See also George L. Mosse, *The Crisis of German Ideology: Intellectual Origins of the Third Reich* (New York, 1964), 50; and Emil Fuchs, *Mein Leben* (Leipzig, 1957), 264–265.

92. See Troeltsch, "Aus der religiösen Bewegung der Gegenwart" (1910), in *Gesammelte Schriften* II, 22–44; idem, "Über die Möglichkeit eines freien Christentums," in *5. Weltkongress für Freies Christentum und Religiösen Fortschritt. Berlin, 5. bis 10. August 1910. Protokoll der Verhandlungen* vol. I ed. Max Fischer and Friedrich Michael Schiele (Berlin, 1910), 333–349; and idem, "Logos und Mythos in Theologie und Religionsphilosophie" (1913), in *Gesammelte Schriften* II, 805–836. For an interpretation of Troeltsch's response to one contemporary pantheist, Arthur Drews, who caused a sensation by asserting that the life of Jesus was myth rather than historical fact, see Brian A. Gerrish, "Jesus, Myth and History: Troeltsch's Stand in the 'Christ-Myth' Debate," in *The Old Protestantism and the New: Essays on the Reformation Heritage* (Chicago, 1982), 230–247.

93. In addition to the essays just named, see Troeltsch's criticisms of educated elitism in *Social Teachings*, 794, 797ff.

94. Ibid., 738–741.

95. Ibid., 740.

96. Ibid., 737.

97. Ibid., 752.

98. Ibid., 795.

99. Ibid., 791–792.

100. Ibid., 794.

101. Ibid., 799.

102. "Das stoisch-christliche Naturrecht und das moderne profane Naturrecht," in Verh. DGS I, 166–214.

103. *Social Teachings*, 150–155, 305–306, 343–344, 499ff., 508, 529, 531–532.

104. "Das stoisch-christliche Naturrecht," 175ff.

105. Ibid., 179–181.

106. Ibid., 183–184.

107. Ibid., 181–183.

108. Ibid., 185–187.

109. Ibid., 189–190.

110. Ibid., 192–196.

111. In his review of *Social Teachings* Tönnies continued this critique, arguing that there was a continuous history of natural right predating and postdating Christianity. Tönnies's other objection to *Social Teachings* was its treatment of mysticism as a social category, whereas in his view it was necessarily a psychological one—Tönnies, *Soziologische Studien und Kritiken* III, 432–438.

112. "Das stoisch-christliche Naturrecht," 204–206.

113. These remarks were at odds with Simmel's tendency elsewhere to reduce religion to a function of social psychology. See the chapter on Simmel, below, 153ff.

114. "Das stoisch-christliche Naturrecht," 196ff.

115. Ibid., 210ff.

116. "Das stoisch-christliche Naturrecht," 186–187.

117. *Religion and Industrial Society*, passim.

118. "Die christliche Ethik und die heutige Gesellschaft," in *Verhandlungen des Evangelisch-Sozialen Kongresses* XV (1904), 11–57. Troeltsch published a slightly revised version of the speech under the title *Politische Ethik und Christentum* (Göttingen, 1904).

119. "Christliche Ethik," 13–15.

120. Troeltsch called himself a "Bismarckianer sans phrase" at the time he met Bousset in winter 1884. See "Kleine Göttinger Fakultät," 281. For his reaction to Treitschke, see his remark of 6 November 1885 that the historian exercised on him "an unexpectedly powerful, almost bewitching influence" (Troeltsch-Bousset, 22). On Troeltsch's political outlook, cf. Marianne Weber's judgment of him in the late 1890s, *Max Weber*, 228: "Troeltsch's views at that time made him part of the older National Liberal generation; social and democratic ideals were alien to his strongly bourgeois instincts. He did not believe in many things that the Webers were striving for—neither in the intellectual and political development of the working classes nor in the intellectual development of women."

121. Cf. "Christliche Ethik," 17–19.

122. Ibid., 19–22.

123. Ibid., 22–26.

124. Ibid., 27–29.

125. Ibid., 29–32.

126. Ibid., 38–40.

127. Ibid., 45–50.

128. Ibid., 51–53.

129. Ibid., 40–43.

130. Ibid., 53–57.

131. Ibid., 54.

132. On the protestant church in Baden, see Hermann Erbacher, ed., *Vereinigte Evangelische Landeskirche in Baden, 1821–1971. Dokumente und Aufsätze* (Karlsruhe, 1971); and Eckhart Lorenz, "Protestantische Reaktionen auf die Entwicklung der sozialistischen Arbeiterbewegung. Mannheim 1890–1933," in *Archiv für Sozialgeschichte* XVI (1976), 371–416, which tells an interesting story of middle-class resistance to church social work, even in relatively enlightened Baden.

133. On Jolly, see Adolf Hausrath, *Alte Bekannte. Gedächtnisblätter* I. *Zur Erinnerung an Julius Jolly* (Leipzig, 1899).

134. On liberalism and Protestantism in nineteenth- and early twentieth-century Baden, see *Badische Geschichte. Vom Grossherzogtum bis zur Gegenwart*, ed. Landeszentrale für politische Bildung Baden-Württembergs (Stuttgart, 1979); Andreas Cser, "Badischer Landtag bis 1918," in Günther Bradler and Franz Quarthal, eds., *Von der Ständeversammlung zum demokratischen Parlament. Die Geschichte der Volksvertretungen in Baden-Württemberg* (Stuttgart, 1982), 153–182; Hans Fenske, *Der liberale Südwesten. Freiheitliche und demokratische Traditionen in Baden und Württemberg 1790–1933* (Stuttgart, 1981); Lothar Gall, *Der Liberalismus als regierende Partei. Das Grossherzogtum Baden zwischen Restauration und Reichsgründung* (Weisbaden, 1963); and Josef Becker, *Liberaler Staat und Kirche in der Ära von Reichsgründung und Kulturkampf. Geschichte und Strukturen ihres Verhältnisses in Baden 1860–1876* (Mainz, 1973). On the period from 1905 to 1914 see Jürgen Thiel, *Die Grossblockpolitik der Nationalliberalen Partei Badens, 1905 bis 1914* (Stuttgart, 1976).

135. On Rothe and the Protestant Association, see Becker, *Liberaler Staat und Kirche*, 179ff. See also the biography by Adolf Hausrath, *Richard Rothe und seine Freunde*, 2 vols. (Berlin, 1902–06).

136. Troeltsch, *Richard Rothe* (Freiburg, Leipzig, and Tübingen, 1899). See also Troeltsch, "Rotheliteratur," in *Die Christliche Welt* XIII (1899), 18–19; idem, "Richard Rothe," in *Die Christliche Welt* XIII (1899), 77–81; and idem, "Rotheliteratur," in *Die Christliche Welt* XIII (1899), 327–338.

137. See Thiel, *Grossblock*, 40ff.

138. Ibid.

139. Troeltsch, *Die Trennung von Staat und Kirche, der staatliche Religionsunterricht und die theologischen Fakultäten* (Heidelberg, 1906). On the conflict over confessional schools, see Manfred Stadelhofer, *Der Abbau der Kulturkampfgesetzgebung im Grossherzogtum Baden, 1878–1918* (Mainz, 1969), 301ff.

140. Troeltsch, *Die Trennung von Staat und Kirche*, 36.

141. Ibid., 36–37.

142. Ibid., 39.

143. *Verhandlungen der Ersten Kammer der Stände-Versammlung des Grossherzogtums Baden*, 45. Landtag 1911/12, Protokollheft CLIV, Sitzung vom 23. Februar 1912, 98.

144. For two early reactions to the war, see Troeltsch's speeches, *Nach Erklärung der Mobilmachung* [2 August 1914] (Heidelberg, 1914), and *Unser Volksheer* [3 November 1914] (Heidelberg, 1914). Troeltsch's mood in the fall of 1914 was more apprehensive than these two propaganda efforts alone would indicate. In a text dated 5 September 1914, "Der Krieg und die Internationalität der geistigen Kultur," in *Internationale Monatsschrift für Wissenschaft, Kunst und Technik* IX (1914), he feared for the unity of European culture and particularly regretted Germany's broken ties to England, 55–56. In "Friede auf Erden," a Christmas reflection in *Die Hilfe* XX (1914), 833–834, Troeltsch warned against deification of the nation and asked his readers to remember the otherworldly spirit of the season.

145. The essay, "Die Ideen von 1914" (1916), in Troeltsch, *Deutscher Geist und Westeuropa* (Tübingen, 1925), was published at a time when the "spirit of 1914" had become a memory—one that Troeltsch perhaps wished to turn into a piece of morale-building mythology by recalling it. On the "Ideas of 1914," see Hermann Lübbe, *Politische Philosophie in Deutschland,* 173–238. Lübbe considers Troeltsch to be the most responsible of the thinkers who propagated the notion, contrasting him favorably to Rudolf Eucken, Paul Natorp, Johann Plenge, Werner Sombart, Georg Simmel, and Max Scheler. See his estimation of Troeltsch, 228ff.

146. Troeltsch, "Die Ideen von 1914," 41–42.

147. Ibid., 42–43, 48. See also Troeltsch's praise for Tönnies's discovery of the community-society schema in "Konservativ und Liberal," in *Die Christliche Welt* XXX (1916), 649–650.

148. For some of Troeltsch's judgments of the general course of the war and its historical significance, see Troeltsch, "Imperialismus," in *Die neue Rundschau* XXVI (1915), 1–14; "Der Ansturm der westlichen Demokratie," in Adolf von Harnack et al., *Die deutsche Freiheit* (Gotha, 1917), 79–113; "Der innere Zusammenhang der politischen Forderungen," in *Von deutscher Volkskraft. Zweite Veröffentlichung des Volksbundes fur Freiheit und Vaterland* (Gotha, 1918), 6–21; "Anklagen auf Defaitismus," in *Deutsche Politik* III (1918), 661–669; and "Das Wesen des Weltkrieges," in *Der Weltkrieg in seiner Einwirkung auf das deutsche Volk,* ed. Max Schwarte (Leipzig, 1918), 7–25.
  For collective portraits of Troeltsch and the moderate academic elite, see Rathje, *Welt des freien Protestantismus,* especially the letters from Troeltsch to Martin Rade (which have since disappeared) cited on 240 and 256–257; Gottfried Mehnert, *Evangelische Kirche und Politik, 1917–1919* (Düsseldorf, 1959), 61–62, 152ff.; Fischer, *Germany's Aims in the First World War,* 172–173, 329–330, 604, and passim; Klaus Schwabe, *Wissenschaft und Kriegsmoral. Die deutschen Hochschullehrer und die politischen Grundfragen des Ersten Weltkrieges* (Göttingen, 1969); and Gustav Schmidt, *Deutscher Historismus und der Übergang zur parlamentarischen Demokratie. Untersuchungen zu den politischen Gedanken von Meinecke-Troeltsch-Max Weber* (Lübeck and Hamburg, 1964). See also the sketch of Troeltsch's political activities in Robert J. Rubanowice, *Crisis in Consciousness: The Thought of Ernst Troeltsch* (Tallahassee, Fla., 1982), 99–130, and the discussion of his wartime and postwar views in Köhler, *Ernst Troeltsch,* 292ff.

149. Troeltsch, *Spektator-Briefe. Aufsätze über die deutsche Revolution und die Weltpolitik 1918/22,* ed. Hans Baron (Tübingen, 1924).

150. Ibid., 16 Nov. 1918, 4ff.; 30 Nov. 1918, 20.

151. Ibid., 19 Dec. 1919, 90; 12 Jan. 1920, 96.

152. Ibid., 23 May 1919, 55; 29 Feb. 1920, 111–112.

153. Cf. Troeltsch's letters to Gertrud von le Fort from 26 Feb. 1917 to 25 April 1922. For example, he wrote on 2 Dec. 1918, "Perhaps things will be easier than I fear now. But I am deathly sad at heart and often think: happy are the dead. As a five-year-old boy I helped celebrate 1870, my most beautiful childhood memory! My heart bleeds when I think that it was a passing episode. From now on there will only be a greater Switzerland if all goes well. I still can't imagine the new order, my heart is still with the old Empire, and I can only slowly work up my feelings for the new world, which will be poor, small, and weak. Of course the community of faith was always more my home than the state. In truth I have now retreated to the former. There all hearts meet for whom love burns brightest." Universitätsbibliothek Heidelberg, Signatur n.3653.14.

Cf. Gertrud von le Fort's remembrance of Troeltsch's melancholy mood in a conversation with her a few months before his death in 1923—Gertrud von le Fort, *Die Hälfte des Lebens* (Munich, 1965), 88–89.

154. Troeltsch, "Walther Rathenau, dem ermordeten Freunde" (1922), idem, *Deutscher Geist und Westeuropa*, 258–264.

155. *Gesammelte Schriften* III.

156. See Frederic Spotts, *The Churches and Politics in Germany* (Middletown, Conn., 1973).

Chapter 4

1. The entry is dated November 1904. Tönnies Papers Cb54.43:02.

2. For Weber's and Tönnies's exchanges and mutual assessments, see *Economy and Society*, 4, 41–43; Weber's letter of 1908 to Tönnies cited in *Werk und Person*, 398–99, 670; Tönnies, "Kulturbedeutung der Religionen" (1919), in Tönnies, *Soziologische Studien und Kritiken* II (Jena, 1926), 353–380; and the exchanges between Weber and Tönnies in *Verh. DGS* I and II.

Weber's response to Tönnies's book *Die Sitte* singled out *Wesenwille* as a problematic concept containing illegitimate value judgments as well as purely heuristic description. See Weber's letter to Tönnies, 29 August 1910, copy in Tönnies Papers Cb56:878b. Original in Zentrales Staatsarchiv, Merseburg, East Germany, Repr. 92 Weber Nr. 30 Bd. 6, Bl. 15–16.

For other evaluations of the relationship see *Biography*, 393; Guenther Roth, introduction to *Economy and Society*, cii; Talcott Parsons, *The Structure of Social Action* II, 686–694; Werner J. Cahnman, "Tönnies and Weber: Comparisons and Excerpts," in Cahnmann, ed., *Ferdinand Tönnies: A New Evaluation*, 257ff.; and idem, "Tönnies and Weber: A Rejoinder," in *European Journal of Sociology* XXII (1981), 154–157.

3. Friedrich Wilhelm Graf suggests that Troeltsch's willingness to criticize the antidemocratic structure of the Wilhelmine political order grew under Weber's influence. See Graf, "Friendship between Experts: Notes on Weber and Troeltsch," in Wolfgang J. Mommsen and Jürgen Osterhammel, *Max Weber and His Contemporaries* (London, Boston, Sydney, 1987, 215–233).

4. The history of the Anglo-American reception of Weber as a positivist and prophet of the end of ideology whose main theme was the development of Western rationality and the reimportation of this interpretation into a post-1945 Germany anxious to be freed of the burdens of its past will bemuse future generations of intellectual historians. For succinct defenses of this point of view, see Ernst Topitsch, "Max Weber and Sociology Today," and Talcott Parsons, "Value-Freedom and Objectivity," in *Max Weber and*

Sociology Today, ed. Otto Stammer, 8–25, 27–50. Of course, we all remain greatly indebted to the efforts of Parsons and others who made Weber so widely known to the English-speaking world; without their labors of translation and interpretation, we would not be in a position to argue about Weber today.

I make no claims to originality in focusing on Weber's allegiance to Protestant *Persönlichkeit;* it is one of the central themes of Marianne Weber's biography. Despite the aspersions that positivist scholars occasionally cast on her work—as if a mere woman could be trusted to chronicle the life of so manly a hero of modern social science!—it is a highly accurate, insightful portrait of a life and an era. My interpretation of the role of *Persönlichkeit* in Weber's thought also owes a great deal to Karl Löwith, *Max Weber and Karl Marx,* ed. Tom Bottomore and William Outhwaite (London and Boston, 1982), and Wolfgang Mommsen, "Universalgeschichtliches und politisches Denken," in *Max Weber. Gesellschaft, Politik und Geschichte* (Frankfurt am Main, 1974), 97–143. Wilhelm Hennis, *Max Webers Fragestellung,* contains an interesting account of *Persönlichkeit* in Weber's thought complementing my concentration on its religious origins.

5. Several important essays have recently examined Weber's work from the 1890s. See Lawrence A. Scaff, "Weber before Weberian Sociology," in *British Journal of Sociology* XXXV (1984), 190–215; Keith Tribe, "Prussian Agriculture—German Politics: Max Weber 1892–97," in *Economy and Society* XII (1983), 181–226; and Martin Riesebrodt, "From Patriarchalism to Capitalism: The Theoretical Context of Max Weber's Agrarian Studies (1892–93)," in *Economy and Society* XV (1986), 476–502.

6. On Weber's father see *Max Weber and German Politics,* 1ff.

7. Hermann Baumgarten, *Der deutsche Liberalismus. Eine Selbstkritik,* ed. Adolf M. Birke (1866; Frankfurt am Main, Berlin and Vienna, 1974), 43.

8. See Birke's introduction, ibid., 19; and *Max Weber and German Politics,* 4ff.

9. Weber to Hermann Baumgarten, 30 April 1888, in *Werk und Person,* 66.

10. Ibid., 67–68.

11. Jean Daniel Souchay (1736–1811) was called to the Frankfurt Reform parish in 1765. His fifth child, Carolina Louisa Emilia Souchay (1805–1881), was Weber's maternal grandmother and married his grandfather, Georg A. E. F. Fallenstein (1790–1853), in 1835. Through the Souchay family, Max Weber was distantly related to Felix Mendelssohn. See *Deutsches Familienarchiv* Bd. XIX (1961), Otto Döhner, ed., *Das Hugenottengeschlecht Souchay de la Duboissière und seine Nachkommen.*

12. Hausrath was married to Henriette Fallenstein, one of Helene's sisters. Cf. *Biography,* 17, 66; cf. Troeltsch's reaction to Hausrath, above, 51.

13. Cf. Weber's attack on "purely external, purely formal bureaucratic religion, as is peculiar to feudalism and conservatism, the officers' corps and feudalized civil service, the penetration of this bureaucratized formal church life into our middle class," in his remarks on the speech by Karl Oldenberg in *Verh. d. Ev.-Soz. Kongresses* VIII (1897), 110.

14. Max Weber to Alfred Weber, 25 March 1884, in *Werk und Person,* 24–25.

15. On Weber and Channing, see *Biography,* 28, 86–90; and Max Weber to Helene Weber in Max Weber *Jugendbriefe,* ed. Marianne Weber (Tübingen, 1936), 8 July 1884, 120–121, and 6 December 1885, 191.

16. On Channing (1780–1842), see William Ellery Channing, *Works* (6 vols.; Boston, 1849); David P. Edgell, *William Ellery Channing: An Intellectual Portrait* (Boston, 1955); Robert L. Patterson, *The Philosophy of William Ellery Channing* (New York, 1952); and Madeleine Rice, *Federal Street Pastor: The Life of William Ellery Channing* (New York, 1961).

17. On the early history of the Protestant Social Congress, see *Religion and Industrial Society*, ch. 1.

18. On Baumgarten, idem, *Meine Lebensgeschichte* (Tübingen, 1929).

19. Adolf von Harnack, *Lehrbuch der Dogmengeschichte* (3 vols.), Freiburg, 1885–1890).

20. See *Economy and Society*, 216.

21. For a succinct statement of his views, see Rudolf Sohm, *Das Verhältnis von Staat und Kirche. Aus dem Begriff von Staat und Kirche entwickelt* (Tübingen, 1873). For his concept of charisma, idem, *Kirchenrecht* vol. I (Leipzig, 1892), 28–38. Cf. Troeltsch's skeptical remarks on Sohm in *Social Teachings*, 98, 825–827, 852.
On Sohm's activities as social reformer in the 1890s see Andreas Bühler, *Kirche und Staat bei Rudolf Sohm* (Zurich, 1965); and Wolfgang Huber, *Kirche und Öffentlichkeit* (Stuttgart, 1973), 88ff.

22. On Naumann, see Theodor Heuss, *Friedrich Naumann. Der Mann, das Werk, die Zeit* (Stuttgart and Berlin, 1937); Werner Conze, "Friedrich Naumann: Grundlagen und Ansatz seiner Politik in der national-sozialen Zeit (1895 bis 1903)," in *Schicksalwege deutscher Vergangenheit. Beiträge zur Deutung der letzten hundertfünfzig Jahre. Festschrift für Siegfried A. Kaehler*, ed. Walter Hubatsch (Dusseldorf, 1950), 355–387; Richard Nürnberger, "Imperialismus, Sozialismus und Christentum bei Friedrich Naumann," *Historische Zeitschrift* CLXX (1950), 525–548; Hermann Timm, *Friedrich Naumanns theologischer Widerruf* (Munich, 1967); William O. Shanahan, "Friedrich Naumann: A German View of Power and Nationalism," in *Nationalism and Internationalism: Essays Inscribed to Carlton J. H. Hayes*, ed. Edward Mead Earle (New York, 1950), 352–398; and Peter Theiner, *Sozialer Liberalismus und Weltpolitik. Friedrich Naumann im wilhelminischen Deutschland (1860–1919)* (Baden-Baden, 1983).
From Naumann's writings, see *Werke I. Religiöse Schriften* (Cologne and Opladen, 1964) and *Demokratie und Kaisertum. Ein Handbuch für innere Politik* (Schöneberg, 1900).

23. Weber, "Was heisst Christlich-Sozial? Gesammelte Aufsätze von Friedrich Naumann," in *Die Christliche Welt* VIII (1894), 472–477.

24. On Naumann's political party, the National Social Union, see Dieter Düding, *Der National-Soziale Verein, 1896–1903. Der Gescheiterte Versuch einer parteipolitischen Synthese von Nationalismus, Sozialismus und Liberalismus* (Munich and Vienna, 1972).

25. On Weber's relationship to Naumann, see *Biography*, passim; *Max Weber and German Politics*, passim; and *Werk und Person*, 615–618.

26. On the Social Policy Association, see the summary in Gordon Craig, *Germany 1866–1945* (New York, 1980), 87; Dieter Lindenlaub, *Richtungskämpfe im Verein für Sozialpolitik. Wissenschaft und Sozialpolitik im Kaiserreich vornehmlich vom Beginn des "Neuen Kurses" bis zum Ausbruch des ersten Weltkrieges (1890–1914)*, Vierteljahrsschrift für Sozial- und Wirtschaftsgeschichte, Beihefte LII–LIII (Wiesbaden, 1967); Marie-Louise Plessen, *Die Wirksamkeit des Vereins für Socialpolitik von 1872–1890. Studien zu Kathesder- und Staatssozialismus* (Berlin, 1975); Martin Heilmann, *Adolf Wagner. Ein deutscher Nationalökonom im Urteil der Zeit. Probleme seiner biographischen und theoriegeschichtlichen Würdigung*

im Lichte neuer Quellen (Frankfurt am Main and New York, 1980); and Albert Müssig-gang, *Die soziale Frage in der historischen Schule der deutschen Nationalökonomie* (Tübingen, 1968).

27. On Weber's research on the agrarian question and the public response see Martin Riesebrodt, introduction to Max Weber, *Gesamtausgabe*, vol. III: *Die Lage der Landarbeiter im ostelbischen Deutschland: 1892* (Tübingen, 1984).

28. The following writings by Weber treat the rural crisis in the context of the Protestant reform movement: "Die Erhebung des Evangelisch-Sozialen Kongresses über die Verhältnisse der Landarbeiter Deutschlands," in *Die Christliche Welt* VII (1893), 535–540; "Die deutschen Landarbeiter," *Verh. d. Ev.-Soz. Kongresses* V (1894), 61–82; and Weber's comment on Karl Oldenberg, "Über Deutschland als Industriestaat," ibid., VIII (1897), 105–113, 122–123.

29. Paul Göhre, *Drei Monate Fabrikarbeiter und Handwerkerbursche. Eine praktische Studie* (Leipzig, 1891).

30. Weber, "Zur Rechtfertigung Göhres," in *Die Christliche Welt* VI (1892), especially 1107.

31. Ernst Troeltsch, "Max Weber," in Troeltsch, *Deutscher Geist und Westeuropa*, 247–252.

32. Paul Göhre, "Die deutschen Landarbeiter," *Verh. d. Ev.-Soz. Kongresses* V (1894), 61.

33. Weber, "Die deutschen Landarbeiter," ibid., 80. Italics are Weber's.

34. Ibid., 87–91.

35. See the reports from the *Kreuzzeitung*, the *Reichsbote*, and the *National-Zeitung*, in *Mitteilungen des Evangelisch-Sozialen Kongresses* III (1894), 4ff.

36. Albin Gladen, *Geschichte der Sozialpolitik in Deutschland. Eine Analyse ihrer Bedingungen, Formen, Zielsetzungen und Auswirkungen* (Wiesbaden, 1974), 80, 169.

37. *Stenographische Berichte über die Verhandlungen des Reichstages*, IX. Legislaturperiode, 3. Session 1894–1895, Bd. I (Berlin 1895), 206ff. On Stumm, see Fritz Hellwig, *Carl Ferdinand Freiherr von Stumm-Halberg, 1836–1901* (Heidelberg and Saarbrücken, 1936), 295–312.

38. *Stenographische Berichte über die Verhandlungen des Abgeordnetenhauses*, XVIII. Legislaturperiode, 2. Session, Bd. II (Berlin, 1895), 1068ff., especially 1080.

39. *Die Christliche Welt* IX/7 (14 February 1895), 167–168; *Mitteilungen des Evangelisch-Sozialen Kongresses* IV (February 1895), 1.

40. Weber, "Der Nationalstaat und die Volkswirtschaftspolitik. Akademische Antrittsrede" (1895), in Weber, *Gesammelte Politische Schriften*, ed. Johannes Winckelmann (Tübingen, 1971), 1–25.

41. Cf. Mommsen, *Max Weber and German Politics*, 91–100, 123ff.

42. *Verh. d. Ev.-Soz. Kongresses* VIII (1897), 105–113, 122–123.

43. On Weber's breakdown see Mitzman, *The Iron Cage*.

44. Weber originally published "Die protestantische Ethik und der 'Geist' des Kapitalis-mus" as two contributions to the *Archiv f. Sozialwiss.* in November 1904 and approxi-mately June 1905. A revised version, prepared in 1919, appeared in the first volume of his *Gesammelte Aufsätze zur Religionssoziologie* (Tübingen, 1920), 17–206. Johannes Winckelmann prepared an edition of the revised version, published (together with re-lated essays) in its sixth edition in 1981. The English translation by Talcott Parsons is also based on the revised version of 1920.

Critical editions of both the first and the second versions of the essay are in prepa-ration as part of the complete edition of Weber's works (Max-Weber-Gesamtausgabe) under way in West Germany. The original edition of the essay has never been re-printed, and subsequent editions do not indicate the changes Weber made in the re-vised version of 1920. Weber himself, angered by criticisms of the original version, declared in a bibliographical note that his changes had not in any significant way weak-ened or altered his argument. Comparison of the 1904/5 and 1920 texts confirms one of Weber's assertions: he did not weaken his argument. His numerous significant ad-ditions, however, had the purpose of fitting *The Protestant Ethic* into the larger context of his studies of the world religions and somewhat obscured the essay's original inten-tions. The "author's introduction" to the Parsons and Winckelmann editions comes from the 1920 version; so does much of the comparative material on Jansenism, Indian religion, ancient Judaism, Islam, and Catholicism. These additions affect one feature of the 1904/5 version that is particularly important for my argument, the stark contrast between Lutheranism and Calvinism. It retains its structural integrity, but loses its ar-chitectonic clarity amid the wealth of added ornamentation: I count at least fifty signif-icant changes, which taken together create an appearance rather different from the original. Readers who seriously wish to test Weber's original historical intentions, as this chapter aims at doing, will have to go back to the original text.

I have cited from the readily available Winckelmann edition and noted significant differences between it and the 1904/5 version. Parsons's translation is serviceable, but does not attempt to render the dense allusiveness of Weber's prose. Although Weber is often criticized for his stylistic carelessness, *The Protestant Ethic* shows a metaphorical complexity rivaling that of great literature. I have therefore preferred to make my own translations from the German, taking special care to preserve stylistic peculiarities such as Weber's heavy use of italics and (not entirely translatable!) his intricate syntax.

On the diverging interpretations of the essay that arise from the two versions Weber wrote, see the excellent discussion in Gordon Marshall, *In Search of the Spirit of Capital-ism: An Essay on Max Weber's Protestant Ethic Thesis* (New York, 1982), 21–22. Cf. the perspectives on Weber's work in Friedrich Tenbruck, "Das Werk Max Webers," in KZSS XXVII (1975), 663–702; Martin Riesebrodt, "Ideen, Interessen, Rationalisierung. Kri-tische Anmerkungen zu F. H. Tenbrucks Interpretation des Werkes Max Webers," in KZSS XXXII (1980), 111–129; Wolfgang Schluchter, *The Rise of Western Rationalism: Max Weber's Developmental History* (Berkeley and Los Angeles, 1981); and Schluchter, "Max Webers Religionssoziologie. Eine werkgeschichtliche Rekonstruktion," in KZSS XXXVI (1984), 342–365.

Several useful guides survey the Protestant ethic controversy. See Ephraim Fischoff, "The Protestant Ethic and the Spirit of Capitalism: The History of a Controversy," in *Social Research* XI (1944), 53–77; Robert W. Green, ed., *Protestantism, Capitalism, and Social Science: The Weber Thesis Controversy* (Lexington, Mass., 1973); the bibliographical essay in David Little, *Religion, Order and Law: A Study in Pre-Revolutionary England* (New York, 1970), 226–237; Gordon Marshall, *Presbyteries and Profits: Calvinism and the Devel-opment of Capitalism in Scotland, 1560–1707* (Oxford, 1980), 325ff.; and Marshall, *In Search of the Spirit of Capitalism.*

45. Riese, *Die Hochschule auf dem Wege zum wissenschaftlichen Grossbetrieb,* 346, 354.

46. Ibid., 210; *Biography,* 228.

47. *Biography*, 227.

48. Cf. Troeltsch chapter, above, 52.

49. Georg Jellinek, *Die Erklärung der Menschen- und Bürgerrechte. Ein Beitrag zur modernen Verfassungsgeschichte* (Leipzig, 1895), 31–32. Cf. Guenther Roth's discussion of Jellinek and Weber in Reinhard Bendix and Roth, *Scholarship and Partisanship: Essays on Max Weber* (Berkeley, Los Angeles and London, 1971), 308–310.
    Cf. the following passage from the original version of *The Protestant Ethic* (1905, 43):

No matter how highly one regards the historical significance of the Enlightenment, its ideals of freedom lacked anchorage in those *positive* impulses that alone guarantee continuity of the kind that gave Gladstone's political work its entire 'constructive' note. For the history of the rise and *political* significance of 'freedom of conscience,' Jellinek's 'Declaration of Human Rights' is by general acknowledgment fundamental. I too am personally indebted to this work for the first stimulus for renewed concern with Puritanism.

This passage, which was omitted from the second version of the essay, indicates that Weber's reflections leading up to *The Protestant Ethic* began no earlier than 1895. Another passage written 1910 in reply to one of the essay's critics (with the purpose of asserting that his concern with the origins of capitalism predated Sombart's *Der Moderne Kapitalismus*, which appeared in 1902) states that Weber had publicly discussed his work on related notions in class twelve years earlier, i.e., in 1898 (*Prot. Ethik Kritiken*, 150). Hence Weber's work on *The Protestant Ethic* began 1895 to 1898, coinciding with his years of political setback.
    At the beginning of 1905, Weber joined the Eranos Circle, a discussion group newly founded by Adolf Deissmann, whose other members included Jellinek, Troeltsch, and other historians, economists, classical scholars, and theologians. The discussions apparently gravitated to a mixture of religious and sociological questions. While writing the second part of *The Protestant Ethic*, Weber gave a talk there on Protestant asceticism. See *Biography*, 356.

50. *Biography*, 199–200. Cf. *Max Weber and German Politics*, 3.

51. *Biography*, 261. I have used "calling" instead of "vocation" to translate *Beruf* and have corrected a grammatical error ("me" instead of the translation's "I"). Cf. Marianne Weber, *Max Weber. Ein Lebensbild* (Heidelberg, 1950), 297.

52. Cf. *Biography*, 263–264.

53. Ibid., 265ff., 278–279, 325–326, 356. Cf. Winckelmann's introduction to *Prot. Ethik*, 5. On the Louisiana Purchase Exposition, see Robert W. Rydell, *All the World's a Fair: Visions of Empire at American International Expositions, 1876–1916* (Chicago, 1984), ch. 6.

54. See the essays by Fischer and Rachfahls in *Prot. Ethik Kritiken*.

55. *Prot. Ethik*, 55ff.; cf. *Prot. Ethik* 1904, 26ff.

56. Ibid. Cf. Sombart, *Der Moderne Kapitalismus* vol. I (Leipzig, 1902), xviii, 3, 11. Sombart's identification of rationality with planful activity (3) closely resembled Marx's definition of human work in contrast to the instinctual labor of other forms of life in *Capital*, transl. Samuel Moore and Edward Aveling (New York, n.d.), 198.

57. *Prot. Ethik*, 85–90.

58. *Ibid.*, 40ff.

59. Ibid., 42.

60. Ibid., 44.

61. Marx, *Das Kapital. Kritik der politischen Ökonomie*, vol. I (1867; Frankfurt am Main, 1976), 147. My translation. Cf. Marx, *Capital*, 150.

62. On this pattern of inversion and its fundamental importance for Marx's thought, see Jerrold Seigel, *Marx's Fate: The Shape of a Life* (Princeton, 1978).

63. *Capital*, 170–171.

64. Weber, "Antikritisches zum 'Geist' des Kapitalismus" (1910), in *Prot. Ethik Kritiken*, 167. Weber came back to the same point in his final reply to Rachfahls, "Antikritisches Schlusswort zum 'Geist' des Kapitalismus" (1910), 319, contrasting the Puritans' unbroken unity of inward *Persönlichkeit* and worldly calling with the disintegration of that unity and contempt for the *Berufsmensch* of his own time.

65. *Prot. Ethik*, 142.

66. Ibid., 201.

67. Ibid. On Gladstone, see *Prot. Ethik* 1905, 43.

68. See *Prot. Ethik*, 118–143. This section includes the following additions on Catholicism and other world religions diluting the first edition's Lutheran-Calvinist comparison: 123, lines 6–21; 132, line 35, to 133, line 31; 133, line 33, to 134, line 1; 134, lines 27–28, 29–31, 32–33.

69. Ibid., 122–123.

70. Ibid., 127ff.

71. Ibid., 129, 145, 207, 223.

72. Ibid., 142.

73. Matthias Schneckenburger, *Vergleichende Darstellung des lutherischen und reformierten Lehrbegriffs* (Stuttgart, 1855).

74. *Prot. Ethik*, 129, 194.

75. According to Schneckenburger, because the Lutheran *unio mystica* was personal and substantive, it drained energy away from the church. But for the Calvinist there was no difference between them; the church as mystical body of Christ *was* the place of the *unio mystica*. Weber argued instead that the Lutheran belonged to a mystical community of persons and that the Calvinist's relationship to the church and its members was impersonal.

Weber, like Troeltsch in *The Social Teachings*, was writing against Ritschl, who argued for the essential identity of Lutheran and Calvinist doctrine, both of which, he maintained, made rebirth possible only through the church community. See Ritschl, *Rechtfertigung und Versöhnung* vol. I, 143–145, 148, 154ff., 185, 203ff. Ritschl specifically attacked Schneckenburger's psychological interpretation of rebirth as an event taking place outside the believer's consciousness of community membership—ibid., 205ff.,

263–264, 212–213, 216. Weber was arguing with Schneckenburger and against Ritschl that official doctrine only covered the individuation that in empirical fact was taking place in the Calvinist psyche. Weber accused Ritschl of letting dogmatic assumptions distort the evidence. See *Prot. Ethik*, 194, 207–208, 222–223.

76. "In its awesome inhumanity," Weber wrote of predestination, "this teaching must have had one consequence above all for the mood of a generation that submitted to its grandiose consequences: a feeling of unbelievable inner *isolation of the single individual*" (*Prot. Ethik*, 122). To support this sentence Weber turned to Edward Dowden for the following observation about Bunyan: "The deepest community is found not in institutions or corporations or churches, but in the secrets of a solitary heart." Weber thought Dowden was talking about the relationship between man and God. The plain sense of Dowden's text makes clear that his point could hardly contradict Weber's more completely, for it actually discussed the mediated relationship between man and man. The full passage read, "Yet through what is most personal in each of us we come upon the common soul; let any man record faithfully his most private experiences in any of the great affairs of life, and his words awaken in other souls innumerable echoes; the deepest community is found not in institutions or corporations, or churches, but in the secrets of the solitary heart. And because Bunyan, rich as his nature was in our common humanity, put into his writings the central facts of his personal life, his books are not for himself alone, but for all men of like passions, who must each tread for himself the same arduous way"— *Puritans and Anglicans* (New York, 1901), 234.

77. On covenant theology see Perry Miller, "The Marrow of Puritan Divinity" and "The Puritan State and Puritan Society," in *Errand into the Wilderness* (New York, 1964), 48–98 and 141–152; William A. Clebsch, *England's Earliest Protestants, 1520–1535* (New Haven and London, 1964), 185–195; David Zaret, *The Heavenly Contract: Ideology and Organization in Pre-Revolutionary Puritanism* (Chicago, 1984); and Marshall, *Presbyteries and Profits*, 109–112.

78. *Prot. Ethik*, 45–46.

79. Ibid., 71.

80. Ibid., 127.
   Weber sketched out his conception of the relationship between eschatology and worldly politics and work more fully in *Economy and Society*. Particularly important are the assertions that nineteenth-century socialism was an eschatological movement—515, 874; that Russian revolutionaries represent the last great movement of this kind—515–516; and that in their eschatological phase, religious movements such as early Christianity, Lutheranism, and Calvinism cut across classes, only developing their "elective affinities" with social strata at the time of their secularization—1180–1181. These remarks show a general tendency toward dehistoricization of eschatology and its integration into a "law" by which eschatological expectations inevitably give way to the routine of everyday existence.

81. *Prot. Ethik*, 75. Cf. the argument that the Civil War turned the Puritan calling from a revolutionary into a socially conservative, more purely ascetic idea in Arnold Eisen, "Called to Order: The Role of the Puritan Berufsmensch in Weberian Sociology," in *Sociology* XIII (1979), 203–218.

82. Weber, "'Objectivity' in Social Science and Social Policy," in Weber, *The Methodology of the Social Sciences*, transl. Edward A. Shils and Henry A. Finch (New York, 1949), 72ff.; and Weber, "Roscher's 'Historical Method'" (1903), in Weber, *Roscher and Knies: The Logical Problems of Historical Economics*, transl. Guy Oakes (New York and London, 1975), 55ff. Cf. *Prot. Ethik*, 39–40.

83. Weber never attempted a systematic exposition of his views on value-freedom. I have introduced the categories of ontological and teleological as a shorthand for the many kinds of errors he attacks.

84. Weber, "Roscher's 'Historical Method,'" in *Roscher and Knies*, 61–62, 71–72, 84, 88, 210–211, 231–232.

85. Cf. "Knies and the Problem of Irrationality" (1906), ibid., 191–194.

86. Lindenlaub, *Richtungskämpfe*, 433–443; *Biography*, 414–418.

87. For other interpretations of the German Sociological Society, see *Biography*, 420–424; Guenther Roth, "Das historische Verhältnis der Weberschen Soziologie zum Marxismus," KZSS XX (1968), 442–445; idem, "'Value-Neutrality' in Germany and the United States," in Bendix and idem, *Scholarship and Partisanship*, 34–54; René König, "Fünfzig Jahre Deutsche Gesellschaft für Soziologie (1909 bis 1959)," in KZSS XI (1959), 1–2; Paul Honigsheim, "Die Gründung der Deutschen Gesellschaft für Soziologie in ihren geistesgeschichtlichen Zusammenhängen," ibid., 3–10; Leopold von Wiese, "Die Deutsche Gesellschaft für Soziologie. Persönliche Eindrücke in den ersten fünfzig Jahren (1909 bis 1959)," ibid., 11–20; Christian von Ferber, "Der Werturteilsstreit 1909/1959. Versuch einer wissenschaftsgeschichtlichen Interpretation," ibid., 21–37; Ursula Karger, "Deutsche Soziologentage in Perspektive," in *Sociologia Internationalis* XIV (1976), 7–21; Bärbel Meurer, "Vom bildungsbürgerlichen Zeitvertreib zu Fachwissenschaft—Die deutsche Soziologie im Spiegel ihrer Soziologentage," in *Soziologie und Praxis*, ed. Bernhardt Heidtmann and Robert Katzenstein (Cologne, 1979), 210–231; Dirk Käsler, "Der Streit um die Bestimmung der Soziologie auf den Deutschen Soziologentagen 1910–1930," in *Soziologie in Deutschland und Österreich 1918–1945* ed. M. Rainer Lepsius, 199–244; and idem, *Die frühe deutsche Soziologie 1909 bis 1934 und ihre Entstehungs-Milieus*, 50–57.

88. *Biography*, 421.

89. Weber, "Rechenschaftsbericht für die abgelaufenen beiden Jahre," in *Verh. DGS* II, 78.

90. See the report on the opening night of the conference in *Frankfurter Zeitung* 20 Oct. 1910, 3. Morgenblatt. On Merton see Hans Achinger, *Wilhelm Merton in seiner Zeit* (Frankfurt am Main, 1965).

91. On the Society for Social Reform, see Ursula Ratz, *Sozialreform und Arbeiterschaft. Die "Gesellschaft für Sozialreform" und die sozialdemokratische Arbeiterbewegung von der Jahrhundertwende bis zum Ausbruch des Ersten Weltkrieges* (Berlin, 1980).

92. *Biography*, 226, mentions Merton's offer; I assume that its reference to a *Sozialwissenschaftliches Institut* is a misnomer. Weber mentions support for his project from the Institute as well as from the Heidelberg Academy of Science and unnamed private donors. "Rechenschaftsbericht," *Verh. DGS* II, 77.

93. See Weber's "Geschäftsbericht" in *Verh. DGS* I, 61–62, and his notice, "Die Deutsche Gesellschaft für Soziologie," published as an insert in *Arch. f. Sozialwiss.* XXXI (1910). (Attributed to Weber by Martin Riesebrodt in his bibliography to the Max Weber-Gesamtausgabe, in the publisher's prospectus, J. C. B. Mohr 1981. See the bibliography, item 1910-I-8.)

94. *Verh. DGS* I, v.

95. Ibid., 39.

96. "Soziologie der Geselligkeit," ibid., 1ff.

97. "Wege und Ziele der Soziologie. Eröffnungsrede," ibid., 17ff.

98. See Tönnies, *Selbstdarstellung*, 226, in which he recalled, "I considered it appropriate to proceed objectively here [in his talk to the 1910 Sociology Conference] in the sense that I let not so much my personal view occupy the foreground as the idea that had brought the persons there together. . . ." On his role in both prewar conferences, he added, "I always kept to the principle: strict limitation to theoretical knowledge. The question whether and to what extent practical sciences such as ethics and politics were possible was left open" (226).

99. Sombart, "Technik und Kultur," in *Verh. DGS* I, 63ff.

100. Cf. above, 63ff.

101. *Verh. DGS* I, 91, 95.

102. Ibid., 142.

103. Ibid., 166; *Frankfurter Zeitung*, 22 Oct. 1910, 3. Morgenblatt.

104. *Verh. DGS* I, 275ff.

105. Ibid., 278–279.

106. See the discussion, ibid., 310ff. Even Weber's Heidelberg colleague, Eberhard Gothein, spoke up against value-freedom in jurisprudence—ibid., 323.

107. Ibid., 323–324; *Biography*, 423.

108. Weber to Tönnies, 18(?) Oct. 1910; 26 Oct. 1910; 8 Nov. 1910. Copies in DGS Akten Cb56:878b. Originals in Zentrales Staatsarchiv, Merseburg, East Germany, Repr. 92 Weber Nr. 30 Bd. 6, Bl. 25, 26, 34–34a.

109. Weber, "Geschäftsbericht" in *Verh. DGS* I, 41.

110. Cf. Weber's "Rechenschaftsbericht für die abgelaufenen beiden Jahre," in *Verh. DGS* II (1912), 75–79.

111. Alfred Weber, "Der soziologische Kulturbegriff," in *Verh. DGS* II, 1–20. "His [Alfred Weber's] theme, the sociological concept of culture, and the way he treated it placed high demands on the intellectual cooperation of the listeners. . . . Professor Simmel thanked the speaker for his talk, whose profundity and difficulty he recognized with the remark that it was fortunate not to have to discuss the talk"—*Frankfurter Zeitung*, 21 Oct. 1912, Abendblatt. Cf. Lukács's critique, "Zum Wesen und zur Methode der Kultursoziologie," *Arch. f. Sozialwiss.* XXXIX (1914–15), 216–222; and Alfred Weber's reply, "Entgegnung," ibid., 223–226.

112. "Die Nationalität in ihrer soziologischen Bedeutung," *Verh. DGS* II, 21ff. On Barth, see the entry "Barth, Paul," by Carl Brinkmann in *Encyclopedia of the Social Sciences* vol. II (New York, 1930), 469–470. See also Troeltsch's review of Barth's book in *Theologische Literaturzeitung* XXIII (1898), 398–401.

113. *Frankfurter Zeitung*, 22 Oct. 1912, 3. Morgenblatt.

114. Ibid.

115. Ibid.

116. "Die Begriffe Rasse und Gesellschaft und einige damit zusammenhängende Probleme," *Verh. DGS* I, 111ff. Ploetz founded the International Society for Racial Hygiene in 1906 and edited the *Archiv für Rassen- und Gesellschaftsbiologie*. Cf. Colette Guillaumin and Léon Poliakov, "Max Weber et les théories bioraciales du XXe siècle," in *Cahiers internationaux de sociologie* LVI (1974), 115–126.

117. *Verh. DGS* I, 151.

118. On Weber's interest in Ploetz's participation, see Ploetz to Hermann Beck (the Society's corresponding secretary), 26 Sept. 1910, and 1 Oct. 1910; and Weber to Beck, 4 Oct. 1910, in DGS Akten, Cb54.61:1.1. For Weber's reaffirmation of the Society's commitment to founding a social biology section, see *Verh. DGS* I, 215.

119. *Verh. DGS* II, 98ff.

120. Ibid., 135.

121. *Vossische Zeitung*, 22 Oct. 1912, Abend.

122. On Sombart, see Arthur Mitzman, *Sociology and Estrangement*, part III.

123. Sombart, *Die Zukunft der Juden* (Leipzig, 1912). On Sombart's lectures and their public impact, see Jehuda Reinharz, *Fatherland or Promised Land: The Dilemma of the German Jew, 1893–1914* (Ann Arbor, 1975).

124. Sombart, *Die Juden und das Wirtschaftsleben* (Leipzig, 1911). The translation leaves out an important reference to Weber on p. 5 of the original. Cf. Sombart, *The Jews and Modern Capitalism*, transl. M. Epstein (New York, 1969). For a recent interpretation of the controversy between Weber and Sombart, see Freddy Raphäel, *Judaïsme et Capitalisme: Essai sur la controverse entre Max Weber et Werner Sombart* (Paris, 1982).

125. *Verh. DGS* II, 185–186.

126. Ibid., 188ff.

127. Ibid., 190.

128. *Biography*, 424–425.

129. *Verh. DGS* II, 75; *Vossische Zeitung*, 21 Oct. 1912, and 22 Oct. 1912, Abend.

130. Vorstand protocols of 5 July 1913, 1 Nov. 1913, 3 Jan. 1914, 10 Jan. 1914, DGS Akten Cb54.61:1.2.10; the petition, Cb54.61:1.2.05; and Beck to Vorstand, Rundschreiben of 19 June 1914, Cb54.61:1.1.5.

131. Correspondence of Emile Waxweiler (director of the Institut Solvay in Belgium) to Beck, 23 July 1909, 12 Dec. 1913; Waxweiler to Vorstand, 13 March 1914; DGS Akten Cb54.61:1.1. Beck to Vorstand, Rundschreiben of 12 Sept. 1914; Cb54.61:1.1.5. On Waxweiler and the Institut Solvay, see Henry H. Frost, Jr., "The Functional Sociol-

ogy of Emile Waxweiler and the Institut de Sociologie Solvay," in Académie royale de Belgique, Classe des lettres et des sciences morales et politiques, *Mémoires*, LV/5 (1960).

132. Beck to Vorstand, Rundschreiben of 9 Oct. 1914 and 26 Nov. 1914, DGS Akten Cb54.61:1.1.5; Vorstand to Mitglieder, Rundschreiben of 13 Nov. 1914, Cb54.61:1.2.04.

133. Cf. Martin Riesebrodt, "Ideen, Interessen, Rationalisierung," 124–125.

134. *Economy and Society*, 241ff., 1112ff.

135. Ibid., 245.

136. Ibid., 1140–1141.

137. Ibid., 1132–1133, 1139.

138. Weber, *The Religion of India: The Sociology of Hinduism and Buddhism*, transl. Hans Gerth and Don Martindale (Glencoe, Ill., 1958). Cf. Wolfgang Schluchter, ed., *Max Webers Studie über Hinduismus und Buddhismus. Interpretation und Kritik* (Frankfurt am Main, 1984).

139. Weber, *The Religion of China: Confucianism and Taoism* (1920; New York, 1951). Cf. Wolfgang Schluchter, ed., *Max Webers Studie über Konfuzianismus und Taoismus. Interpretation und Kritik* (Frankfurt am Main, 1983).

140. Max Weber, *Ancient Judaism*, transl. Hans Gerth and Don Martindale (1921; New York, 1952). Cf. Wolfgang Schluchter, *Max Webers Studie über das antike Judentum. Interpretation und Kritik* (Frankfurt am Main, 1981).

141. Weber, "Politics as a Vocation" and "Science as a Vocation" in *From Max Weber*, 77–128 and 129–156.

142. On the dates and setting of Weber's lectures, see the comments by Wolfgang Schluchter, "Wertfreiheit und Verantwortungsethik. Zum Verhältnis von Wissenschaft und Politik bei Max Weber," in Schluchter, *Rationalismus der Weltbeherrschung. Studien zu Max Weber* (Frankfurt am Main, 1980), 236–241.

Chapter 5

1. Hans Simmel, "Auszüge aus den Lebenserinnerungen," in *Ästhetik und Soziologie*, 265.

2. Ibid., 247–248.

3. *Buch des Dankes*, 17–21.

4. See *Buch des Dankes* and the memoirs included in Böhringer, *Ästhetik und Soziologie*. On Simmel's cultural identity see also David Frisby, *Sociological Impressionism: A Reassessment of Georg Simmel's Social Theory* (London, 1981); idem, *Fragments of Modernity: Theories of Modernity in the Work of Simmel, Kracauer and Benjamin* (Cambridge, Mass., 1986), ch. 2; and the essays in Heinz-Jürgen Dahme and Otthein Rammstedt, eds., *Georg Simmel und die Moderne. Neue Interpretationen und Materialien* (Frankfurt am Main, 1984).

5. Immanuel Kant, *Critique of Pure Reason*, transl. Norman Kemp Smith (New York, 1965), 233ff. I have greatly benefited from the discussions of interaction in H. J. Paton, *Kant's Metaphysics of Experience*, vol. II (London and New York, 1936), 294–331, and in P. F. Strawson, *The Bounds of Sense: An Essay on Kant's Critique of Pure Reason* (London, 1966), 139–140.

6. See the discussions of interaction in *Über soziale Differenzierung*, 13–14; Simmel, *Soziologie*, 4ff., 25, 29, 30; and *The Philosophy of Money*, 53–56, 129. The latter's preface uses the word *Gegenseitigkeit* but to exactly the same effect as *Wechselwirkung;* Simmel, *Philosophie des Geldes* (1900, 1907; Berlin, 1977), viii. In addition see the important "Anfang einer unvollendeten Selbstdarstellung" in *Buch des Dankes,* 9–10.
For a penetrating discussion of the Kantian foundations of Simmel's thought see Karin Schrader-Kleberg, "Der Begriff der Gesellschaft als regulative Idee. Zur transzendentalen Begründung der Gesellschaft bei Georg Simmel," in *Soziale Welt* XIX (1968), 97–118. See also the discussions of interaction in Frisby, *Sociological Impressionism,* 36ff., 61ff.; Heribert J. Becher, *Georg Simmel. Die Grundlagen seiner Soziologie* (Stuttgart, 1971); and Heinz-Jürgen Dahme, *Soziologie als exakte Wissenschaft. Georg Simmels Ansatz und seine Bedeutung in der gegenwärtigen Soziologie,* 2 vols. (Stuttgart, 1981), 465.

7. On the modernization of Berlin, see Annemarie Lange, *Das wilhelminische Berlin. Zwischen Jahrhundertwende und Novemberrevolution* (Berlin, 1976), 66ff.; Jochen Boberg, Tilmann Fichter, Eckhart Gillen, eds., *Exerzierfeld der Moderne. Industriekultur in Berlin im 19. Jahrhundert* (Munich, 1986); and Boberg, Fichter, and Gillen, *Die Metropole. Industriekultur in Berlin im 20. Jahrhundert* (Munich, 1986).

8. Cf. Simmel's review of Ignaz Jastrow, "Die Aufgaben des Liberalismus in Preussen. Sozialliberal," in *Archiv für soziale Gesetzgebung und Statistik* VI (1893), 622–627.
On Simmel's friendship with Jastrow, see *Buch des Dankes,* 13. Jastrow, *Privatdozent* in economics and editor of *Soziale Praxis,* was fined for insulting a state minister in print, according to Simmel's anonymous article, "Zur Privatdozenten-Frage," *Die Zeit,* 2 May 1896. On Jastrow's dismissal from the editorship of *Soziale Praxis* and replacement by a more reliably bourgeois social reformer, Ernst Francke, see Ratz, *Sozialreform und Arbeiterschaft,* 13–14, 24–25.

9. Simmel, "Ein Wort über soziale Freiheit," in *Sozialpolitisches Zentralblatt* I (1892), 333–335.

10. Simmel, "Weltpolitik," in *Die Neue Zeit* XII (1893–94), vol. II, 165–170.

11. *Über soziale Differenzierung,* 97–99. See also Simmel, "Rosen. Eine soziale Hypothese" (1897), in Simmel, *Schriften zur Soziologie. Eine Auswahl,* ed. Heinz-Jürgen Dahme and Otthein Rammstedt (Frankfurt am Main, 1983), 169–172.

12. Simmel, "Massenpsychologie," in *Die Zeit,* 23 Nov. 1895.

13. Simmel, "Der Frauenkongress und die Sozialdemokratie," in *Die Zukunft* XVII (1896), 84.

14. Simmel, "Soziale Medizin," *Die Zeit,* 13 Feb. 1897.

15. On Simmel's early positivism and its significance for his later work, see Dahme, "Das 'Abgrenzungsproblem' von Philosophie und Wissenschaft bei Georg Simmel. Zur Genese und Systematik einer Problemstellung," in Dahme und Rammstedt, eds., *Simmel und die Moderne,* 202–230.

16. *Über soziale Differenzierung,* 21ff.

17. Ibid., 108.

18. Ibid., 10–12.

19. Ibid., 10, 12–14.

20. Ibid., 14.

21. Cf. Marshall Berman, *All That Is Solid Melts into Air: The Experience of Modernity* (New York, 1982).

22. Tönnies-Paulsen, *Briefwechsel,* 31 Dec. 1890, 290.

23. *Über soziale Differenzierung,* 43.

24. Tönnies, review of *Über soziale Differenzierung* in *Jahrbücher für Nationalökonomie und Statistik* LVI (1891), 272.

25. Ibid., 273.

26. Tönnies, "Simmel als Soziologe," in *Frankfurter Zeitung,* 9 Oct. 1918.

27. Cf. Gustav Schmoller, "Simmels Philosophie des Geldes," in *Schmollers Jahrbuch* XXV (1901), 1–18.

28. Cf. Hans Blumenberg, "Geld oder Leben. Eine metaphorologische Studie zur Konsistenz der Philosophie Georg Simmels," in *Ästhetik und Soziologie,* 121–134.

29. *The Philosophy of Money,* 55.

30. Cf. Hegel, *Philosophy of Right* (1821; New York, 1967), 11.

31. *Biography,* 252–253. Weber makes playful reference to *Philosophie des Geldes* by calling Franklin's credo a *"Philosophie des Geizes"*—*Prot. Ethik,* 42.

32. *The Philosophy of Money,* 254.

33. *Protestant Ethic,* 183.

34. *The Philosophy of Money,* 56.

35. Ibid., 54.

36. Ibid., 101ff.

37. Max Weber, "Georg Simmel as Sociologist," transl. Donald N. Levine in *Social Research* XXXIX (1972), 155–163.

38. On the metaphor of consumption, see Victor Bromberg, *The Novels of Flaubert: A Study of Themes and Techniques* (Princeton, 1966), 51–52.

39. *Protestant Ethic,* 180–181.

40. *The Philosophy of Money,* 232–234.

41. Cf. Tönnies's nostalgia for the traditional town and diatribe against the metropolis in *Community and Society,* 226–228.
For Simmel's rejection of the neohumanist belief in Greek cultural superiority to modernity, see "Humanistisches Märchen," in *Die Neue Zeit* X (1891–92), vol. II, 713–718; "The Future of Our Culture" (1909), in *Simmel: Sociologist and European,* 250–251; "Rodin," in *Philosophische Kultur,* 146; "Vom Tode in der Kunst," in *Frankfurter Zeitung,* 2 April 1915, first morning edition; and *Rembrandt* (1916; Munich, 1985), 6, 79.

42. *The Philosophy of Money,* 404.

43. *Theory of the Novel,* 64. Cf. the interesting discussion of second nature and reification in Russel Jacoby, *Dialectic of Defeat: Contours of Western Marxism* (Cambridge and New York, 1981), 118–120.

44. Cf. *Religion and Industrial Society,* 52ff.

45. *Soziologie,* 4–6.

46. Ibid., 6.

47. Ibid., 24–30; cf. Schrader-Klebert, "Begriff der Gesellschaft als regulative Idee," 110ff.

48. *Soziologie,* ch. 2.

49. Ibid., ch. 5.

50. Ibid., ch. 7, 509ff.

51. Ibid., ch. 4, especially 196.

52. Ibid., chs. 6, 10.

53. Ibid., 8–10, 15–16.

54. Cf. Simmel, "The Meaning of Culture" (1908), in *Simmel: Sociologist and European,* 243–249; "The Future of Our Culture," ibid., 250–252; and "The Concept and Tragedy of Culture" (1911), in *The Conflict in Modern Culture and Other Essays,* ed. K. Peter Etzkorn (New York, 1968), 27–46.

55. Lukács, "Georg Simmel" (1918), in *Buch des Dankes,* 171.

56. Cf. *Buch des Dankes,* 13, and Simmel's essay, "Sociological Aestheticism" (1896), in Simmel, *The Conflict in Modern Culture,* 68–80.

57. *The Philosophy of Money,* 376–380.

58. Ibid., 390–391.

59. Ibid., 390.

60. Nietzsche, *Beyond Good and Evil,* transl. Walter Kaufmann (1886; New York, 1968), 291.

61. Simmel, review of Tönnies, *Der Nietzsche-Kultus. Eine Kritik* (1897), in *Deutsche Literaturzeitung* XVIII (1897), 1645–1651. On the concept of distance in Simmel and Nietzsche, cf. Klaus Lichtblau, "Das 'Pathos der Distanz.' Präliminarien zur Nietzsche-Rezeption bei Georg Simmel," in Dahme and Rammstedt, eds., *Georg Simmel und die Moderne*, 231–281. Cf. the remarks on Simmel in Horst Baier, "Die Gesellschaft. Ein langer Schatten des toten Gottes. Friedrich Nietzsche und die Entstehung der Soziologie aus dem Geist der Dekadenz," in *Nietzsche-Studien* X–XI (1981–82), 6–33.

62. *Gesammelte Schriften* III, 141.

63. Simmel, *Schopenhauer und Nietzsche. Ein Vortragszyklus* (1907; Munich and Leipzig, 1923), 170–192. Cf. Simmel, "Zum Verständnis Nietzsches," *Das freie Wort* II (1902–3), 9ff.

64. Simmel, *Schopenhauer und Nietzsche*, 171.

65. Nietzsche, *Jenseits von Gut und Böse*, in *Werke*, vol. VI/2 (Berlin, 1968), 417–418.

66. See Mommsen, "Universalgeschichtliches und politisches Denken," idem, *Max Weber. Gesellschaft, Politik und Geschichte* (Frankfurt am Main, 1974), 255–256, 261–262. Cf. Eugène Fleischmann, "De Weber à Nietzsche," in *European Journal of Sociology* V (1964), 190–238; and Robert Eden, *Political Leadership and Nihilism: A Study of Weber and Nietzsche* (Tampa, 1983), 257–276.

67. Simmel, *Schopenhauer und Nietzsche*, 171ff.

68. The letters were recently published by Michael Landmann in Dahme and Rammstedt, eds., *Simmel und die Moderne*, 430–437.
      On Simmel and George, see Landmann's essay in the same volume, "Georg Simmel und Stefan George," 147–173; Günther Freymuth, "Georg Simmel und Stefan George," in *Neue deutsche Hefte* XVII (1970), 41–50; and Werner Kraft, *Stefan George* (Munich, 1980), 123–134.

69. Cf. Sabine Lepsius, *Stefan George. Geschichte einer Freundschaft* (Berlin, 1939), and *Ein Berliner Künstlerleben um die Jahrhundertwende* (Munich, 1972), 62–65, 172ff.

70. See the meetings listed in H.-J. Seekamp, R. C. Ockenden, and M. Keilson, *Stefan George. Leben und Werk. Eine Zeittafel* (Amsterdam, 1972).

71. Stefan George and Friedrich Gundolf, *Briefwechsel*, ed. Robert Böhringer and Georg Peter Landmann (Munich and Düsseldorf, 1962), 81.

72. Simmel, "Stefan George. Eine kunstphilosophische Betrachtung" (1898), in *Stefan George in seiner Zeit. Dokumente zur Wirkungsgeschichte* vol. I, ed. Ralph-Rainer Wuthenow (Stuttgart, 1980), 27–40.

73. Simmel, "Stefan George. Eine kunstphilosophische Studie" (1901), ibid., 75–87.

74. I am greatly indebted here to the interpretation of Claude David in *Stefan George. Sein dichterisches Werk* (Munich, 1967), 163–200.
      The Tapestry of Life is included in *The Works of Stefan George*, transl. Olga Marx and Ernst Morwitz (Chapel Hill, 1974), 163–214; the original is in George, *Werke. Ausgabe in Zwei Bänden* (Düsseldorf and Munich, 1968), 169–223.

75. Simmel to George, 24 Feb. 1903, in Dahme and Rammstedt, eds., *Simmel und die Moderne,* 434.

76. See Paret, *The Berlin Secession.*

77. Memo attached to Simmel's letter to George of 24 Feb. 1903 in Stefan-George-Archiv, Württembergische Landesbibliothek, Stuttgart.

78. Seekamp, *Zeittafel,* 21 May 1903.

79. Simmel to George, 4 March 1903, in Dahme and Rammstedt, eds., *Simmel und die Moderne,* 436.

80. Ibid., 435. Simmel lists only the last names. He also mentions "Mommsen" without specifying which family member.

81. Ibid.

82. Claude David, "Le Jahrbuch für die geistige Bewegung (1910–1911)," in *Etudes Germaniques* X (1955), 276–277.

83. On George's transformation from aesthete to prophet see the two previously cited works by David. In addition see Bodo Würffel, *Wirkungswille um Prophetie. Studien zu Werk und Wirkung Stefan Georges* (Bonn, 1978); and Klaus Landfried, *Stefan George—Politik des Unpolitischen* (Heidelberg, 1975). See also Walter Benjamin, "Rückblick auf Stefan George. Zu einer neuen Studie über den Dichter" (1933), in *Gesammelte Schriften* vol. III, 392–399 (Frankfurt am Main, 1972); and Theodor W. Adorno, "The George-Hoffmansthal Correspondence, 1892–1906," in *Prisms* (Cambridge, Mass., 1981), 189–226.

84. Simmel, "Der siebente Ring" (1909), in Simmel, *Zur Philosophie der Kunst. Philosophische und kunstphilosophische Aufsätze* (Potsdam, 1922), 75.

85. See Gertrud Simmel to Stefan George, 2 Dec. 1911, George Archive; Simmel to Heinrich Rickert, 29 Dec. 1911, in *Buch des Dankes,* 109; and Friedrich Gundolf, *Briefe, Neue Folge,* ed. Lothar Helbin and Claus Victor Bock (Amsterdam, 1965), 228–230.

86. The first meeting between Weber and George probably took place on 17 September 1910, the last meeting on 20 June 1912. See Seekamp, *Zeittafel;* and *Biography,* 454–464.

87. Cf. Weber's remarks in *Economy and Society,* 245, 640, 1114, 1157.

88. Edgar Salin, *Um Stefan George* (Godesberg, 1948), 157–163, is a witness from George's point of view.

89. On Gertrud Simmel, see Marianne Weber, *Lebenserinnerungen* (Bremen, 1948), 375–409.

90. *Buch des Dankes,* 347.

91. The following discussion concentrates on Simmel's philosophy of religion during the middle period of his thought. Even during his positivist early years, Simmel did not take a purely reductionist approach to religion, but distinguished between a genuine immanent spirituality and a contrived other-worldly spirituality. Cf. Simmel, "Rudolf

Euckens 'Lebensanschauungen,'" part III, *Vossische Zeitung*, 28 June 1891, Sonntagsbeilage 26; and Simmel, "Etwas vom Spiritismus" in *Vorwärts*, 12 July 1892, 1. Beilage. Several of the essays in *Philosophische Kultur* dramatize the tension between modern man's longing for transcendence and his imprisonment in immanent relationships. See especially "Das Abenteuer," 13ff., "Die Alpen," 113ff., and "Michaelangelo," 119ff.

92. Simmel, "Zur Soziologie der Religion," *Neue deutsche Rundschau* IX (1898), 111–123, and "Beiträge zur Erkenntnistheorie der Religion" (1902), in *Individuum und Freiheit*, 100–109.

93. Cf. Simmel, *Schopenhauer und Nietzsche*, 1ff.

94. Simmel, "Vom Heil der Seele" (1902), in *Individuum und Freiheit*, 114–119.

95. Simmel, "Die Soziologie der Religion"; contribution to "Religiöse Grundgedanken und moderne Wissenschaft. Antwort auf eine Umfrage" (1909), in *Individuum und Freiheit*, 110–113; "Die Persönlichkeit Gottes. Ein philosophischer Versuch" (1911), in *Philosophische Kultur*, 154–168; and *Die Religion* (Frankfurt am Main, 1906). The English translation of the latter, *The Sociology of Religion*, transl. Curt Rosenthal (New York, 1959), is unreliable.

96. Simmel, "Vom Pantheismus," in *Das freie Wort* II (1902/3), 306–312, especially 310–311. See also "Sozialismus und Pessimismus" in *Die Zeit*, 3 Feb. 1900.

97. "Vom Pantheismus," 311. Cf. Simmel, "Das Christentum und die Kunst" (1907), in *Individuum und Freiheit*, 120.

98. "Die Persönlichkeit Gottes," 163.

99. *Soziologie*, 30, 558ff.

100. Cf. ibid., 561.

101. Schrader-Klebert, "Begriff der Gesellschaft als regulative Idee," 116–118. While an analysis of Simmel's introductory a prioris alone might justify such a judgment, the body and conclusion of *Soziologie* require a more complex reading.

102. Cf. *Buch des Dankes*, 26, 32, 145.

103. Troeltsch, review of *Grundfragen der Soziologie* and *Der Konflikt der modernen Kultur* in *Theologische Literaturzeitung* XLIV (1919), 207.

104. Troeltsch, *Gesammelte Schriften* III, 593.

105. Troeltsch, "Eschatologie: IV. Dogmatisch," 622–632.
   In addition to the sources already cited, see Troeltsch, "Zur modernen Religionsphilosophie" (review of Simmel, *Die Religion*), in *Deutsche Literaturzeitung* XXVIII (1907), 837–841; review of Simmel, *Das Problem der historischen Zeit* (1916), in *Theologische Literaturzeitung* XLII (1917), 343–344; review of Simmel, *Lebensanschauung* (1918), in *Theologische Literaturzeitung* XLVI (1921), 211–212; "Der historische Entwicklungsbegriff in der modernen Geistes- und Lebensphilosophie," in *Historische Zeitschrift* CXXIV (1921), 421–447; the remarks by Simmel and Weber in the discussion following Troeltsch's paper on "Das stoisch-christliche Naturrecht," in *Verhandlungen des 1. deutschen Soziologentages*, 204ff.; and the recollections of Simmel's relationship to Troeltsch by Charles Hauter in *Buch des Dankes*, 254.

106. Simmel, "Deutschlands innere Wandlung" (1914), in *Der Krieg und die geistigen Entscheidungen* (Munich and Leipzig, 1917), 10. Italics are Simmel's.

107. Ibid., 11–12.

108. Ibid., 14; Simmel, "Die Umwertung der Werte. Ein Wort an die Wohlhabenden," in *Frankfurter Zeitung*, 5 March 1915, second morning edition; "The Crisis of Culture" (1916) in *Simmel: Sociologist and European*, 260–262; and "Eine Fastenpredigt. Von dem Opfer der Wohlhabenden," in *Frankfurter Zeitung*, 18 March 1918, first morning edition.

109. Simmel, "The Idea of Europe" (1915), in *Simmel: Sociologist and European*, 267–271.

110. Cf. the remarks in a letter from Simmel to Hermann Count Keyserling, 18 May 1918, in Simmel, *Das Individuelle Gesetz*, 246.

111. For a particularly naive example of this kind of critique, see Randall Collins, *Weberian Sociological Theory* (Cambridge and New York, 1986), ch. 10.

Chapter 6

1. On Lukács's relationship to Hungarian and to German culture see Congdon, *The Young Lukács;* Gluck, *Georg Lukács and His Generation 1900–1918;* and Ernst Keller, *Der junge Lukács. Antibürger und wesentliches Leben. Literatur- und Kulturkritik 1902–1915* (Frankfurt am Main, 1984).

2. Cf. the introduction to Lukács, *Briefwechsel*, 12.

3. G. W. F. Hegel, *Phänomenologie des Geistes* (1807; Frankfurt am Main, 1970), 36: "But the life of the mind is not one that shuns death, and keeps clear of destruction; it endures death and in death maintains its being. It only wins its truth when it finds itself utterly torn asunder" [from Hegel, *The Philosophy of Mind*, transl. J. B. Baillie (New York and Evanston, 1967), 93].

4. On the Thalia Society, see Lukács, *Briefwechsel*, 7; Congdon, *The Young Lukács*, 15ff.; and Gluck, *Lukács and His Generation*, 62–64.

5. Bánóczi to Lukács, 5 Aug. 1906, in *Briefwechsel*, 26—my translation. Cf. *Correspondence*, 30.

6. Alexander to Lukács, 21 Jan. 1908, in *Briefwechsel*, 26.

7. Cf. Andrew Arato and Paul Breines, *The Young Lukács and the Origins of Western Marxism*, 14; and Ferenc Fehér, "Die Geschichtsphilosophie des Dramas, die Metaphysik der Tragödie und die Utopie des untragischen Dramas. Scheidewege der Dramentheorie des jungen Lukács," in *Die Seele und das Leben*, ed. Agnes Heller, et al. (Frankfurt am Main, 1977), 10.

8. Cf. *Dramengeschichte*, 43–44.

9. Ibid., 57–60.

10. Ibid., 12–13, 569.

11. Ibid., 12.

12. Ibid., 10–12, 44.

13. Ibid., 91ff.

14. Ibid., 133ff.

15. Ibid., 180ff.

16. Ibid., 47.

17. Ibid., 50.

18. Ibid., 242, 274–275, 332–333, 499.

19. Ibid., 499ff.

20. Lukács, "Bürgerlichkeit und l'art pour l'art: Theodor Storm," in Lukács, *Die Seele und die Formen* (Berlin, 1911), 121–169. The title is incorrectly translated as "The Bourgeois Way of Life and Art for Art's Sake" in *Soul and Form*, transl. Anna Bostock (Cambridge, Mass., 1974), 55–78. Throughout the essay, Bostock indiscriminately translates *Bürger* and *bourgeois* as "bourgeois" (see especially 123–126 in the original and 56–57 in the translation) and translates *Novelle* as "short story" (156 in the original and 72 in the translation). These errors make it impossible to understand the essay, since *Bürger* refers in it to the traditional townsman and *bourgeois* to the modern urbanite, while *Novelle* refers to a type of traditional tale fundamentally different from the short story, a modern literary genre. Hereafter I cite from the German original.

21. "Theodor Storm," in *Die Seele und die Formen*, 140–142.

22. Ibid., 156–160.

23. Ibid., 133–136; and Tönnies, *Theodor Storm zum 14. September 1917. Gedenkblätter* (Berlin, 1917), 20, 26. For a comprehensive interpretation of Storm's life and work in English, see Arthur T. Alt, *Theodor Storm* (New York, 1973).

24. "Theodor Storm," 125.

25. Ibid., 121–122.

26. Ibid., 142ff.

27. Ibid., 165.

28. Lukács, *Gelebtes Denken. Eine Autobiographie im Dialog*, ed. Istvan Eörsi (Frankfurt am Main, 1981), 58.

29. The foreword is dated Berlin, 10 December 1909, in *Dramengeschichte*, 15.

30. Ibid., 55; see also the discussion of objective culture, 96–103.

31. Ibid., 63.

32. Ibid., 271–274.

33. Ibid., 113.

34. Ibid., 499–507.

35. Lukács, "The New Solitude and Its Poetry: Stefan George" (1908), in *Soul and Form*, 79–81.

36. Ibid., 85–87.

37. Ibid., 88.

38. *Dramengeschichte*, 495ff., 538.

39. Lukács, "The Metaphysics of Tragedy," in *Soul and Form*, 152–163, cited below as "Metaphysics of Tragedy." An important supplement to the first section of the essay is Lukács's correspondence in *Briefwechsel*. See especially Lukács to Salomo Friedländer, mid-July 1911, 230–231; and Lukács to Leopold Ziegler, 13 Aug. 1911, 241–242.

40. "Metaphysics of Tragedy," 152.

41. Ibid., 159–160.

42. Ibid., 163.

43. On the meeting with Ernst, see *Dokumente einer Freundschaft*, xvii. On the dating of the writing of "Metaphysik der Tragödie," see Fehér, "Geschichtsphilosophie des Dramas," 53.

44. See *Dokumente einer Freundschaft*, 151–205.

45. Kutzbach, *Dokumente einer Freundschaft*, xxv–xxvi.

46. Cf. the editor's introduction to Karl August Kutzbach, ed., *Die Neuklassische Bewegung um 1905. Paul Ernst in Düsseldorf* (Emsdetten, 1972), ix–xix.

47. Ernst, "Die Möglichkeit der klassischen Tragödie" (1904), in Ernst, *Der Weg zur Form. Abhandlungen über die Technik vornehmlich der Tragödie und Novelle* (Munich, 1928), 121.

48. See Ernst's descriptions of the friendship and the correspondence in *Buch des Dankes*, 67–81, 139–142. See also Ernst's praise for the second edition of Simmel's *Probleme der Geschichtswissenschaft* as a book refuting materialism and restoring modern man's consciousness of his autonomy amid the constraints of modern society in an unpublished review included in Kutzbach, ed., *Neuklassische Bewegung*, 54.

49. Ernst, "Möglichkeit der klassischen Tragödie," 130–131.

50. Ernst, *Brunhild. Trauerspiel in drei Aufzügen* (1909; Berlin, 1911).

51. "Metaphysics of Tragedy," 163–166.

52. Cf. ibid., 165; Lukács to Ziegler, around mid-July 1911, in *Briefwechsel*, 232.

53. Simmel to Ernst, 14 March 1908, in *Buch des Dankes*, 70; 1 Jan. 1910, ibid., 75.

54. Ernst to Lukács, 23 March 1916, in *Dokumente einer Freundschaft*, 85.

55. "Georg Simmel" (1918), in *Buch des Dankes*, 171, 172.

56. Cf. *Metaphysics of Tragedy*, 167.

57. Ibid., 167–172.

58. See Agnes Heller, "Das Zerschellen des Lebens an der Form: György Lukács und Irma Seidler," in Agnes Heller et al., *Die Seele und das Leben*, 54–98; and the introduction to *Briefwechsel*, 7ff.

59. Introduction to *Briefwechsel*, 9ff.

60. Cf. *Die Seele und die Formen*, dedication, 3–39.

61. Cf. introduction to *Briefwechsel*, 12; and Lukács's diary, "Naplo-Tagebuch," in Georg Lukács, *Naplo-Tagebuch (1910–1911). Das Gericht (1913)*, ed. Ferenc L. Lendvai (Budapest, 1981), especially the entry for 27 Oct. 1911, 44ff.

62. Zoltan Andor Feher, "Georg Lukács's Role in Dostoyevsky's European Reception at the Turn of the Century: A Study in Reception" (Dissertation, UCLA, 1978), 107.

63. Cf. Congdon, *The Young Lukács*, 58–61; and Gluck, *Lukács and His Generation*, 57–62, 100–101.

64. Introduction to *Briefwechsel*, 13–14.

65. For biographical background, see Wayne Hudson, *The Marxist Philosophy of Ernst Bloch* (New York, 1982), 1–20.

66. Ernst Bloch, "Kritische Erörterungen über Rickert und das Problem der modernen Erkenntnistheorie" (Dissertation, Würzburg, 1908).

67. Lukács, *Record of a Life* transl. Rodney Livingstone (London, 1983), 38.

68. Cf. Introduction to *Briefwechsel*, 15, and Simmel to Lukács, 25 May 1912, in *Correspondence*, 200.

69. Cf. *Briefwechsel*, introduction, 14–15.

70. Lask to Lukács, 11 June 1912, in *Correspondence*, 201. Cf. *Record of a Life*, 38.

71. Joszef Lukács to Georg Lukács, 13 Aug. 1912, in *Briefwechsel*, 294.

72. Weber to Lukács, 22 July 1912, ibid., 204–205.

73. Marianne Weber, *Max Weber*, 468.

74. *Record of a Life*, 37–38.

75. Weber, "Science as a Vocation," in *From Max Weber*, 154.

76. "Theodor Storm," 123–124.

77. Cf. *Max Weber and German Politics*, 190–211.

78. Weber to Tönnies, 15 Oct. 1914, in *Gesammelte Politische Schriften* (1st ed.; Munich, 1921), 458.

79. Cf. the newspaper reports of a speech of 1 August 1916 reprinted in Mommsen, *Max Weber und die deutsche Politik, 1890–1920* (Tübingen, 1974), 489–490, 506—omitted in the English translation.

80. Lukács, preface to *Theory of the Novel*, 11. Cited below as *Theory of the Novel*.

81. Simmel to Marianne Weber, 14 Aug. 1914, in *Buch des Dankes*, 133.

82. Lukács, "Die deutschen Intellektuellen und der Krieg," in *Text und Kritik* XXXIX/XL (October 1973), 65. Lukács mentioned to Ernst in a letter of 2 August 1915 that he had promised to write the essay for the *Archiv;* see *Dokumente einer Freundschaft*, 81.

83. See Ernst, "Nationalcharakter und Staat," a newspaper article in the *Vossische Zeitung* (27 May 1915) reprinted in *Dokumente einer Freundschaft*, 76–80.

84. For the recounting of the dialogue, ibid., 86–95.

85. Ibid., 86–87.

86. Ibid.

87. Cf. Lukács's account of his conversation with Marianne Weber in his introduction to *Theory of the Novel*, 11.

88. *Theory of the Novel*, 153.

89. Ibid., 132.

90. Ibid., 132, 135.

91. Ibid., 142.

92. Ibid., 138–143.

93. Lukács to Irma Seidler, around 18 April 1911, in *Briefwechsel*, 212. Cf. *Correspondence*, 156.

94. Lukács, "Von der Armut am Geiste. Ein Gespräch und ein Brief," in *Neue Blätter*, II. Folge, Heft 5–6 (1912), 70–72.

95. Ibid., 74–75.

96. Lukács to Ernst, 4 May 1915, in *Dokumente einer Freundschaft*, 74.

97. Ibid., 88.

98. *Theory of the Novel*, 146–147.

99. Ibid., 152.

100. Ibid., 153.

101. Lukács, *Dostojewski Notizen und Entwürfe*, ed. J. C. Nyiri (Budapest, 1985). Cf. the text of some of the notes and the valuable commentary in Ferenc Fehér, "Am Scheideweg des romantischen Antikapitalismus. Typologie und Beitrag zur deutschen Ideologiegeschichte gelegentlich des Briefwechsels zwischen Paul Ernst und Georg Lukács," in Heller et al., *Die Seele und das Leben*, 275ff.

102. I have closely followed the analysis of Lukács's reading of Dostoevsky in Z. A. Feher, "Georg Lukács's Role in Dostoevsky's European Reception," 180ff.

103. See the notes reprinted in Feher, "Am Scheideweg des romantischen Antikapitalismus," 299–301.

104. Ibid., 291–293.

105. Ibid., 293–294, 299–300.

106. Troeltsch to Lukács, 1 Aug. 1912, in *Correspondence*, 205–206.

107. *Dostojewski Notizen*, 104–107. On Dostoevsky as prophet of the post-German era, see Lukács's review of Solovjeff, *Die Rechtfertigung des Guten*, in *Arch. f. Sozialwiss.* XLII (1916–1917), 979.

108. Weber to Lukács, 14 Aug. 1916, in *Correspondence*, 264.

109. Cf. Lukács to Weber, mid-Dec. 1915, in *Correspondence*, 253–254.

110. Marianne Weber, *Max Weber*, 327.

111. Weber, "Zur Lage der bürgerlichen Demokratie in Russland," *Arch. f. Sozialwiss.* XXII (1906), 255. Lukács was familiar with this essay and its discussions of the relationship between religious and political radicalism. See his note on another passage describing a Christian sect in Russia committed to revolutionary overthrow of private property—Lukács, *Dostojewski Notizen*, 107–109.

112. Weber, *From Max Weber*, 122, 126.

113. Ibid., 127.

114. See Weber, *Politische Schriften*, third edition, 123, 126, 132, 157, 169, 214–215, for Weber's views from late 1915 to April 1917.

115. See David Kettler, "Culture and Revolution: Lukács in the Hungarian Revolution of 1918," in *Telos* X (winter, 1971), 54ff. Cf. Gluck, *Georg Lukács and His Generation*, ch. 6; and the source collection edited by Karádi and Vezér, *Georg Lukács, Karl Mannheim und der Sonntagskreis* (Frankfurt am Main, 1985).

116. Kettler, "Culture and Revolution," 68–69.

117. Cf. Arato and Breines, *The Young Lukács and the Origins of Western Marxism*, 78, and Michael Löwy, *Georg Lukács: From Romanticism to Bolshevism*, 149.

118. Kettler, "Culture and Revolution," 77–81.

119. Michael Löwy points out that by 1920 Lukács's thought was already becoming less purely "ethical"—Löwy, *Georg Lukács*, 148–167.

120. Lukács, *History and Class Consciousness: Studies in Marxist Dialectics* (1923; Cambridge, Mass., 1983), 83–92.

121. Ibid., 88–89.

122. See the references to Weber, ibid., 210–211, 220–221, and to *The Philosophy of Money*, 95.

123. See ibid., 149ff., especially the critique of Simmel, 156–157. Cf. Lukács's remarks in the essay "Class Consciousness," ibid., 48.

124. Ibid., 166.

125. Lukács, *Geschichte und Klassenbewusstsein* (1923; Darmstadt and Neuwied, 1977), 257. Cf. the English translation: the problem of commodities must be considered "as the central, structural problem of capitalist society in all its aspects"—*History and Class Consciousness*, 83.

126. *Geschichte und Klassenbewusstsein*, 313. Cf. above, 185.

127. Ibid., 355.

128. Ibid., 362.

129. *History and Class Consciousness*, 191–192.

130. Bloch, *Geist der Utopie*.

131. Bloch, *Thomas Münzer als Theologe der Revolution*.

132. See Bloch's articles in *Die freie Zeitung*: "An der schönen blauen Donau" (15 Dec. 1917); "Deutsche Annexationsfrühling" (30 March 1918); "Jusqu'au bout, jetzt mehr als je" (22 May 1918); "Belgien und die Faustpfandtheorie" (24 July 1918); and "Mensch und Idee. Eine Antwort an Stefan Zweig" (14 Aug. 1918). Cf. the listings of Bloch's contributions to this newspaper in *Bloch-Almanach*, 2. Folge (1982), 99–179.

133. Lukács, *History and Class Consciousness*, 192–193.

134. Ernst Bloch, "Aktualität und Utopie. Zu Lukács' *Geschichte und Klassenbewusstsein*," in *Philosophische Aufsätze zur Objektiven Phantasie* (Frankfurt am Main, 1969), 618.

135. Cf. ibid., 621.

Bibliography

Primary Sources: Archives

Göttingen. Niedersächsische Staats- und Universitätsbibliothek. Paul de Lagarde Nachlass.

Heidelberg. Universitätsbibliothek. Correspondence from Ernst Troeltsch to Gertrud von le Fort. Hs. 3653.7–3653.24.

Kiel. Schleswig-Holsteinische Landesbibliothek. Ferdinand Tönnies Nachlass.

Stuttgart. Württembergische Landesbibliothek. Stefan George Archiv.

Primary Sources: Published

Anonymous. Review of Ferdinand Tönnies, *Gemeinschaft und Gesellschaft* (second edition, 1912). *Revue de métaphysique et de morale*, May 1914.

Bachofen, Johann Jakob. *Gesammelte Werke*. 10 vols. Basel: Schwabe, 1948–1967.

Baltzer, (?). Review of Ferdinand Tönnies, *Gemeinschaft und Gesellschaft* (second edition, 1912). *Mecklenburger Tageblatt* 23 May 1912, Beilage zu Nr. 118.

Barth, Paul. *Die Philosophie der Geschichte als Soziologie*. Leipzig: Reisland, 1897.

Baumgarten, Hermann. *Der deutsche Liberalismus. Eine Selbstkritik*. Introduction by Adolf M. Birke. Frankfurt am Main: Ullstein, 1974. (First edition, 1866.)

Baumgarten, Otto. *Meine Lebensgeschichte*. Tübingen: J. C. B. Mohr, 1929.

Bernstein, Eduard, et al. *Die Geschichte des Sozialismus in Einzeldarstellungen*, vol. I. Stuttgart: Dietz, 1895.

Bloch, Ernst. "Kritische Erörterungen über Rickert und das Problem der modernen Erkenntnistheorie." Dissertation. University of Würzburg, 1908.

Bloch, Ernst. "An der schönen blauen Donau." *Die freie Zeitung* 15 December 1917.

Bloch, Ernst. "Deutscher Annexationsfrühling." *Die freie Zeitung* 30 March 1918.

Bloch, Ernst. "Jusqu'au bout, jetzt mehr als je." *Die freie Zeitung* 22 May 1918.

Bloch, Ernst. "Belgien und die Faustpfandtheorie." *Die freie Zeitung* 24 July 1918.

Bloch, Ernst. "Mensch und Idee. Eine Antwort an Stefan Zweig." *Die freie Zeitung* 14 August 1918.

Bloch, Ernst. *Geist der Utopie.* Frankfurt am Main: Suhrkamp, 1971. (First edition, 1918.)

Bloch, Ernst. "Aktualität und Utopie. Zu Lukacs' Geschichte und Klassenbewusstsein" (1923). In *Philosophische Aufsätze zur Objektiven Phantasie:* 598–621. Frankfurt am Main: Suhrkamp, 1969.

Bloch, Ernst. *Thomas Münzer als Theologe der Revolution.* Frankfurt am Main: Suhrkamp, 1969. (First edition, 1921.)

Blunt, Herbert. Review of Ferdinand Tönnies, *Gemeinschaft und Gesellschaft. Mind* L (1888): 143.

Braun, Lily. *Gesammelte Werke.* 5 vols. Berlin-Grunewald: H. Klemm, n.d.

Brockdorff, Cay von. Review of Ferdinand Tönnies, *Gemeinschaft und Gesellschaft* (second edition, 1912). *Schulblatt für die Herzogtümer Braunschweig und Anhalt* XXV (1912): 765–768.

Channing, William Ellery. *Works.* 6 vols. Boston: G. G. Channing, 1849.

"D." [Adolf Damaschke?] Review of Ferdinand Tönnies, *Gemeinschaft und Gesellschaft* (second edition, 1912). *Bodenreform* XXIV (1913):255–256.

Die Christliche Welt.

Dietrich, Albert. "Troeltsch, Ernst." In *Deutsches Biographisches Jahrbuch,* vol. V (1923), 348–368. Edited by Verbände der Deutschen Akademien. Berlin and Leipzig:Deutsche Verlags-Anstalt Stuttgart, 1930.

Dowden, Edward. *Puritans and Anglicans.* New York: Holt, 1901.

Durkheim, Emile. Review of Ferdinand Tönnies, *Gemeinschaft und Gesellschaft* (1887). *Revue Philosophique* XXVII (1889): 416–422. Translated in Werner Cahnman, ed., *Ferdinand Tönnies: A New Evaluation. Essays and Documents,* 240–247.

Engels, Friedrich. *The Origin of the Family, Private Property and the State: In the Light of the Researches of Lewis H. Morgan.* New York: International Publishers, 1942. (First edition, 1884.)

Ernst, Paul. *Brunhild. Trauerspiel in drei Aufzügen.* Berlin: Verband Deutscher Bühnen-schriftsteller, 1911. (First edition, 1909.)

Ernst, Paul. *Der Weg zur Form. Abhandlungen über die Technik vornehmlich der Tragödie und Novelle.* Munich: G. Müller, 1928.

Frankfurter Zeitung.

George, Stefan. *Werke. Ausgabe in Zwei Bänden.* Düsseldorf and Munich: H. Küpper, 1968.

George, Stefan. *The Works of Stefan George.* Translated by Olga Marx and Ernst Morwitz. Chapel Hill: University of North Carolina Press, 1974.

George, Stefan, and Gundolf, Friedrich. *Briefwechsel.* Edited by Robert Böhringer and Georg Peter Landmann. Munich and Düsseldorf: H. Küpper, 1962.

Göhre, Paul. *Drei Monate Fabrikarbeiter und Handwerkerbursche. Eine praktische Studie.* Leipzig: F. W. Grunow, 1891.

Gumplowicz, Ludwig. Review of Ferdinand Tönnies, *Gemeinschaft und Gesellschaft* (1887). *Deutsche Literaturzeitung* (1888): 132–140.

Gundolf, Friedrich. *Briefe. Neue Folge.* Edited by Lothar Helbing and Claus Victor Bock. Amsterdam: Castrum Peregrini, 1965.

Harnack, Adolf von. *Lehrbuch der Dogmengeschichte.* 3 vols. Freiburg: J. C. B. Mohr. 1885–1890.

Harnack, Adolf von, et al. *Die deutsche Freiheit.* Gotha: F. A. Perthes, 1917.

Hegel, G. W. F. *Phänomenologie des Geistes.* Frankfurt: Suhrkamp, 1970. Translated by J. B. Baillie as *The Phenomenology of Mind.* New York and Evanston: Harper and Row, 1967. (First edition, 1807.)

Hegel, G. W. F. *Philosophy of Right.* New York: Oxford University Press, 1967. (First edition, 1821.)

Hobbes, Thomas. *Behemoth, or The Long Parliament.* London: Simpkin Marshall and Co., 1889.

Hobbes, Thomas. *The Elements of Law: Natural and Politic.* London: Simpkin Marshall and Co., 1889.

Hobbes, Thomas. *Leviathan.* Edited by C. B. Macpherson. Middlesex and New York: Penguin, 1968. (First edition, 1651.)

Humboldt, Wilhelm von. *Werke,* vol. IV. *Schriften zur Politik und zum Bildungswesen.* Edited by Andreas Flitner and Klaus Giel. Stuttgart: Cotta, 1964.

Jellinek, Georg. *Die Erklärung der Menschen- und Bürgerrechte. Ein Beitrag zur modernen Verfassungsgeschichte.* Leipzig: Duncker and Humblot, 1895.

Kant, Immanuel. *Critique of Pure Reason.* Translated by Norman Kemp Smith. New York: St. Martin's, 1965.

Kautsky, Karl. "Der urchristliche Kommunismus." In Eduard Bernstein et al., eds., *Die Geschichte des Sozialismus in Einzeldarstellungen,* vol. I, 16–35.

Köhler, Walter. Review of Ernst Troeltsch, *Die Soziallehren der christlichen Kirchen und Gruppen. Historische Zeitschrift* CXIV (1915): 598–605.

Bibliography

Lask, Emil. *Fichtes Idealismus und die Geschichte.* Tübingen: J. C. B. Mohr, 1902.

Loofs, Friedrich. Review of Ernst Troeltsch, *Die Soziallehren der christlichen Kirchen und Gruppen. Deutsche Literaturzeitung* XXXIV (1913):2885–2893.

Lukács, Georg. *Die Seele und die Formen.* Berlin: E. Fleischel, 1911. Translated by Anna Bostock as *Soul and Form.* Cambridge, Mass.: MIT Press, 1974.

Lukács, Georg. "Von der Armut am Geiste. Ein Gespräch und ein Brief." *Neue Blätter* II. Folge, Heft 5–6 (1912): 67–92.

Lukács, Georg. "Zum Wesen und zur Methode der Kultursoziologie." *Archiv für Sozialwissenschaft und Sozialpolitik* XXXIX (1914–1915): 216–222.

Lukács, Georg. Review of Wladimir Solovjeff, *Die Rechtfertigung des Guten* (1916). *Archiv für Sozialwissenschaft und Sozialpolitik* XLII (1916–1917): 978–980.

Lukács, Georg. *Die Theorie des Romans. Ein geschichtsphilosophicher Versuch über die Formen der grossen Epik.* Neuwied and Berlin: Luchterhand, 1971. Translated by Anna Bostock as *The Theory of the Novel: A Historico-Philosophical Essay on the Forms of Great Epic Literature.* Cambridge, Mass.: MIT, 1971. (First edition, 1920.)

Lukács, Georg. "Die deutschen Intellektuellen und der Krieg." *Text und Kritik* 39/40 (October 1973): 65–69.

Lukács, Georg. *Entwicklungsgeschichte des modernen Dramas.* Edited by Frank Benseler. Darmstadt and Neuwied: Luchterhand, 1981. (First edition, 1911.)

Lukács, Georg. *Naplo-Tagebuch (1910–1911). Das Gericht (1913).* Edited by Ferenc L. Lendvai. Budapest: Akadémiai Kiado, 1981.

Lukács, Georg. *Briefwechsel 1902–1917.* Edited by Éva Karádi and Éva Fekete. Stuttgart: J. B. Metzler, 1982.

Lukács, Georg. *Geschichte und Klassenbewusstsein.* Neuwied and Berlin: Luchterhand, 1968. Translated by Rodney Livingstone as *History and Class Consciousness: Studies in Marxist Dialectics.* Cambridge, Mass.: MIT Press, 1983. (First edition, 1923.)

Lukács, Georg. *Gelebtes Denken. Eine Autobiographie im Dialog.* Edited by Istvan Eörsi. Frankfurt am Main: Suhrkamp, 1981. Translated by Rodney Livingstone as *Record of a Life.* London: Verso, 1983.

Lukács, Georg. *Dostoyewski Notizen und Entwürfe.* Edited by J. C. Nyiri. Budapest: Akadémiai Kiado, 1985.

Lukács, Georg. *Selected Correspondence 1902–1920.* Edited by Judith Marcus and Zoltán Tar. Columbia University Press: New York, 1986.

Marcard, K. Review of Ferdinand Tönnies, *Gemeinschaft und Gesellschaft* (second edition, 1912). *Die Hilfe* XLIV (31 Oct. 1912): 700–701.

Marx, Karl, and Engels, Friedrich. *Werke,* vol. XXXIX. Berlin: Institute for Marxism-Leninism, 1968.

Marx, Karl. *Das Kapital. Kritik der politischen Ökonomie,* vol. 1. Frankfurt am Main: Marxistische Blätter, 1976. Translated by Samuel Moore and Edward Aveling as *Capital.* New York: Random House, n.d. (First edition, 1867.)

Metzger, Wilhelm. Review of Ferdinand Tönnies, *Gemeinschaft und Gesellschaft* (second edition, 1912). *Weltwirtschaftliches Archiv* II (1913): 184–187.

Mill, John Stuart. *Autobiography*. Boston: Houghton Mifflin, 1969. (First edition, 1873.)

Mitteilungen des Evangelisch-Sozialen Kongresses.

Nathusius, Martin von. *Die Mitarbeit der Kirche an der Lösung der sozialen Frage. Auf Grund einer kurzgefassten Volkswirtschaftslehre und eines Systems der christlichen Gesellschaftslehre (Sozialethik).* Leipzig: Hinrichs, 1897.

Naumann, Friedrich. *Demokratie und Kaisertum. Ein Handbuch für innere Politik.* Schöneberg: Buchverlag der *Hilfe,* 1900.

Naumann, Friedrich. *Werke,* vol. I. *Religiöse Schriften.* Cologne and Oplaten: Westdeutscher, 1964.

Nietzsche, Friedrich. *The Birth of Tragedy* and *The Genealogy of Morals.* Translated by Francis Golffing. Garden City, New Jersey: Doubleday, 1956. (First edition of *The Birth of Tragedy,* 1872.)

Nietzsche, Friedrich. *Werke. Kritische Gesamtausgabe.* Edited by Giorgio Colli and Mazzino Montinari. Berlin and New York: de Gruyter, 1967ff.

Nietzsche, Friedrich. *Beyond Good and Evil.* Translated by Walter Kaufmann. New York: Knopf, 1968. (First edition, 1886.)

Paulsen, Friedrich. Review of Ferdinand Tönnies, *Gemeinschaft und Gesellschaft* (1887). *Vierteljahrsschrift für wissenschaftliche Philosophie* XII (1888): 111–119.

Paulsen, Friedrich. *System der Ethik. Mit einem Umriss der Staats- und Gesellschaftslehre.* Stuttgart and Berlin: F. G. Cotta, 1913. (First edition, 1889.)

Paulsen, Friedrich. *An Autobiography.* Translated and edited by Theodor Lorenz, with foreword by Nicholas Murray Butler. New York: Columbia University Press, 1938.

Die Religion in Geschichte und Gegenwart. Handwörterbuch in gemeinverständlicher Darstellung. Edited by Hermann Gunkel, Otto Scheel, et al. 5 vols. Tübingen: J. C. B. Mohr, 1909–1913.

Rickert, Heinrich. *Die Grenzen der Naturwissenschaftlichen Begriffsbildung.* 2 vols. Tübingen: J. C. B. Mohr, 1896–1902.

Ritschl, Albrecht. *Die christliche Lehre von der Rechtfertigung und Versöhnung.* 6 vols. Bonn: A. Marcus, 1870–1874.

Ritschl, Albrecht. *Three Essays.* Translated and edited by Philip Hefner. Philadelphia: Fortress Press, 1972.

Rosenbaum, Eduard. Review of Ferdinand Tönnies, *Gemeinschaft und Gesellschaft* (second edition, 1912). *Schmollers Jahrbuch* XXXVIII (1914): 445–492.

Schmidt, Raymund, ed. *Die Philosophie der Gegenwart in Selbstdarstellungen.* 3 vols. Leipzig: F. Meiner, 1922. (Second edition, 1923.)

Schmoller, Gustav. Review of Ferdinand Tönnies, *Gemeinschaft und Gesellschaft* (1887). *Schmollers Jahrbuch* XII (1888): 327–329.

Schmoller, Gustav. "Simmels Philosophie des Geldes." *Schmollers Jahrbuch* XXV (1901): 1–18.

Schneckenburger, Matthias. *Vergleichende Darstellung des lutherischen und reformierten Lehrbegriffs.* 2 vols. Stuttgart: J. B. Metzler, 1855.

Schwarte, Max, ed. *Der Weltkrieg in seiner Einwirkung auf das deutsche Volk.* Leipzig: Quelle and Meyer, 1918.

Simmel, Georg. "Rudolf Euckens 'Lebensanschauungen,'" part 3. *Vossische Zeitung* 14 June 1891, Sonntagsbeilage 24, 1–3; 21 June 1891, Sonntagsbeilage 25, 3–6; 28 June 1891, Sonntagsbeilage 26, 4–8.

Simmel, Georg. "Humanistisches Märchen." *Die Neue Zeit* X (1891–2), vol II: 713–718.

Simmel, Georg. "Etwas vom Spiritismus." *Vorwärts* 12 July 1892, 1. Beilage.

Simmel, Georg. *Die Probleme der Geschichtsphilosophie.* Leipzig: Duncker and Humblot, 1892.

Simmel, Georg. "Ein Wort über soziale Freiheit." *Sozialpolitisches Zentralblatt* I (1892): 333–335.

Simmel, Georg. Review of Ignaz Jastrow, *Die Aufgaben des Liberalismus in Preussen. Sozialliberal. Archiv für soziale Gesetzgebung und Statistik* XI (1893): 622–627.

Simmel, Georg. "Weltpolitik." *Die Neue Zeit* XII (1893–94) vol. II: 165–170.

Simmel, Georg. "Massenpsychologie." *Die Zeit* (Vienna) 23 November 1895.

Simmel, Georg. "Berliner Kunstbrief." *Die Zeit* (Vienna) 21 March 1896.

Simmel, Georg. "Der Frauenkongress und die Sozialdemokratie." *Die Zukunft* XVII (1896): 80–84.

Simmel, Georg. "Zur Privatdozenten-Frage." *Die Zeit* (Vienna) 2 May 1896.

Simmel, Georg. Review of Ferdinand Tönnies, *Der Nietzsche-Kultus. Eine Kritik.* (1897). *Deutsche Literaturzeitung* XVIII (1897): 1645–1651.

Simmel, Georg. "Rosen. Eine soziale Hypothese" (1897). In Georg Simmel, *Schriften zur Soziologie,* 169–172.

Simmel, Georg. "Soziale Medizin." *Die Zeit* (Vienna) 13 February 1897.

Simmel, Georg. "Zur Soziologie der Religion." *Neue deutsche Rundschau* IX (1898): 111–123.

Simmel, Georg. "Stefan George. Eine kunstphilosophische Betrachtung" (1898). In *Stefan George in seiner Zeit. Dokumente zur Wirkungsgeschichte,* vol. I, ed. Ralph-Rainer Wuthenow, 27–40.

Simmel, Georg. "Sozialismus und Pessimismus." *Die Zeit* (Vienna) 3 February 1900.

Simmel, Georg. "Stefan George. Eine kunstphilosophische Studie" (1901). In *Stefan George in seiner Zeit. Dokumente zur Wirkungsgeschichte,* vol. I, ed. Ralph-Rainer Wuthenow, 75–87.

Bibliography

Simmel, Georg. "Zum Verständnis Nietzsches." *Das freie Wort* vol. II (1902–3): 6–11.

Simmel, Georg. "Vom Pantheismus." *Das freie Wort* vol. II (1902/3): 306–312.

Simmel, Georg. *Die Religion.* Frankfurt am Main: Rutten and Loening, 1906. Translated by Curt Rosenthal as *The Sociology of Religion.* New York: Philosophical Library, 1959.

Simmel, Georg. "Die Umwertung der Werte, Ein Wort an die Wohlhabenden." *Frankfurter Zeitung* 5 March 1915, second morning edition.

Simmel, Georg. "Vom Tode in der Kunst." *Frankfurter Zeitung* 2 April 1915, first morning edition.

Simmel, Georg. *Grundfragen der Soziologie (Individuum und Gesellschaft).* Berlin: G. J. Göschen, 1917.

Simmel, Georg. *Der Krieg und die geistigen Entscheidungen.* Munich and Leipzig: Duncker and Humblot, 1917.

Simmel, Georg. "Eine Fastenpredigt. Von dem Opfer der Wohlhabenden." *Frankfurter Zeitung* 18 March 1918, first morning edition.

Simmel, Georg. *Zur Philosophie der Kunst. Philosophische und kunstphilosophische Aufsätze.* Potsdam: G. Kiepenheuer, 1922.

Simmel, Georg. *Schopenhauer und Nietzsche. Ein Vortragszyklus.* Munich and Leipzig: Duncker and Humblot, 1923. (First edition, 1907.)

Simmel, Georg. *Über soziale Differenzierung.* Amsterdam: Liberae, 1966. (First edition, 1890).

Simmel, Georg. *The Conflict in Modern Culture and Other Essays.* Edited by K. Peter Etzkorn. New York: Teachers College Press, 1968.

Simmel, Georg. *Das Individuelle Gesetz.* Edited by Michael Landmann. Frankfurt am Main: Suhrkamp, 1968.

Simmel, Georg. *Soziologie.* Berlin: Duncker and Humblot, 1968. (First edition, 1908.)

Simmel, Georg. *Georg Simmel: Sociologist and European.* Edited by Peter Lawrence. Sunbury-on-Thames: Thomas Nelson, 1976.

Simmel, Georg. *Philosophie des Geldes.* Leipzig: Duncker and Humblot, 1958. Translated by Tom Bottomore and David Frisby as *The Philosophy of Money.* London: Routledge and Kegan Paul, 1978. (First edition, 1900.)

Simmel, Georg. *Philosophische Kultur. Über das Abenteuer, die Geschlechter und die Krise der Moderne—Gesammelte Essais.* Berlin: Wagenbach, 1983. (First edition, 1911.)

Simmel, Georg. *Schriften zur Soziologie. Eine Auswahl.* Edited by Heinz-Jürgen Dahme and Otthein Rammstedt. Frankfurt am Main: Suhrkamp, 1983.

Simmel, Georg. *Das Individuum und die Freiheit. Essais.* Berlin: Wagenbach, 1984.

Simmel, Georg. *Rembrandt. Ein kunstphilosophischer Versuch.* Munich: Matthes und Seitz, 1985. (First edition, 1916.)

Simmel, Hans. "Auszüge aus den Lebenserinnerungen." In Hannes Böhringer and Karlfried Gründer, eds., *Ästhetik und Soziologie um die Jahrhundertwende. Georg Simmel,* 247–268.

Sohm, Rudolf. *Das Verhältnis von Staat und Kirche. Aus dem Begriff von Staat und Kirche entwickelt.* Tübingen: H. Laupp, 1873.

Sohm, Rudolf. *Kirchenrecht* I. *Die geschichtlichen Grundlagen.* II. *Katholisches Kirchenrecht.* 2 vols. Leipzig: Duncker and Humblot, 1892–1923.

Sombart, Werner. *Der Moderne Kapitalismus.* 2 vols. Leipzig: Duncker and Humblot, 1902.

Sombart, Werner. *Die Juden und das Wirtschaftsleben.* Leipzig: Duncker and Humblot, 1911. Translated by M. Epstein as *The Jews and Modern Capitalism.* New York: Ben Franklin, 1969.

Sombart, Werner. *Die Zukunft der Juden.* Leipzig: Duncker and Humblot, 1912.

Stammler, Rudolf. "Besprechung von Ferdinand Tönnies, 'Gemeinschaft und Gesellschaft' [1887]" (1890). In *Rechtsphilosophische Abhandlungen und Vorträge,* vol. I. Aalen: Scientia Verlag, 1970, 43–48. (First edition, 1925.)

Stenographische Berichte über die Verhandlungen des Abgeordnetenhauses [Prussia].

Stenographische Berichte über die Verhandlungen des Reichstages.

Tönnies, Ferdinand. "Anmerkungen über die Philosophie des Hobbes." *Vierteljahrsschrift für wissenschaftliche Philosophie* III (1879): 453–466; IV (1880): 55–74, 428–453; V (1881): 186–220.

Tönnies, Ferdinand. "Studie zur Kritik des Spinoza." *Vierteljahrsschrift für wissenschaftliche Philosophie* VII (1883): 158–183.

Tönnies, Ferdinand. "Studie zur Entwicklungsgeschichte des Spinoza." *Vierteljahrsschrift für wissenschaftliche Philosophie* VII (1883): 334–364.

Tönnies, Ferdinand. Review of Georg Simmel, *Über soziale Differenzierung. Jahrbücher für Nationalökonomie und Statistik* LVI (1891): 269–277.

Tönnies, Ferdinand. *Ethische Cultur und ihr Geleite* [in der "Zukunft" und in der "Gegenwart."] *1. Nietzsche-Narren. 2. Wölfe in Fuchspelzen* [2 Kirchenzeitungen]. Berlin: F. Dümmler, 1893.

Tönnies, Ferdinand. "In Sachen der 'Ethischen Kultur.'" *Burschenschaftliche Blätter* (1893): 126–127.

Tönnies, Ferdinand. "Ethische Betrachtungen." *Ethische Kultur* III (1895): 212–213, 218–221, 228–229.

Tönnies, Ferdinand. *Hobbes Leben und Lehre.* Stuttgart: F. Frommans Verlag, 1896.

Tönnies, Ferdinand. "Die ethische Bewegung." *Die Umschau* III (1899): 842–845.

Tönnies, Ferdinand. "Die Zerrüttung der liberalen Partei in England." *Das freie Wort* I (1901): 289–292.

Bibliography

Tönnies, Ferdinand. "Moderne Geschichtsphilosophie." *Theologische Rundschau* VI (1903): 3–28, 57–72, 103–117.

Tönnies, Ferdinand. "Political Parties in Germany." *The Independent Review* III (1904): 365–381.

Tönnies, Ferdinand. "Der Massenstreik in ethischer Beleuchtung." *Das freie Wort* V (1905): 537–543.

Tönnies, Ferdinand. "Zum Verständnis des politischen Parteiwesens." *Das freie Wort* V (1906): 752–759.

Tönnies, Ferdinand. "Politische Stimmungen und Richtungen in England." *Das freie Wort* VI (1906): 337–343.

Tönnies, Ferdinand. "Ethik und Sozialismus." *Archiv für Sozialwissenschaft und Sozialpolitik* XXV (1907): 573–612; XXVI (1908): 56–95; XXIX (1909): 895–930.

Tönnies, Ferdinand. "Französisch-deutsche Beziehungen. Ein Vorwort zur Haager Konferenz." *Das freie Wort* VII (1907): 121–129.

Tönnies, Ferdinand. "Das Reichstagswahlrecht für Preussen?" *Das freie Wort* VII (1907): 492–497.

Tönnies, Ferdinand. "Die Gleichheit des Wahlrechts." *Das freie Wort* VIII (1908): 165–169.

Tönnies, Ferdinand. "Die Weltlage." *Das freie Wort* VIII (1908): 286–288.

Tönnies, Ferdinand. Review of Ernst Troeltsch, *Die Soziallehren der christlichen Kirchen und Gruppen* (1912). In *Theologische Literaturzeitung* XXXIX (1914):8–12. Reprinted in Ferdinand Tönnies, *Soziologische Studien und Kritiken* III, 432–438.

Tönnies, Ferdinand. "Der Friede." *Ethische Kultur* XXIII (1915): 25–27.

Tönnies, Ferdinand. "Marokko und der Weltkrieg." *Neue Rundschau* XXVI (1915): 1540–1546.

Tönnies, Ferdinand. *Warlike England as Seen by Herself.* New York: G. W. Dillingham, 1915.

Tönnies, Ferdinand. "Der Wiederbeginn geistiger Gemeinschaftsarbeit zwischen den Völkern." *Ethische Kultur* XXIII (1915): 105–106.

Tönnies, Ferdinand. "Frohmut und Ernst in der Kriegszeit." *Ethische Kultur* XXIV (1916): 81–82.

Tönnies, Ferdinand. "Machtgedanken." *Neue Rundschau* XXVII (1916): 261–265.

Tönnies, Ferdinand. "Boz-Dickens." *Ethische Kultur* XXV (1917): 5–7.

Tönnies, Ferdinand. *Theodor Storm zum 14. September 1917. Gedenkblätter.* Berlin: K. Curtius, 1917.

Tönnies, Ferdinand. "Simmel als Soziologe." *Frankfurter Zeitung* 9 October 1918.

256

Bibliography

Tönnies, Ferdinand. *Germany's War Guilt Disproved, Russia's Responsibility as Instigator of the Great War Established by Documentary Evidence of the Year 1914.* Amsterdam and Rotterdam: C. L. van Langenhuysen, 1919.

Tönnies, Ferdinand. "Kulturbedeutung der Religionen" (1919). Reprinted in *Soziologische Studien und Kritiken* II: 353–380.

Tönnies, Ferdinand. "Selbstdarstellung (1922)." In *Die Philosophie der Gegenwart in Selbstdarstellungen,* ed. Raymund Schmidt, vol. III, 199–236.

Tönnies, Ferdinand. *Der Zarismus und seine Bundesgenossen 1914. Neue Beiträge zur Kriegsschuldfrage.* Berlin: Deutsche Verlagsgesellschaft für Politik und Geschichte, 1922.

Tönnies, Ferdinand. *Soziologische Studien und Kritiken.* 3 vols. Jena: G. Fischer, 1925–1929.

Tönnies, Ferdinand, and Paulsen, Friedrich. *Ferdinand Tönnies-Friedrich Paulsen. Briefwechsel 1876–1908.* Edited by Olaf Klose, E. G. Jacoby, and Irma Fischer. Kiel: F. Hirt, 1961.

Tönnies, Ferdinand. *Gemeinschaft und Gesellschaft. Grundbegriffe der reinen Soziologie.* Darmstadt: Wissenschafliche Buchgesellschaft, 1979. Reprint of the 8th edition, 1935. Translated by Charles P. Loomis as *Community and Society.* New York: Harper and Row, 1963. (First edition, 1887.)

Tönnies, Ferdinand. *On Sociology: Pure, Applied and Empirical Selected Writings.* Edited by Werner J. Cahnman and Rudolf Heberle. Chicago and London: University of Chicago Press, 1971.

Tönnies, Ferdinand. *Studien zur Philosophie und Gesellschafslehre im 17. Jahrhundert.* Edited by E. G. Jacoby. Stuttgart-Bad Cannstatt: Frommann Holzboog, 1975.

Tönnies, Ferdinand. "Lebenserinnerungen aus dem Jahre 1935 an Kindheit, Schulzeit, Studium und erste Dozentenzeit (1855–1894)." Edited by Rainer Polley. *Zeitschrift der Gesellschaft für Schleswig-Holsteinische Geschichte* CV (1980): 187–227.

Traub, Gottfried. Review of Ernst Troeltsch, *Die Soziallehren der christlichen Kirchen und Gruppen* (1912). *Die Christliche Welt* XXVIII (1914): 339–346.

Troeltsch, Ernst. *Vernunft und Offenbarung bei Johannes Gerhard und Melanchthon. Untersuchung zur Geschichte der altprotestantischen Theologie.* Göttingen: Vandenhoeck and Ruprecht, 1891.

Troeltsch, Ernst. *Die historischen Grundlagen der Theologie unseres Jahrhunderts.* Karlsruhe: Gutsch, 1895.

Troeltsch, Ernst. "Religion und Kirche." *Preussische Jahrbücher* LXXXI (1895): 215–249.

Troeltsch, Ernst. Review of Paul Barth, *Die Philosophie der Geschichte als Sociologie* I. Teil. *Einleitung und kritische Übersicht* (1897). *Theologische Literaturzeitung* XXIII (1898): 398–401.

Troeltsch, Ernst. Review of Heinrich Rickert, *Kulturwissenschaft und Naturwissenschaft* (1898). *Theologische Literaturzeitung* XXIV (1899): 375–377.

Bibliography

Troeltsch, Ernst. Review of Friedrich Paulsen, *Kant der Philosoph des Protestantismus* (1899). *Deutsche Literaturzeitung* XXI (1900): 157–161.

Troeltsch, Ernst. *Richard Rothe.* Tübingen: J. C. B. Mohr, 1899.

Troeltsch, Ernst. "Rotheliteratur." *Die Christliche Welt* XIII (1899): 18–19.

Troeltsch, Ernst. "Richard Rothe." *Die Christliche Welt* XIII (1899): 77–81.

Troeltsch, Ernst. "Rotheliteratur." *Die Christliche Welt* XIII (1899): 327–328.

Troeltsch, Ernst. Review of Otto Ritschl, *Die Causalbetrachtung in den Geisteswissenschaften* (1901). *Theologische Literaturzeitung* XXVII (1902): 387–389.

Troeltsch, Ernst. Review of Emil Lask, *Fichtes Idealismus und die Geschichte* (1902). *Theologische Literaturzeitung* XXVIII (1903): 244–251.

Troeltsch, Ernst. "Moderne Geschichtsphilosophie." *Theologische Rundschau* VI (1903): 3–28, 57–72, 103–117.

Troeltsch, Ernst. *Politische Ethik und Christentum.* Göttingen: Vandenhoeck and Ruprecht, 1904.

Troeltsch, Ernst. Review of Maria Raich, *Fichte. Seine Ethik und seine Stellung zu dem Problem des Individualismus* (1905). *Göttingische gelehrte Anzeigen* CLXVIII (1906): 680–682.

Troeltsch, Ernst. *Die Trennung von Staat und Kirche, der staatliche Religionsunterricht und die theologischen Fakultäten.* Heidelberg: J. Hoerning, 1906.

Troeltsch, Ernst. "Zur modernen Religionsphilosophie." *Deutsche Literaturzeitung* XXVIII (1907): 837–841.

Troeltsch, Ernst. "Die Soziallehren der christlichen Kirchen." *Archiv für Sozialwissenschaft und Sozialpolitik* XXVI (1908): 1–55, 292–342, 649–692; XXVII (1908): 1–72, 317–348; XXVIII (1909): 1–71, 387–416, 621–653; XXIX (1909): 1–49, 381–416; XXX (1910): 30–65, 666–720.

Troeltsch, Ernst. "Eschatologie: IV. Dogmatisch." In *Die Religion in Geschichte und Gegenwart,* vol. II (1910), 622–632.

Troeltsch, Ernst. "Die Kulturbedeutung des Calvinismus" (1910). In Max Weber, *Die protestantische Ethik* II. *Kritiken und Antikritiken,* 188–215.

Troeltsch, Ernst. "Über die Möglichkeit eines freien Christentums." In *5. Weltkongress für Freies Christentum und Religiösen Fortschritt, Berlin, 5. bis 10. August 1910. Protokoll der Verhandlungen,* 333–349.

Troeltsch, Ernst. *Die Bedeutung des Protestantismus für die Entstehung der modernen Welt.* Munich: R. Oldenbourg, 1911. (First edition, 1906.)

Troeltsch, Ernst. *Religiöser Individualismus und Kirche.* Karlsruhe: Gutsch, 1911.

Troeltsch, Ernst. *Gesammelte Schriften.* Vol. I: *Die Soziallehren der christlichen Kirchen und Gruppen.* Vol. II: *Zur religiösen Lage, Religionsphilosophie und Ethik.* Vol. III: *Der Historismus und seine Probleme. Erstes Buch: Das logische Problem der Geschichtsphilosophie.* Vol. IV:

Aufsätze zur Geistesgeschichte und Religionssoziologie. Edited by Hans Baron. Tübingen: J. C. B. Mohr, 1912–1925.

Troeltsch, Ernst. Review of Heinrich Rickert, *Kulturwissenschaft und Naturwissenschaft* (2nd ed., 1910). *Theologische Literaturzeitung* XXXVIII (1913): 440.

Troeltsch, Ernst. Review of Fritz Münch, *Erlebnis und Geltung. Eine systematische Untersuchung zur Transzendental-philosophie als Weltanschauung* (1913). *Theologische Literaturzeitung* XXII (1915): 470–472.

Troeltsch, Ernst. *Nach Erklärung der Mobilmachung 2 August 1914.* Heidelberg: C. Winters, 1914.

Troeltsch, Ernst. "Der Krieg und die Internationalität der geistigen Kultur." *Internationale Monatsschrift für Wissenschaft, Kunst und Technik* IX (1914): 51–58.

Troeltsch, Ernst. *Unser Volksheer. 3 November 1914.* Heidelberg: C. Winters, 1914.

Troeltsch, Ernst. "Friede auf Erden." *Die Hilfe* XX (1914): 833–834.

Troeltsch, Ernst. "Imperialismus." *Die neue Rundschau* XXVI (1915): 1–14.

Troeltsch, Ernst. Review of Heinrich Rickert, *Wilhelm Windelband.* (1915). *Theologische Literaturzeitung* XLI (1916): 469–471.

Troeltsch, Ernst. "Konservativ und Liberal." *Die Christliche Welt* XXX (1916): 647–651.

Troeltsch, Ernst. "Der Ansturm der westlichen Demokratie" (1917). In Adolf von Harnack et al., *Die deutsche Freiheit,* 79–113.

Troeltsch, Ernst. Review of Georg Simmel, *Das Problem der historischen Zeit (1916). Theologische Literaturzeitung* XLII (1917): 343–344.

Troeltsch, Ernst. "Der innere Zusammenhang der politischen Forderungen." In *Von deutscher Volkskraft. Zweite Veröffentlichung des Volksbundes für Freiheit und Vaterland,* 6–21. Gotha: Verlag F. A. Perthes, 1918.

Troeltsch, Ernst. "Das Wesen des Weltkrieges." In *Der Weltkrieg in seiner Einwirkung auf das deutsche Volk,* ed. Max Schwarte, 7–25.

Troeltsch, Ernst. "Anklagen auf Defaitismus." *Deutsche Politik* III (1918): 661–669.

Troeltsch, Ernst. Review of Georg Simmel, *Grundfragen der Soziologie* (1917) and *Der Konflikt der modernen Kultur* (1918). *Theologische Literaturzeitung* XLIV (1919): 207–208.

Troeltsch, Ernst. "Die 'Kleine Göttinger Fakultät' von 1890." *Die Christliche Welt* XXXIV (1920): 281–283.

Troeltsch, Ernst. Review of Georg Simmel, *Lebensanschauung* (1918). *Theologische Literaturzeitung* XLVI (1921): 211–212.

Troeltsch, Ernst. "Der historische Entwicklungsbegriff in der modernen Geistes- und Lebensphilosophie." *Historische Zeitschrift* CXXIV (1921): 421–447.

Troeltsch, Ernst. "Die Geisteswissenschaften und der Streit um Rickert. Aus Anlass von Erich Becher, Geisteswissenschaften und Naturwissenschaften. Untersuchungen zur Theorie und Einteilung der Realwissenschaften." *Schmollers Jahrbuch* XLVI (1922): 35–64.

Troeltsch, Ernst. "Meine Bücher" (1923). In *Die Philosophie der Gegenwart in Selbstdarstellungen*, ed. Raymund Schmidt, vol. I, 165–182.

Troeltsch, Ernst. *Spektator-Briefe. Aufsätze über die deutsche Revolution und die Weltpolitik 1918/22.* Edited by Hans Baron. Tübingen: J. C. B. Mohr, 1924.

Troeltsch, Ernst. *Deutscher Geist und Westeuropa. Gesammelte kulturphilosophische Aufsätze und Reden.* Edited by Hans Baron. Tübingen: J. C. B. Mohr, 1925.

Troeltsch, Ernst. *The Social Teaching of the Christian Churches.* 2 vols. Translated by Olive Wyon. New York: Macmillan, 1931.

Troeltsch, Ernst. *Briefe an Friedrich von Hügel 1901–1923.* Edited by Karl-Ernst Apfelbacher and Peter Neuner. Paderborn: Bonifacius-Druckerei, 1974.

Verhandlungen der Ersten Kammer der Stände-Versammlung des Grossherzogtums Baden.

Verhandlungen des deutschen Soziologentages.

Verhandlungen des Evangelische Sozialen Kongresses.

Vossische Zeitung.

Weber, Alfred. "Entgegnung." *Archiv für Sozialwissenschaft und Sozialpolitik* XXXIX (1914–1915): 223–226.

Weber, Marianne. *Max Weber: Ein Lebensbild.* Heidelberg: L. Schneider, 1950. Translated by Harry Zohn as *Max Weber: A Biography.* New York: Wiley, 1975. (First edition, 1926.)

Weber, Marianne. *Lebenserinnerungen.* Bremen: J. Storm, 1948.

Weber, Max. "Zur Rechtfertigung Göhres." *Die Christliche Welt* VI (1892): 1104–1109.

Weber, Max. "Die Erhebung des Evangelisch-Sozialen Kongresses über die Verhältnisse der Landarbeiter Deutschlands." *Die Christliche Welt* VII (1893): 535–540.

Weber, Max. "Was heisst Christlich-Sozial? Gesammelte Aufsätze von Friedrich Naumann." *Die Christliche Welt* VIII (1894): 472–477.

Weber, Max. "Die protestantische Ethik und der 'Geist' des Kapitalismus. I. Das Problem. II. Die Berufsidee des asketischen Protestantismus." *Archiv für Sozialwissenschaft und Sozialpolitik* XX (1904): 1–54, XXI (1905): 1–110. Translated by Talcott Parsons as *The Protestant Ethic and the Spirit of Capitalism.* New York: Scribner's, 1958.

Weber, Max. "Zur Lage der bürgerlichen Demokratie in Russland." *Archiv für Sozialwissenschaft und Sozialpolitik* XXII (1906): 234–353.

Weber, Max. "Die Deutsche Gesellschaft für Soziologie." *Archiv für Sozialwissenschaft und Sozialpolitik* XXXI (1910).

Weber, Max. *Gesammelte Aufsätze zur Religionssoziologie.* 3 vols. Tübingen: J. C. B. Mohr, 1920–1921.

Weber, Max. *Gesammelte Politische Schriften*. Munich: Drei Masken Verlag, 1921 (first edition, edited by Marianne Weber). Tübingen: J. C. B. Mohr, 1971 (third edition, edited by Johannes Winckelmann).

Weber, Max. *Jugendbriefe*. Edited by Marianne Weber. Tübingen: J. C. B. Mohr, 1936.

Weber, Max. *The Methodology of the Social Sciences*. Translated by Edward A. Shils and Henry A. Finch. New York: Free Press, 1949.

Weber, Max. *The Religion of China: Confucianism and Taoism*. Translated by Hans Gerth. Glencoe, Ill: Free Press, 1951. (First edition, 1920.)

Weber, Max. *Ancient Judaism*. Translated by Hans Gerth and Don Martindale. New York: Free Press, 1952. (First edition, 1921.)

Weber, Max. *From Max Weber*. Edited and translated by Hans Gerth and C. Wright Mills. New York: Oxford University Press, 1958.

Weber, Max. *The Religion of India: The Sociology of Hinduism and Buddhism*. Translated by Hans Gerth and Don Martindale. Glencoe, Ill.: Free Press, 1958. (First edition, 1921.)

Weber, Max. "Georg Simmel as Sociologist." Translated by Donald N. Levine. *Social Research* XXXIX (1972): 155–163.

Weber, Max. *Roscher and Knies: The Logical Problems of Historical Economics*. Translated by Guy Oakes. New York, London: Free Press, 1975.

Weber, Max. *Economy and Society*. Translated by Guenther Roth and Claus Wittich. Berkeley, Los Angeles, and London: University of California Press, 1978. (First edition, 1921.)

Weber, Max. *Die Protestantische Ethik*. Vol. I: *Eine Aufsatzsammlung*. Vol. II: *Kritiken und Antikritiken*. Edited by Johannes Winckelmann. Gütersloh: G. Mohn, 1981.

Weber, Max. *Gesamtausgabe*. Vol. III: *Die Lage der Landarbeiter im ostelbischen Deutschland. 1892*. Edited by Martin Riesebrodt. Tübingen: J. C. B. Mohr, 1984.

Weiss, Johannes. *Jesus' Proclamation of the Kingdom of God*. Edited by R. H. Hiers and D. L. Holland. Philadelphia: Fortress Press, 1971. (First edition, 1892.)

Wernle, Paul. Review of Ernst Troeltsch, *Die Soziallehren der christlichen Kirchen und Gruppen* (1912). *Zeitschrift für Theologie und Kirche* XXII (1912): 329–368: XXIII (1913): 18–80.

Wuthenow, Ralph-Rainer, ed. *Stefan George in seiner Zeit. Dokumente zur Wirkungsgeschichte*, 2 vols. Stuttgart: Klett-Cotta, 1980.

Secondary Sources

Achinger, Hans. *Wilhelm Merton in seiner Zeit*. Frankfurt am Main: W. Kramer, 1965.

Adorno, Theodor W. *Prisms*. Translated by Samuel and Shierry Weber. Cambridge, Mass.: MIT Press, 1983.

Bibliography

Albisetti, James C. *Secondary School Reform in Imperial Germany*. Princeton: Princeton University Press, 1983.

Alt, Arthur T. *Theodor Storm*. New York: Twayne, 1973.

Arato, Andrew, and Breines, Paul. *The Young Lukács and the Origins of Western Marxism*. New York: Seabury Press, 1979.

Aron, Raymond. *German Sociology*. Translated by Mary and Thomas Bottomore. New York: Arno, 1979.

Badische Biographien. VI. Teil (1901–1910). Edited by A. Krieger and K. Obser. Heidelberg: Winter, 1935.

Baier, Horst. "Die Gesellschaft. Ein langer Schatten des toten Gottes. Friedrich Nietzsche und die Entstehung der Soziologie aus dem Geist der Dekadenz." In *Nietzsche-Studien* X–XI (1981–1982): 6–33.

Bauer, Karl. *Adolf Hausrath. Leben und Zeit*. Heidelberg: C. Winter, 1933.

Baumgarten, Eduard. *Max Weber: Werk und Person*. Tübingen: J. C. B. Mohr, 1964.

Becher, Heribert J. *Georg Simmel. Die Grundlagen seiner Soziologie*. Stuttgart: F. Enke, 1971.

Becker, Josef. *Liberaler Staat und Kirche in der Ära von Reichsgründung und Kulturkampf. Geschichte und Strukturen ihres Verhältnisses in Baden 1860–1876*. Mainz: Matthias-Grünewald, 1973.

Beiträge zur Deutung der letzten hundertfünfzig Jahre. Festschrift für Siegried A. Kaehler, 355–387.

Bellebaum, Alfred. *Das soziologische System von Ferdinand Tönnies unter besonderer Berücksichtigung seiner soziographischen Untersuchungen*. Meisenheim an der Glan: Hain, 1966.

Bellebaum, Alfred. "Ferdinand Tönnies." In Dirk Käsler, ed., *Klassiker des soziologischen Denkens*, vol. I: *Von Comte bis Durkheim*, 232–266.

Bendix, Reinhard. *Force, Fate, and Freedom: On Historical Sociology*. Berkeley, Los Angeles, and London: University of California Press, 1984.

Bendix, Reinhard, and Roth, Guenther. *Scholarship and Partisanship: Essays on Max Weber*. Berkeley, Los Angeles, and London: University of California Press, 1971.

Benjamin, Walter. *Illuminations*. Edited with an introduction by Hannah Arendt. New York: Schocken, 1969.

Benjamin, Walter. *Gesammelte Schriften*. Frankfurt am Main: Suhrkamp, 1972 ff.

Benjamin, Walter. *The Origins of German Tragic Drama*. Translated by John Osborne. London: New Left Books, 1977.

Benz, Richard. *Heidelberg, Schicksal und Geist*. Sigmaringen: J. Thorbecke, 1975.

Berglar, Peter. *Wilhelm von Humboldt in Selbstzeugnissen und Bilddokumente*. Reinbek bei Hamburg: Rowohlt, 1970.

Bibliography

Berman, Marshall. *All That Is Solid Melts into Air: The Experience of Modernity.* New York: Simon and Schuster, 1982.

Besnard, Philippe, ed. *The Sociological Domain: The Durkheimians and the Founding of French Sociology.* Cambridge and New York: Cambridge University Press, 1983.

Bickel, Cornelius. "Ferdinand Tönnies. Soziologie zwischen geschichtsphilosophischem 'Pessimismus', wissenschaftlicher Ratio und sozialethischem 'Optimismus.'" in Sven Papcke, ed., *Ordnung und Theorie. Beiträge zur Geschichte der Soziologie in Deutschland,* 307–334.

Binion, Rudolph. *Frau Lou: Nietzsche's Wayward Disciple.* Princeton: Princeton University Press, 1968.

Bloch-Almanach.

Blüm, Norbert. *Willenslehre und Soziallehre bei Ferdinand Tönnies. Ein Beitrag zum Verständnis von 'Gemeinschaft und Gesellschaft.'* Bonn: Rheinische Friedrich-Wilhelms-Universität, 1967.

Blumenberg, Hans. "Geld oder Leben. Eine metaphorologische Studie zur Konsistenz der Philosophie Georg Simmels." In Hannes Böhringer and Karlfried Gründer, eds., *Ästhetik und Soziologie um die Jahrhundertwende. Georg Simmel,* 121–134.

Boberg, Jochen, Fichter, Tilmann, and Gillen, Eckhart, eds. *Exerzierfeld der Moderne. Industriekultur in Berlin im 19. Jahrhundert.* Munich: C. H. Beck, 1986.

Boberg, Jochen, Fichter, Tilmann, and Gillen, Eckhart, eds. *Die Metropole. Industriekultur in Berlin im 20. Jahrhundert.* Munich: C. H. Beck, 1986.

Böckenförde, Ernst-Wolfgang. *Die deutsche verfassungsgeschichtliche Forschung im 19. Jahrhundert. Zeitgebundene Fragestellungen und Leitbilder.* Berlin: Duncker and Humblot, 1961.

Böckenförde, Ernst-Wolfgang. "Die Historische Rechtsschule und das Problem der Geschichtlichkeit des Rechts," in Ernst-Wolfgang Böckenförde et al., *Collegium Philosophicum. Studien. Joachim Ritter zum 60. Geburtstag,* 9–36.

Böckenförde, Ernst-Wolfgang, et al. *Collegium Philosophicum. Studien. Joachim Ritter zum 60. Geburtstag.* Basel and Stuttgart: Schwabe, 1965.

Böhringer, Hannes, and Gründer, Karlfried, eds. *Ästhetik und Soziologie um die Jahrhundertwende. Georg Simmel.* Frankfurt am Main: V. Klostermann, 1976.

Born, Karl Erich. *Staat und Sozialpolitik seit Bismarcks Sturz.* Wiesbaden: F. Steiner, 1957.

Bradler, Günther, and Quarthal, Franz, eds. *Von der Ständeversammlung zum demokratischen Parlament. Die Geschichte der Volksvertretungen in Baden-Württemberg.* Stuttgart: K. Theiss, 1982.

Brandt, Otto, Kluver, Wilhelm, and Jankuhn, Herbert. *Die Geschichte Schleswig-Holsteins. Ein Grundriss.* Kiel: Mühlau, 1976.

Brinkmann, Carl. "Barth, Paul." In *Encyclopedia of the Social Sciences,* vol. II, 469–470.

Bibliography

Brockstedt, Jürgen. "Frühindustrialisierung in den Herzogtümern Schleswig und Holstein. Ein Überblick." In Jürgen Brockstedt, ed., *Frühindustrialisierung in Schleswig-Holstein, anderen norddeutschen Ländern und Dänemark*, 19–77.

Brockstedt, Jürgen, ed. *Frühindustrialisierung in Schleswig-Holstein, anderen norddeutschen Ländern und Dänemark*. Neumünster: Wachholtz, 1983.

Bromberg, Victor. *The Novels of Flaubert: A Study of Themes and Techniques*. Princeton: Princeton University Press, 1966.

Brunner, Otto, Conze, Werner, and Koselleck, Reinhart, eds., *Geschichtliche Grunbegriffe. Historisches Lexikon zur politisch-sozialen Sprache in Deutschland*. Stuttgart: Klett-Cotta, 1975.

Bühler, Andreas. *Kirche und Staat bei Rudolf Sohm*. Zurich: EVZ, 1965.

Cahnman, Werner J., ed. *Ferdinand Tönnies: A New Evaluation—Essays and Documents*. Leiden: E. J. Brill, 1973.

Cahnman, Werner J. "Tönnies and Weber: Comparisons and Excerpts." In Werner J. Cahnman, ed., *Ferdinand Tönnies: A New Evaluation—Essays and Documents*, 257–283.

Cahnman, Werner J. "Tönnies and Weber: A Rejoinder." *European Journal of Sociology* XXII (1981): 154–157.

Cahnman, Werner J. and Heberle, Franziska. "Tönnies and National Socialism: Two Documents and a Commentary." In Werner J. Cahnman, ed., *Ferdinand Tönnies: A New Evaluation—Essays and Documents*, 284–290.

Calleson, Gerd. "Die Arbeiterbewegung in Nordschleswig 1872–1878—Haupzüge ihrer Entwicklung." *Zeitschrift der Gesellschaft für Schleswig-Holsteinische Geschichte* C (1975): 193–216.

Clark, T. J. *The Painting of Modern Life: Paris in the Art of Manet and His Followers*. New York: Knopf, 1984.

Clark, T. N. *Prophets and Patrons: The French University and the Emergence of the Social Sciences*. Cambridge: Cambridge University Press, 1973.

Clausen, Lars, and Pappi, Franz Urban. *Ankunft bei Tönnies, Soziologische Beiträge zum 125. Geburtstag von Ferdinand Tönnies*. Kiel: W. Mühlau, 1981.

Clebsch, William A. *England's Earliest Protestants, 1520–1535*. New Haven and London: Yale University Press, 1964.

Collins, Randall. *Weberian Sociological Theory*. Cambridge and New York: Cambridge University Press, 1986.

Congdon, Lee. *The Young Lukács*. Chapel Hill: University of North Carolina Press, 1983.

Conze, Werner. "Friedrich Naumann: Grundlagen und Ansatz seiner Politik in der national-sozialen Zeit (1895 bis 1903)." In Walther Hubatsch, ed., *Schicksalwege deutscher Vergangenheit*.

Conze, Werner, and Groh, Dieter. *Die Arbeiterbewegung in der nationalen Bewegung. Die deutsche Sozialdemodratie vor, während, und nach der Reichsgründung.* Stuttgart: Klett-Cotta, 1966.

Conze, Werner, and Kocka, Jürgen, eds. *Bildungsbürgertum im 19. Jahrhundert. Bildungssystem und Professionalisierung in internationalen Vergleichen.* Stuttgart: Klett-Cotta, 1984.

Craig, Gordon. *Germany 1866–1945.* New York: Oxford University Press, 1980.

Cser, Andreas. "Badischer Landtag bis 1918." In Günther Bradler and Franz Quarthal, eds., *Von der Ständeversammlung zum demokratischen Parlament. Die Geschichte der Volksvertretungen in Baden-Württemberg,* 153–182.

Dahme, Heinz-Jürgen. "Das 'Abgrenzungsproblem' von Philosophie und Wissenschaft bei Georg Simmel. Zur Genese und Systematik einer Problemstellung." In Heinz-Jürgen Dahme and Otthein Rammstedt, eds., *Simmel und die Moderne. Neue Interpretationen und Materialien,* 202–230.

Dahme, Heinz-Jürgen. *Soziologie als exakte Wissenschaft. Georg Simmels Ansatz und seine Bedeutung in der gegenwärtigen Soziologie.* 2 vols. Stuttgart: F. Enke, 1981.

Dahme, Heinz-Jürgen, and Rammstedt, Otthein, eds. *Georg Simmel und die Moderne. Neue Interpretationen und Materialien.* Frankfurt am Main: Suhrkamp, 1984.

Dahrendorf, Ralf. *Society and Democracy in Germany.* New York: Norton, 1967.

David, Claude. "Le Jahrbuch für die geistige Bewegung (1910–1911)," *Etudes Germaniques* X (1955): 276–299.

David, Claude. *Stefan George. Sein dichterisches Werk.* Munich: C. Hanser, 1967.

Deutsches Familienarchiv. Vol. XIX (1961): *Das Hugenottengeschlecht Souchay de la Duboissière und seine Nachkommen.* Edited by Otto Döhner.

Dinkler-von Schubert, Erika, ed. "Ernst Troeltsch. Briefe aus der Heidelberger Zeit an Wilhelm Bousset, 1894–1914." *Heidelberger Jahrbücher* XX (1976): 19–52.

Duchrow, Ulrich, Huber, Wolfgang, and Reith, Louis. *Umdeutungen der Zweireichenlehre Luthers im 19. Jahrhundert.* Gütersloh: G. Mohn, 1975.

Düding, Dieter. *Der National-Soziale Verein, 1896–1903. Der gescheiterte Versuch einer parteipolitischen Synthese von Nationalismus, Sozialismus und Liberalismus.* Munich and Vienna: Oldenbourg, 1972.

Earle, Edward Mead, ed. *Nationalism and Internationalism: Essays Inscribed to Carlton J. H. Hayes.* New York: Columbia University Press, 1950.

Eden, Robert. *Political Leadership and Nihilism: A Study of Weber and Nietzsche.* Tampa: University of Florida Press, 1983.

Edgell, David P. *William Ellery Channing: An Intellectual Portrait.* Boston: Beacon, 1955.

Eisen, Arnold. "Called to Order: The Role of the Puritan Berufsmensch in Weberian Sociology." In *Sociology* XIII (1979): 203–218.

Bibliography

Encyclopedia of the Social Sciences. Edited by R. A. Seligman. New York: Macmillan, 1930–1935.

Erbacher, Hermann, ed. *Vereinigte Evangelische Landeskirche in Baden, 1821–1971, Dokumente und Aufsätze.* Karlsruhe: Evangelischer Presseverband, 1971.

Ernst, O. A. "Merx, Adalbert." in *Badische Biographien* VI. Teil (1901–1910), 44–56.

Feaver, George. *From Status to Contract: A Biography of Sir Henry Maine, 1822–1888.* London: Longmans, 1969.

Fechner, Rolf, ed. *Der Dichter und der Soziologe. Zum Verhältnis zwischen Theodor Storm und Ferdinand Tönnies. Referate der Arbeitstagung im November 1984 in Husum.* Hamburg: Ferdinand-Tönnies-Arbeitsstelle an der Universität Hamburg, Materiaien Bd. 2, 1985.

Fehér, Ferenc. "Am Scheideweg des romantischen Kapitalismus. Typologie und Beitrag zur deutschen Ideologiegeschichte gelegentlich des Briefwechsels zwischen Paul Ernst und Georg Lukács." In Agnes Heller et al., *Die Seele und das Leben,* 241–327.

Fehér, Ferenc. "Die Geschichtsphilosophie des Dramas, die Metaphysik der Tragödie und die Utopie des untragischen Dramas. Scheidewege der Dramentheorie des jungen Lukács." In Agnes Heller et al., *Die Seele und das Leben,* 7–53.

Feher, Zoltan Andor. "Georg Lukács's Role in Dostoyevsky's European Reception at the Turn of the Century: A Study in Reception." Ph.D. Dissertation, UCLA, 1978.

Fenton, Steve, Reiner, Robert, and Hamnett, Ian. *Durkheim and Modern Sociology.* Cambridge and New York: Cambridge University Press, 1984.

Fenske, Hans. *Der liberale Südwesten. Freiheitliche und demokratische Traditionen in Baden und Württemberg 1790–1933.* Stuttgart: Kohlhammer, 1981.

Ferber, Christian von. "Der Werturteilsstreit 1901/1959. Versuch einer wissenschaftsgeschichtlichen Interpretation." *Kölner Zeitschrift für Soziologie und Sozialpsychologie* XI (1959): 21–37.

Fischer, Fritz. *Germany's Aims in the First World War.* New York: Norton, 1968.

Fischoff, Ephraim. "The Protestant Ethic and the Spirit of Capitalism: The History of a Controversy." *Social Research* XI (1944): 53–77.

Fleischmann, Eugène. "De Weber à Nietzsche." *European Journal of Sociology* V (1964): 190–238.

Freymuth, Günther. "Georg Simmel und Stefan George." *Neue deutsche Hefte* XVII (1970): 41–50.

Friedrichs, Robert W. *A Sociology of Sociology.* New York: Free Press, 1970.

Frisby, David. *Sociological Impressionism: A Reassessment of Georg Simmel's Social Theory.* London: Heinemann, 1981.

Frisby, David. *Fragments of Modernity: Theories of Modernity in the Work of Simmel, Kracauer and Benjamin.* Cambridge, Mass.: MIT, 1986.

Frommel, Otto. "Heinrich Bassermann." In *Badische Biographien* VI.Teil (1901–1910), 525–527.

Frost, Henry H., Jr. "The Functional Sociology of Emile Waxweiler and the Institut de Sociologie Solvay." In *Académie royale de Belgique, Classe des lettres et des sciences morales et politiques, Mémoires* LV/5 (1960).

Fuchs, Emil. *Mein Leben.* Leipzig: Koehler and Amelang, 1957.

Gall, Lothar. *Der Liberalismus als regierende Partei. Das Grossherzogtum Baden zwischen Restauration und Reichsgründung.* Wiesbaden: F. Steiner, 1963.

Gassen, Kurt, and Landmann, Michael. *Buch des Dankes an Georg Simmel. Briefe, Erinnerungen, Bibliographie. Zu seinem 100. Geburtstag am 1. März 1958.* Berlin: Duncker and Humblot, 1958.

Gerrish, Brian A. *The Old Protestantism and the New: Essays on the Reformation Heritage.* Chicago: University of Chicago Press, 1982.

Gladen, Albin. *Geschichte der Sozialpolitik in Deutschland. Eine Analyse ihrer Bedingungen, Formen, Zielsetzungen und Auswirkungen.* Wiesbaden: F. Steiner, 1974.

Glassman, Ronald M., and Murvar, Vatro. "Introduction." In Ronald M. Glassman and Vatro Murvar, *Max Weber's Political Sociology: A Pessimistic Vision of a Rationalized World,* 3–11.

Glassman, Ronald M., and Murvar, Vatro. *Max Weber's Political Sociology: A Pessimistic Vision of a Rationalized World.* Westport, Conn., and London: Greenwood, 1984.

Gluck, Mary. *Georg Lukács and His Generation.* Cambridge, Mass.: Harvard University Press, 1985.

Gmür, Rudolf. *Savigny und die Entwicklung der Rechtswissenschaft.* Münster: Aschendorff, 1962.

Gouldner, Alvin W. *The Coming Crisis of Western Sociology.* New York and London: Basic, 1970.

Graf, Friedrich Wilhelm. "Der 'Systematiker' der 'Kleinen Göttinger Fakultät.' Ernst Troeltschs Promotionsthesen und ihr Göttinger Kontext." In Horst Renz and Friedrich Wilhelm Graf, eds., *Troeltsch-Studien. Untersuchungen zur Biographie und Werkgeschichte,* 235–290.

Graf, Friedrich Wilhelm. "Friendship between Experts: Notes on Weber and Troeltsch." In Wolfgang J. Mommsen and Jürgen Osterhammel, eds., *Max Weber and His Contemporaries,* 215–233.

Graf, Friedrich Wilhelm. "Licentiatos theologiae und Habilitation." In Horst Renz and Friedrich Wilhelm Graf, *Troeltsch-Studien. Untersuchungen zur Biographie und Werkgeschichte,* 78–102.

Grass, H. "Erlanger Schule." In *Die Religion in Geschichte und Gegenwart,* 3rd ed., vol. II: 566–568.

Green, Robert W., ed. *Protestantism, Capitalism, and Social Science: The Weber Thesis Controversy.* Lexington, Mass.: Heath, 1973.

Groh, John E. *Nineteenth-Century German Protestantism: The Church as Social Model.* Washington, D.C.: University Press of America, 1982.

Guillaumin, Colette, and Poliakov, Léon. "Max Weber et les théories bioraciales du XXe siècle." *Cahiers internationaux de sociologie* LVI (1974): 115–126.

Hakamies, Ahti. "Der Begriff 'Eigengesetzlichkeit' in der heutigen Theologie und seine historischen Wurzeln." *Studia Theologica* XXIV (1970): 117–129.

Hamann, Richard, and Hermand, Jost. *Naturalismus.* Munich: Nymphenburger, 1972.

Hausrath, Adolf. *Carl Holsten. Worte der Erinnerung.* Heidelberg: Petters, 1897.

Hausrath, Adolf. *Alte Bekannte. Gedächtnisblätter,* vol. I: *Zur Erinnerung an Julius Jolly.* Leipzig: S. Hirzel, 1899.

Hausrath, Adolf. *Geschichte der theologischen Fakultät zu Heidelberg im 19. Jahrhundert.* Heidelberg: J. Hörning, 1901.

Hausrath, Adolf. *Richard Rothe und seine Freunde.* 2 vols. Berlin: G. Grote, 1902–06.

Hawthorn, Geoffrey. *Enlightenment and Despair: A History of Sociology.* Cambridge and New York: Cambridge University Press, 1976.

Hefner, Philip. *Faith and the Vitalites of History: A Theological Study Based on the Work of Albrecht Ritschl.* New York: Harper and Row, 1966.

Heidtmann, Bernhardt, and Katzenstein, Robert. *Soziologie und Praxis,* Cologne: Pahl-Rugenstein, 1979.

Heilmann, Martin. *Adolf Wagner. Ein deutscher Nationalökonom im Urteil der Zeit. Probleme seiner biographischen und theoriegeschichtlichen Würdigung im Lichte neuer Quellen.* Frankfurt am Main and New York: Campus, 1980.

Heller, Agnes. "Das Zerschellen des Lebens an der Form. György Lukács und Irma Seidler." In Agnes Heller et al., *Die Seele und das Leben,* 54–98.

Heller, Agnes, et al. *Die Seele und das Leben.* Frankfurt am Main: Suhrkamp, 1977.

Hellwig, Fritz. *Carl Ferdinand Freiherr von Stumm-Halberg, 1836–1901.* Heidelberg, Saarbrücken: Westmark, 1936.

Hennis, Wilhelm. "Max Weber's 'Central Question.'" *Economy and Society* XII (1983): 135–180.

Hennis, Wilhelm. *Max Webers Fragestellung. Studien zur Biographie des Werks.* Tübingen: J. C. B. Mohr, 1987.

Hentschel, Volker. *Geschichte der deutschen Sozialpolitik (1880–1908). Soziale Sicherung und kollektives Arbeitsrecht.* Frankfurt am Main: Suhrkamp, 1983.

Herrigel, Oskar. "Zum Gedächtnis von Adalbert Merx." *Protestantische Monatshefte* XIV (1910): 41–50, 89–103.

Hess, W. "Carl Holsten." *Allgemeine deutsche Biographie* L (1905): 450–454.

Heuss, Theodor. *Friedrich Naumann. Der Mann, das Werk, die Zeit.* Stuttgart and Berlin: Deutsche Verlagsanstalt, 1937.

Hinz, Gerhard, ed. *Ruperto-Carola Sonderband. Aus der Geschichte der Universität Heidelberg und ihrer Fakultäten.* Heidelberg: Brausdruck, 1961.

Hoffmann, Friedrich. "Ferdinand Tönnies im Gedenken seiner heimatlichen Verbundenheit zu seinem 100. Geburtstag." *Zeitschrift der Gesellschaft für Schleswig-Holsteinische Geschichte* LXXIX (1955): 301–316.

Honigsheim, Paul. "Die Gründung der Deutschen Gesellschaft für Soziologie in ihren geistesgeschichtlichen Zusammenhängen." *Kölner Zeitschrift für Soziologie und Sozialpsychologie* XI (1959): 3–10.

Hubatsch, Walter, ed. *Schicksalwege deutscher Vergangenheit. Beiträge zur Deutung der letzten hundertfünfzig Jahre. Festschrift für Siegfried A. Kaehler.* Dusseldorf: Droste, 1950.

Huber, Ernst Rudolf, and Huber, Wolfgang, eds. *Staat und Kirche im 19. und 20. Jahrhundert. Dokumente zur Geschichte des deutschen Staatskirchenrechts,* vol. I: *Staat und Kirche vom Ausgang des alten Reichs bis zum Vorabend der bürgerlichen Revolution.* Berlin: Duncker and Humblot, 1973.

Huber, Wolfgang. *Kirche und Öffentlichkeit.* Stuttgart: E. Klett, 1973.

Huber, Wolfgang. "Die Schwierigkeit evangelischer Lehrbeanstandung. Eine historische Erinnerung aus aktuellem Anlass." *Evangelische Theologie* XL (1980): 517–536.

Hudson, Wayne. *The Marxist Philosophy of Ernst Bloch.* New York: St. Martin's Press, 1982.

Jacoby, E. G. *Die moderne Gesellschaft im sozialwissenschaftlichen Denken von Ferdinand Tönnies. Eine biographische Einführung.* Stuttgart: F. Enke, 1971.

Jacoby, Russel. *Dialectic of Defeat: Contours of Western Marxism.* Cambridge and New York: Cambridge University Press, 1981.

Janssen, Albert. *Otto von Gierkes Methode der geschichtlichen Rechtswissenschaft. Studien zu den Wegen und Formen seines juristischen Denkens.* Göttingen, Frankfurt am Main, and Zurich: Musterschmidt, 1974.

Jelavich, Peter. *Munich and Theatrical Modernism: Politics, Playwriting, and Performance, 1890–1914.* Cambridge, Mass.: Harvard University Press, 1985.

Karádi, Éva, and Vezér, Erzsébet, eds. *Georg Lukács, Karl Mannheim und der Sonntagskreis.* Frankfurt am Main: Sendler, 1985.

Karger, Ursula. "Deutsche Soziologentage in Perspektive." *Sociologia Internationalis* XIV (1976): 7–21.

Käsler, Dirk, ed. *Klassiker des soziologischen Denkens.* 2 vols. Munich: Beck, 1976.

Käsler, Dirk. "Der Streit um die Bestimmung der Soziologie auf den deutschen Soziologentagen 1910–1930." in M. Rainer Lepsius, ed., *Soziologie in Deutschland und Österreich 1918–1945,* 199–244.

Käsler, Dirk. *Die frühe deutsche Soziologie 1909 bis 1934 und ihre Entstehungs-Milieus. Eine wissenschafts-soziologische Untersuchung.* Opladen: Westdeutscher Verlag, 1984.

Keller, Ernst. *Der junge Lukács. Antibürger und wesentliches Leben. Literatur- und Kulturkritik 1902–1915.* Frankfurt am Main: Sendler, 1984.

Kettler, David. "Culture and Revolution: Lukács in the Hungarian Revolution of 1918." *Telos* X (winter 1971): 35–92.

Kettler, David, Meja, Volker, and Stehr, Nico, eds. *Karl Mannheim.* New York: Tavistock, 1984.

Kleyser, Friedrich. *Kleine Kieler Wirtschaftsgeschichte von 1242 bis 1945.* Kiel: W. G. Juhlau, 1969.

Köhler, Walter, *Ernst Troeltsch.* Tübingen: J. C. B. Mohr, 1941.

König, René. "Die Begriffe Gemeinschaft und Gesellschaft bei Ferdinand Tönnies." *Kölner Zeitschrift für Soziologie und Sozialpsychologie* VII (1955): 348–420.

König, Rene. "Fünfzig Jahr Deutsche Gesellschaft für Soziologie (1909 bis 1959)." *Kölner Zeitschrift für Soziologie und Sozialpsychologie* XI (1959): 1–2.

Kraft, Werner. *Stefan George.* Munich: Edition Text und Kritik, 1980.

Kuklick, Bruce. *Churchmen and Philosophers: From Jonathan Edwards to John Dewey.* New Haven: Yale University Press, 1985.

Kutzbach, Karl August, ed. *Die Neuklassische Bewegung um 1905. Paul Ernst in Düsseldorf.* Emsdetten: Lechte, 1972.

Kutzbach, Karl August, ed. *Paul Ernst und Georg Lukács. Dokumente einer Freundschaft.* Emsdetten: Lechte, 1974.

Landeszentrale für politische Bildung Baden-Württembergs. *Badische Geschichte. Vom Grossgherzogtum bis zur Gegenwart.* Stuttgart: Theiss, 1979.

Landfried, Klaus. *Stefan George—Politik des Unpolitischen.* Heidelberg: L. Stiehm, 1975.

Landmann, Michael. "Georg Simmel and Stefan George." In Heinz-Jürgen Dahme and Otthein Rammstedt, eds, *Simmel und die Moderne,* 147–173.

Lange, Annemarie. *Das wilhelminische Berlin. Zwischen Jahrhundertwende und Novemberrevolution.* Berlin: Dietz, 1976.

le Fort, Gertrud von. *Die Hälfte des Lebens.* Munich: Ehrenwirth, 1965.

Lent, Kurt. "Das tragische Bewusstsein in der deutschen Soziologie." *Kölner Zeitschrift für Soziologie und Sozialpsychologie* XVI (1964): 257–287.

Lepenies, Wolf, ed. *Geschichte der Soziologie. Studien zur kognitiven, sozialen und historischen Identitat einer Disziplin.* 4 vols. Frankfurt am Main: Suhrkamp, 1981.

Lepenies, Wolf. *Die drei Kulturen. Soziologie zwischen Literatur und Wissenschaft.* Munich and Vienna: Hanser, 1985.

Lepsius, M. Rainer, ed. *Soziologie in Deutschland und Österreich 1918–1945. Materialien zur Entwicklung, Emigration und Wirkungsgeschichte. Kölner Zeitschrift für Soziologie und Sozialpsychologie* Sonderheft XXIII. Opladen: Westdeutscher, 1981.

Lepsius, Sabine. *Stefan George. Geschichte einer Freundschaft.* Berlin: Die Runde, 1939.

Lepsius, Sabine. *Ein Berliner Künstlerleben um die Jahrhundertwende.* Munich: G. Müller, 1972.

Lichtblau, Klaus. "Das 'Pathos der Distanz.' Präliminarien zur Nietzsche-Rezeption bei Georg Simmel." In Heinz-Jürgen Dahme and Otthein Rammstedt, eds., *Georg Simmel und die Moderne,* 231–281.

Liebersohn, Harry. *Religion and Industrial Society: The Protestant Social Congress in Wilhelmine Germany.* Philadelphia: Transactions of the American Philosophical Society, vol. LXXVI, part 6, 1986.

Lindenlaub, Dieter. *Richtungskämpfe im Verein für Sozialpolitik. Wissenschaft und Sozialpolitik im Kaiserreich, vornehmlich von Beginn des "Neuen Kurses" bis zum Ausbruch des ersten Weltkrieges (1870–1914). Vierteljahrsschrift für Sozial- und Wirtschaftsgeschichte,* Beihefte LII/LIII. Wiesbaden: F. Steiner, 1967.

Little, David. *Religion, Order and Law: A Study in Pre-Revolutionary England.* New York: Harper and Row, 1970.

Loader, Colin. *The Intellectual Development of Karl Mannheim.* Cambridge and New York: Cambridge University Press, 1985.

Long, Rose-Carol Washton. "Expressionism, Abstraction, and the Search for Utopias in Germany." In *The Spiritual in Art: Abstract Painting, 1890–1985,* 201–217.

Lorenz, Eckhart. "Protestantische Reaktionen auf die Entwicklung der sozialistischen Arbeiterbewegung. Mannheim 1890–1933." *Archiv für Sozialgeschichte* XVI (1976): 371–416.

Löwith, Karl. *Max Weber and Karl Marx.* Edited by Tom Bottomore and William Outhwaite. London and Boston: George Allen & Unwin, 1982.

Löwy, Michael. *Georg Lukács—from Romanticism to Bolshevism.* London: New Left Books, 1979.

Lübbe, Hermann. *Politische Philosophie in Deutschland. Studien zu ihrer Geschichte.* Basel and Stuttgart: Schwabe, 1963.

Mannheim, Karl. *Ideology and Utopia: An Introduction to the Sociology of Knowledge.* Translated by Louis Wirth and Edward Shils. New York: Harcourt, Brace and World, 1936.

Manuel, Frank. *The Prophets of Paris.* Cambridge, Mass.: Harvard University Press, 1962.

Marcuse, Herbert. "Industrialism and Capitalism." In Otto Stammer, ed., *Max Weber and Sociology Today,* 133–186.

Marshall, Gordon. *Presbyteries and Profits: Calvinism and the Development of Capitalism in Scotland, 1560–1707.* Oxford: Oxford University Press, 1980.

Bibliography

Marshall, Gordon. *In Search of the Spirit of Capitalism: An Essay on Max Weber's Protestant Ethic Thesis.* New York: Columbia University Press, 1982.

Massing, Paul W. *Rehearsal for Destruction: A Study of Political Anti-Semitism in Imperial Germany.* New York: Harper, 1949.

McClelland, Charles E. *State, Society and University in Germany, 1700–1914.* Cambridge and New York: Cambridge University Press, 1980.

McKinney, John C., and Loomis, Charles. "The Application of Gemeinschaft and Gesellschaft as Related to Other Typologies." In Ferdinand Tönnies, *Community and Society,* 12–29.

Mehnert, Gottfried. *Evangelische Kirche und Politik, 1917–1919.* Düsseldorf: Droste, 1959.

Menze, Clemens. *Die Bildungsreform Wilhelm von Humboldts.* Hannover: Schroedel, 1975.

Meuli, Karl. "Nachwort. Bachofens Leben." In Johann Jakob Bachofen, *Gesammelte Werke,* vol. III: *Das Mutterrecht,* 1011–1079.

Meurer, Bärbel. "Vom bildungsbürgerlichen Zeitvertreib zu Fachwissenschaft—Die deutschen Soziologie im Spiegel ihrer Soziologentage." In Bernhardt Heidtmann and Robert Katzenstein, *Soziologie und Praxis,* 210–231.

Miller, Perry. *Errand into the Wilderness.* New York: Harper and Row, 1964.

Mitzman, Arthur. *The Iron Cage: An Historical Interpretation of Max Weber.* New York: Grosset and Dunlap, 1969.

Mitzman, Arthur. *Sociology and Estrangement: Three Sociologists of Imperial Germany.* New York: Knopf, 1973.

Mommsen, Wolfgang. *Max Weber und die deutsche Politik, 1890–1920.* Tübingen: J. C. B. Mohr, 1974. Translated by Michael Steinberg as *Max Weber and German Politics, 1890–1920.* Chicago and London: University of Chicago Press, 1984.

Mommsen, Wolfgang. *Max Weber. Gesellschaft, Politik und Geschichte.* Frankfurt am Main: Suhrkamp, 1974.

Mommsen, Wolfgang, and Osterhammel, Jürgen, eds. *Max Weber and His Contemporaries.* London, Boston, Sydney: Allen & Unwin, 1987.

Mosse, George L. *The Crisis of German Ideology: Intellectual Origins of the Third Reich.* New York: Grosset and Dunlap, 1964.

Mueller, David L. *An Introduction to the Theology of Albrecht Ritschl.* Philadelphia: Westminster Press, 1969.

Muirhead, John Henry. *Reflections by a Journeyman in Philosophy in the Movements of Thought and Practice in His Time.* Edited by John W. Harvey. London: Allen & Unwin, 1942.

Müssiggang, Albert. *Die soziale Frage in der historischen Schule der deutschen Nationalökonomie.* Tübingen: J. C. B. Mohr, 1968.

Nürnberger, Richard. "Imperialismus, Sozialismus und Christentum bei Friedrich Naumann." *Historische Zeitschrift* CLXX (1950): 525–548.

Oberschall, Anthony. *Empirical Social Research in Germany, 1848–1914.* New York: Basic Books, 1965.

Oberschall, Anthony. "The Empirical Sociology of Tönnies." In Werner J. Cahnman, ed., *Ferdinand Tönnies: A New Evaluation—Essays and Documents,* 160–180.

Papcke, Sven, ed. *Ordnung und Theorie. Beiträge zur Geschichte der Soziologie in Deutschland.* Darmstadt: Wissenschaftliche Buchgesellschaft, 1986.

Paret, Peter. *The Berlin Secession: Modernism and Its Enemies in Imperial Germany.* Cambridge, Mass.: Harvard University Press, 1980.

Parsons, Talcott. *The Structure of Social Action: A Study in Social Theory with Special Reference to a Recent Group of European Writers.* 2 vols. New York: Free Press, 1968.

Parsons, Talcott. "Value-Freedom and Objectivity." In Otto Stammer, ed., *Max Weber and Sociology Today,* 27–50.

Paton, H. J. *Kant's Metaphysics of Experience.* 2 vols. London and New York: Allen & Unwin, 1936.

Patterson, Robert L. *The Philosophy of William Ellery Channing.* New York: Bookman Associates, 1952.

Pfeiffer, G. "Bayern: Evangelische Kirche." in *Die Religion in Geschichte und Gegenwart,* 3rd. ed., vol. I, 939–947.

Plessen, Marie-Louise. *Die Wirksamkeit des Vereins für Socialpolitik von 1872–1890. Studien zu Katheder- und Staatssozialismus.* Berlin: Duncker and Humblot, 1975.

Pocock, J. G. A. *Politics, Language and Time: Essays on Political Thought and History.* New York: Atheneum, 1971.

Pollmann, Klaus Erich. *Landesherrliches Kirchenregiment und soziale Frage.* Berlin: de Gruyter, 1973.

Pulzer, Peter G. J. *The Rise of Political Anti-Semitism in Germany and Austria.* New York: Wiley, 1964.

Raphäel, Freddy. *Judaïsme et Capitalisme: Essai sur la controverse entre Max Weber et Werner Sombart.* Paris: Presses Universitaires de France, 1982.

Rathje, Johannes. *Die Welt des freien Protestantismus. Ein Beitrag zur deutsch-evangelischen Geistesgeschichte dargestellt am Leben und Werk von Martin Rade.* Stuttgart: E. Klotz, 1952.

Ratz, Ursula. *Sozialreform und Arbeiterschaft. Die "Gesellschaft für Sozialreform" und die sozialdemokratische Arbeiterbewegung von der Jahrhundertwende bis zum Ausbruch des Ersten Weltkrieges.* Berlin: Colloquium, 1980.

Regling, Heinz Volkmar. *Die Anfänge des Sozialismus in Schleswig-Holstein.* Neumünster: K. Wachholtz, 1965.

Bibliography

Reinharz, Jehuda. *Fatherland or Promised Land: The Dilemma of the German Jew, 1893–1914.* Ann Arbor: University of Michigan Press, 1975.

Die Religion in Geschichte und Gegenwart. Handwörterbuch für Theologie und Religionswissenschaft. Third edition. Edited by Kurt Galling, Hans Freiherr von Campenhausen, et al. 7 vols. Tübingen: J. C. B. Mohr, 1957–1965.

Renz, Horst. "Augsburger Jahre. Grundlagen der geistigen Entwicklung von Ernst Troeltsch." In Horst Renz and Friedrich Wilhelm Graf, eds., *Troeltsch-Studien. Untersuchungen zur Biographie und Werkgeschichte,* 13–32.

Renz, Horst. "Troeltschs Theologiestudium." In Horst Renz and Friedrich Wilhelm Graf, eds., *Troeltsch-Studien. Untersuchungen zür Biographie und Werkgeschichte,* 48–59.

Renz, Horst, and Graf, Friedrich Wilhelm, eds. *Troeltsch-Studien. Untersuchungen zur Biographie und Werkgeschichte.* Gütersloh: Mohn, 1982.

Resek, Carl. *Lewis Henry Morgan: American Scholar.* Chicago: University of Chicago Press, 1960.

Rice, Madeleine. *Federal Street Pastor: The Life of William Ellery Channing.* New York: Bookman Associates, 1961.

Richter, Melvin. *The Politics of Conscience: T. H. Green and His Age.* London: Weidenfeld and Nicholson, 1964.

Riedel, Manfred. "Gemeinschaft, Gesellschaft." In Otto Brunner, Werner Conze, and Reinhart Koselleck, *Geschichtliche Grundbegriffe. Historisches Lexikon zur politisch-sozialen Sprache in Deutschland,* vol. II, 801–832.

Riese, Reinhard. *Die Hochschule auf dem Wege zum wissenschaftlichen Grossbetrieb. Die Universität Heidelberg und das badische Hochschulwesen, 1860–1914.* Stuttgart: Klett-Cotta, 1977.

Riesebrodt, Martin. "Ideen, Interessen, Rationalisierung: Kritische Anmerkungen zu F. H. Tenbrucks Interpretation des Werkes Max Webers." *Kölner Zeitschrift für Soziologie und Sozialpsychologie* XXXII (1980): 111–129.

Riesebrodt, Martin. "From Patriarchalism to Capitalism: The Theoretical Context of Max Weber's Agrarian Studies (1892–1893)." *Economy and Society* XV (1986), 476–502.

Ringer, Fritz. *The Decline of the German Mandarins: The German Academic Community, 1890–1933.* Cambridge, Mass.: Harvard University Press, 1969.

Ringer, Fritz. *Education and Society in Modern Europe.* Bloomington, Indiana: Indiana University Press, 1979.

Ritschl, Otto. *Albrecht Ritschls Leben,* 2 vol. Freiburg: J. C. B. Mohr, 1892–1896.

Rode, Horst, and Kluge, Ekkehard. "Ferdinand Tönnies' Verhältnis zu Nationalsozialismus und Faschismus." In Lars Clausen and Franz Urban Pappi, eds., *Ankunft bei Tönnies. Soziologische Beiträge zum 125. Geburtstag von Ferdinand Tönnies,* 250–274.

Rosenberg, Hans. *Grosse Depression und Bismarckzeit. Wirtschaftsablauf, Gesellschaft und Politik in Mitteleuropa.* Berlin: de Gruyter, 1967.

Roth, Guenther. "Das historische Verhältnis der Weberschen Soziologie zum Marxismus." *Kölner Zeitschrift für Soziologie und Sozialpsychologie* XX (1968): 429–447.

Rothacker, E. "Savigny, Grimm, Ranke. Ein Beitrag zur Frage nach dem Zusammenhang der historischen Schule." *Historische Zeitschrift* CXXVIII (1923): 415–445.

Rubanowice, Robert J. *Crisis in Consciousness: The Thought of Ernst Troeltsch.* Tallahassee, Florida: University Presses of Florida, 1982.

Rydell, Robert. *All the World's a Fair: Visions of Empire at American International Expositions, 1876–1916.* Chicago: University of Chicago Press, 1984.

Salin, Edgar. *Um Stefan George.* Godesberg: Helmut Kuper, 1948.

Scaff, Lawrence A. "Weber before Weberian Sociology." *British Journal of Sociology* XXXV (1984): 190–215.

Schaefer, Rolf. *Ritschl. Grundlinien eines fast verschollenen dogmatischen Systems.* Tübingen: J. C. B. Mohr, 1968.

Schluchter, Wolfgang. *Rationalismus der Weltbeherrschung. Studien zu Max Weber.* Frankfurt am Main: Suhrkamp, 1980.

Schluchter, Wolfgang, ed. *Max Webers Studie über das antike Judentum. Interpretation und Kritik.* Frankfurt am Main: Suhrkamp, 1981.

Schluchter, Wolfgang. *The Rise of Western Rationalism: Max Weber's Developmental History.* Translated by Guenther Roth, Berkeley and Los Angeles: University of California Press, 1981.

Schluchter, Wolfgang. *Max Webers Studie über Konfuzianismus und Taoismus. Interpretation und Kritik.* Frankfurt am Main: Suhrkamp, 1983.

Schluchter, Wolfgang. "Max Webers Religionssoziologie. Eine werkgeschichtliche Rekonstruktion." *Kölner Zeitschrift für Soziologie und Sozialpsychologie* XXXVI (1984): 342–365.

Schluchter, Wolfgang, ed. *Max Webers Studie über Hinduismus und Buddhismus. Interpretation und Kritik.* Frankfurt am Main: Suhrkamp, 1984.

Schmidt, Gustav. *Deutscher Historismus und der Übergang zur parlamentarischen Demokratie. Untersuchungen zu den politischen Gedanken von Meinecke-Troeltsch-Max Weber.* Lübeck and Hamburg: Matthiesen, 1964.

Scholz, Gunter. "Drittes Reich. Begriffsgeschichte mit Blick auf Blochs Originalgeschichte." *Bloch-Almanach* II (1982): 19–38.

Schrader-Klebert, Karin. "Der Begriff der Gesellschaft als regulative Idee. Zur transzendentalen Begründung der Gesellschaft bei Georg Simmel." *Soziale Welt* XIX (1968): 97–118.

Schwabe, Klaus. *Wissenschaft und Kriegsmoral. Die deutschen Hochschullehrer und die politischen Grundfragen des Ersten Weltkrieges.* Göttingen: Musterschmidt, 1969.

Seekamp, H.-J., Ockenden, R. C., and Keilson, M., eds. *Stefan George. Leben und Werk. Eine Zeittafel.* Amsterdam: Castrum Peregrini, 1972.

Seigel, Jerrold. *Marx's Fate: The Shape of a Life.* Princeton: Princeton University Press, 1978.

Shanahan, William O. "Friedrich Naumann: A German View of Power and Nationalism." In Edward Mead Earle, ed., *Nationalism and Internationalism: Essays Inscribed to Carlton J. H. Hayes,* 352–398.

Sheehan, James J. *German Liberalism in the Nineteenth Century.* Chicago: University of Chicago Press, 1978.

Soliday, Gerald L. *A Community in Conflict: Frankfurt Society in the Seventeenth and Early Eighteenth Centuries.* Hanover, N.H.: University Press of New England, 1974.

The Spiritual in Art: Abstract Painting, 1890–1985. Exhibition Catalog. Los Angeles: Los Angeles County Museum of Art, 1986.

Spotts, Frederic. *The Churches and Politics in Germany.* Middletown, Conn.: Wesleyan University Press, 1973.

Stadelhofer, Manfred. *Der Abbau der Kulturkampfgesetzgebung im Grossherzogtum Baden, 1878–1918.* Mainz: Matthias-Grünewald-Verlag, 1969.

Stammer, Otto, ed. *Max Weber and Sociology Today.* Translated by Kathleen Morris. New York: Harper and Row, 1971.

Stern, Bernard J. *Lewis Henry Morgan: Social Evolutionist.* New York: Russell and Russell, 1967.

Strawson, P. F. *The Bounds of Sense: An Essay on Kant's Critique of Pure Reason.* London: Methuen, 1966.

Sweet, Paul R. *Wilhelm von Humboldt: A Biography.* Columbus, Ohio: Ohio State University Press, 1978.

Tenbruck, Friedrich. "Das Werk Max Webers." *Kölner Zeitschrift für Soziologie und Sozialpsychologie* XXVII (1975): 663–702.

Theiner, Peter. *Sozialer Liberalismus und Weltpolitik: Friedrich Naumann im wilhelminischen Deutschland (1860–1919).* Baden-Baden: Nomos, 1983.

Thiel, Jürgen. *Die Grossblockpolitik der Nationalliberalen Partei Badens, 1905 bis 1914.* Stuttgart: W. Kohlhammer, 1976.

Timm, Hermann. *Theorie und Praxis in der Theologie Albrecht Ritschls und Wilhelm Herrmanns. Ein Beitrag zur Entwicklungsgeschichte des Kulturprotestantismus.* Gütersloh: G. Mohn, 1967.

Timm, Hermann. *Friedrich Naumanns theologischer Widerruf.* Munich: Kaiser, 1967.

Tompert, Helene. *Lebensformen und Denkweisen der akademischen Welt Heidelbergs im wilhelminischen Zeitalter vornehmlich im Spiegel zeitgenössischer Selbstzeugnisse.* Lübeck and Hamburg: Matthiesen, 1969.

Topitsch, Ernst. "Max Weber and Sociology Today." In Otto Stammer, ed., *Max Weber and Sociology Today,* 8–25.

Trautmann, Gunter. "Liberalismus, Arbeiterbewegung und Staat in Hamburg und Schleswig-Holstein, 1862–1869." *Archiv für Sozialgeschichte* XV (1975): 51–110.

Tribe, Keith. "Prussian Agriculture—German Politics: Max Weber 1892–1897." *Economy and Society* XII (1983): 181–226.

Turner, Bryan S. *For Weber: Essays on the Sociology of Fate.* Boston, London, and Henley: Routledge and Kegan Paul, 1981.

Turner, R. Stephen. "The Bildungsbürgertum and the Learned Professions in Prussia, 1770–1830: The Origins of a Class." *Histoire Sociale-Social History* (1980): 105–135.

Verheule, Anthonie F. *Wilhelm Bousset. Leben und Werk. Ein theologiegeschichtlicher Versuch.* Amsterdam: Van Bottenburg, 1973.

Vidich, Arthur J., and Lyman, Stanford M. *American Sociology: Worldly Rejections of Religion and Their Directions.* New Haven: Yale University Press, 1985.

Vosskamp, Wilhelm. "Einleitung." In Wilhelm Vosskamp, ed., *Utopieforschung. Interdisziplinäre Studien. zur neuzeitlichen Utopie,* 1–10.

Vosskamp, Wilhelm, ed. *Utopieforschung. Interdisziplinäre Studien zur neuzeitlichen Utopie.* 3 vols. Frankfurt am Main: Suhrkamp, 1985.

Walker, Mack. *German Home Towns.* Ithaca and London: Cornell University Press, 1971.

Wer Ist's 1928. Edited by Herrmann Degener. Berlin: H. Degener, 1928.

White, Dan S. *The Splintered Party: National Liberalism in Hessen and the Reich, 1867–1918.* Cambridge, Mass.: Harvard University Press, 1976.

Wiese, Leopold von. "Die Deutsche Gesellschaft für Soziologie. Persönliche Eindrücke in den ersten Fünfzig Jahren (1909–1959)." *Kölner Zeitschrift für Soziologie und Sozialpsychologie* XI (1959): 11–20.

Williams, Raymond. *Modern Tragedy.* Stanford: Stanford University Press, 1966.

Wiltshire, David. *The Social and Political Thought of Herbert Spencer.* Oxford and New York: Oxford University Press, 1978.

Winkler, Heinrich August. "Vom linken zum rechten Nationalismus. Der deutsche Liberalismus in der Krise von 1878/79." *Geschichte und Gesellschaft* IV (1978): 5–28.

Wolf, Erik. *Grosse Rechtsdenker der deutschen Geistesgeschichte.* Tübingen: J. C. B. Mohr, 1963.

Würffel, Bodo. *Wirkungswille um Prophetie. Studien zu Werk und Wirkung Stefan Georges.* Bonn: Bouvier, 1978.

Zander, Jürgen. "Ferdinand Tönnies und Friedrich Nietzsche. Mit einem Exkurs: Nietzsches 'Geburt der Tragödie' als Impuls zu Tönnies' 'Gemeinschaft und Gesellschaft.'" In Lars Clausen and Franz Urban Pappi, *Ankunft bei Tönnies,* 185–227.

Zaret, David. *The Heavenly Contract: Ideology and Organization in Pre-Revolutionary Puritanism.* Chicago: University of Chicago Press, 1984.

Index